Parker on the Iroquois

NEW YORK STATE STUDIES

ARTHUR C. PARKER

(Courtesy Rochester Museum of Arts and Sciences)

Parker on the Iroquois

Iroquois Uses of Maize and Other Food Plants
The Code of Handsome Lake, the Seneca Prophet
The Constitution of the Five Nations

ARTHUR C. PARKER

Edited with an Introduction by

WILLIAM N. FENTON

SYRACUSE UNIVERSITY PRESS

Acknowledgments

In writing this critique of Parker's work I incurred the following debts of gratitude to colleagues and staff of the State Museum for their assistance: the concept of lateralization, an idea which I recalled in evaluating Parker's career, comes from the writings and discussions of Professor Burt Aginsky, for many years at City College of New York; the use of this tool for interpretation was reinforced by the analysis of Parker as a pan-Indianist by Hazel Hertzberg, a former social studies teacher now at Teachers College of Columbia University, who finds Parker continually dealing in equivalents. At the Museum, Paul Weinman checked the references in "Maize" and afterward read the manuscript. Dr. William A. Ritchie, for many years at the Rochester Museum and now the State Archeologist, refreshed my memory of Parker's literary materials, described Parker's work habits, and gave me the benefit of his criticism. At Rochester, Parker used to have a desk in a room adjacent to the director's office, where he hoped to repair to work on ethnological notes that he had brought from Albany. The drawers were full of notes and manuscripts in various stages of completion. But the demands of his position left him little time for literary pursuits. And M. H. Deardorff of Warren, Pennsylvania, reminded me that there was a closet, in Parker's Rochester apartment, that was literally stuffed with manuscripts and papers. Parker, within my experience, was an impulsively generous man. I still have copies of scarce books on the Iroquois that he thrust into my hands during one of these visits when I was yet a graduate student. Years later I bought his remaining library for the New York State Library, which also has his unpublished manuscript, "The Amazing Iroquois," to which he devoted his later years.

v

A C K N O W L E D G M E N T S

Rounding up the illustrations for the three *Bulletins* has presented some difficulties. The Manuscript Section of the New York State Library has the Jesse Cornplanter pen and ink drawings, which illustrate "The Code of Handsome Lake." These have been reproduced through the kindness of Miss Juliet Wolohan. The photographs presented more of a problem since few of the negatives are still at the State Museum while more of them are in the Rochester Museum where Parker carried them when he became director. The latter include several of the glass plate negatives of illustrations on "Maize," and there are yet others from his reports as Archeologist to the Director of the State Museum. Evidently, when Parker removed from Albany to Rochester he took with him both his field notebooks and glass plate negatives, slides, and photographic prints covering the period of his official work for the State Museum, 1905–1920. Section 233 of the Education Law governing the State Museum is quite specific that any scientific collection, field notes, and photographs made by a member of the Museum staff during his term of office belong to the State of New York and form part of the State Museum. Parker chose to ignore this. Instead he held that no one in Albany was interested in these materials. And he was probably right.

I am accordingly most grateful to W. Stephen Thomas, the present director of the Rochester Museum, and to Charles Hayes, curator of Anthropology, for making the Parker collection of Iroquois photographs available. Charles Gillette, curator of Archeology, identified the many illustrations and specimens in his care; Mrs. Gwyneth Gillette retouched the prints from old negatives and the Cornplanter drawings; Harold Furlong produced the crisp prints for the half tones. Where original negatives have not been available, facsimile substitutions have been made. Miss Eileen Wood, my secretary at the Museum, typed the final draft. To all of these helpful people I return thanks.

W. N. F.

Slingerlands, New York
February, 1968

Contents

Editor's Introduction

The scientific literature on the Iroquois Indians of New York State has been growing for over a century, commencing in 1851 with Lewis Henry Morgan's *League of the Ho-dé-no-sau-nee, or Iroquois,* the work of a Rochester lawyer who is the acknowledged father of American ethnology. It now numbers several hundred titles and has always enjoyed an avid readership, but unfortunately, important basic works are no longer in print. The Iroquois themselves have contributed to this literary outpouring, and they covet and guard the books about their customs as if they were tribal wampum belts, which are the records of their transactions. Ely S. Parker, of Tonawanda, a Sachem, an engineer, and afterward a general in the Union Army, collaborated with Morgan.

Parker's grand-nephew (his brother's grandson) Arthur C. Parker, who became an anthropologist and a museum curator during the second decade of this century, published as *Bulletins* of the New York State Museum three monographs that have become famous. Much sought after by collectors and the Iroquois and now only infrequently listed in Americana booksellers' catalogs, these monographs are now scarce books that command a premium price. They have not been reprinted because it is not the policy of the New York State Museum to re-issue out-of-print works, but to devote its limited printing budgets to the publication of new research by the present staff. It was only when the "Iroquois Indians" attained national recognition as a resource for teaching seventh-grade social studies, since the publication of a guide, "Teaching a Pre-Columbian Culture: the Iroquois," [1]

---

[1] Hertzberg, Hazel W., published by the University of the State of New York, State Education Department, Bureau of Secondary Curriculum Development, Albany, 1966.

that the demand for teaching materials, both at the introductory level and in undergraduate anthropology courses, warranted asking for their release and justified meeting the demand. We are therefore grateful to the officers of the State Education Department and to the Regents of the University of the State of New York for releasing these titles to the Syracuse University Press. In bringing them out together within hard covers as a trilogy—"Maize, Handsome Lake, and the Constitution of the Five Nations"—one is reminded of another famous triad—maize, beans, and squash, which are the "Three Sisters" of Iroquois agriculture, of whom the Iroquois fondly say, "They on whom our lives depend." "Parker gave us the three monographs, and we are also grateful." It is in this spirit of fulfillment that we offer these monographs today in homage to their author.

II

Gáwasowaneh, or "Big Snowsnake," as the Iroquois called him, or Arthur C[aswell] Parker (1881–1955), as he was known to the world of letters, belongs to a rare genre of writers who are indeed native sons of the New World. Of distinguished Seneca Iroquois ancestry through his father and of New England heritage through his mother, Arthur Parker was at home on either side of the buckskin curtain, and he was certainly the most distinguished American Indian savant of his generation. Neither Francis La Flesche, the Osage, nor J. N. B. Hewitt, a Tuscarora, both ethnologists at the Smithsonian Institution, covered as broad a spectrum of achievement in American life as Parker. His many roles included folklorist, ethnologist, archeologist, museologist (a word he coined), defender of Indian rights, writer of children's books, historian, and museum director. A man of so many roles was necessarily complex in character, but as I knew him in his later years, the Indian facets of his personality came through and dominated his outlook. Parker had traveled many miles since his youth on the reservation of the Seneca nation, had earned his living and died on the white side of the buckskin curtain, and was buried with the rites of the Masonic order, yet the Seneca leaders who attended his graveside and spoke their condolences in the metaphors of the forest reminded those present that their brother had never left the longhouse.

Thirty miles south of Buffalo, Cattaraugus Indian Reservation of the Seneca nation extends fifteen miles along the fertile bottoms of Cattaraugus Creek between the town of Gowanda and Lake Erie, which the Indians named for its "smelly banks" caused by marsh gas. In the 1880's these flats and neighboring banks were the refuge of 1,500 Seneca and related people, of whom a minority were Christians and lived clustered around the mission church and school, occupying the best lands between Four Corners and the Lake, and the rest were "pagans," comprising three neighborhoods: Newtown on the hill toward Lawtons, Plank Road toward Buffalo, and Four Mile Level toward Gowanda. In the 1840's the Senecas had undergone a revolution. After losing Buffalo Creek Reservation, they "dehorned" their life chiefs, withdrew to Cattaraugus, and set up a constitutional form of government. The rebels, still in power, were young, educated Christians. They were the bright pupils of Asher Wright (1803–1875), the missionary, who, after learning their language, set up a printing press to publish teaching materials in the Seneca language. He established the first effective schools among the Senecas and then retired with them from Buffalo, having devoted fifty-seven years of his life to their service. His saintly wife and collaborator in the mission, Laura Sheldon Wright (1809–1886), who survived him by eleven years, was affectionately called "Auntie Wright" by the younger generation of Parkers. The memory of these two wonderful people who had brought literacy to the Senecas was very much alive in the members of Arthur Parker's generation, and the tradition of learning which they fostered was to affect all their lives.[2] Just as the "pagans" or longhouse people were strong be-

---

[2] Caswell, Mrs. Harriet S., *Our Life among the Iroquois Indians* (Boston, 1892), 303; Parker, Arthur C., "The Life of General Ely S. Parker," Buffalo Historical Society *Publications*, XXIII (1919), 192, 206, 302, 309, 314; Fenton, W. N., "Toward the Gradual Civilization of the Indian Natives: the Missionary

lievers in the doctrine of their prophet, Handsome Lake, celebrated ancient agricultural festivals, and continued their obligations to the medicine societies, so the Christian party around the mission expounded the Gospel with vigor, read the Scriptures, attended worship, and sang with agreeable harmony from Asher Wright's Seneca hymnal. Seneca was indeed the first language of most households, but many Senecas knew a few words of English, although most everyone employed a dialect of English nouns strung on Iroquoian syntax that was to be known as "Reservation English," or "Asylum-geh." The Parkers, however, spoke English well. The Seneca nation made contact with the surrounding world at two levels: they called on and received officials from Washington and Albany, and they bartered farm goods, peddled baskets, and hired out as laborers to neighboring Yankee, English, and German farmers.

The most important Indian then living at Cattaraugus and one of its more successful farmers was Nicholson H. Parker (183?–1892), Arthur's paternal grandfather, and the U.S. Interpreter, who exerted a marked influence on his grandson's character. Younger brother to General Ely S. Parker (1828–1895), Nick Parker was born and raised at Tonawanda, attended Albany State Normal School in 1854, and returned to manage the family farm at Tonawanda for three years before moving to Cattaraugus, where he bought the farm of Daniel Two Guns. During his association with the Wrights and their work at the mission, Parker was employed as interpreter, printer, and clerk by Dr. Wright, who had set up the first press at Buffalo Creek in 1838 for publishing the *Mental Elevator*. Nicholson met and courted Martha Hoyt, who for many years served the mission household and was Mrs. Wright's niece.[3] Possessed of real intellectual curiosity, Nicholson was a lifelong reader. He intoned the Scriptures and *Pilgrim's Progress* aloud to his household, and he reviewed his algebra periodically. He taught his sons the uses of the carpenter's square,

---

and Linguistic Work of Asher Wright (1803–1875) among the Senecas of Western New York," *Proceedings,* American Philosophical Society, 100(6):567–81.
   [3] Caswell, 36.

and together, in the manner of their ancestors, they built the Parker homestead from lumber sawed on the place. It was here that Mrs. Wright repaired in 1876, after the death of her husband, and it was here, on the family farm, that Arthur Parker spent his first formative eleven years.

In the biography of his great uncle, the Civil War general, which is also a Parker family history, Arthur employs typical Seneca humor in characterizing the close proximity of farm, mission, fairground, stage route, school, dispensary, and national cemetery: "Members of the family by this rare situation get the daily paper, can be married and preached to, attend the fair, get sick, call a doctor, die and be buried, with all the rites of the church, without even leaving the neighborhood,—so 'civilized' has the reservation become." [4]

The Parkers, believing in education, sent their several children to school on the reservation and beyond to the neighboring cities. They were partly motivated by the rule of matrilineal descent, which is still observed among the Iroquois. Children born of a white mother and an Indian father could never be enrolled legally in the Seneca Nation. Frederick Ely, Arthur's father, graduated from Fredonia State Normal School and soon became an accountant with the New York Central Railroad. Like his father, he too married a white woman, Geneva H. Griswold, of Scottish and English descent, who was herself a teacher for a number of years among the Seneca.[5] Arthur Parker was certainly no more than one-fourth Seneca, and probably nearer one-eighth.

It was into this household of mixed Iroquois and New England heritage that Arthur Caswell Parker was born April 5, 1881. Here amid Presbyterian piety he learned the virtues of work, temperance, and self-improvement. Nor could he escape the rich oral literature of a politically minded family who boasted chiefs in every generation going back to Handsome Lake and Old Smoke and beyond to the beginnings of the Iroquois Confederacy. For

---

[4] Parker (1919), 192.
[5] *Ibid.*, viii; Thomas, W. Stephen, "Arthur Caswell Parker: 1881–1895: Anthropologist, Historian and Museum Pioneer," *Rochester History,* XVII(3) :1–20 (1955).

the lore of the folk and techniques of woodcraft and hunting he need only ask his grandfather. There were plenty of old men accessible and willing to tell stories to gangs of young boys that roamed the creek banks of the reservation, and on winter nights storytellers came to the Parker kitchen. A bright boy had only to listen. Since his mother did not speak Seneca, nor did his father's mother, English was Arthur's first language, but during his first ten years he learned to comprehend and make himself understood in Seneca, which was spoken by his agemates, for many of whom it was the first language. Having learned it early, it would stand him in good stead in later field work.[6]

The Parkers were an extended clan, having representation in other communities. Uncle Ely was a life chief at Tonawanda, where other siblings of his father's father resided, and his father's sister, Caroline Parker Mountpleasant, was married to a Tuscarora chief and lived on the Tuscarora reserve near Niagara Falls. It was to the Parker homestead near the ford in Tonawanda Creek, at the east end of the reservation, that Lewis H. Morgan first came to begin ethnological studies with the generation of Arthur's great-grandparents, and Morgan inscribed his classic on the League to Ely S. Parker, his collaborator.[7] Caroline, then a young girl, modeled the Seneca woman's costume for the frontispiece to Book II of the *League,* and the skirt she wore then, the finest surviving piece that Morgan collected for the Regents of the University of the State of New York, is now in the New York State Museum. Arthur C. Parker was thus linked by kinship and intellectual tradition to the history of American ethnology; he had only to return to the hearth of the longhouse with welcome assured in three communities.

At several points in his career Arthur Parker wrote succinct sketches of his life, stressing what he then valued. From his correspondence in the State Museum I have been able to flesh out the bones of these telegraphic statements.

During his first season of archeological field work for the State Museum, Parker wrote a typically Indian letter to an Albany re-

---

[6] Personal observation; confirmed by Dr. W. A. Ritchie.

[7] Morgan, Lewis H. *League of the Ho-dé-no-sau-nee, or Iroquois* (Rochester, 1851).

porter who had asked him for a vita. The table of contents for the first decade of reservation life lists "Colic; green apples; fights; lickings; Indian district school; hookey; bow and arrow hunts; fishing and swimming; visits to old warriors in the woods; visits of 'the big white chiefs from Washington.' " [8] By his ninth year he had made his first natural history collection, commencing with birds' eggs.[9] And Devonian fossils, which abound in the rocky cliffs of Cattaraugus Creek, where the old Senecas say the Little People live, fascinated him.

Rural life of western New York differs from suburban life in Westchester, but a gulf separates life in White Plains from Seneca life at Cattaraugus. This was even more true in the 1890's, when Arthur, at age eleven, and his sister followed their father's career to the environs of the big city and entered the public schools. Although Arthur was to graduate from White Plains High School in 1897 and merit the recommendation of his Presbyterian minister to study for the ministry, the reservation exerted a strong pull. The Parker family went home whenever they could, and Arthur mentions a later period of "more district school." It was then that he made the acquaintance of "more big chiefs"; experienced "Injun boy adventures"; he even mentions "dream fasts" and "sweat lodges" (both of which were already obsolete and dying usages), visiting "medicine men," and "pagan dances" (much alive yet); he became a "novice in secret orders of the Senecas," although this was much later during his entrance to ethnology in 1904; and "more pagan dances." He met a girl (Parker mentions her in his writings but does not identify her) and they both went to college. This is the most obscure period of his life.

What began as the two cultures of White Plains and Cattaraugus created an ambivalence that Parker was never able to shake. He is a naturalist one moment, a divinity student the next, aspiring anthropologist, then Indianist. The formal rituals and requirements of white culture repelled him, but he would succeed by lateralization, as we shall see below. Parker was quite aware of

---

[8] Parker to W. W. Judd of the Press-Knickerbocker Office, Albany, 7/10/07. See also *Skunny Wundy* in Thomas, 2.

[9] Thomas, 3.

this ambivalence in Indians who emerged from behind the buckskin curtain, and he writes revealingly about his grandfather's
many roles :

Besides being clerk of the nation, United States interpreter, census
agent, marshal . . . , orator, agriculturist, and civil engineer, . . .
[he] was drum major of the Seneca Indian Silver Cornet Band. He
was a versatile and useful citizen of the Seneca Republic. Like his
other brother Ely, he never could completely accept civilization's
teachings or wholly neglect the philosophy of his fathers. Seeing true
virtue in each, according to his mood he argued for each. Many Indians have this same characteristic and often appear vacillating and
uncertain in judgment when in reality the quality is merely the in-
voluntary mental struggle between hereditary impressions and pro-
clivities and those acquired.[10]

Notwithstanding the fallacy that Indian culture was inherited, un-
like white culture which was acquired, Parker was really describing himself. In his ambivalence he never followed a direct path,
but, as an Indian path goes around a log, he bypassed the hurdles
to academic achievement.

It is probably to his credit that he shifted careers early, before
discovering his life's work. For three years after 1900 he was
enrolled in Williamsport Dickinson Seminary at Williamsport,
Pennsylvania, but he left without finishing the course. And he
tried his hand at writing, first in school, then as a newspaper reporter. But in the years before electing to study for the ministry,
he haunted the halls and met the staff of the American Museum of
Natural History, and there he gravitated whenever home on vaca-
tion. He met F. W. Putnam, of Harvard, who was then at the
Museum, and Mark Raymond Harrington, who a few years ago
retired from the Southwest Museum and who recalls that he took
Parker digging on Long Island.[11] This small expedition to the
shell heaps of Oyster Bay was Parker's introduction to archeology.
The trip marked the beginning of a lifelong friendship between the
two men, a tie that was further strengthened when Harrington
married Parker's sister. In the next few years they would make

---

10 Parker (1919), 198.
11 Thomas, 5; Harrington to Fenton, 9/30/67.

joint forays to the Mohawk Valley, to the St. Lawrence, to the hills of Chautauqua County. In turn, Parker introduced Harrington to the Iroquois, who gave him the name of *Jiskogo* (Robin). Collecting ethnographic specimens for museums was a way of financing these field trips.

New York City was an exciting place for amateur archeologists in 1901. Professor Putnam, of Mound Builder fame, was temporarily curator of anthropology at the American Museum of Natural History. Putnam had a magic touch with collectors, and he welcomed young men who became his "boys" regardless of their academic attainment, encouraging them to come and work at the Museum and bring their collections. Putnam's "boys" soon included Harrington, Parker, Alanson B. Skinner, and John W. Fenton, my father, who had just come from western New York to teach in the city schools, a career that he combined with painting for nearly forty years. Frank G. Speck, afterward professor of Anthropology at the University of Pennsylvania, was a student at Columbia where Franz Boas had recently founded the Department of Anthropology, having moved uptown from the Museum. Downtown, Harriet Maxwell Converse held open house for the friends of the American Indian, especially for the Iroquois and their friends. Mrs. Converse (*Ya-ié-wa-noh*) enjoyed a special relationship with the Senecas; in return for her good works they had made her an honorary female chief, and she collected their folklore and reinterpreted it into romantic poetry which she contributed to the newspapers and to various literary journals. When Mrs. Converse died in 1903, Arthur became her literary executor and ultimately edited and published her collection of Seneca folklore.[12]

III

American anthropology in 1901 was turning the corner from the Museum period of converted naturalists represented by Put-

<hr/>

[12] Parker, A. C., ed., "Myths and Legends of the New York State Iroquois, By Harriet Maxwell Converse (Ya-ié-wa-noh)," *New York State Museum Bulletin* 125 (1908).

nam, from the romantic view of the Indian's literature and music, epitomized by Mrs. Converse, to folklore, to the rigorous training of ethnologists in the universities, a tradition that Boas brought from Germany. Of the young naturalists Speck saw this trend most clearly. Speck took Parker around to meet Boas, who encouraged Parker to enroll in the university and come up to anthropology through Columbia College. But Parker, having made up his mind to become a professional archeologist, found the long academic route impractical for him and returned to the congenial and informal tutorials of Professor Putnam at the Museum. The decision to turn his back on the doctorate in anthropology would haunt his professional career, for it was an achievement that he very much coveted and envied in others, allowing himself to be called "Doctor" Parker for years before Union College sanctioned the long usage with an honorary degree in 1940.[13]

Instead, Parker was to advance himself by a process of lateralization, by discovering and gaining admission to "secret" medicine societies of the Seneca, by moving up in fraternal orders that were open to him, by seeking identification with and fellowship in professional societies, and, as a prophet, creating new orders, new societies, and new honors in which he enjoyed founding membership and was the ultimate recipient of kudos. These activities continued throughout his life, in many ways a creative process, advancing archeology and museology immeasurably; and the list of societies, memberships, and honors is incredibly long.

Parker served his apprenticeship as a field assistant to Harrington on archeological expeditions under Professor Putnam's direction for the American Museum of Natural History and the Peabody Museum of Harvard during the summers of 1903 and 1904. He would soon be ready to strike out on his own. Between field trips and while tutoring at the American Museum he worked as a reporter on the *New York Sun,* learning to write quickly and concisely and developing a style which makes his scientific reports easy reading. He could always be depended upon for a good

---

[13] Personal conversations with Professor F. G. Speck, Professor Edward Sapir, Dr. W. A. Ritchie, and Parker himself after 1933; Thomas, 4–5.

story, and his literary output is voluminous, comprising 350 titles, including 14 books.[14] This energetic and talented young man of Seneca descent was soon commended to the educational authorities in Albany.

It was undoubtedly Harriet Maxwell Converse who brought Parker to the attention of Melvil Dewey, secretary of the Board of Regents and State Librarian. Dewey was responsible for advancing the Indian Museum in the State Capitol which began with the articles collected for the Regents of the University by L. H. Morgan, of Rochester, fifty years earlier; with Mrs. Converse he had secured the Iroquois wampum belts for the state. After their purchase, the Regents accepted them in a special convocation held in 1898 in the Assembly Chamber. The Iroquois contributed their own ceremony on this occasion and Dewey served as the principal speaker for the Regents. In 1904 Dewey convinced the new commissioner of education, Andrew S. Draper, that the State of New York should "secure all possible information concerning the history, customs, ceremonies, festivals, songs, traditions, etc. of the tribes constituting the Iroquois Confederacy," and collect "any articles of dress, household goods or utensils, implements . . ." and all else "indicative of the manner and life and habits of the Indian people." This heritage should be passed on to the people of later generations. Parker was commissioned to carry out this charter for ethnography by visiting the tribes and getting all the information he could. In addressing this appeal "to the Indian people of the State" Draper hoped that "a young man of Indian descent" might be welcome among them, and he expressed confidence in Parker's integrity.[15] This document, now much creased and soiled, must have impressed the Iroquois, although Parker first had to win the confidence of the longhouse leaders. The arrangement was that Parker should report biweekly to Howard J. Rogers, the first assistant commissioner of education, and re-

---

[14] Thomas, 5; "Arthur Caswell Parker: Leader of the Museum World," *Museum Service* (February, 1955), Bulletin of the Rochester Museum.

[15] Andrew S. Draper, Commissioner of Education, November 10, 1904, "To the Indian People of the State of New York," Parker Papers, New York State Museum, Box 1.

ceive a fee based on the manuscripts sent to the State Library and specimens collected for the State Museum. When items were purchased he was to be reimbursed upon presentation of proper receipts. It was a trial arrangement at best, pending results and the reactions of the Indians. The administrative details deserve mention because they produced an accession record that is still not found in the Museum catalog and does not appear in printed reports. It tells us how Parker worked and describes the field conditions that he encountered.[16] The years 1905 and 1906 were Parker's best period as a field worker. He gradually gained the confidence of the Keepers of the Faith in the Newtown Longhouse at Cattaraugus. He was admitted to ceremonies of the medicine societies that were previously unknown to science; he obtained texts of the speeches and the song cycles; he undertook a translation of the Code of Handsome Lake, and he filled his notebooks with information on gardening, subsistence, technology, folk tales, and games. In addition, in the summer of 1906 he made the first systematic excavation of an Iroquois village site and prepared a report.[17] Like many other anthropologists he was most productive early in life, before being burdened with the duties of a regular job.

Just how difficult it was to gain the confidence of the longhouse leaders and to do productive field work he explains to Melvil Dewey, who was unable to honor Parker's invitation to come out for the Midwinter ceremonies which Parker promises to describe for him.

It takes a long time for the Indians to give their confidence to anyone and for some time, although they accepted my statements and gave me preveleges [sic], I was conscious of a certain reserve on their part. The trouble was the fact that I was brought up under mission influence and the "pagans" are always more or less suspicious of such a person's motives. I have therefore, sought in every way to remove all obstacles that would cause the people to withhold information from me. I was much gratified, therefore, when the council of chiefs as-

---

[16] See correspondence with Howard J. Rogers, 6/15/05–4/20/06, *ibid.*
[17] Parker, Arthur C., "An Erie Indian Village and Burial Site at Ripley, Chautauqua Co., N.Y.," New York State Museum *Bulletin* 117 (1907).

sured me through their chairman that after watching my movements and noted my methods they would give me their complete confidence in all matters and give me a place that only Mrs. Converse had enjoyed. My work immediately became easier and I am admitted to secret ceremonies that I was formerly barred from and this with the full knowledge that I am taking notes for publication . . . I am just beginning to appreciate my people myself. The work at hand at present is the translation of the twelve native orders. To facilitate this work I am using the phonograph to record some of the more important ceremonial chants and speeches.[18]

Parker's notebooks are not now available for study, but he seems to have written and published promptly the best of his field notes, a habit which he acquired as a reporter. While it is a pity that he worked before the invention of the tape recorder, there is always the possibility that his wax cylinder recordings will turn up in Albany or Rochester.

Parker was one of those people who make news. Wherever he went he was soon followed by reporters, so there are abundant clippings on his activities in the Buffalo, Albany, and Rochester papers of the day. While these press notices would be helpful to a biographer, his official correspondence is a better source on how he did his field work. He was evidently adopted into the Bear Clan early, as happens to most ethnologists who work among the Iroquois, and given one of the "free" names from the clan set. *Gáwasowaneh* means "Big Snowsnake," and not "Talking Leaves," as some writers have suggested;[19] it is a typical adult male's name of distinction, and it has no personal reference to Parker, although he did write up the Snow Snake Game.[20] The purpose and function of Indian names arise from the persistent belief that every person will have a tag by which he can be referred to or mentioned in the ceremonies. The name itself bears a rank as child, adult, warrior, matron, chief, or ceremonial officer

---

[18] Parker to Melvil Dewey, Gowanda, 4/7/06; Parker to Joseph Keppler, 1/22/06.
[19] Thomas, 18.
[20] Parker, A. C., "Snow Snake as Played by the Senecas," *American Anthropologist,* XI(2) :250–56.

that everyone recognizes, and it also serves to place the individual
in the society because each clan has its own set of names. Awarding
Indian names, through the custom of adoption, has been going on
for centuries, and the Iroquois are not unaware of its public relations value. The people at Newtown Longhouse, who adopted
Mrs. Converse, gave Cornplanter's old name, "Giantwake," from
the Wolf Clan set, to Joseph Keppler, the New York publisher of
Puck, who helped them financially while he was collecting for the
Heye Museum. Naturally Parker, wanting to honor Dewey, his
sponsor, turned to Keppler for support in getting the Senecas to
give an Indian name to Dewey "as founder of the Iroquois museum at the Capitol and lifelong friend of *Yaiewanoh* [Mrs. Con-
verse]," and suggested "a baby's name for him." [21] In a manner
of speaking, these adopted Senecas—white men having Indian
names—formed a rather exclusive club at the opening of the
century.

During 1905 Parker completed a preliminary translation of
Gáiwio [Káiwi :yo :h], the "Good Message" or Code of Handsome
Lake, from Chief Edward Cornplanter's version which was written in a crude orthography in a "butcher book." He also discovered and reported the Little Water Medicine Society and was
at work on the False Face Company, recording the rites and collecting the masks. Late in the year he set out to document the
Code and the life of the Prophet. In the course of these inquiries
he discovered "A List of Names of the Indians of the Six Nations
of New York who Served in the War of 1812 between Britain
and the United States," which he says gives the names of the
warriors, their Indian names, and their totems; and this he sent to
Commissioner Rogers for preservation by the State.[22]

Parker left no stone unturned. Edward Cornplanter had a
talented son Jesse who liked to draw, and Parker promptly commissioned Jesse to illustrate various activities in Seneca cere-

---

[21] Parker to Jos. Keppler, 1/26/06.
[22] Parker to H. J. Rogers, First Asst. Commissioner of Education, 6/15/05;
12/18/05; 1/30/06. "List of Indians of the Six Nations who Served in the War
of 1812 . . . ," Parker Papers, Henry E. Huntington Library, San Marino,
California, Box 1.

monial life. The discovery of Jesse Cornplanter, the Seneca boy artist, was to have interesting consequences for both men: Jesse became famous, and his association with Parker's early work made him the best living interpreter of Seneca culture during my own first field work a generation later. A set of Jesse Cornplanter's drawings was the instrument for raising the fund to cast the first Cornplanter Medal for Iroquois Research, which Parker ultimately received. These drawings added a dimension to Parker's monographs in subjects where no photographs are available.[23]

Parker even got access to the attic of the Newtown Longhouse. There after the Midwinter Festival he found "the last dog pole" where it had been put overhead twenty-five years earlier and lain unused since the species of white dog that the Senecas traditionally strangled, hung, and burned had become extinct. This was the reason given by the Keepers of the Faith for abandoning the sacrifice, although they were also reacting to white pressure. The longhouse officers gave the pole, which was striped with ceremonial red paint, to Parker "for preservation by the State," an unusually generous act on which he comments, "The pagans do not easily part with the treasured rites of their ancestors and have long guarded them from publicity. . . ." [24]

By this time Parker was able to take texts in Seneca, and that spring he gained admission to Yei?do:s, which is the celebration group for those who hold charms or have themselves been cured by the Little Water Medicine. To get permission to attend the rites, Parker had to interview thirty people who belonged to the society, a fact which conveys an idea of its size, his persistence, and his opportunity. Up until April of 1906 Parker was a real ethnologist.[25]

Inevitably the stream of correspondence, specimens for the State Museum, and manuscripts and pictures for the State Library led to a decision concerning Parker's future. It was decided to set up the position of Archeologist in the Science Division of the State Museum and invite Parker to accept the job temporarily, pending

[23] Parker to Rogers, 2/20/06.
[24] *Ibid.*, 3/20/06.
[25] *Ibid.*, 4/2/06.

a qualifying examination, at an annual salary of $900. Patently
Parker was working to fulfill the guidelines of such a position
all along. Once he attained the position, however, he discovered
that having a job imposed other obligations beyond his own
choice of field work, i.e., assignments that he did not plan, inter-
ruptions from taxpayers on questions of mutual interest which he
must answer, demands to speak that he must fulfill, and competi-
tion from other state scientists in older and better established
disciplines which were bound to frustrate and curb his activities.

The then director of the Division of Science and of the New
York State Museum was John M. Clarke (1857–1925), who had
gained eminence as a paleontologist under the great James Hall,
and retained both titles of State Geologist and State Paleontologist
after acceding to the directorship. Proud of his honors, Clarke
was a tight administrator and a good money raiser, and he put
the programs of his division ahead of the desires of individual
scientists. Archeology being understandably more congenial to his
background than ethnology, he almost immediately ordered Parker
to suspend his present work (which explains why Parker stopped
when he was doing so well) and turn to archeology which offered
a better hope of filling the museum cases. In fact he later ordered
Parker to devote his prime attention to exhibits. Clarke was preparing for the removal of the Museum from Geological Hall and
the Capitol to the new State Education Building, which was then
on the drawing boards, and, as now, offered a great opportunity
for display of collections.[26] The Museum report of that year mentions "the archeologic collections, . . . enriched by the archives
of the Six Nations [the famous wampum belts] formally transferred to the State in 1898, and by the Morgan, Converse, and
Maxwell collections together with constant occasional additions,"
as being "of superior and in large measure unique value." Clarke
urged a persistent effort to recover those remains yet in the soil.[27]

---

[26] John M. Clarke to Parker 4/11/06, 4/18/06, Parker Papers, New York
State Museum, Box 1, and Clarke Papers in State Libary, Division of Manuscripts.
[27] 59th Annual Report of the State Museum for 1905, New York State Museum (Second Report of the Director 1905), 51.

Field work began on the first of May, 1906. The previous summer, Parker had explored a group of sites in the valley of Cattaraugus Creek and in Chautauqua County, including, farther west on Lake Erie, the Ripley site which John Fenton had first reported to Putnam in 1901, and which Parker and Harrington had afterward tested. That summer Parker planned to concentrate on Ripley, and his report on the site made his reputation as an archeologist.[28] The report is a landmark in the history of American archeology since it represents one of the first attempts to describe the complete excavation of a large site and then interpret the results as the description of a local culture. Parker's presumption, however, that the site was protohistoric Erie, or was one of the Erie towns sacked by the Iroquois in 1654, is currently not accepted by prehistorians. Ripley yielded a series of skeletons which somehow did not appeal to Clarke, who wanted spectacular displays. In addition Clarke thought the work terribly expensive. Clarke was continually second-guessing Parker: that he ought to know where to dig and then on rich sites, that collections could be purchased more cheaply for the Museum from amateurs, and that Parker's crew worked without supervision while Parker was off doing ethnology. Parker, nevertheless, added some important objects of ceremonial equipment to the ethnological collections—a set of Eagle Dance fans, the feather headpiece of *Ainowa,* who had the distinction of both weighing 320 lbs. and being a great athlete and agile dancer, having caught a ball at the goal in a lacrosse match at the Pan American Exposition and thrown it through the opposite goal, not to mention Tall Peter's silver crown or head band from Tonawanda.[29]

Parker very much wanted the job of archeologist at the State Museum, and he wanted to succeed at it. He evidently mustered support for his appointment, judging by the letters of congratula-

---

[28] Parker (1907).
[29] 60th Report of the State Museum for 1906, New York State Museum (Third Report of the Director of the Science Division 1906), 73, 79–80

tions received and acknowledged in the autumn of 1906. The Civil Service examination was held October 13, and on the 16th Clarke duly recommended his appointment to the Commissioner. It must have been particularly gratifying to receive the plaudits of F. W. Putnam, who wrote, "From what you have done in the past I am sure you will do credit to the State, and in realizing your own ambitions you have brought about the consummation of my hopes for you. . . ." Parker followed up this opening by indicating his desire to affiliate with professional societies and asking for sponsorship. As one of Putnam's "boys," Parker appealed to Putnam's secretary for the reports of the Peabody Museum at Harvard and received a generous gift box of various anthropological publications and a list of books for order by the State Library.[30]

Considerations of program for his new division weighed on Parker's mind that first year. Although he was appointed as archeologist in the State Museum, he immediately began to sign his mail as "State Archeologist," after the manner of his colleagues who enjoyed statutory titles. This ultimately got him into trouble with Clarke and with Commissioner Draper, who called this misuse of title to Clarke's attention. It is just another example of Parker's dealing in equivalents. Parker foresaw the archeological section of the State Museum developing into a department of anthropology having subsections for archeology, ethnology, folklore, philology, and physical anthropology; but in the twenty years that he singlehandedly carried on all of these activities, he never could get Clarke to see the broader concept. As a curator it was also required that Parker install and rearrange collections and exhibits.[31] Full of enthusiasm, Parker wrote to William Beauchamp who, as member of an *ad hoc* committee on the Indian Collection, published a series of monographs. Saying that he was an admirer of the latter's writings, Parker urged that they press folklore studies but acknowledged that "the Onondagas are

[30] Joseph Keppler to Parker, 10/29/06; Parker to Keppler, 11/6/06; Parker to F. W. Putnam, 10/25/06; Putnam to Parker, 10/26/06; Parker to Putnam, 11/2/06. Parker to Mead, 11/20/06; Mead to Parker, 12/28/06, Parker Papers, New York State Museum, Box 1.
[31] Clarke to Parker, 2/12/1912; 61st Annual Report of the State Museum, New York State Museum *Bulletin* 121, 85.

properly your field and the Senecas, perhaps, mine." Parker proposed a systematic comparison between the two nations, with a view to getting "out a work on Iroquois ceremonials at least equal to Alice Fletcher's [Pawnee] *Hako.*" [32]

There is a familiar saying in government circles, "The money goes where the program is." Parker did make his program explicit. He devotes the Introduction to the Ripley site report to an extensive review of the beginnings of archeology and ethnology in the State Museum. Parker foresaw that the State Indian collection would become something more than what Morgan first thought, merely "a memento to the red race. . . ." He credits Dewey with awakening the Board of Regents to their responsibility toward ethnology, recounts how the wampum belts were acquired by legislation, purchase, and ceremony, and tells how Richmond, Converse, and Beauchamp increased the collections. And so that administrators and the public might understand how one may still do salvage ethnology among an acculturated people, Parker writes a vivid sketch contrasting the expectancies of Iroquois culture from museum ethnology with the dress and behavior of pagan and Christian Indians of the day.

Among these modern people of the ancient Five Nations one must conduct his researches in ethnology, folklore and philology. It is late, far too near the hour when a new epoch will dawn and there will be no more red men as such. Yet in the short time that remains it is our purpose to save at least part of the tattered fringe of the ancient fabric that was, and from this small part learn something of its entirety. It is apparent that as far as collecting ethnological material from the Indians themselves is concerned, there is little to be obtained, except slowly and in small quantities.[33]

Morgan made this same plea, and yet Iroquois culture persists as a recognizable entity on the reservations. What Parker was

[32] Parker to William M. Beauchamp, c. 1906; Beauchamp to Parker, 11/27/06; Fletcher, Alice, "The Hako: a Pawnee Ceremony," 22nd *Annual Report,* Bureau of American Ethnology, Smithsonian Institution, Pt. 2.
[33] Parker (1907), 461–66.

saying is that ethnology is not something to put in the museum, but it is an affair of the mind. Since it is often difficult to explain intellectual pursuits to those who are object minded, Parker experienced continuing frustrations with his program.

Parker learned early that men of authority who might cause him trouble could be bought off with honors. So when Clarke, who was now "custodian of the archives," that is, the wampum belts of the Iroquois Confederacy, wrote him a personal note suggesting an Indian title for the Director of the State Museum, and indicated a few days later that he was willing to bear the expense officially, Parker went into action. Parker wrote to Baptist Thomas, then president of the Onondaga Nation, reminding him that the nation had made the State the Keeper of the Six Nations' wampums and informing him that the status of Keeper rests with the Director of the State Museum. After asking Baptist Thomas for the ancient title of the Onondaga Wampum Keeper, Parker suggested that the transfer of this specific title or the creation of a new one should be ratified by the Council of Chiefs and validated by a paper bearing the name in Onondaga and English, for which he enclosed a model certificate. Since the chiefs were willing to consider the matter and apparently looked forward to the ceremony, Parker assured them that the expenses would be met and held out the hope of a gift for Thomas' trouble. For their part, Parker assured Thomas they would have a large engraved sheepskin for the chiefs to sign, if this were consistent with their customs. The ceremony took place June 29, 1908, and three days later Parker explained to Clarke that his title *Ho-sen-na-géh-teh,* means "He carries the name" or "The name bearer." And this is the story behind the certificate which today hangs in the office of the Director of the State Museum. There is besides a red yoke on which the title is spelled out in glass beads, a present from Onondaga women. Indeed, it was "a name hung about the neck." [34]

Parker wanted to do field work, and Clarke ordered him to concentrate on exhibits. How Parker resolved this conflict is a

---

[34] Clarke to Parker, 12/27/1907; Parker to Baptist Thomas, 1/7/1908, 1/13/1908; Parker to Clarke, 1/27/1908.

tribute to the man's energy and versatility. Parker made the need to authenticate information for the Indian Groups, for which Clarke had received a large bequest, justify further ethnological forays to the Seneca and to the Six Nations Reserve in Canada, which enabled him at the same time to maintain a steady stream of publications. Parker corresponded with his old informants at Newtown, especially with Delos Kittle, his agent, and Edward Cornplanter, his principal source. He was coming out to do field work, but first needed the pictures which he commissioned Jesse Cornplanter to do for Mrs. Converse's book in which he had billed Jesse as a Seneca boy artist of promise. The next year Parker inquired about the date of the Strawberry Festival, the first fruits ceremony in the annual cycle, so that he could attend, and he wanted Delos Kittle to arrange for one Jonas to carve a False Face in the ancient manner on a large basswood tree for a Museum exhibit and to have a certain Mr. Luke make a bark barrel, such as is described in the early literature, to his specifications. Later he ordered certain ceremonial equipment appropriate for each of the medicine societies. These letters got results, judging by the pictures printed and the accessions listed in annual reports of the period.[35]

Parker kept his other eye on his professional colleagues. From Alanson B. Skinner he learned that Frank Speck, who chose the academic route, was now established in Philadelphia at the University Museum, and had urged that Parker bring out his Seneca texts in some up-to-date phonetic system, since the word was that J. N. B. Hewitt, ethnologist at the Smithsonian Institution in Washington, was on the verge of publishing his Seneca folklore materials in text form.[36] Parker, concerned, discussed the question of his field materials with Clarke, but he was already overcommitted. And the Indian Groups took precedence over everything else. The story of how the Indian Groups were planned, financed, researched, produced, and installed, fascinating in itself, is abundantly documented. It belongs, however, to Parker's career as a museologist, and it deserves separate treatment.

---

[35] Parker to Delos Kittle, 12/7/08, 6/3/09, 6/8/09.
[36] Alanson B. Skinner to Parker, 11/10/08.

IV

Parker's reputation as an ethnologist rests on his contributions to Iroquois studies. These comprise a book and four monographs, three of which are reprinted here, and a half-dozen brief papers in the *American Anthropologist*. Except for the book, which was delayed until 1923, most of the work was done before 1912.

On the death of Mrs. Converse, Keppler and Parker were put in charge of her Iroquois manuscripts with the understanding that Parker would try to get them into publishable form. He sold them to the State Library on the condition that they would soon be published.[37] One of the earliest assignments given to the new "State Archeologist" was carrying out this trust by editing the notes of Mrs. Converse on Iroquois folklore and mythology. This remarkable and energetic woman had been most active among the Iroquois, notably the Onondaga and Seneca; she had espoused their causes, and they had entrusted to her their oral literature, their ceremonies, and much ritual equipment for safekeeping by the State of New York. That she did not always understand them seems plausible when one considers that she was not trained as an ethnologist or linguist, and in their eagerness to impart "tribal secrets" that they would entrust to no one else, they did not always succeed in communicating concepts which they thought her sympathy and intelligence comprehended. Her notes are therefore full of misconceptions, and, being a poet besides, her interpretations of what she says was communicated to her lie beyond the possibility of substantiation. Had I realized this when I commenced my own field work among the Senecas in 1933, I would have saved myself much frustration. I knew what she had written about the masks, or False Faces, but I was unable to verify what she claimed to have learned from informants. Later, when I tracked down the accession notes of specimens that she collected for museums, I encountered labels bearing fanciful type names—bird

---

[37] Parker to H. J. Rogers, 2/1/08.

mask, maternity masks, etc.—which implied a classification and certain functions that I had not found in my own observations or learned from informants and that I have never been able to substantiate.

Parker transmitted the edited manuscript in late May and asked Clarke to write the Preface. The book was out within the year 1908. In his Introduction Parker discussed the problems and techniques of collecting folklore among the Seneca. While editing the Converse collection, Parker went back to Mrs. Converse's sources and re-collected much of the material that was finally published, and this new material and a great deal more that he did not use appeared afterward in his own book on Seneca folklore in 1923. Nevertheless, he added enough new material to the original Converse manuscript to double its length, assuring Clarke that his own contribution voided any prior claim to the manuscript by the State Library. In a manner of speaking, Clarke rose to the bait and was hooked, signing his piece with his new Indian title, so that the publication was strictly an affair of adopted Iroquois.

Parker, in the Introduction to the Converse bulletin, tells how stories are told and how they are listened to. Then he contrasts methods of collecting folklore—the compulsive accuracy of taking texts in phonetics, and then translating them literally, with Converse's more "interpretive" approach to the material which preserves its "native beauty." Parker evidently followed the latter technique, using an interpreter. But he says this only resulted in a caricature of the original. He resorted to another extreme, recasting the material in the author's own mold, which he also rejected.

Parker describes still another method which combines some of the worthy features previously suggested—making what was essentially his own version. He thought its merits outweighed its drawbacks. "By this method the transcriber attempts to assimilate the ideas of the myth tale as he hears it, seeks to become imbued with the spirit of its characters, and, shutting out from his mind all thought of his own culture, and momentarily transforming

himself into the culture of the myth teller, records his impressions
as he recalls the story. His object is to produce the same emotions
in the mind of civilized man which is produced in the primitive
mind, which entertains the myth, without destroying the native
style or warping the facts of the narrative." This effort to communicate the connotations of the narrative in English is substantially the method which was employed by Harriet Converse, and
Parker's notes show where he differs from her interpretation. The
difference between the two collectors is that Parker sticks closer
to the original, which he essentially understood, and from his
jottings he produced materials of varying levels of literary sophis-
tication. Of his children's books, *Skunny Wundy* is a good example.[38]

Parker applied his method to an account of the Little Water
Medicine Society, on which Mrs. Converse left a newspaper article, and appended it to the monograph. This was not a new discovery, but Parker was accepted fully, becoming a lifelong holder
of the medicine. He soon extended his description of its rites to
other societies, which he did discover. The publication of "Secret
Medicine Societies of the Seneca" in the *American Anthropologist*
coincided with current work on secret societies and ceremonial
associations of the Plains Indians which Wissler was directing
from the American Museum.[39] It projected Parker into the main-
stream of ethnology.

But Parker was unable to give full attention to field work and
writing, and he feared that the field would be preempted by others.
Following one conversation with Clarke, Parker wrote, "One of
the understandings which I have with other ethnologists is that
inasmuch as I am actively interested in working up Iroquoian
ethnology with the idea of publishing the results, other ethnologists
will out of courtesy keep out of my territory. . . ."[40] He was

---

[38] Converse and Parker, 1908; Parker to Clarke, 5/26/1908: Parker,
"Seneca Myths and Folk Tales," Buffalo Historical Society *Publications,*
XXVII (1923); Parker, *Skunny Wundy and Other Indian Tales* (New York:
Doran, 1927).

[39] Parker, "Secret Medicine Societies of the Seneca." *American Anthropologist,* XI:161–85 (1909); Lowie, R. H., "Ceremonialism in North America, *ibid.,*
XVI:602–31 (1914).

[40] Parker to Clarke, 4/16/09.

particularly apprehensive about the topic of folklore, and soon the field of social organization would be invaded. In June he tells Clarke, "My summer plans include further ethnological studies and I am collecting notes for a work on Iroquois ethnology and culture history that I am vain enough to hope will out-Morgan Morgan. I have a large amount of data now." [41] Clarke was just as ambivalent as Parker about some things. That fall he acknowledged reprints of the two papers in the *Anthropologist*—"Snowsnake" and "Societies"—but chided Parker for not using his official title and connection on the title page, especially when he was using illustrations of specimens in the State Museum which should be so identified: "We must keep our Department as much in the foreground as possible." [42]

V

Iroquois Uses of Maize and Other Food Plants put ethnology at the State Museum and Parker on the scientific map. A work of fundamental importance, it has remained one of three pioneer studies of the subsistence of American Indian societies, at least one of which was inspired by Parker's monograph. Parker gave the manuscript to Clarke for publication in April, 1910. It was evidently written in longhand, for he asked to have it typed, which may account for the many typographical errors which are found in the printed text. But Parker saw it again in June when he resubmitted it as the "result of some years of research," trusting that it would merit approval for publication as a bulletin.[43] Parker was in the field much of that year while his work was going through the press. We may assume that the manuscript followed the usual Education Department channels after leaving the Museum, going first to the Commissioner's Room, where Clarke submitted it September 27, 1910. It was approved for publication

[41] *Ibid.,* 6/16/09.
[42] Clarke to Parker, 10/19/09.
[43] Parker to Clarke, 4/9/10, 6/7/10; Parker to Skinner, 4/13/10; Parker to Speck, 4/19/10.

the next day, after which it rested in the tender hands of the editors and proofreaders in the Bureau of Publications. The Education Department *Bulletin* was then published fortnightly, and ordinarily printed in its own shop. Parker was much concerned with what was happening to it. From Geological Hall he wrote to Clarke on July 31 to say that it was now accepted usage to refer to American Indian tribes in the singular, the tribal appellation *Seneca* being regarded as a collective noun, and "to save our selves criticism," Parker asked Clarke to "instruct those who handle our proof or edit our manuscript in accordance with the Regents' system" to adhere to the new scientific usage.[44] This seems to have been done. In fact, judging by present standards, the press was relatively speedy, having issued the bulletin on November 1.

Parker had indeed "out-Morganed Morgan" on this single topic. Had he continued to produce a material culture and technology and monographs on arts and decorations, designs and clothing, on all of which he was doing research, and on which he alone commanded the material, we would not be today without an adequate study of the arts and industries of the Iroquois. But let us be thankful for what he did and see how well he did it.

Like many ethnologists Parker discovered that once he commenced to ask questions informants recalled "many interesting facts" that were "brought out from almost hidden recesses of their minds." *Iroquois Uses of Maize* represents the fruits of ten years of original inquiry of many informants both on the New York Iroquois reservations and at Six Nations Reserve in Canada. The main ones are listed (p. 6). All of the names cited in the text are in the language of the Seneca, whom he says are the most conservative of the Iroquois; but theirs was the dialect he knew. He made an attempt to employ the orthography for phonetic transcription of Iroquoian terms that Hewitt (whom he spells Hewett) had recently published. His command of Seneca constructs was

---

[44] Parker to Clarke, 7/31/10.

really quite good, as witness his information of the role of Seneca matrons (p. 24); but his phonetics are primitive by today's standards, and rightfully every term in the text should be corrected to the "Handbook of the Seneca Language" (1963),[45] by Wallace L. Chafe, who used Parker as a source for eliciting the terms in the field.

The strengths of Parker's monograph are in the descriptions of social customs attending the maize cycle and the eating customs of the Seneca in which activities he was himself both participant and observer (p. 62). He might have cited Asher Wright's correspondence with Morgan on mutual aid customs and property in fields (pp. 29–30), although it may not have been then available to him.[46] His next strength lies in observations and systematic descriptions of the varieties of maize (p. 43), although this topic is subject to refinement by Waugh,[47] who considerably lengthened the list and added a color plate, which moved Parker to comment to me, "Waugh beat me!" A third strength is the notes and illustrations on the manufacture and use of objects of material culture: baskets, bowls, ladles, stirrers, elm-bark trays and dishes, etc. (p. 45 ff.). Here again Waugh has more to say but nothing essentially new. The same can be said of the cook book (p. 66 ff.). In general, Parker excels at relating what he describes to the ethos of Iroquois culture, while Waugh's training in natural history led him to be systematic to the point of setting up a matrix through which the culture escaped.

But it is not until one consults Waugh's more scientific study, which has the advantage of having been done in the years after the appearance of Parker's bulletin, that one begins to see the deficiencies in Parker. Waugh was an exceedingly meticulous scholar, but on rereading Parker recently, I found many obvious inconsistencies that have not been previously mentioned. Here is a work

---

[45] New York State Museum and Science Service *Bulletin* 388, 50–56; Hewitt, J. N. B., "Iroquoian Cosmology (Part I)," *Annual Report,* Bureau of American Ethnology, XXI:127–339 (1900).
[46] Stern, Bernhard J., "The Letters of Asher Wright to Lewis Henry Morgan," *American Anthropologist,* XXXV(1):138–45.
[47] Waugh, F. W., "Iroquois Foods and Food Preparation," *Memoirs,* Canada Department of Mines, Geological Survey, 86 (1916): 1–235.

that has all the apparatus of a scholarly research paper, including the call numbers of books in the State Library, but some names of important authors are misspelled; Morgan of all persons is "Louis" instead of Lewis H.; and titles of works are inaccurate and frequently wrong. After asking one member of my staff, Mr. Paul Weinman, who had been doing an Iroquois bibliography, to check some of the more obvious references to Morgan, Heckewelder, and any other work of his choice, I spent some discouraging hours comparing the bulletin and books that Parker used.

The mistakes comprise essentially failure to follow copy in the originals quoted, including punctuation, accents, spelling, singular and plural forms, and paragraphing. There are two quotes attributed to Heckewelder that are not on the pages cited, unless Parker used a different edition than the one cited, and he gives the wrong title for the work. Parker apparently did not know French, but he had the help of Marchand, the sculptor, who was working with him on the Indian Groups, in translating passages from Lahontan, Lafitau, and Bacqueville de la Potherie, although the latter does not appear in the bibliography. Of the four references to Lafitau (pp. 24, 31, 34, 71), the original French is incorrectly cited once, two references are on the page cited, and none is given on the last. But even when using American sources like the journals of Sullivan's soldiers in the campaign of 1779, Parker is not precise, although his slips do not alter the enormity of destruction of Indian lands (p. 19). There is a point to all this nit-picking. Parker, in representing himself as a scholar to the learned world, took some short cuts, and he never got caught. It is another example of lateralization. Had Parker indeed studied at Harvard, as so many thought, and had Roland B. Dixon, who had an eagle eye for the literature of anthropology, been on his degree committee, Parker would have been sent back to the library to check his sources. Lacking this kind of supervision and hurriedly going it alone, he deserves praise for what he accomplished.

And Parker was just that lucky with reviewers. His old friend Frank Speck read the bulletin for the *American Anthropologist,* appraising it as "a most careful and detailed study of an important topic in the ethnology of the Iroquois." He noted that Parker enjoyed a "particularly favorable position to investigate these important tribes which have for so long remained in a state of neglect on the part of trained ethnologists." If this was a sample of what might be expected in further topical studies by Parker "we shall have a comprehensive library on the life of these Indians." Speck was not satisfied with the level of analysis employed in translating native terms of plants and implements, a deficiency he had previously communicated to Parker through Skinner about the importance of taking texts phonetically in the original Iroquoian language.[48] But he praised Parker's style and encouraged him.

Genuine recognition of Parker's solid scientific achievement came in Wissler's survey of the material culture of the North American Indians and in the subsequent classic, *The American Indian* (1917, 1922).[49] Parker's field study demonstrated two things: First, "how completely that people drew upon the contiguous flora," and second, "how completely the white colonists absorbed the maize complex of the Indians." Indeed as Parker wrote, "And thus the maize plant was the bridge over which English civilization crept, tremblingly and uncertainly, at first, then boldly and surely to a foothold and a permanent occupation of America"[50] (p. 15). Wissler readily perceived that, despite the importance of this historical transfer and although "the homely art of maize culture is still practiced by many surviving natives, the only field studies we have approaching a satisfactory standard are those of Parker, . . . Hough for the Hopi, and Wilson for the Hidatsa." Wissler goes on to say that the very best of literature can never take the place of field studies. Only the work of Parker and Wilson enables us to judge "how closely the cultivation of maize of white farmers follows aboriginal patterns."[51]

By this time Waugh's work appeared, too late to preempt the field, and was only listed in the bibliography of Wissler's second

---

[48] Speck, Frank G., reviewer, "Iroquois Uses of Maize . . . ," *American Anthropologist*, XIII:135–36 (1911).
[49] Wissler, Clark, "The Material Culture of North American Indians," *ibid.*, XVI:447–505.
[50] Parker (1910), 15.
[51] Wissler (1922), 19, 21.

edition. George F. Will and George F. Hyde were inspired by
reading Parker to make a study of *Corn among the Indians of
the Upper Missouri* (1917). Will and his father were plant
breeders at Bismarck, North Dakota, and he once told me that
Parker's work had influenced the direction of their experiments
with drought-resistant corn.[52] And the long chain of dependence
on Parker runs down to the great botanical works on maize of
our day.[53]

Food habits and preferences are among man's most conservative behavior patterns. Several of the cooking and eating customs
(p. 59 ff.) and corn foods (p. 66 ff.) persist today in Seneca
homes in western New York and among the Six Nations near
Brantford, Canada. The old corn foods are prepared for the festivals in the longhouse, but hulled corn soup, besides being the
staple fare at family feasts honoring the medicine societies, is
offered for sale at longhouse socials and at ball games. Mush is
still made for the False Faces. Jesse Cornplanter used to distinguish "corn soup-eating people near the longhouse" from "salad
eating Indians" of the church socials; but even the Christian
Iroquois are nostalgic about the old foods. In recent years the
ladies of the Jimersontown United Presbyterian Church at the
Allegany Reservation of the Seneca Nation have put on an annual
Indian food dinner for the Salamanca community. The menu
varies with available garden vegetables and the luck of hunters.
There is invariably hulled corn soup and frequently venison. The
menu for ca. 1958 carries recipes for five items of corn foods,
besides colored beans, Ghost Bread (fried white-flour bread),
and salt pork. Dema Crouse Stoffer contributed the menu notes
from which I select a few pertinent recipes.

Wah-da-sgion-dah [watéskon:tak, "it's been baked"; also called
ʔonɛ:ʔtaʔ], Burnt, or Roasted Corn Soup. This is made of white corn

[52] Will, George F. and Hyde, George E., *Corn among the Indians of the Upper Missouri*, Little Histories of the North American Indians, No. 5 (St. Louis,
1917); see Wissler (1922); George F. Will personal communication, 1932.
[53] Mangelsdorf, P. C., and Reeves, R. G., "The Origin of Indian Corn and
Its Relatives," Texas Agricultural Experimental Station *Bulletin* No. 574
(College Station, Texas, 1939), 313. (The bibliography lists Parker but not
Waugh.)

roasted on top of the stove until it is black. It is then taken off the cob and dried out of doors under a screen. When soup is desired it is cooked in water with colored beans and salt port in a large open kettle.

O-noh-gwah [ʔonó:hkwaʔ], Hulled Corn Soup. This is made from white corn gathered from the fields after it has ripened on the stalk. The husks are braided together and the long braids are hung in a dry place until . . . [one] wishes to shell some for use. The shelled corn is boiled with hard wood ashes until the hull loosens and comes off. It then goes through many water baths until it is clear . . . usually . . . by placing the kernels in a basket and swishing it . . . in running water. It then is cooked with colored beans and salt pork as [above] . . . (Cf. Parker, 74)

Oh-sonh-wenh [ʔoshonwɛ:ʔ], Parched Corn Mush (Parker, corn pudding, p. 75). This is made of white shelled corn placed in a large iron kettle and parched. This is then pounded into flour and cooked for several hours until a mush is formed. It is then seasoned with bacon and maple syrup.

Ga-gai-te-ta-a-kwa- [kakaehtɛ'htaʔ or kakaeht'htonh ʔä:hkwaʔ] Boiled Corn Bread. For this . . . purple, calico, or hominy corn is used. After shelling the corn it is boiled in water with hard wood ashes for about one-half hour. It then is washed clear and the hulls are discarded. The kernels are then placed in the mortar and pulverized with a pestle. The granules are then sifted. The meal is mixed with boiling water and shaped into cakes. These cakes are then plunged into boiling water and boiled until they float. Beans are now used in the cakes with the corn. In some instances, dried blackberries are used. This is eaten with butter. (Parker, p. 69. A little boiled bread goes a long way, and it takes a strong digestive tract.—W.N.F.)

O-non-daat [ʔonontä:ʔ], Hominy . . . is prepared from the colored corn (*Ha-go-wah*) [héhko:wa:h, *Zea mays indurata,* "flint corn"]. The corn is placed in the mortar and moistened with a small amount of water. To make the pounding easier a small amount of soda is used. When the hulls begin to come off easily the pounding quickens until the corn is broken into small pieces. It is then sifted. The hominy passes through the basket and the uncracked kernels are returned to the mortar for further pounding. The hominy is tossed to . . . [winnow out] the hulls. This is cooked in water and then sweetened with sugar. (Parker, p. 73. After hulled-corn soup, hominy is the favorite. Today, hominy is available commercially as a canned good, and Iroquois cooks no longer take the trouble to pound and winnow flint corn.—W.N.F.)

VI

Iroquois Uses of Maize represented the subsistence pattern of the conservative longhouse people who are the followers of the Gaíwi :yo :h, or the "Good Message" of Handsome Lake. The Code of Handsome Lake is still being preached in the longhouses, or at the several "fires," of the Iroquois today. What was once a cult has now established itself as a religion: It has regularly established churches called "fires"; it has ordained ministers, called "preachers" in English or "speakers" in Seneca; it has a duly appointed body of elders, or "Keepers of the Good Message"; and it has put out missions to formerly Christian parts. Parker's bulletin containing the Code, for want of anything better, has become the Bible of the "new religion." The original edition of 2,000 copies printed in 1913 has long since sold out, and the book is now a collector's item. Its readers are both Iroquois, who need the book, and anthropologists, psychologists, and a host of other academicians, who study messianic movements, of which this has become one of the classic types. Reprinting it here fulfills a double need.

When Arthur Parker went to Cattaraugus Reservation to collect manuscripts for the State Library, Edward Cornplanter, or Sosondó :wa (Deep Night), for two years had devotedly been copying the Code from memory into an old minute book of the Seneca Lacrosse Club. Sosondó :wa was one of several authorized holders of the Gaíwi :yo :h, and in this capacity regularly preached the Good Message to the Longhouse fold at Newtown, and annually traveled on call to the other fires of the longhouse religion in western New York and Canada. Sosondó :wa was aware that the Code was subject to a process of drift because his version was not identical to that preached by other holders of the Good

Message. Thus theological arguments were developing among the "Guardians of the Good Message" at the several centers where it was celebrated as to the precise word order and the proper number of "words," as the chapters and paragraphs are called. This was his motivation in writing it out. The argument over content and order was still going on during my field work at Allegany Reservation in the thirties.

Parker arrived at the strategic moment. I find it amazing in the light of my own experience in such matters that he succeeded in persuading Chief Cornplanter to finish the writing and then entrust the conservation of the document to the State of New York. Parker enlisted the services of William Bluesky as interpreter, and then brought Cornplanter to accept this Baptist preacher as the vehicle for preserving the Longhouse religion. This ecumenical exercise is unmatched in the annals of native religions. Apparently, according to Parker's introduction (p. 8), the two native preachers developed a mutual respect.

Parker did try to secure an accurate Seneca text. Evidently Cornplanter read from his minute book or recited from memory, Bluesky rendered it into English, and Parker wrote it down. At that, it is a remarkable job of translation—Senecas who have heard the Code recited can take the English text and render it back into Seneca. But there are some things, they say, which are lacking in the English version, and these lapses are both stylistic and contextual.

The proof is in the recitation. Of the Handsome Lake preachers whom I have known and heard, Henry Redeye of Allegany got his version from Oscar Crow, and he claimed it was somewhat different from the Cornplanter-Bluesky-Parker version, but Henry Redeye died before I could get him to commit the Seneca text to tape, and Henan Scrogg of Tonawanda told me that he learned the Code from Parker's publication. Yet when I heard him recite it on several occasions, and I tried to follow him with the book, stylistic considerations lengthened the passages considerably. So Parker got the gist of it in the order that Cornplanter put it down in his halting, written Seneca. His son Jesse Cornplanter, whom

I knew in his later years, said that when his father preached from his own book, much of the meaning was not captured in the English text.

Recent attempts to capture Gaíwi:yo:h have all ended with failure or only partial success. Wallace L. Chafe, then a graduate student and now a professor at Berkeley, and the writer persuaded Ed Curry, the present speaker at the Coldspring Longhouse, to tape the current Coldspring version. It went fine for two days until public criticism began to mount and Ed succumbed to diffuse sanctions: people talked. The project remains incomplete. On another occasion, Chief Corbett Sundown of Tonawanda arranged to have me send recording apparatus to the Tonawanda Longhouse. The preacher agreed to being taped, but delegates there from other longhouses objected, and the matter was set aside. All of this is pertinent to the uniqueness of Parker's accomplishment and underscores how indispensable his work has become.

Since Parker published in 1913 much has been learned about the historical circumstances of Handsome Lake's vision. Quakers who were present at Cornplanter, in Warren County, Pennsylvania, mention the vision and revelation in their journals, which now are in print, on the basis of which M. H. Deardorff has reconstructed the events that are recalled in the oral tradition.[54] There is no better example of the authentication of oral literature by historical fact. None of this was available to Parker.

The whole question of Nativistic Movements came up for discussion at the Centenary of the American Ethnological Society in 1942, for which the late Professor Ralph Linton, then at Columbia, prepared a perceptive paper which proposes a fourfold typology.[55] Nowhere is Handsome Lake mentioned, but marginally I noted that he fits the prophet role perfectly, and his doctrine is what Linton calls "Revivalistic-magical." The perpetuation of the old successful ceremonies would ensure survival

---

[54] Deardorff, M. H., "The Religion of Handsome Lake: Its Origin and Development," Symposium on Local Diversity in Iroquois Culture, W. N. Fenton, ed., Bureau of American Ethnology *Bulletin* 149, Smithsonian Institution (Washington, 1951), No. 5, 77–107.

[55] Linton, Ralph, "Nativistic Movements," *American Anthropologist*, XLV: 230–240.

of the society. In recent years, since interest in Nativistic Movements has exploded, the literature on them has increased enormously. Professor Wallace, Speck's student and now his successor at the University of Pennsylvania, speculates that such religious productions, including myths and rituals, arise in periods of social and cultural stress and "come into existence as parts of a program or code of religious revitalization movements." His analysis of the Handsome Lake Code receives summary statement in his recent book on *Religion*,[56] and the career of the prophet is the subject of a full-length study by Wallace soon to be published.

The relevance of all this is that Parker had his finger on the pulse of something quite vital. Although his treatment of the life and times of the prophet are now somewhat altered by later research, he still gives us a rounded picture of the situation during the first decade of this century. Twice before the book went to the printer Parker went over the translation with Edward Cornplanter, and, as Parker reports, "this is Cornplanter's own translation of the 'New Religion.' . . ."[57] The next year, when the bulletin was in preparation, he predicted, "It will be a free translation . . . and should prove of some psychological as well as sociological interest. It was Handsome Lake who revolutionized in 16 years the disintegrating Seneca and Onondaga tribes and recrystallized their native beliefs. This was accomplished at the critical moment in [their] history—immediately after the Revolutionary War, when the Iroquois League was broken and disheartened. Handsome Lake's teaching gave new life and new hope. . . ."[58]

At the same time Handsome Lake's Code documented some shifts in the structure of Iroquois society. Wallace has called these the decline of the Iroquois matriarchate. For example, the prophet manifests concern over the fragile nature of the Iroquois family nucleus since the main line of loyalty runs through the mother's

---

[56] Wallace, A. F. C., *Religion: an Anthropological View* (New York: Random House, 1966), 30–32.
[57] Parker, in Report of the Director of the State Museum for 1911, New York State Museum *Bulletin* 158, 65–66.
[58] Parker, Report of the Director . . . for 1912, *ibid.*, 164, 56.

lineage. This led to a situation of brittle monogamy supported only by the mutual satisfaction of the spouses. With the decline in importance of the clan and lineage and the rise of social disorganization in the frontier situation, especially drinking and its consequences, the nuclear family was unable to stand the strains of quarreling, gossip, parental irresponsibility, and infidelity. Handsome Lake devotes several sections to these problems. He also speaks of the responsibility of grandchildren for the old people. And he creates the model of a new man. Wallace goes on to explain why Handsome Lake held such views. The forces at work were economic and a new kind of kinship dominance was coming into being. The nuclear family was going to be more important in an agrarian society.[59]

The Code prescribes the maintenance of much ancient Iroquois ritual behavior. The Code sanctions the celebration of the Four Ceremonies, which are addressed to the Creator, and these— Great Feather Dance, the Thanksgiving or Drum Dance, Personal Chant, and Bowl Game—comprise the core of the two great ceremonial marks at Midwinter or New Year and at Green Corn, which segment the annual cycle. Between them come the smaller thanksgiving rites for the increase of the crops, while the medicine society rites, which come at unstated intervals scattered throughout the year, are held mainly in winter. Handsome Lake preached against these smaller feasts because in the last decade of the eighteenth century they were occasions for drunken brawls. But gradually they crept back into favor, sometimes with changed functions to fit the newer times.

Preaching the Code annually fortifies the ceremonies. The second day of the preaching is devoted to virtues of hospitality, mutual aid, and the maintenance of the reinforcing ceremonies mentioned above that enhance the growth and maturation of the agricultural staples on which the life of society depends. Thus, the life of the Handsome Lake adherent is passed virtually in ful-

---

[59] Wallace, A. F. C., "Handsome Lake and the Decline of the Iroquois Matriarchate." (Unpublished paper, prepared for seminar on Kinship and Culture, Burg Wartenstein, Austria, 1966; to appear in his forthcoming biography of Handsome Lake.)

filling his ceremonial obligations. Sketches of these particular rites and ceremonies, therefore, make up the second part of Parker's monograph. Parker does not treat the annual cycle of ceremonies which he observed at the Newtown Longhouse as a unified whole, but parts of it are represented in full or outline form from his notebooks of the early 1900's. Several of the texts of prayers and ritual addresses appear in translation, but these are now available in the original Seneca texts to the extent that Wallace Chafe recovered them from Solon Jones fifty years later.[60] Parker included in his monograph two articles reprinted from learned journals. The then sensational discovery of the Secret Medicine societies, which first appeared in the *American Anthropologist,* stimulated the writer to do a full-scale monograph on the Eagle Dance, and to undertake museum and field research on the False Faces and the Society of Faces.[61] The entire form and function of these rites as they foster conservatism on the Six Nations Reserve have been treated in books by Speck and Shimony, and for the New York Onondaga by Blau.[62] Parker's second article on sun myths is reprinted from the *Journal of American Folklore* (1910).

No adherent of the Handsome Lake religion is laid to rest without the words of the Funeral Address (p. 107) being said over his body by an appointed preacher of the cousin clans, or the opposite moiety of society. And at the wake, during the lull in the Moccasin Game (which two sides play by hiding a bullet in one of four moccasins while drumming to keep the mourners awake) someone may relate the legend of the coming of death (p. 107). Then ten days later, the bereaved relatives thank those who per-

---

[60] Chafe, Wallace L., "Seneca Thanksgiving Rituals," Bureau of American Ethnology *Bulletin* 183.

[61] Parker (1909) ; Fenton, "The Iroquois Eagle Dance: an offshoot of the Calumet Dance," Bureau of American Ethnology *Bulletin* 156 (1953) ; "Masked Medicine Societies of the Iroquois," *Annual Report* of Smithsonian Institution for 1940, 397–430; "Some Questions of Classification, Typology, and Style Raised by Iroquois Masks," *Trans.,* New York Academy of Science, Ser. (2) XVIII(4) :347–57 (1956).

[62] Speck, Frank G., *Midwinter Rites of the Cayuga Long House* (Philadelphia: University of Pennsylvania Press, 1949) ; Shimony, Annemarie Anrod, "Conservatism among the Iroquois of the Six Nations Reserve," *Yale University Publications in Anthropology,* No. 65 (1961) ; Blau, Harold, "Function and the False Faces," *Journal of American Folklore,* LXXIX, No. 314 (1966).

formed the ceremony and dug the grave with a memorial feast which stems from the deepest roots of Iroquois culture history (p. 110).

Although Parker's key to the pronunciation of Seneca is not in accordance with modern standards of descriptive linguistics, the glossary of Seneca terms is rich in cultural content. Both are updated and corrected in Chafe's "Handbook of the Seneca Language." [63] So much for the heart of Parker's ethnology.

VII

The so-called *Constitution of the Five Nations,* our third item, is a compilation of native manuscripts of which Parker is in reality the editor. The material was discovered by him, commencing in 1910 during a visit to the Six Nations Reserve on Grand River, Ontario, when Parker went there to secure casts of representative Mohawks and Cayugas for the Indian Groups which were then in preparation. He then met Seth Newhouse, the native scribe, and other chiefs of the Six Nations, and learned to his amazement that ancient forms and rites were still practiced there as if the League of the Iroquois had never covered up its fire or the member tribes disbanded. This was not a new discovery. Horatio Hale made known to the learned world the continued existence of the League by the publication of *The Iroquois Book of Rites* (1883), and J. N. B. Hewitt of the Smithsonian was regularly communicating papers on the subject to scholarly journals.[64] Further, Hewitt knew and rejected some of the sources which Parker assembled and edited. Hewitt was working with the native texts slowly and patiently; Parker was ill-equipped to go behind the native literature that came to him in Indian-English manuscripts, and he was anxious to publish. His belated publication was to bring him ac-

---

[63] Chafe (1963).
[64] Hale, Horatio, *The Iroquois Book of Rites* (Philadelphia, 1883, reprinted by University of Toronto Press, 1963) ; Hewitt, J. N. B., "Era of the Formation of the Historic League of the Iroquois," *American Anthropologist,* VII, 61–67 (1894).

claim in some quarters and invite critical scorn from two fellow Iroquoianists. How this came to pass is a tale worth telling.

Seth Newhouse, or *Dayodakane* (1842–1921), was an Onondaga of the Six Nations Reserve who spoke Mohawk eloquently and represented the Warrior's party in nativist causes. He was often at odds with the policies of the Council of Life Chiefs, but he was with them solidly in opposition to the Canadian government. Above all he strove to adapt the institutions of the Iroquois Confederacy to the problems of local government on the reserve. From the 1880's on, these institutions were under attack by the progressive elements on the reserve, by the missionaries, and by the representatives of the Dominion government. Like all reformers Newhouse was a bit of a prophet. He questioned the old men on the lore of the League, and he patiently wrote down their cultural memories in his limited but picturesque English. Having codified the law and custom, he earnestly carried petitions to the Council of Chiefs to get them to accept his manuscript draft which he had ready by 1885. But the chiefs failed to heed the Speaker for the Warriors and the Women, and he died in 1921 as the movement for the elective system and the abolition of the life chiefs was gaining headway. Dekanawidah's prediction was about to come true. The skull of the old League would roll three years later.

The chiefs, having twice rejected Newhouse's construction of their laws, appointed a committee of themselves to draw up a substitute version which they approved in 1900. Parker acknowledges this source (p. 13) and lists the committee (p. 61), but fails to mention that the document was already in print, having been communicated to the Royal Society of Canada by Duncan Campbell Scott in 1911.[65] By far the most learned member of the committee of chiefs was Chief John A. Gibson, with whom Hewitt was working at the time, recording in Onondaga what the

[65] Scott, Duncan Campbell, "Traditional History of the Confederacy of the Six Nations," Royal Society of Canada, *Proc. and Trans.*, 3rd ser., V (Ottawa, 1912), Sec. II, 195–246.

committee set over into flawless English. The authenticity and conformity with ancient tradition of the committee version can be largely attributed to Gibson's intellect, but Chief Gibson seems not to have been satisfied either with the version of Newhouse, who was opinionated, or of the committee. There was a second occasion in 1912 when Chief Gibson dictated the Onondaga text of the origin of the Confederacy, this time to Professor Alexander A. Goldenweiser, in a much expanded form to comprise the ritual of the Condolence Council, amounting to 525 manuscript pages. Together these two texts, the first of which I translated with Simeon Gibson, and the latter still largely untranslated, constitute the most satisfactory single native account of the League.[66] Such was the state of native Iroquois ethnohistory when Parker made his discovery.

A certain ethnic and psychological identity drew Newhouse and Parker together. They were both Indians, Iroquois patriots, and fellow ethnologists with complementary talents. Parker, in addition, held an official position with a great museum that might make a book of the "traditional history and constitution of the Iroquois Confederacy" which Hewitt, at the Smithsonian, had failed to accept. Perhaps, also, Newhouse was weary of trying to convert his labored English back into Mohawk for Hewitt. Newhouse and Parker were in correspondence for several years in an effort to recover the Six Nations wampum belts, once on the reserve and now in the hands of a trader in Wisconsin. Newhouse particularly wanted to recover the "Pledge," given by George III, of the independence of the confederated tribes. But Parker failed to get the trader to admit that he had it. In addition to these joint endeavors, Newhouse also solicited the help of Director Clarke and Parker to locate and verify the written treaty behind this agreement, thinking it might be in Albany or Ottawa. Further, he wanted copies of the printed New York Colonial Documents.[67]

---

[66] Fenton, W. N., "Seth Newhouse's Traditional History and Constitution of the Iroquois Confederacy," *Proceedings,* American Philosophical Society, 93(2):141–58, 158–59.

[67] Seth Newhouse to Clarke, 10/3/1908; Newhouse to Parker, 3/21/1910; Parker to Newhouse, 3/22/1910, 4/13/1910.

But Parker had the chief's version in hand a year before he received the Newhouse manuscript. His report for the year 1909 complains that work on folklore and ceremonials was retarded by other duties, but that "some notes were taken, however, on a very important manuscript secured through the courtesy of Rev. A. J. Farney of Ohsweken, Ontario. . . ." It was the official version of how Dekanawidah founded the League, ending with the Condolence ceremony verbatim from Hale, which Parker attributed to to the accuracy of Hale's work.[68]

It was the next June when the Newhouse manuscript came into the "possession of the division." Parker speaks of it as "the Dekanawideh code of the Iroquois by Seth Newhouse, a Canadian Mohawk" who has been compiling it "for twenty years." Parker believed that its essential accuracy was attested by similarities with the Chiefs' version, "the two being written independently." He adds that Newhouse wrote in "Indian-English and affords a quaint example of the transcription of Indian thought and concept into English." [69] In writing to Newhouse that he had returned home and was prepared to receive the manuscript, Parker assured the author that he could guarantee its safekeeping, and that it would not be copied or used to his detriment. "My aim is to have it published among the documents on Indian history which we issue from time to time . . . ," and one hundred copies go to the author gratis. He was also to send his Mohawk text of the Condolence ceremony and any other such documents. Instructions were to send it express under the enclosed label, addressed to the Education Department, and declare it as a historical manuscript. It arrived safely in Albany, and Parker showed it to Clarke late in June, obtained a partial commitment to publish it, and again reassured Newhouse about free copies and his rights. Within a fortnight the requested Mohawk texts were received, and Parker began to prepare the author for editorial changes.[70]

Parker's method of editing the manuscripts has an interesting

[68] 63rd Annual Report of the New York State Museum for 1909. New York State Museum *Bulletin* 140, 63.

[69] Report of the Director, 1910, *ibid.,* 149:48–49.

[70] Parker to Newhouse, 5/23/1910, 6/23/1910, 7/7/1910.

bearing on the results. He submitted the Newhouse manuscript for criticism and correction to Albert Cusick, an Onondaga-Tuscarora who had worked as informant with Hale and then Beauchamp, and Cusick devoted more than a month's expert service to the task of making it a satisfactory translation (p. 12). Parker next "made a codified version of the Constitution for comparative purposes and placed similar articles together regardless of the original form. . . ." He explained to Newhouse that this was "just as a barrister would do." This re-ordered version was then typed and the carbon copy offered to Newhouse, with the promise of a copy of his own text later. The Newhouse manuscript was originally divided into three sections: (1) "The Tree of the Long Leaves"; (2) "The Emblematical Union Compact"; and (3) "Skanawatih's Law of Peace and War." Each of these sections or laws was supported by a wampum belt or string, and the number of the mnemonic and the section of the code from which it is taken appears after each law in Parker's edition (p. 13). The system is explained in a foot-note (p. 30). Parker explained further to Newhouse that he had seen fit to change the language so that "our readers may understand," making the style conform to the "Regents editing system." "The meaning," Parker assures him, "is not changed at all, as you will see when the manuscript reaches you," hopefully in a few days. But Parker did not mention Albert Cusick or any similar outside opinions.[71]

The State of New York evidently never acquired title to the Newhouse manuscript and supplements. Newhouse was simply treated as an outside author who was submitting his manuscript to the Museum for publication, and Parker was expected to put it in shape. Indeed Parker wrote to William Beauchamp of Syracuse saying, "Last year when I was on the Grand River Six Nations' Reservation I borrowed a manuscript which embraced the Condolence Rite or Peace Hymn, the legend of the origin of the League and the code of the wampum laws." Parker notes a remarkable similarity between Newhouse's version of the Condolence rite and that published in Beauchamp's monograph. "Mr.

[71] *Ibid.*, 2/21/1911.

Newhouse wants us to publish his version." Parker wondered whether Beauchamp had seen it because the Museum did not wish to duplicate work already in print.[72]

March 29, 1911, was a grim mark on the cultural calendar of Albany. In the fire which destroyed the west end of the Capitol and the State Library that night more than two-thirds of the ethnographical collection went up in flames, including a collection of costumes and fabrics acquired for the Regents by L. H. Morgan, a similar proportion of the small but valuable Converse collection, and 200 of the nearly 300 objects which Parker had personally collected since joining the staff. Parker and his assistant rushed into the burning building and rescued more valuable items within reach, and although his reports make much of this role, his letters written afterward reveal the depth of his depression at the loss. "It was an awful experience, I assure you, to see the fruits of one's labors and the results of 60 years by others shrivel up in the merciless flame . . . the most discouraging feature of it all is that most of this material can never be replaced." [73] Fortunately, two weeks previously Parker had withdrawn about half of his manuscripts from the State Library and put them in his office in Geological Hall, down State Street. Thus, they escaped the holocaust. But editing the Newhouse manuscript was necessarily put aside for the more crucial task of conserving the surviving collections. There was no money for publication now since funds were diverted to the great expense of the emergency. Newhouse would have to wait.

But Parker was beset by other tides. It was years since the Regents had raised his salary from $900 to $1200 per annum, which was still inadequate to meet family expenses although it was halfway up the pay scale for state scientists. He was lecturing widely and entertaining publisher's offers, and he was considering a career

[72] Parker to Beauchamp, 2/17/1911; Beauchamp, W. M., "Civil, Religious and Mourning Councils and Ceremonies of Adoption of the New York Indians," New York State Museum *Bulletin* 113.
[73] Parker to Barrett, 5/13/1911.

in the Indian rights movement. Building the Indian Groups occupied his workdays, and difficulties were arising in the staff
among designers, artists, and planners. Nevertheless, Parker
tried to continue his writing at home, and in April he petitioned
Director Clarke for release of a treatise on Indian law in which
he planned to include the "basic codes of the Iroquois. . . ."
Since no part of it was "done on State time or paid for by State
money," Parker asked for reassurance and relief from censure if
he published it commercially. To his credit, Clarke endorsed the
letter, "I see no objection whatever to this plan," and returned it
to Parker.[74] Neither the plan to bring out a limited edition in
Albany nor the suggestion to have it published by the National
Museum of Canada ever came to fruition.

By now the "code" had become a "constitution," which, says
Parker, is how the Iroquois refer to it, as do both Hale and
Morgan. His 1911 report devotes five pages to a gloss on its content.[75] Both Albert Cusick, already mentioned, and Chief John A.
Gibson died during 1912, removing from the scene the two most
competent native critics of the Iroquois political tradition. Parker
went off to Washington for a year to serve the Society of American Indians, and his book was finally published four years later.

It is fortunate that Parker's reputation as an ethnologist does
not rest on the two reviews which greeted the Constitution in
succeeding years in the *American Anthropologist*. Goldenweiser,
who himself had worked with Chief Gibson, analyzed and compared the two principal manuscripts which comprise Parker's
bulletin. Goldenweiser calls the Newhouse manuscript "MS 1"
and the chiefs' version "MS 2," noting that MS 1 is an enumera-
tion of laws and MS 2 gives the fullest coverage of the origin
legend then in print. He then politely notes "the absence of any
reference [to Scott's publication, already cited, which] must be
due to a regrettable oversight." Following a long point-for-point
comparison, he concluded, "An analysis . . . can leave no doubt

---

[74] Parker to Clarke, 4/25/1911.
[75] Report of the Director for 1911. New York State Museum *Bulletin* 158:66.

that MS 1 reflects Iroquois society at a much later stage in its development than is the case in MS 2. The impression, in fact, derived from a study of MS 1 is one of ancient Iroquois society distorted by abnormal social conditions and the intrusion of modern traits. . . ." Goldenweiser inferred from his analysis what can now be demonstrated historically, as we have seen, namely "the breakdown of a highly complex and coherent socio-political system, under the stress of modern conditions." "MS 2 represents an exceedingly old traditional record, but weakly rationalized by the intrusion of later interpretations. . . ." In short, Newhouse's manuscript cannot be "regarded as a genuine native product," and "The Constitution of the Five Nations" is a figment. It does not exist. For, apart from the legend of Dekanawidah, the Indians of the Iroquois League had no constitution, either written or unwritten.[76] Newhouse was protesting and rationalizing a situation on the Grand River Reserve in 1885–1900; and the chiefs had stuck to the oral tradition.

Hewitt, who wrote the second review, knew the strengths and weaknesses of the informants, Cusick, Newhouse, and Gibson, for he had worked with them all. Moreover, he knew the languages or could control the translations from the languages in which the originals were given. The history of Newhouse's literary efforts was quite familiar to him, commencing with the first draft of the "Constitution" in 1880; Hewitt could have bought the 1885 draft in 1888 for the Smithsonian, and he knew well that the Committee of Chiefs was commissioned by the Council to prepare a substitute for the Newhouse document, since he, Hewitt, was a guest of Chief Gibson at the time. Moreover, Hewitt and all friends of the Council derived satisfaction from the fact that no less a literary luminary than Duncan Campbell Scott of Ottawa communicated the chiefs' version to the Royal Society of Canada, and it appeared in the *Transactions*. Parker might better have explained this. Hewitt's long review article picks up technical errors

[76] Goldenweiser, A. A., reviewer, "The Constitution of the Five Nations. Arthur C. Parker," *American Anthropologist*, XVIII:431–36 (1916).

in Parker's publication, but it does not include Goldenweiser's theoretical argument.[77] Hewitt's main points were these: First, that "Parker tells us that two main manuscripts form the basis of his publication," but "fails to point out the value of either manuscript, or to explain the significance of the serious conflict of statements of essential facts . . . between the two." Second, Parker should have told us that the version of the Committee of Chiefs was prepared as a substitute for the Newhouse document. Third, Parker represents that these two manuscripts were "discovered" in 1910 on the Six Nations Reserve, while it is a fact that the Newhouse "Constitution" had been known in briefer form since 1880. The remainder of Hewitt's points are of a technical nature: errors of translation by Newhouse who thought in Mohawk and wrote in English; the number of federal chiefs, whether fifty or forty-nine, as Hewitt claimed; matters of orthography; that the religious festivals all antedated the time of Handsome Lake; and the inclusion by Newhouse in Sections 93 to 96 of matter which Hewitt himself had translated from Lafitau's *Moeurs* for Newhouse's benefit and made available to him.

If Parker could not forget these two reviews, the rest of the learned world soon did. Historians then and now cite his *Constitution* (for it stood alone until Paul Wallace's *White Roots of Peace,* published in 1946, gave us a gloss on the Hewitt and Gibson version of Dekanawidah); and the work is still occasionally referenced in general works on cultural anthropology.[78]

Thus Parker's career as an ethnologist came to a close. He was a pioneer in describing the subsistence patterns and food resources of an American Indian people. His study of maize and its uses set a standard for such studies and was used as a model for similar

[77] Hewitt, J. N. B., reviewer, "Constitution; Traditional History of the Confederacy of the Six Nations. Duncan Campbell Scott; and Civil, Religious and Mourning Councils . . . Beauchamp," *ibid.,* XIX(3):429–38 (1917).

[78] Murdock, G. P., *Our Primitive Contemporaries* (New York, 1934); Linton, Ralph, *The Tree of Culture* (New York, 1955), 604; Gipson, L. H., *The British Empire before the American Revolution,* V (New York: Knopf, 1942), 69.

work on the Plains Indians and in the American southwest. His recovery of the Code of Handsome Lake was another first step along the path to understanding revitalization movements among native peoples of the world. His so-called Constitution of the Five Nations represents the effort of native scribes to codify custom law and usage in the face of pressures from without and to answer criticism from within a native society. Seen from the present day, it is now easier to reflect on what Seth Newhouse was attempting for the people of the Six Nations Reserve on Grand River than it was in Parker's day. If the Constitution was not a model of aboriginal political structure, as Parker thought—and his critics maintained it was not—what he collected from the then living sources cannot be had again, and what he salvaged in the mesh of undeveloped ethnological theory can fortunately be reinterpreted and perhaps even reworked with living Iroquois informants who are the grandsons of his sources.

BOOK ONE

Iroquois Uses of Maize and Other Food Plants

Contents

Iroquois Uses of Maize and Other Food Plants

ARTHUR C. PARKER

PREFATORY NOTE

These notes on the preparation and uses of maize and other vegetable foods by the Iroquois have been gathered during a period of 10 years, while the writer has been officially concerned with the archeology and ethnology of the New York Iroquois and their kindred in Canada. They embrace all it has been possible for him to gather from the Iroquois themselves concerning the uses of their favorite food plants. Scores of Indians were questioned and many interesting facts were brought out from almost forgotten recesses of their minds.

The greater part of this treatise is the result of a purely original inquiry. An attempt has been made to cite the records of early explorers and travelers where the case seemed of interest or importance, but no general historical review of the subject is given.[1] The aim is rather to present an ethnological study of the Iroquois uses of food plants. This it is hoped will also have an economic and sociologic value.

Maize played an important part in Iroquois culture and history. Its cultivation on the large scale to which they carried it necessitated permanent settlements, and it was, therefore, an influential factor in

---

[1] For a general review of the subject of Indian foods consult Thomas. Mound Explorations, Bureau of Ethnology, 1890–91; Carr. Mounds of the Mississippi Valley, Smithsonian Rep't, 1891; Carr. Foods of Certain American Indians, Am. Antiq. Soc.\ 1895.

determining and fixing their special type of culture. They had ceased to be nomadic hunters when their corn fields and vegetable gardens flourished. Many of the tribes of eastern North America were agriculturalists to an extent hardly realized by those unfamiliar with early records and this is especially true of the Huron-Iroquois family, though it is not to be disputed that the Algonquin tribes of the east and southeast had large fields and raised corn and other vegetables on a large scale.

My principal informants as to names and recipes are the following Iroquois Indians: on the Tonawanda Seneca Reservation, Lyman Johnson, Otto Parker, Peter Sundown; on the Allegany Reservation, Mrs Henry Logan, Mrs Fred Pierce and others; on the Cattaraugus Reservation, Mrs Aurelia Jones Miller, George Dolson Jimerson, Thomas Silverheels, Mrs Frank Patterson, Mrs Emily Tallchief, Mrs Julia Crouse (Aweniyont), Chief and Mrs Edward Cornplanter, Chief and Mrs Delos Big Kettle, John Jake, George Pierce, John Lay jr, Skidmore Lay, Mrs Emily C. Parker (Tuscarora), Mrs Cassie Gordon (Cayuga), Job King, Mrs Naomi Jimeson and many others; on the Onondaga Reservation, Chief and Mrs Baptist Thomas, Marvin Crouse and others; on the Grand River Reservation of the Six Nations, Canada, Albert Hill, Chief and Mrs D. C. Loft, Mr and Mrs Seth Newhouse (all Mohawks), Chief Michael Anthony and Lawson Montour (Delaware), Chief Josiah Hill (Nanticoke), Chief Jacob Johnson, Fred Johnson (Oneida), Chief Gibson (Seneca) and many others, of the Oneida of Muncytown, Ontario, Chief Danford, Elijah Danford, and of the Caughnawaga Mohawk, Mr and Mrs Longfeather (James Hill), Mrs Dibeux, Mrs Saylor and others.

As far as practicable the writer has followed the system of orthography used by the Smithsonian Institution in recording American languages, and especially that employed by Hewett in his *Cosmology*. For certain reasons there are a few minor departures from the system as employed by Hewett but in general there is little difference.

Alphabet and abbreviations

a   as in *father, bar;* Germ. *haben*
ā   the same sound prolonged
ă   as in *what;* Germ. *man*
ä   as in *hat, man, ran*
ā̈   the same sound prolonged
â   as in *law, all;* Fr. o in *or*

ai   as in *aisle,* as i in *mine, bind;* Germ. *Hain*

au   as ou in *out,* as ow in *how;* Germ. *Haus*

c   as sh in *shall;* Germ. sch in *schellen;* Fr. ch in *charmer*

ç   as th in *wealth*

d   pronounced with the tip of the tongue touching the upper teeth
      as in enunciating the English th; this is the only sound of d
      in the language

e   as e in *they,* as a in *may;* Fr. *ne*

ĕ   as in *met, get, then;* Germ. *denn;* Fr. *sienne*

g   as in *gig;* Germ. *geben;* Fr. *gout*

h   as in *has, he;* Germ. *haben*

i   as in *pique, machine*

ī   the same sound prolonged

ĭ   as in *pick, pit*

k   as in *kick, kin*

n   as in *no, nun, not*

ñ   as ng in *ring, sing*

o   as in *note, boat*

q   as ch in Germ. *ich*

s   as in *see, sat*

t   pronounced with the tip of the tongue on the upper teeth, as in
      enunciating the English th, this being the only sound of t in
      the language

u   as in *rule;* Germ. *du;* Fr. ou in *doux*

ŭ   as in *rut, shut*

w   as in *wit, win*

y   as in *yes, yet*

dj   as j in *judge*

hw   as wh in *what*

tc   as ch in *church*

ⁿ   marks nasalized vowels as aⁿ, eⁿ, ĕⁿ, oⁿ, ăⁿ, aiⁿ, etc.

'   indicates an aspiration or soft emission of the breath which is
      initial or final, thus 'h, ĕⁿ', o', etc.

'   marks a sudden closure of the glottis preceding or following a
      sound, thus 'a, o', ä', ă', etc.

'   marks the accented syllable of a word

th   in this system are always pronounced separately

In abbreviating the names of the various languages the following
have been used: Mk., Mohawk; Od., Oneida; Onon., Onondaga;
Ca., Cayuga, and Sen., Seneca.

Unless otherwise specified the Iroquois names and words used in the body of this paper are all Seneca. The writer is more familiar with this dialect of the Iroquois than the others, and this coupled with the fact that the Seneca are the most conservative of the Iroquois and remember more concerning their ancient usages, it is hoped will justify the employment of that tongue to the exclusion of the others.

In a work of this character one is always tempted to add in full the myths which hover about the subject and to describe the various rites and ceremonies that attend it. These things, interesting as they are, are reserved however for notice in other works where they will be more properly correlated.

ARTHUR C. PARKER

I MAIZE OR INDIAN CORN IN HISTORY

1 **The origin of maize.** From the Greek ζαω meaning to live has come the Latin *zea,* the family name of Z e a m a y s Linn., Indian corn or maize. The term *zea* as applied to the name of maize is highly significant and most appropriate for with the Iroquois as with many other Indian tribes maize was the principal and favorite vegetable food. So important was it to the Iroquois that they called it by a name meaning " our life " or " it sustains us."

That maize is a native American plant there is now no question. The testimony of archeology, history and botany all point to this conclusion. From botanical studies its origin in southern Mexico can be practically demonstrated.[1]

Several early investigators have endeavored to show that Z e a m a y s is not indigenous to America by referring to the corn of Egypt and the Levant.[2] Most of these writers, if not all, have based their premises upon statements by no means unassailable. It is difficult to imagine what advantage is to be derived from creating or fostering misstatements as to the origin of maize but this has been done by several writers.[3] In 1810 Molinari, a European writer, published a work called *Storia d'Incisa* in which there was a reference to ". . . a purse containing a kind of seed of a golden color and partly white, and unknown in the country and brought from Anatolia."[4] This strange seed was supposed to have been given by two crusaders, companions of Boniface III, to the town of Incisa. This reference to the seed " of golden color " caused some discussion at the time and many believed it to be maize, but after much controversy the celebrated *Storia* was found by the Comte de Riant to be a pure forgery, but not until it had been cited widely as proof of the Old World origin of maize.[5] There are many historical references as vague and unreliable as this which nevertheless seemed to have a certain weight.

---

[1] For origin and botanical character of maize *see* Harshburger. Botanical Studies, Univ. Pa. and Iowa Agric. Exp. Sta. Bul. 36, 1907. *See also* Brown, P. A. Farmer's Cabinet, v. 2. Albany 1838; Brown, D. J. Amer. Inst. Trans. 1846.

[2] *Cf.* Van der Donck. New Netherlands. Amsterdam 1656. 1:158. Reprint Hist. Soc. Trans. Ser. 2.

[3] Compare the account of Lundy, John P. Zea Mays, as it is Related to the Incipient Civilization of Red Men all the World Over. Numismatic & Antiq. Soc. Phila. 1883.

[4] De Candolle. Origin of Cultivated Plants, p. 388, Internat. Sci. Ser. N. Y. 1885.

[5] Riant. La Charte d'Incisa. 1877. Reprinted from Revue des Questions Historiques.

The names applied to maize during the 16th century in Europe have confused some writers. It was variously called Roman corn, Turkish wheat, Sicilian corn, Spanish corn, Guinea corn, Egyptian corn and Syrian dourra. The people or localities after which the corn was named, however, universally disclaimed all knowledge of its origin and referred it to some other source, and so named it; thus the Turks called it Egyptian corn and the Egyptians always referred to it as Syrian dourra, each in turn disclaiming its origin. Possibly the most widespread name by which maize was known in Europe was Turkish wheat which was the name generally used by the English. The name seems to have been first used by the botanist, Reullins,[1] in 1536, and later, in 1552, Tragus represented a maize plant in his *Stirpium* calling it F r u m e n t u m   t ù r c i c u m, but afterward, having read some vague reference to a plant thought to be similar he conceived the idea that it must be a species of Typhia grown in Bactriana. Other writers, however, denied this, Matthiole in 1570, Dodens in 1583 and Camerarius in 1588, all asserting its American origin.[2]

D'Herbelot, the oriental scholar, thought he had discovered maize in the references of the Persian historian, Mourkoud, who lived in the 15th century and who recorded that Rous, son of Japhet, sowed a certain seed on the shores of the Caspian sea.[3] He could not, of course, substantiate his belief but his statements at the time had a certain weight. Candolle[4] cites the finding of an ear of corn in an Egyptian sarcophagus at Thebes by Rifaud but says that the incident was probably the result of a trick played by an Arab imposter.[5] If maize had grown in Egypt, says Candolle, " it would have been connected with religious ideas like all other remarkable plants." He further cites that Ebn Baithar, an Arab physician, who had traveled through all the territory lying between Spain and Persia mentions no plant which may be taken for maize. Maize was so little known as a food plant in India in the 18th century that it was only grown in gardens as an ornamental grass.[6] In China it has been cultivated since the middle of the 17th century [7] although there are attempts to show earlier introduction, which, however, are denied by the best Chinese authorities.

---

[1] Reullins. De Natura Stirpium, p. 428. *Cf.* Candolle, p. 339.
[2] Candolle. Origin of Cultivated Plants, p. 389. N. Y. 1885.
[3] *Ibid.* p. 390.
[4] *Ibid.* p. 390.
[5] *See* Reply of President Price to Lundy's Paper *Zea Mays.* Numismatic & Antiq. Soc. Trans. Phila. 1883.
[6] Roxburgh. Flora Indica, III :568.
[7] Candolle. Origin of Cultivated Plants, p. 392.

A review of the subject [1] leads to the fact that there is no authentic reference to maize in the writings of travelers or naturalists prior to the discovery of America by Columbus. Hebrew parchments and Sanscrit scrolls are alike silent. With the opening up of the New World and the discovery of the great staple grain of the western continent, maize cultivation spread with lightning rapidity throughout the eastern hemisphere. It became a definitely known and accurately described food plant.

One early writer,[2] who no doubt had read with interest the early discussions as to the origin of maize says: " Maize was carried from America to Spain and from Spain into other countries of Europe, to the great advantage of the poor, though an author of the present day, would make America indebted to Europe for it, an opinion the most extravagant and improbable which ever entered the human brain."

If the grain had been known before the Columbian epoch it would have spread quite as rapidly as it did subsequently, which is good evidence of its American origin and this origin is no longer disputed by competent authorities.[3] Edward Enfield in his book on maize is so positive that maize is an American plant that he declares that ". . . if any further evidence were wanting on this point it may be found in the impossibility that a grain so nutritious, prolific and valuable, so admirably adapted to the wants of man could have existed in the eastern world before the discovery of America without coming into general use and making itself universally known. Had this cereal existed there at that period it would have made its record too clearly and positively to leave any doubt on the subject." [4]

The researches of Harshburger and others indicate that maize is a development of a Mexican grass known as teosinte (E u c h l a e n a m e x i c a n a Schrad.). Maize and teosinte by cross fertilization produce fertile hybrid plants known as Z e a c a n i n a Watson, or

---

[1] *See* Salisbury. History and Chemical Investigation of Corn, p. 8. Albany 1846.

[2] Clavigero. History of Mexico; trans. by Charles Cullen, Lond. 1787. I :26.
Clavigero in a footnote further states that the name *Grano di Turchia*, by which it (maize) is at present known in Italy, must certainly have been the only reason for Bomares adopting an error, so contrary to the testimony of all writers on America, and the universal belief of nations. The wheat is called by the Spaniards of Europe and America, *maize*, taken from the Haitina language which was spoken in the island Hispaniola or St Domingo."

[3] *Cf.* Beverly. Hist. of Va. Lond. 1722. p. 125.
" They say that they had their corn and beans from the southern Indians, who received their seed from a people who resided still farther south." *Van der Donck, New Netherlands,* (1656). Reprint N. Y. Hist. Soc. Trans. I :137.

[4] *See* Bailey. Cyclopedia of American Agriculture, I :404.

as the Mexicans call it, *mais de coyote* (L u p u s   l a t r a n s).
Harshburger says that our cultivated maize is of hybrid origin probably starting as a sport of teosinte which then crossed itself with its
normal ancestor, producing our cultivated corn.[1] Plants which by
hybridizing and cultivation will produce maize are not found outside
of Mexico and for this reason, if no other, it would seem conclusive
that maize had its origin there. As to the exact locality, Harshburger who has made a special study of the plant and its origin, says
that it originated in all probability north of the Isthmus of Tehuan-
tepec, and south of the 22° of north latitude near the ancient seat
of the Maya tribes.[2] In this connection it is worthy of notice that
nearly all the traditions of the Indians, not pure myths, point to the
far southwest as the mother country of the corn plant.

An important proof of the cultivation of maize in America before
the Columbian epoch is the fact that the kernels and cobs in a charred
state have been found in ancient pits and refuse heaps all over eastern
North America. Impressions of the kernels have been taken from
Precolumbian mounds and the actual ears and cobs from the
storage places of the Pueblos, Cliff Dwellers, Aztecs and Peruvians
where time and crumbling ruins had sealed up the stores. No American archeologist doubts the cultivation of maize in America in Pre-
columbian times. The revelations of his own spade and trowel assert
the fact in no uncertain way.

The name *maize* is derived from the Arawak *mahiz*. Columbus
found maize growing on the island of Hayti and his mention of it is
the first record of that plant. In the *Life of Columbus, By His Son,*
under the date of November 5, 1492, is the following note:

> There was a great deal of tilled land some sowed with those roots,
> a sort of beans and a sort of grain they call maize, which was well
> tasted, baked, or dried and made into flour.[3]

This is the first historical reference to maize which it is possible to
find in any work and the first use of the term maize.[4]

---

[1] Harshburger.   Contributions from the Botanical Laboratory of the
University of Pennsylvania, v. 1, no. 2.

[2] Harshburger.   Bailey's Cyclopedia of American Agriculture, 1 :399.

[3] Life of Christopher Columbus, By His Son, in Pinkerton's Voyages and
Travels.   Lond. 1832.   12 :38.

[4] Among the first probable references to Indian corn is one by Capt.
John De Verazzano, who early in the 16th century coasted along the middle
Atlantic coast. In his report to the King of France, under date of 1524,
32 years after the discovery, he said in describing the Indians whom he
saw: " Their food is a kind of pulse which there abounds, different in
color and size from ours and of a very delicious flavor."   In the light of
subsequent descriptions by other explorers it seems very probable if not
certain that the *pulse* was maize.

2 **Importance of maize in the early English colonies.** There is no plant more vitally or more closely interwoven into the history of the New World [1] than maize or Indian corn.[2] At the most critical stages in colonial history corn [3] played an important part. Our Pilgrim fathers and the less hardy cavaliers of Jamestown and Maryland were rescued from starvation more than once when it was hard upon them by foods made from the corn given them by the Indians who had cultivated and harvested it. Had it not been for the corn of the Indians the stories of Jamestown and Plymouth instead of being stirring accounts of perseverance and endurance might have been brief and melancholy tragedies. The settlement and development of the New World would have been delayed for years.[4] History would have been changed, the foothold of the English colonists weakened and another tongue spoken along the Atlantic coast.

---

[1] Prescott in reviewing this subject says: "The great staple of the country, as indeed of the American continent, was maize, or Indian corn, which grew freely along the valleys and up the steep sides of the Cordilleras to the high level of the tablelands. The Aztecs were as curious in its preparation, and as well instructed in its manifold uses, as the most expert New England housewife. Its gigantic stalks, in these equinoctial regions, afford a saccharine matter not found to the same extent in northern latitudes, and supplied the natives with sugar little inferior to that of cane itself . . ." *Conquest of Mexico.* N. Y. 1866. 1:112.

John Fiske in his *Discovery of America,* writes: "Maize or Indian corn has played a most important part in the history of the New World, as regards both white and red men. It could be planted without clearing or plowing the soil. It was only necessary to girdle the trees with a stone hatchet, so as to destroy their leaves and let in the sunshine. A few scratches and digs were made in the ground with a stone digger, and the seed once dropped in took care of itself. The ears could hang for weeks after ripening and could be picked off without meddling with the stalk; there was no need of threshing or winnowing. None of the Old World cereals can be cultivated without much more industry and intelligence. At the same time when Indian corn is sown on tilled land it yields with little labor more than twice as much per acre than any other grain." *Fiske, Discovery of America,* 1 :27.

[2] In using the term *corn* hereinafter we refer exclusively to maize.

[3] Lawson very emphatically describes the utility of maize in the following: "The Indian corn or Maize proves the most useful Grain in the World; and had it not been for the fruitfulness of this species, it would have proved very difficult to have settled some of the Plantations in America. It is very nourishing whether in Bread, sodden or otherwise; and those poor Christian Servants in Virginia, Maryland and the other northerly Plantations, that have been forced to live wholly upon it do manifestly prove that it is the most nourishing Grain for a Man to subsist on, without any other Victuals." History of Carolina. Lond. 1714. *Cf.* Cartier Voyages. Tross ed.

[4] . . . we are indebted to the Indians for maize, without which the peopling of America would have been delayed for a century." Cyrus Thomas. Agriculture, in Hand-Book of American Indians. Bureau of Ethnology Bul. 30.

Almost the first discovery which the Pilgrim historian records is that of a cache of Indian corn found along the shore. On November 11, 1620 the historian writes:

They found a pond of clear fresh water and shortly after a good quantitie of clar ground where ye Indeans had formerly set corne and some of their graves. And proceeding furder they saw new-stuble wher corne had been set ye same year, also they found where latly a house had been wher some planks and a great ketel was remaining and heaps of sand newly padled with their hands, which they digging up found in them diverce faire Indean baskets filled with corne and some in eares faire and good of diverce colours . . . and took with them parte of ye corne and buried ye rest . . . And here is to be noted a spetiall providence of God . . . that hear they got seed to plant them corne ye next year, or els they might have starved for they had none, nor any liklyhood to get any.[1]

Few of us in these modern days realize the frightful struggles of these early pioneers to obtain food enough to sustain even the spark of life. It is recorded that some of the desperate Pilgrims, driven by the despair of hunger would even cut wood and fetch water for the Indians for a cap of corn. Others, we are told, " fell to plaine stealing both night & day from ye Indeans of which they (the Indians) greviously complained." [2]

The bitter experiences of the winter of 1622–23 compelled them to think how they might raise as much corn as they could and " obtaine a beter crop then they had done, that they might not still thus languish in miserie." [3] The struggle for existence was a hard one with all the colonists until they had mastered the methods of corn cultivation. The Indians who were the teachers soon found that they had students that outclassed them in many ways. Bradford's account of how the settlers learned to plant and cultivate is both interesting and enlightening. He writes: [4]

Afterwards they, as many as were able, began to plant ther corne, in which servise Squanto stood them in great stead, showing them both ye maner how to set it, and after how to dress and tend it. He also tould them excepte they gott fish and set with it in these old grounds it would come to nothing.

Trumbull also tells that the Connecticut Indians instructed the first settlers in the manner of planting and dressing corn.[5]

---

[1] Bradford. History Plymouth Plantation, p. 49. Cols. Mass. Hist. Soc. Ser. 4. III :87. Bost. 1856.
[2] *Ibid.* p. 130.
[3] *Ibid.* p. 134.
[4] *Ibid.* p. 100.
[5] Trumbull. History of Connecticut, Hartford 1797. I :46.

It was the success of the corn crop that made it possible for the eager colonists to live and to become the Pilgrim Fathers. The experiences of the Connecticut colonists did not differ, for as one historian says,". . . by selling them corn when pinched with famine they relieved their distress and prevented them from perishing in a strange land and uncultivated wilderness." [1]

Significant also is the statement of Capt. John Smith in his *History of Virginia:* ". . . such was the weakness of this poor commonwealth, as had not the salvages fed us we directlie had starved. And this relyfe, most gracious queen (Anne), was brought by this lady Pocahontas; . . . during the time of two or three years, shee next under God, was still the instrument to preserve this colonie from death, famine and utter confusion." [2]

Corn saved the colony as it had others before and after Smith's time, and as in other instances, our historian naïvely remarks, to obtain it, ". . . many were billited among the savages." [3]

And thus it is that the maize plant was the bridge over which English civilization crept, tremblingly and uncertainly, at first, then boldly and surely to a foothold and a permanent occupation of America.

II EARLY RECORDS OF CORN CULTIVATION AMONG THE IROQUOIS AND COGNATE TRIBES

As early as 1535, Jacques Cartier, pushing his way up the St Lawrence, saw fields of waving corn on the island of Hochelaga where he found a thriving village occupied by Iroquois people. He left us the record that these Indians had large fields and that they stored the harvested corn in garrets " at the tops of their houses." [4] Cartier also described the Hochelagans as " given to husbandrie . . . but are no men of great labour." [5]

Nearly every explorer who left a detailed record of his voyages recorded in a minute way his impressions of Indian agriculture and particularly of their cultivation of corn. Henry Hudson repeatedly mentioned in his records the maize which he saw on his voyage up the river which takes its name from him. Recording the events of

---

[1] Trumbull. History of Connecticut, 1 :47.
[2] Smith, Capt. John. History of Virginia. Lond. 1632. p. 121.
[3] *Ibid.* 2 :229. Richmond reprint. 1819.
[4] Hakluyt. Voyages. Lond. 1810. 3 :272.
[5] *Ibid.*

September 13, 1609, and giving the latitude [1] as 42° 18', Hudson wrote: [2]

I saw there a house well constructed of oak bark . . . a great quantity of maize or Indian corn and beans of last year's growth, and there lay near the house for the purpose of drying enough to load three ships, besides what was growing in the fields.

In the journal of Robert Juet,[3] mate on the Half Moon, is a statement under date of September 4, 1609, that " . . . they have a great store of corn whereof they make good bread." This corn was undoubtedly maize, if we are to judge by contemporary descriptions that name the corn specifically.

Sagard has left us a good description of corn cultivation among the Huron, and his account being one of the earliest and most detailed, we quote it in full.

The wheat (Indian corn) being thus sown in the manner that we do beans, of a grain obtained only from a stalk or cane, the cane bears two or three spikes, and each spike yields a hundred, two hundred, sometimes 400 grains, and some yield even more. The cane grows to the height of a man and more, and is very large, (it does not grow so well or so high, nor the spike as large nor the grain so good in Canada nor in France, as there) in the Huron country. The grain ripens in four months and in some places three. After this they gather and bind the leaves (husks), turned up at the top and arrange it in sheaves (braids), which they hang all along the length of the cabin from top to bottom on poles, which they arrange in the form of a rack descending to the front edge of the bench. All this is so nicely done that it seems like a tapestry hung the whole length of the cabins. The grain being well dried and suitable to press (or pound) the women and girls take out the grains, clean them and put them in their large tubs (tonnes) made for this purpose, and placed in their porch or in one corner of the cabins.[4]

It, however, remained for Champlain to give us the first detailed accounts of the cornfields and the methods of cultivation by the Indians in the region of the St Lawrence and lower lake district. Champlain in the beginning probably believed much as many per-

---

[1] The present city of Hudson lies in lat'tude 42° 14'.
[2] De Laet. New Netherlands. N. Y. Hist. Soc. Col. Ser. 2. N. Y. 1841. 1 :300.
[3] Extract from the *Journal of the Voyage of the Half Moon, Henry Hudson, Master, From the Netherlands to the coast of North-America in the Year 1609* by Robert Juet, Mate. Republished by the N. Y. Hist. Soc. Col. Ser. 2. N. Y. 1841. 1 :323.
[4] Sagard. Voyage to the Hurons. (*Le Grand Voyage du pays des Hurons*, 1632). Tross ed. Paris, 1865. 1 :135.

Plate I

View of Seneca farm lands and cornfields in the Cattaraugus flats. This is a typical farm of the conservative Seneca. It may be regarded as typical also of the Seneca farms of a century ago.

sons do even now, that the Indians were hunters only but his changed opinion is recorded as follows:

July the tenth, 1605.

They till and cultivate the soil, something which we have not hitherto observed. In place of ploughs, they use an instrument of hard wood, shaped like a spade. This river is called by the inhabitants of the country Chouacoet. The next day Sieur de Monts and I landed to observe their tillage on the banks of the river. We saw their Indian corn which they raise in gardens. Planting three or four kernels in one place they then heap up about it a quantity of earth with shells of the signoc before mentioned. Then three feet distant they plant as much more, and this in succession. With this corn they put in each hill three or four Brazilian beans which are of different colours. When they grow up they interlace with the corn which reaches to the height of from five to six feet; and they keep the ground very free from weeds. We saw many squashes and pumpkins and tobacco which they likewise cultivate . . . The Indian corn which we saw at that time was about two feet high and some as high as three. The beans were beginning to flower as also the pumpkins and squashes. They plant their corn in May and gather it in September.[1]

When the Iroquois took possession of the territory which we now know as New York State, they carried on corn culture on a large scale and so important an article of food and commerce was it that most of the European invaders of their territory burned their cornfields and destroyed their corncribs instead of shooting the Iroquois themselves but, as one writer says, the power of the Confederacy remained unbroken.[2]

The French made a mistake fatal to French supremacy in the middle Atlantic region. In 1609 under Champlain they fired upon a small detachment of Iroquois at Ticonderoga and thereafter the Iroquois were the bitter enemies of the French, while they espoused the cause of the English.[3] The French realized their error most

---

[1] Voyages of Samuel de Champlain, 2:64–65. Prince Soc. Reprint 1878. Cf. also p. 81–82.

[2] Carr. Mounds of the Mississippi Valley, p. 515. Smithsonian Report. 1891.

[3] The Iroquois, especially the Seneca, were not always uniformly consistent in their alliances with the British, but in general their arms were at the disposal of the English colonial authorities. The espousal of the English cause by the Iroquois greatly strengthened the hold of the British in eastern North America and led to the expulsion of French domination from the continent.

In an address before the New York Historical Society in 1847, Dr Peter Wilson, a Cayuga-Iroquois, reminded the society of this fact in the following

keenly when they found the Iroquois a barrier between them and the trails to central New York and down the Ohio river. To break the power of the Iroquois Confederacy, expedition after expedition was sent out against them, notably those of Champlain in 1615, of Courcelles in 1655, of De Tracy in 1666, of De la Barre in 1684, of Denonville in 1687 (whose work was particularly destructive to cornfields), and of Frontenac in 1692 and 1696. All these gallant commanders failed to accomplish the destruction of Iroquois power perhaps for reasons such as given by Denonville in the following:

I deemed it our best policy to employ ourselves laying the Indian corn which was in vast abundance in the fields, rather than to follow a flying enemy to a distance and excite our troops to catch only some straggling fugitives. . . We remained at the four Seneca villages until the 24th; the two larger distant four leagues and the others two. All that time was spent in destroying the corn which was in such great abundance that the loss including old corn which was in cache which we burnt and that which was standing, was computed according to the estimate afterwards made at 400 thousand minots (about 1,200,000 bushels) of Indian corn. . . A great many both of our Indians and French were attacked with a kind of rheum which put everyone out of humor.[1]

The quantity of corn here destroyed by Denonville is claimed by some authorities to be overestimated and perhaps this is true, as being " out of humor," the amount may have seemed larger than it really was.

The corn-destroying habit of the invaders of the Iroquois dominion was still active when later, in 1779, Maj. Gen. John Sullivan made his famous raid against the Iroquois. The accounts of his officers and soldiers which have come down to us in their journals are most illuminating, when aboriginal corn statistics are sought. " The Indians," said Gen. Sullivan in discussing the subject, " shall see that there is malice enough in our hearts to destroy everything that contributes. to their support." How well he fulfilled his threat may be known by reviewing the record of his campaign.

The journals of Sullivan's campaign through the Iroquois country are replete with descriptions of the Iroquois cornfields and the fre-

---

words: " Had our forefathers spurned you from it (the Iroquois " Long House ") when the French were thundering at the opposite end, to get a passage and drive you into the sea, whatever had been the fate of other Indians, the Iroquois might still have been a nation and I too might have had a country."
[1] Doc. Hist. of the State of N. Y. 1:328–29. Albany 1849. *Cf.* Charlevoix. Nouvelle France, 2:355; Lahontan. Voyages, I, p. 101.

quent mention indicates the importance of corn as a food to the Iroquois. The destruction of the corn supply was a greater blow to the Iroquois than the burning of their towns. Huts might easily have been built again but fields would not yield another harvest after September.

In the journal of Maj. John Burrowes, as in other journals covering the Sullivan campaign, there are many references to the Indian fields. Some instances follow:

Friday, August 27, 1779. Observations. We got this night at a large flat three miles distant from Chemung where corn grows such as can not be equalled in Jersey. The field contains about 100 acres, beans, cucumbers, Simblens, watermelons and pumpkins in such quantities (were it represented in the manner it should be) would be almost incredible to a civilized people. We sat up until between one and two o'clock feasting on these rarities.

Monday, Middletown, 30th Aug. The army dont march this day but are employed cutting down the corn at this place which being about one hundred and fifty acres, and superior to any I ever saw . . . (*Observations*) The land exceeds any I have ever seen. Some corn stalks measured eighteen feet and a cob one foot and a half long. Beans, cucumbers, watermelons, muskmelons, cimblens are in great plenty. . .

Camp on the Large Flats 6 Miles from Chenesee 15th Sep. Wednesday morning. The whole army employed till 11 o'clock destroying corn, there being the greatest quantity destroyed at this town than any of the former. It is judged that we have burnt and destroyed about sixty thousand bushels of corn and two or three thousand of beans on this expedition.

In his letter to John Jay under date of September 30, 1779, General Sullivan reported among other things:

Colonel Butler destroyed in the Cayuga country five principal towns and a number of scattering houses, the whole making about one hundred in number exceedingly large and well built. He also destroyed two hundred acres of excellent corn with a number of orchards one of which had in it 1500 fruit trees. Another Indian settlement was discovered near Newtown by a party, consisting of 39 houses, which were also destroyed. The number of towns destroyed by this army amounted to 40 besides scattering houses. The quantity of corn destroyed, at a moderate computation, must amount to 160,000 bushels, with a vast quantity of vegetables of every kind. . . I flatter myself that the orders with which I was entrusted are fully executed, as we have not left a single settlement or a field of corn in the country of the Five Nations. . .

In his report of Sept. 16, 1779, to General Washington concerning his raid against the Seneca on the Allegany, Daniel Brodhead said:

The troops remained on the ground three whole days destroying the Towns & Corn Fields. I never saw finer corn altho' it was

planted much thicker than is common with our Farmers. The
quantity of Corn and other vegetables destroyed at the several
Towns, from the best accounts I can collect from the officers employed to destroy it must certainly exceed five hundred acres which
is a low estimate and the plunder is estimated at 30m Dollars[1] . . .

1 Meaning probably $30,000.

Quotations from the journals of soldiers and officers could be mul-
tiplied to some length with but one result, that of corroborating the
fact that the Iroquois cultivated corn, beans, squashes, pumpkins
and other vegetables in large quantities and to an extent hardly appreciated by the general student of history.[2]

The beautiful valley of the Genesee, renowned among the Indians
as the fertile garden region of the Seneca was cultivated for miles
of its length.   Luxuriant fields, patches of forest land and wide
openings of grass land were found throughout the valley.   The im-
petuous army of Sullivan, inflamed by the depredations of the Iroquois and bent upon wreaking vengeance upon a tribe of ignorant
savages entered the Genesee valley with feelings of utmost surprise
for they found the land of the savages to be, not a tangled wilderness but a smiling blooming valley, and the savages domiciled in
permanent houses and settled in towns.   General Sullivan describes
the town of Genesee, for example, as containing 128 houses, mostly
large and elegant, and names it as one of the largest.   It was beautifully situated, he added, " almost encircled with clear flat land extending a number of miles ; over which extensive fields of corn were
waving, together with every kind of vegetable that could be conceived."   Forty towns were obliterated, 60,000 bushels of corn destroyed, fruit orchards uprooted, girdled or chopped down, one
containing 1500 trees.   Ruin was spread like a blanket over the Iroquois country and their garden valley reduced to a desolate blighted
and forsaken region dotted with blackened ruins.   Hardly a food
plant remained for the oncoming winter.[3]

2 See Stone. Life of Brandt. N. Y. 1838. v. 2, ch. 1; Journals of the
Military Expedition of Major General John Sullivan against the Six Nations, 1779. Auburn 1887.

3 Cf. Stone. Brant, 2:33.

III IROQUOIS CUSTOMS OF CORN CULTIVATION

1 **Land clearing and the division of labor.** Land for cornfields was cleared by girdling the trees in the spring, and allowing
them to die. The next spring the underbrush was burned off. By
burning off tracts in the forests large clearings were made suitable
for fields and towns. Early travelers in western New York called
these clearings "oak openings." [1] Certain tracts, however, seem
always to have been open lands and it is a mistake to believe that
the country was entirely wooded.

Van der Donck was much impressed by the "bush burnings" of
the Indians of New Netherlands and records that they present a
"grand and sublime appearance." [2] Unless the trees were girdled
or dead they were not ordinarily injured by the "bush burning."

The work of girdling the trees [3] and of burning the underbrush
was that of the men. [4] With the tall trees girdled and the underbrush burned off it was an easy matter to scrape up the soft loam
and plant the corn but the field was not considered in fit form until
the small shrubbery and weeds had been subdued. Fields with
standing dead trees were not regarded as safe after the first year

---

[1] *See* Ketchum. Buffalo and the Senecas, 1 :17–19. *Cf.* Dwight. Travels
in New England and New York

[2] Van der Donck. New Netherlands. Amsterdam 1656.

[3] La Potherie. Paris 1722, 3 :18.

[4] Sagard in his *Voyages des Hurons* has left us a good description of
this work among the Hurons. The translation which follows is taken from
Carr's *Mounds of the Mississippi Valley.*

"The Indians belt (coupent) the trees about two or three feet from the
ground, then they trim off all the branches and burn them at the foot of the
tree in order to kill it and afterwards they take away the roots. This being
done, the women carefully clean up the ground between the trees and at every
step they dig a round hole, in which they sow 9 or 10 grains of maize which
they have first carefully soaked for some days in water."

Peter Kalm, whose observations of Indian usages were accurate and
detailed, records :

"The chief use of their [stone] hatchets was according to the unanimous accounts of all the Swedes to make good fields for maize-plantations;
for if the ground where they intended to make a maize-field was covered
with trees they cut off the bark all round the trees with their hatchets,
especially at the time when they lost their sap. By that means the tree becomes dry and could not take any more norishment and the leaves could
no longer obstruct the rays of the sun from passing. The smaller trees
were pulled out by main force, and the ground was turned up with crooked
or sharp branches." Kalm, 515, Pinkerton's Voyages

and speedy means were taken thereafter to burn them down.   In the
Seneca invocations to the Creator at the midwinter thanksgiving is
a prayer that the dead branches may not fall upon the children in
the fields.

In time the trees were burned or rotted away to leave cleared
patches.   The Iroquois men[1] did very little in the way of field work
but it is said that they sometimes helped clear the land but never
allowed any one to see them.   Some of the old Indians whom the
writer interviewed told laughable stories of grim old " warriors " who
had been caught with a hoe and how they excused themselves.

One early writer even goes so far as to say that if a man loved
his wife devotedly he often helped her with the field work.   As a
rule, however, among the Iroquois the men disdained the work which
they deemed peculiarly that of women.

One writer remarks that the Iroquois were too busy with their
conquests to engage in field work and this is largely true.   In the
age of barbarism the condition of society is one of constant emergency.   Invasion and the destruction of property is momentarily
expected.   The Iroquois by dividing the labors necessary to sustain
life in the manner in which they did contributed much to the strength
of their nation and its arms.   The function of the men was to
hunt, to bring in the game and stand ever ready to defend their
people and their property and to engage in war expeditions.   An
Iroquois man must be ever generous and give to every one who
asked for his arms or his meat.   If he brought his bear to the village it became public property, to the material injury of himself and
family.   He therefore left his game hidden in the outskirts of his
town and sent his wife[2] to bring it in.[3]   She was not bound to
give of her husband's bounty and could properly refuse the appeals

---

[1] La Potherie in his *Historie de l'Amérique,* volume III, page 18 et seq.
says that the men cleared the ground and assisted in braiding the harvested
ears. *Cf.* Lawson. Carolina.

[2] The writer in mentioning Indian females never uses the term *squaw.*
As a name in colonial days it may have been proper but it is no longer good
form and its use is frowned upon by the Iroquois women of this State and
Canada.   It has come with them to mean a degraded female character.
The Superintendent of the Six Nations of Canada was severely rebuked
several years ago by an old Mohawk woman who resented the term as applied to the women of her nation.   The term is of course of Algonquin
origin.   An Allegany Seneca once explained to me that this word was no
longer good language, just as Shakspere's word *wench* is no longer good
English as applied to a housewife, or *villian* as applied to a farmer.

[3] *Cf.* Carr. Food of Certain American Indians, p. 167; Tanner. Narrative, p. 362; Cadillac in Margry 68, Charlevoix, v. 171.

Plate 2

Husking Tuscarora corn for braiding. Note how husks are pulled back
and the ear stood nose up against the basket.

Plate 3

Seneca women plucking Tuscarora corn. The ear of corn is plucked
from the stalk and thrown over the shoulder into the picking basket.

of the hungry, lazy or others who loved to prey upon generosity. After the meat was cooked, however, the case was different and she was bound to feed any who came to her door.

The Iroquois and other Indians have frequently been reproached by writers for allowing or forcing their women to do field labor while the men enjoyed the hunt[1] or lazily fished, or perchance went " high ho! " on the war path. It should be remembered, however, that hunting in those raw days was no easy task. It was not sport then as it is now but work that demanded the use of every faculty. Heckewelder[2] remarks most aptly that the " fatigues of hunting wear out the body and constitution more than manual labor." Another writer says, and there is a sense in which his description might apply in these modern times, that " their manner of rambling through the woods to kill deer is very laborious exercise, as they frequently walk 25 or 30 miles through rough and smooth grounds, and fasting, before they return to camp loaded." [3]

Heckewelder sums up the case when he says that woman's labor in the fields consumed but six weeks out of the year while " the labor of the husband to maintain his family lasts throughout the year." [4]

Woman's part in the division of labor was not a hard one nor even a compulsory one. The labor of the fields was a time welcomed by the women then as modern people now welcome an outing. It was the occasion of productive pleasure. As Heckewelder says,[5] " . . . The cornfield is planted by her and the youngsters in a vein of gaiety and frolic. It was done in a few hours and taken care of in the same spirit."

In the *Life of Mary Jemison,*[6] the white captive of the Genesee, she states:

Our labor was not severe, and that of one year was exactly similar in almost every respect to that of others, without that endless variety that is to be observed in the common labor of white people. Notwithstanding the Indian women have all the fuel and bread to procure, and the cooking to perform, their task is probably not harder than that of white women who have those articles provided for them; and their cares certainly not half as numerous, nor as great. In the summer season we planted, tended and harvested our corn, and

---

[1] *Cf.* Lawson, p. 188.

[2] Heckewelder. Historical Account of the Indian Nations, p. 146.

[3] Adair. History of the American Indians. Lond. 1755. p. 402.

[4] Heckewelder. Historical Account of the Indian Nations, p. 142

[5] *Ibid.* p. 142.

[6] Seaver. Life of Mary Jemison, p. 69.

generally had our children with us; but had no masters to oversee or drive us, so that we could work as leisurely as we pleased.

With the breaking up of the military power of the Iroquois and the subjection of all Indian tribes to the federal government, the men were left freer. War with them was over. The disdain which they had for field labor, and the feeling that it was not a part of their work clung for some time, but as the old reason for abstaining from field work passed away and as the environment of the white man was forced upon them, the Iroquois man gradually became the man with the hoe and thought it no disgrace. This was hardly the case, however, a century ago.

The women of each settlement each year elected a chief matron, onän'o gäin'dago^n et'igowäně[1] to direct their work in the communal fields. She ordered all the details of planting, cultivation and harvesting. She also had the right to choose one or two lieutenants who could give out her orders.

Certain fields were reserved for the use of the nation, that is, to supply food for the councils and national festivals. These fields were called Kěndiŭ''gwă'ge' hodi'yěn'tho'.

2 Preparation of the soil and planting. In preparing the soil a digging implement made of wood, somewhat resembling a short hoe was used. The blade was sometimes a large flat bone or simply a piece of wood worked flat. The hoe in this case was of one piece, the trunk of a sapling serving as a handle and the tough bulbous root end which ran off at right angles, shaped into a blade, served as the digging end.[2]

---

[1] Literally meaning " corn plant, its field's female chief."

[2] " Use wooden hoes," Williams. Key, p. 130.

" Spades made of hard wood." Bossee. Travels Through Louisiana, p. 224

" Ils ont un instrument de bois fort dur, faict en facon d'une besche." Champlain, 1 :95.

" Il leur suffit d'un morceau de bois recourbe de trois doigts de largeur, attaché a un long mauche qui leur sert a sarcler le terre et a la remuer legerment." Lafitau. Moeurs des Sauvages Ameriquains, II :76.

" Use shoulder blade of a deer or a tortoise shell, sharpened on a stone and fastened on a stick instead of a hoe." Loskiel. Missions of North America, p. 67.

" Performed the whole process of planting and hoeing with a small tool that resembled in some respects a hoe with a very short handle." Seaver, Life of Mary Jemison, p. 70.

Cf. Hakluyt. Voyages, III :329.

" In order to sow Indian Corn they make Pick-Axes of Wood." A Continuation of the New Discovery, Hennepin, Father L. Lond. 1698.

The writer has found in various old sites pieces of flattened antler[1] [*see* fig. 1] with one worn edge and the lower surfaces well polished which seem to have been hoe blades. In the Mississippi valley and often in New York hoe heads of picked and chipped stone were used.

Fig. 1   Antler hoe blade (Cut is ⅓ actual size.)

Where wooden hoes were used it is probable that the digging ends were hardened in the fire by a semicharring of the surface. Hardening in this manner was usual where a resisting surface was needed.

Thomas Hariot, a keen and reliable observer though not always a good speculator, has left us in his *Brief and True Report* an excellent description of the cultivation of maize by the coastal Indians of Virginia. In 1587 he writes:

All the aforesaid commodities for victuals are set or sowed sometimes in grounds apart and severally by themselves, but for the most part together in one ground mixtly: the manner thereof with the dressing and preparing of the ground, because I will note unto you the fertility of the soil, I think good briefly to describe.

The ground they never fatten with muck, dung, or anything, neither plow or dig it as we in England but only prepare it in a sort as followeth: A few days before they sow or set the men with wooden instruments made almost in the form of mattocks or hoes with long handles, the women with short peckers or parers, because they use them sitting, of a foot long and five inches in breadth, do only break the upper part of the ground, to raise up the weeds grass and old stubs of cornstalks with their roots. The which after a day or two days drying in the sun, being scraped up into many small heaps, to save them the labor of carrying them away, they burn to ashes. And whereas some may think that they use the ashes for to better the ground, I say that then they would either disperse the ashes abroad, which we observe they do not, except the heaps be too great, or else would take special care to set their corn where the ashes lie, which also we find they are careless of. And this is all the husbanding of their ground that they use.

Then their setting or sowing is after this manner. First, for their corn, beginning in one corner of the plot with a pecker they make a

_____
[1] *Cf.* Parker, A. C. Excavations in an Erie Indian Village. N. Y. State Mus. Bul. 117. p. 535.

hole wherein they put out four grains, with care that they touch not one another (about an inch asunder), and cover them with the mould again; so throughout the whole plot, making such holes and using them in such manner, but with this regard, that they be made in ranks, every rank differing from the other half a fathom or a yard and the holes also in every rank. By this means there is a yard of spare ground between every hole; where according to discretion here and there they set as many beans and pease; in divers places also among the seeds of Macocqwer, Melden and Planta Soles. . .

Another early description of corn and its cultivation is given by Harris in his *Discoveries and Settlements*. For the purpose of comparison with the foregoing, as well as for its information, this description is given verbatim:

The manner of planting is in holes or trenches, about five or six feet distance from each other; the earth is opened with a hoe (and of late years, with a plough), four inches deep, and four or five grains thrown into each hole or trench, about a span distant from each other, and then covered with earth; they keep weeding it from time to time, and as the stalk grows high they keep the mould about it like the hillocks in a hop garden; they begin to plant in April but the chief plantation is in May, and they continue to plant till the middle of June; what is planted in April is reaped in August; what is planted in May is reaped in September; and the last in October.[1]

While the ground is being prepared for sowing, the seed corn is soaked[2] in warm water or in a decoction made of helebore[3] root and some other herb which the writer has not yet identified. These roots are said to be a " medicine for the corn " but in reality the " medicine " is a poison for crows and other field pests which might eat the seed corn. A bird eating this " doctored " corn becomes dizzy and flutters about the field in a way which frightens the others.

---

[1] Harris. Discoveries and Settlements Made by the English. *In* Pinkerton. Voyages, 12:242. *Cf.* Beverly, p. 126–27.

Cf. Their manner of planting it is to make with the finger or with a little stick, separate holes in the ground, and to drop into each one eight or nine grains which they cover with the same soil that had been taken out to make the hole." Jesuit Relations, 67:143. (Rale's letter to his brother.)

Cf. Beverly. History of Virginia, p. 127.

[2] *Cf.* Sagard. Voyages des Hurons, p. 134. Paris 1632.

[3] *Cf.* Kalm. Travels in North America. Lond. 1772; Pinkerton. Voyages, 13:527.

Peter Kalm is the only observer in whose writings the author has found the use of the poison decoction mentioned.[1]

Handsome Lake, the prophet, in his code commanded that these herbs always be used.

The corn was carefully dropped in the hills so as not to break the germs which had nearly burst through. Among the Senecas, in planting corn the seeds of the squash and bean were sown in every seventh hill because it was thought that the spirits of these three plants were inseparable. They were called Diohe"ko, *these sustain us*.[2]. In the Green Corn Thanksgiving the leader rises and says, " Diettino$^{n'}$nio' diohe"ko^{n}, *we give thanks to our sustainers*."

Certain women banded themselves together in a society called the Toñwisas[3] or To^{n}wi'sas Oä'no. They propitiated the spirits of the three sisters by certain ceremonies. In their ceremonial march, Wenŭntoñwi'säs, the leader holding an armful of corn and a cake of corn bread leads her band in a measured march about a kettle of corn soup. The ritual of this society has been translated by the writer. A pen drawing of the march of the Toñwi'sas made by a Seneca youth is shown in figure 2.

Each year at planting time each community observed a planting festival in which the Creator was implored to continue his bounty and his accustomed ways. Sacrifices of tobacco and wampum were made to the spirits of growth and to the pygmies, Djo^{n}gä'o^{n}, and a general thanksgiving for past blessings was given. Especial favor was asked in the growth of the corn.[4]

The Planting Thanksgiving was called by a council of elders in whose charge this festival was placed and lasted for a full day. The addresses to the Creator, however, were all given in the early morn-

---

[1] *Ibid.* p. 531.
See also Kalm on bird pests, *Ibid.* p. 523, 527, 531.

[2] The Aztecs called the corn goddess Tonacaygohua, *She feeds us*. She was sometimes called Centeotl. She was also regarded as the goddess of the earth and was the most beloved deity worshiped by the ancient Mexicans and was the only one that did not require the sacrifice of human victims. It is interesting to note that the Corn goddess was also called Tzinteotl, the original goddess. Her name changed to Xilonen, Iztacaccuteotl, and Tlatlauhquicenteotl according to the various stages in the growth of the corn.

[3] For a fuller description *see* American Anthropologist. New Ser. 1909. v. 11, no. 2. Parker, A. C. Seneca Medicine Societies.

[4] Clark, J. H. V. Onondaga. Syracuse 1849. 1 :54.

Fig. 2 Ceremonial march of the Toñ'wisas Company. The leader carries an armful of ears of corn in one arm and a tortoise

ing. The office of speaker belonged of course to a man but other
offices were held by women.

The address to the Creator as given by Morgan, follows:

Great Spirit, who dwellest alone, listen now to the words of thy
people here assembled. The smoke of our offering arises. Give
kind attention to our words, as they arise to thee in the smoke. We
thank thee for this return of the planting season. Give us a good
season, that our crops may be plentiful.
Continue to listen, for the smoke yet arises. [Throwing on
tobacco] Preserve us from all pestilential disease. Give strength to
us that we may not fall. Preserve our old men among us and protect the young.
Help us to celebrate with feeling the ceremony of this season.
Guide the minds of thy people, that they may remember thee in all
their actions, na-ho.[1]

Earlier in the spring the Thunder dance was held to honor He"-
non Ti'sōt, *Thunder, our grandfather.* He was asked to remember
the fields with a proper amount of rain and prevent the maize fields
from parching. If rain failed to come another Thunder ceremony
might be held.[2]

Cornfields were not always owned by the tribe or clan. Indi-
viduals might freely cultivate their own fields[3] if they were willing
to do their share in the tribal fields. If they did not do this they
could not claim their share of the communal harvest. Individual
fields were designated by a post on which was painted the clan totem
and individual name sign. Any distressed clansman, however, might
claim a right in the individual field and take enough to relieve his
wants, provided he notified the owner.

The first hoeing[4] is called de'owĕnyē', and takes place when the
corn is a span high. The second and final hoeing is called the *hilling
up,* ĕyen'on' or hadiyĕns', and is called for when the corn is knee
high.

3 **Communal customs.** The women of a community who own
individual fields and their husbands or male friends may form a

---

[1] Morgan. League, p. 196.
[2] *Ibid.* p. 196–97.
[3] *Cf.* Margry 1 :123; Jesuit Relations, 52 :165.
[4] " The Indians used to give it one or two weedings, and make a hill about
it, and so the labor was done." Beverly. Hist. of Virginia. Ed. 2. p. 125–28.
Lond. 1722.

mutual aid society[1] known as "(*In the*) *Good Rule they assist one another*," Gai'wiu Oⁿdănnide'oshä, (Sen). This society chooses a matron of the cornfields, eti'gowănĕ, who inspects the individual fields or gets reports regarding their progress and who orders the rest of the band to go to the field she wishes cultivated at a certain day and hour. She commences the hoeing and ranges her helpers in equal numbers on either side and a little to the rear and hoes to the end of the row a little in advance of the rest, counts off the unhoed rows and takes her position again.

---

[1] Roger Williams in his *Key* notes this custom among the New England Algonquins. "When a field is to be broken up," he says, "they have a very loving, sociable, speedy way to dispatch it; all the neighbors, men and women, forty, fifty or a hundred, do joyne and come in to help freely with friendly joyning they break up their fields and build their forts."

"As an organized body of workers, the women of each gens formed a distinct agricultural corporation." Stites, Sara H. Economics of the Iroquois, p. 31, Bryn Mawr Col. Monographs v. 1, no. 3.

In Seaver's *Life of Mary Jemison* [*see* p. 70–71] we find a detailed description of this cooperative work:

"We pursued our farming business according to the general custom of Indian women, which is as follows: In order to expedite their business, and at the same time enjoy each other's company, they all work together in one field, or at whatever job they have at hand. In the spring they choose an old active squaw to be their driver and overseer, when at labor for the ensuing year. She accepts the honor and they consider themselves bound to obey her.

When the time for planting arrives and the soil is prepared, the squaws are assembled in the morning and conducted into a field where each one plants a row. They then go into the next field and plant once across and so on until they have gone through the tribe. If any remains to be planted, they again commence where they did at first (in the same field) and so keep on till the whole is finished. By this rule, they perform their labor of every kind and every jealousy of one having done more or less than another is effectually avoided."

This custom of helping is continued to this day. Among the Christian Iroquois such work is called a "bee" but among the followers of the old ways the mutual aid societies still exist and they continue "in the good rule (gai'wiū) to assist one another." *A. C. P.*

Compare also Lawson's *Carolina*, page 179. "They are very kind and charitable to one another, but more especially to those of their own Nation . . . The same assistance they give to any Man that wants to build a Cabin, or make a Canoe. They say it is our Duty, thus to do; for there are several Works that one Man can not effect, therefore we must give him our Help, otherwise our Society will fall, and we shall be deprived of those urgent Necessities which Life requires."

Cf. Adair. p. 407.

Cf. Cullen. Clavigero's Mexico.

It is the duty of the owner of the field to provide a feast at the end of the hoeing and each helper takes home her supply of corn soup, hominy or ghost bread. After the hoeing and before eating the women flock to the nearest stream or pond and bathe. The whole work is accompanied by singing, laughing, joking and inoffensive repartee[1] and the utmost humor prevails, topped off by a splash in the water to remove dust and fatigue.

This hoeing " bee " is called ĕndwă"twenogwaʻ, (Sen.).

4 The harvest. In the autumn when the corn is ripe, when the " great bear chase is on in the heavens," the harvesting begins. The corn standing in the fields may be stripped of the ears by the harvesters who throw the ears over their shoulders, generally the left, into a great harvesting basket, ye'nistĕⁿnĕk'wistă'. The corn is then deposited in piles in the field or carried to the lodge. Sometimes the cornstalks are pulled up by the roots and carted to the house where they are piled up in layers crosswise for future husking. The plucking bee was called hadĭ'nest'e'oes or if engaged in by women alone, wadi''nĕst'eoes.

The husking bee that followed was called hadinowe'yă'keʻ or if women only engaged in the work, wadinowi'yă'keʻ. Husking time was another time for a long season of merry industrial gatherings. Work was play in those days when mutual helpfulness made money unnecessary. It was not uncommon for men to engage in this work.[2] They were lured to the scene by the promise of soup, song and the society of wise old matrons and shy maidens.[3] The old women carefully noted the industry of their younger assistants and scheming parents were able to obtain information about prospective mates for their children.

The older men did some work but not much. They aired their wisdom by making wise observations but soon lost their reserve in narrating exciting stories of personal adventure or by relating folk tales, gagä'äʻ. They knew full well that a pail full of soup awaited them when the husking ceased whether they worked or not. Often

---

[1] *Cf.* Adair. p. 407.

[2] Lafitau, volume 2, page 78, says that the men braided corn, but that this was the only time when they were called upon to do such menial work.

[3] Lafitau, volume 2, page 79, writing of harvest customs says: "At harvest time the corn is gathered with the leaves surrounding the ears which serve as cords to keep the ears together. The binding of the ears belongs to a peculiar ceremony which takes place at night and it is the only occasion where the men, who do not trouble themselves about harvesting or field work, are called by the women to help."

the " bee " would be enlivened by a marching dance, and for this emergency the men brought their water drums[1] and horn rattles and cleared their throats for singing.

The men smoked incessantly of native tobacco mixed with dried sumac leaves and red willow bark. Some of the older women, if not all, claimed the same privilege. The writer has attended some of these " bees " and though he never saw a pipe in a young woman's mouth,[2] he sometimes thought he saw a quid of store tobacco tucked away in a bloomy brown cheek, no doubt used as a toothache preventive.

The " bees " were often conducted out of doors under the white moonlight. A roaring fire of sumac brush or logs tempered the crisp air of the night but left it sufficiently invigorating to keep up spirit and keep the workers active. There was nothing unhealthful in these night carnivals where the smell of the corn plant, the breath of the pines blown by the autumn wind, the smoke of the fragrant burning wood and the pure merriment of the workers and the knowledge of good work furnished the sole exhilaration.

Husked ears may be placed in a corncrib, onän'o' iadä'kwa, or arranged for roasting. When the husk is stripped back for braiding the ears are stood up in rows, against the wall or log with the husks on the floor or ground. When the worker arose for rest the others covered the husks with corn leaves and loose husks to keep them moist. The work of braiding was called waest"shâni' (com. gen.), or wastĕⁿ'shâni (fem. gen.).

Sick and injured members of the " mutual aid company " were always assisted by the company even in the matter of preparing the soil, planting and harvesting. This help was considered as a right and never as a charity.

In the work of tillage plows or digging sticks are called yetogatŏt'thä ; hoes are called gâu"djishä'. The bone husking pin is called yĕⁿnowiyä"thä.

Husking pins are shaped much like the ancient bone and antler awls but generally have a groove cut about a third of their length about which is fastened a loop, through which it is designed that the middle finger be thrust. The point of the husking pin is held against the thumb. In husking the hand is held slightly open, the ear grasped

---

[1] Cf. Adair, p. 407.
[2] Cf. Jesuit Relations, 67 :141.

Plate 4

Braid of Seneca calico-hominy cor n. This is the native method of preserving dried corn on the cob, now widely adopted by white people and
others.

Plate 5

Seneca elm bark storage barrel, now obsolete among the Iroquois.
Specimen is 31 inches high.   Collected 1908 by A. C. Parker

in the left hand, ear butt downward, the point of the husker thrust into the nose of the ear and under the husk, by a sidewise shuttle motion, the thumb closes quickly over the pin and tightly against the

Fig. 3   Seneca husking pin (specimen is 4¼ inches in length)

husk, and a pull of the arm downward and toward the body tears away the husk.   Many of the ancient bone awls found in refuse pits may be husking pins as well as leather awls.

a Abnormal ears.   When harvesters find a red ear all the harvesters give the finder for his or her own use two ears of corn with the husk pulled back ready for braiding.   The red ear is called the " King ear " or Hosan'nowa'nĕn'.

When one finds an ear with only two diametrically placed rows filled out the finder receives as a reward an ear of corn ready for braiding from each harvester.   This ear is called oa'de meaning *the roadway.*   The unfilled space is " caused by the devil who has licked the cob with his tongue! "

When a large ear is found on which no kernels have grown or on which they are undeveloped, it is called gagĕn'tci, *it is an old one.* The finder is rewarded by the gift of a single ear of normal corn with the husk pulled back ready for braiding.   The finding of one of these abnormal ears is the cause of much merriment.   The gagĕn'tci ear is short and of unusual diameter,— " it is all gone to cob."   Sometimes these ears are collected and braided in strings for decorative purposes.

When the husk is pulled back for braiding the ear is called ganoñyon or onoñ'yon.   If men, boys, girls and women engage in this work the process is called hadi'nonyoñtă'.   If only women are working the work is called wa'dinonnyoñtă'.

When the ears are entirely stripped of husks the ear is called ganowiyă"gon.   The work of husking by a mixed company is called hă'dinowiyas, or if by women alone, wadi'nowiyas.

Corn smut is called odjingwĕnsho' (syphilis).   The smut-blighted ear is termed odjingwĕs o'nisdă"ge.[1]   The blighted cornstalk and its fruit is not used but cast aside and burned.

---

[1] The pink azaleas, Rhododendron nudiflorum, are known as odji'gwĕndă'wĕno', syphilitic flowers.

5 **Storage of corn.** The braided bunches[1] of corn[2] were hung on poles in the house or in a protected outbuilding. The shelled corn was preserved in bark barrels and might either be natural kernels or charred. When the braided strings of corn were stored in the house the pole hung from the ridge pole or from the cross beams. Cartier noticed this method in all probability when he wrote that they preserved it in garrets at the tops of their houses.[3]

Champlain mentions that corn was stored in the tops of the houses and enough cultivated to last three or four years.[4]

Lafitau[5] described minutely the Iroquois long house and said that it had storerooms for barrels and bark shelves above for storing provisions. Certain spaces below also were reserved for this purpose.

The description left us by Sagard previously quoted in this work, of the rows of braided corn, is a most vivid one. He says it hung like a tapestry the whole length of the cabin.[6]

The Iroquois harvested corn in greater quantities than they could consume and thus generally had a surplus for trade or emergency. Should one of the five nations have ill luck with their crops the others would respond to the need, for a consideration or gratuitously, as the case demanded.

The storage of corn was an important matter. Morgan, however, says:[7] " The red races seldom formed m˙ ˙azines of grain to guard against distant wants." A little examinat˙ n of the works of early writers contradicts this statement which M˙ ˙an knew did not apply at any rate to the Iroquois.

Referring to the custom of burying corn and vegetables in pits Lafitau wrote:[8]

Didore of Sicile said that the first people of la grande Bretagne, having gathered their corn, kept it in subterranean granaries and it was only taken out in quantites immediatelv necessary. The Indian women have some sort of an underground granary where also they keep pumpkins (citroulles) and other fruits. It is a hole four to

---

[1] *Cf.* Sagard. Voyages des Hurons. Ed. n. 1865. pt I, p. 135; or *see* footnote p. 31 of this work.

[2] *Ibid.* p. 93.

[3] Cartier in Hakluyt's Voyages, 3:271.

[4] Champlain. Voyages. Paris 1682. p. 301.

[5] Lafitau. Moeurs des Sauvages. Paris 1724. 2:12 et seq.

[6] *Cf.* Morgan. League, p. 318.

[7] Morgan. League, p.372.

[8] Lafitau, 2:80.

Plate 6

Corn pit excavated by Harrington and Parker, 1903 (Peabody Museum of Archeology and Ethnology Expedition) on the Silverheel's site, Brant township, Erie county, N. Y.

Plate 7

1 Vegetable storage pits near Chief E. Cornplanter's house, Cattaraugus Reservation. 2 Seneca corncrib on the James Sandy place, Cattaraugus Reservation

five feet deep, lined with bark and covered with earth. Their fruits
keep perfectly sound during the winter without any injury from the
frost. As for the corn,— it is different,— instead of burying it, except in the case of necessity, they allow it to dry on scaffolds and
under the eaves or in sheds outside of their houses.

At Tsonnontouann[1] they make bark granaries round and place
them on elevations, piercing the bark from all sides so that the air
will get in and prevent the moisture from spoiling the grain.

Morgan in his League[2] describes the *cache* in a somewhat similar
way:

The Iroquois were accustomed to bury their surplus corn and also
their charred green corn in caches, in which the former would preserve uninjured through the year, and the latter for a much longer
period. They excavated a pit, made a bark bottom and sides, and
having deposited their corn within it, a bark roof, water tight, was
constructed over it, and the whole covered with earth. Pits of
charred corn are still found near their ancient settlements.

The writer has found these corn pits throughout the Iroquois region in New York, one of them shown in plate 6. Many of these
ancient pits show that they had been lined with long grass or with
hemlock boughs,[3] for after the corn had been removed the pit was
filled with rubbish and the entire matter burned or charred. In
this manner the grass lining, if it were carbonized, was preserved
and when excavated the charred grass lining could be removed in
chunks or sheets. Mr Harrington has also noted this occurrence
throughout his field of investigation in New York. The Iroquois
have not abandoned this custom even now. Among the more primitive the custom of burying parched corn and other vegetables is still in
vogue. In plate 7 is shown a group of pits on the Cattaraugus
Seneca Reservation in Erie county. In the background the Council

---

[1] Also known as Sonnontouan, Totiacton and La Conception. The site
of this old Seneca town is in the present town of Mendon, Monroe co., 1½
miles from Honeoye Falls.

[2] Morgan, p. 319.

[3] In describing corn storage, Kalm writes: "After they reaped their maize,
they kept it in holes underground during winter; they dug these holes
seldom deeper than a fathom, and often not so deep; at the bottom and
sides they put broad pieces of bark. The A n d r o p o g o n   b i c o r n e,
a grass which grows in great plenty here, and which the English call Indian
grass . . . supplies the want of bark; the ears of maize are then thrown
into the hole, and covered to a considerable thickness with the same grass
and the whole is again covered by a sufficient quantity of earth; the maize
keeps extremely well in these holes and each Indian has several such subterranean stores where his corne lay safe though he travel far from it."
Kalm. Pinkerton's Voyages, 13:539.

or Long House is to be seen. These pits are near the house of Edward Cornplanter and were photographed in the spring of 1909 after the store had been removed.

The custom of caching vegetables in the ground is, of course, one now followed by white people generally. Beauchamp[1] says the Mohawk word for making a *cache* is asaton. The Seneca word is similar, being wae'sado^n, meaning *she buried it*. *It is buried* would be, gasa'do^n.

The modern *caches* are lined with hemlock boughs instead of bark although wood is sometimes used and sometimes bark instead of boughs at the top. Over this is placed a mound of earth.[2]

Champlain is the first writer to describe the pit method of storing corn. He says: " They make trenches in the sand on the slope of the hills some five to six feet deep more or less. Putting their corn and other grains into large grass sacks[3] they throw them into these trenches and cover them with sand three or four feet above the surface of the earth, taking out as their needs require. In this way it is preserved as well as it would be possible in our granaries."

The corn found by the Pilgrims in November 1620 was buried in a similar manner.

In the Journal of a Dutch agent, by some supposed to be Arent Van Curler, who journeyed among the Mohawks and Oneidas in 1634–35, is a statement that the houses were full of corn, some of them containing more than 300 bushels.[4]

Corncribs are an Indian invention and for general construction have been little improved upon by white men. Figure 2 in plate 7 shows a modern Seneca crib.

IV   CEREMONIAL AND LEGENDARY ALLUSIONS TO CORN

In the cosmologic myth of the Senecas corn is said to have sprung from the breasts of the Earth-Mother who died upon delivering the twins, Good Minded and Evil Minded. Thus the food of the mother's bosom still continued to give life to her offspring. Esquire Johnson, an old Seneca chief, in an interview with Mrs Asher

---

[1] Beauchamp, *Dr* W. M. N. Y. State Mus. Bul. 89. p. 193.

[2] Compare the following: " The Indians thrash it as they gather it. They dry it well on mats in the sun and bury it in holes in the ground, lined with moss or boughs, which are their barns." Pinkerton. Voyages, 12:258.

[3] *Cf.* Hennepin. Voyages. Lond. 1698. p. 104.

[4] Amer. Hist. Ass'n Trans. 1895. Wilson, *Gen.* J. G. Arent Van Curler, Journal of, 1634–35, p. 91.

Wright, the missionary, in 1876 said that the beans, squashes, potatoes and tobacco plants sprang also from the grave. Some of the writer's informants declare that the squash grew from the grave earth directly over the Earth-Mother's navel, the beans from her feet and the tobacco plant from her head. Thus it is said of the latter plant, " It soothes the mind and sobers thought."

From the manuscript of Mrs Wright's interview with Johnson, the following is quoted:

Johnson says that a long time ago squashes were found growing wild. He says that he has seen them and that they were quite unpalatable, but the Indians used to boil and eat them. He says that in their ancient wars with the southern Indians they brought back squashes that were sweet and palatable and beans which grow wild in the south, calico colored, and which were very good, and he thinks the white folks have never used them. Also the o-yah-gwa-oweh (oyen'kwaoñ'we^n, tobacco) they brought from the south where it grows wild, also various kinds of corn, black, red and squaw corn, they brought from the prairie country south where they found it growing wild. All these things they found on their war expeditions and brought them here and planted them and thus they abound here, but he does not know where they first found the potato.

The mythology of the Iroquois is full of allusions to corn, its cultivation and uses. The story of its origin from the breasts of the mother of the two spirits, previously referred to, is generally accepted as the proper version, but there are other stories which, however, are regarded simply as *gaga"*, or amusement tales, rather than religious explanations. One story relates that an orphaned nephew who had been adopted by an eccentric uncle with strange habits thought that he would discover how his uncle obtained food. He pretended to be asleep and looking through a peephole in his skin coverlet found that the old man had a strange lot of nuts fastened on a stick (a corncob). Cautiously removing a nut (kernel) he placed it in a small pot of water and making some mysterious passes over it as he crooned a mysterious song, he caused the vessel to expand to a great size and fill with a delicious food. The next day the old man went on a journey to a distant gorge and the young man determined to try the experiment which he had seen his uncle perform. He shelled all the corn from the cob, threw it in the pot, sang and motioned until the pot swelled up so large that it filled the house and burst the walls. A great mound was formed and when the old man returned he cried out in dismay, " You have killed me," and gave as his reason that he was the custodian of the corn which

was the only ear in the country, the remainder being in the possession of a ferocious company of women who killed by their very
glances. Beasts and serpents guarded the path to their houses and
as there was nothing else to eat the nephew and uncle must starve.
The nephew laughed and set out to conquer all the difficulties. The
story of his conquest of all these things is detailed and exciting.
However, he chased the women up a tree and made them promise
to deliver up the corn, which they did and the hero went home, step-
ping disdainfully over the carcasses of monsters and serpents. Since
then corn has been plentiful.

Beauchamp refers to this tale which he found among the Onondaga but thinks it of European origin. Hewett in his *Cosmology*[1]
gives this tale substantially as outlined above. The reference in the
tale to the nuts on the stick has given some Iroquois the idea that
chestnuts were meant and the story is given as the origin of chestnuts. The Seneca names for chestnuts and corn kernels are not
dissimilar, the former being o'nĭs'tă' and the latter o'nie'stă'.

Dr Beauchamp relates another tale which he had from Joseph
Lyon, an Onondaga. A fine young man lived on a small hill, so the
story runs, and being lonely he desired to marry some faithful, agreeable maiden. With his long flowing robes and tasseled plumes he
lifted up his voice and sang, " Say it, say it, some one I will marry."
He kept up his song day after day and at last there came a fair
maiden, arrayed in a flowing green mantle over which were fastened
beautiful yellow bells. " I have come to marry you," she smiled, but
the tall young warrior responded, " No, you are not the one, you
wander too much from home and run over the ground so fast that
I can not keep you by my side." The poor rejected pumpkin maiden
went sorrowfully away and floating after her came the echo of the
song, " Some one I will marry."

One morning a tall slender maiden appeared drawn toward the
singer by the magic of the song (which even we of these degenerate
days must confess, though even inaudible, is a song that attracts).
The maiden was covered with clusters of flowers and gracefully
dangling leaves. The tall young man needed but to look and there
was an immediate consciousness of affinity. The two embraced each
other and to this day in the Indian's cornfield the two plants are
inseparable. The cornstalk bean twines around her lover still.

---

[1] Bureau of Ethnology Rep't. 1903.

Dr Beauchamp adds that they are inseparable even in death " for the beans make a part of Indian corn bread." [1]

Mrs Converse relates a very pretty story of the three plant sisters in her *Myths and Legends*. [2] The writer has heard the same story. The corn, however, is a female and not a pining, singing lover. The corn plant in the old days produced a heavy grain rich in an oil which was most delicious. The Evil Minded spirit, jealous of the good gifts which the Good Minded had given *men beings* watched his opportunity to capture the spirit of the corn. Detaining the spirit he sent his messengers to blight the fields. The sun sent a ray of light to liberate the captive spirit but ever since corn has been less productive and required greater care. Morgan also mentions this legend in the *League*. [3]

There is an allusion to the spirit of the corn plant in the code of Handsome Lake, as follows:

It was a bright day when I went into the planted field and alone I wandered in the planted field and it was the time of the second hoeing. Suddenly a damsel appeared and threw her arms about my neck and as she clasped me she spoke saying " When you leave this world for the new world above it is our wish to follow you." I looked for the damsel but saw only the long leaves of corn twining round my shoulders. And then I understood that it was the spirit of the corn who had spoken, she the sustainer of life. [*See* Code of Ga-nio-dai-o,[4] § 48, ¶ 2]

---

[1] Jour. Am. Folk Lore, p. 195.

[2] Converse. Myths and Legends of the Iroquois; ed. by A. C. Parker. N. Y. State Mus. Bul. 125.

[3] Morgan. League of the Iroquois. Rochester 1854. p. 161.

[4] Manuscript in N. Y. State Library, trans. by Parker, A. C. and Bluesky, William.

Fig. 4 The Spirit of the Corn speaking to Handsome Lake, the Seneca prophet. (From a drawing by Jesse Cornplanter, a Seneca boy artist)

V VARIETIES OF MAIZE USED BY THE IROQUOIS AND OTHER EASTERN INDIANS

1 **Varieties mentioned by historians.** Few authorities agree as to the varieties of Indian corn. Beverly[1] mentions four "sorts" among the Virginia Indians, two of which he says are early ripe and two late ripe. He describes the four varieties carefully and ends by saying that his description is without respect to what he calls the "accidental differences in color, some being blue, some red, some yellow, some white and some streaked." He continues that the real difference is determined by the "plumpness or shriveling of the grain." To him the smooth early ripe corn was flint corn and the "other . . . with a dent on the back of the grain . . . they call *she-corn*." This is probably the *Poketawes* of the Powhatan Indians.

In Harris's *Discoveries*[2] is another description of corn giving the variety of colors as "red, white, yellow, blue, green and black and some speckled and striped but the white and yellow are most common."[3]

Thomas Hariot in his *Brief and True Report,* reports[4] the "divers colors" as red, white, yellow and blue which in the light of the descriptions of his contemporaries would seem to make his report true but not the whole truth.

Morgan[5] is even more unsatisfactory in his descriptions and records

---

[1] Beverly. Virginia, p. 126.

[2] Pinkerton. Voyages and Travels, 12:242.

[3] " . . . maise or Indian corn, which is not our pease in taste, but grows in a great ear or head as big as the handle of a large horse whip, having from three hundred to seven hundred grains in one ear, and sometimes one grain produces two or three such ears or heads; it is of various colours, red, white, yellow, blue, green and black, and some speckled and striped, but the white and yellow are most common; the stalk is as thick as an ordinary walking cane, and grows six or eight feet high, in joints, having a sweet juice in it, of which a syrup is sometimes made, and from every joint there grow long leaves in the shape of sedge leaves." *Ibid.* p. 242.

[4] Pagatowr, a kind of grain so called by the inhabitants; the same is called mayze, Englishmen call it Guinywheat or Turkey-wheat, according to the names of the countries from whence the like has been brought. The grain is about the bigness of our ordinary English pease, and not much different in form and shape; but of divers colors, some white, some red, some yellow and some blue. All of these yield a very white and sweet flour being used according to his kind, it maketh a very good bread." Hariot. Reprint. N. Y. 1872. p. 13–16.

[5] League of the Iroquois, p. 370.

only three kinds of corn among the Seneca. He enumerates them as white, O-na-o-ga-ant, red, Tic-ne, and white flint, Ha-go-wa. These were the varieties which he collected and sent the State Cabinet (Museum) in 1850.

It is difficult to say what kind of corn Columbus saw on the island which he discovered, but we may be reasonably sure that Cartier mentioned the white flint corn when he described the corn of the Hochelagans. Morgan[1] mentions this as the bread corn of the Seneca mistaking it for the white Tuscarora or squaw corn.

Sweet corn was long known to the Indians and its seed was first obtained by Sullivan's soldiers from the Seneca fields on the Susquehanna.[2]

Purple or blue corn is mentioned in the Journal of Lieut. Erkuries Beatly, an officer under Sullivan. In describing the events of Friday the 3d of September he says ". . . the Indians had just left their kettles on the fire boiling fine corn and beans which we got, but what was most remarkable — the corn was all purple . . ."

Esquire Johnson, an aged Seneca chief, in an interview with Mrs Laura Wright in 1879 said, ". . . They brought it from the south, also various kinds of corn black, red and squaw corn. . . All these things they found on their war expeditions and brought them here and planted them and thus they abound." The object of Iroquois raids, according to many of the old Indians, was to get new vegetables and slaves as well as to subjugate insubordinate tribes.

Dent corn, with the Iroquois (Seneca), is called ono'dja, *tooth*. Tradition relates that this is a western form derived from Sandusky Iroquois in Ohio.

The writer has conducted a lengthy inquiry as to the varieties of corn cultivated by the Iroquois during the last 100 years and the result is embodied in the list, which is found below.[3] At the present day while they conserve the forms with a zeal that has in it a religious and patriotic sentiment, they also cultivate the new varieties with equal ardor for in the modern types is found the corn which produces the most money in the markets.

---

[1] *Ibid.* p. 370.

[2] *Cf.* Journal of Capt. Richard Begnall.

[3] *Cf.* Harrington. Seneca Corn Foods, Am. Anthropologist, new ser. v. 10, no. 4, p. 575, 576. Four varieties are mentioned.

Plate 8

Scenes about an Iroquois bark house, from a drawing by Jesse Corn-planter, a Seneca youth. Note the manner in which the corn braids are placed on the drying pole.

Plate 9

Varieties of Iroquois corn. From left to right the ears are: 1 Tuscarora. 2, 3 Red. 4, 5 Purple. 6 Calico. 7 White flint. 8 Short-eared calico. There are seven other varieties cultivated as native corn. Specimens are one third natural size.

2 Varieties of corn used by the Iroquois

Zea mays amylacea, soft corns

Tuscarora or Squaw, Onä'oñga^n== [1] *white corn*
Tuscarora short eared, Onyuñ'gwĭktă'== *growing over the tip*
Purple soft, Oso^ngwŭdji' == *purple*
Red soft, gwĕ^ndä'ä == *red*

Zea mays indurata, flint corns

Hominy or flint, dionĕo"stäte'==the corn glistens
Hominy or flint, long eared, hĕ"kowă

Calico, $\begin{cases} \text{yodjisto'goñnyi} == it\ spotted\ is \\ \text{deyuneo}^n\text{'de}^n\text{iŭs} == \text{mixed colors} \end{cases}$

Yellow, djitgwä^n'ä^n hĕ"kowă == yellow hĕ"kowă

Zea mays saccharata, sweet corns

Sweet, diyut'gotnogwi == *puckered corn*
Black sweet, oso^ngwud'dji deutgo^n'negaidĕ == *black puckers*

Zea mays everta, pod corn

Red pop, gwĕ^n"dä'ä wata'toñgwus == red, *it bursts*
White pop, wata'toñgwus == *it bursts*

Zea mays (variety ?), pod corn

Sacred corn, onä'o^nwĕ == original corn

The Mohawks cultivate some of these varieties now. Mr William
Loft, a Mohawk Indian of the Six Nations Reservation in Canada,
gives the Mohawk names for the following:

Tuscarora, ono^nstaga^n'rha
Tuscarora, short, ono^nstaoan'nal
Sweet corn, degon'derho^nwix
Hominy or white flint, onust'teoñwe'
Hominy, longeared, ga'hrades
Yellow, o'jinegwa"onuste'
Purple, orhon'ya'
Husk or pod, oo^n'na^t
Pop, wadada'gwas oniuste'

---

[1] Seneca terminology.

VI CORN CULTIVATION TERMINOLOGY[1]

1 The process of growing

SENECA	ENGLISH
a Onä'o'	Corn
b waeeyŭnt'to'	She plants
c ohwĕⁿo'dadyiĕ'	It is just forming sprouts
d oga''hwäodaⁿ	It has sprouted
e otgaä'häät	The blade begins to appear
f otga'äähät	The blade has appeared
g deyuähă'o	The blade is already out
h ogwäⁿ'dääodyiĕ'	The stalk begins to appear
i ogwäⁿ'dää'e'	The stalk is fully out
j oge''odadyie'	It is beginning to silk
k owäⁿ'dă'	The ears are out
l o'geot	It has silked out
m ogwäⁿdŭ'äe', ogwäⁿ'däⁿe'	The tassels are fully out
n ono''gwaat	It is in the milk
o dĕju'göⁿsäät	It is no longer in the milk
p oweäⁿdäädyĕ', owĕⁿdädyĕ'	The ears are beginning to set
q onĕ'oda'dyiē'	The kernels are setting on the cob
r hadí'nonyoⁿcos	They are husking (indefinite as to method)
s yestä'änyoⁿnyano'	She is braiding
t dŭstaⁿ'shoni	It is braided
u gasdäⁿt'shudoho'	It is hung over a pole
v ganoⁿ'gadi'	It is strung along a pole

2 Terminology of cultivation

a waĕ'yuntto'	She plants
b yeeo'do'gwŭs	She weeds
c deyonanyaoh, or deyo'wĕnnyē'	She stirs up the earth
d wae'oaoⁿ, or wa'eä	She hills it up

3 Parts of corn

a oea'	Leaves
b odjoⁿ'wa'sa	Leaves of corn
c oaya', oe'ä'	Stalk

[1] Based upon manuscript lexicon of Rev. Asher Wright. For the sake of uniformity the Wright system of orthography has been changed to that used in the body of this work.

d onoⁿ'gwaⁿ'a'	Cob
e gagosswa"ge', ogoishă"ge	Butt of cob (meaning nose)
f oji'jut	Tassels
g onäo onius'ta or o'nis'ta'	Kernels
h onyo'nia'	Husk
i oaya okdayä, or ok'te'ä	Roots
j okta'a	Hulls
k ogai'tă'	Waste matter
l onäo'a'wĕn'niăsă'	Germ = heart
m ogŭdjidä'	Pollen when it comes off
n ganäoñgwe'	Seed corn
o o"gioⁿt	Silk

VII UTENSILS EMPLOYED IN THE PREPARATION OF CORN FOR FOOD

The implements and utensils employed for the planting, cultivating and harvesting and the preparation of corn for food embraced the larger part of Iroquois domestic furniture. To a large extent many of the old-time corn utensils are still made and used by the Iroquois who prefer the " old way " and it is surprising to find that even the Christianized Iroquois, who generally live in communities away from their " pagan " brothers, cling to their corn mortars and the other articles which go with them. Today on all the Iroquois reservations both in New York and Canada the corn articles form the great part of their Indian material, and in fact constitute much of their aboriginality. As far as the writer can learn this same observation applies to all of the Indian tribes or remnants of such east of the Mississippi river.

Corn mortars are still made in the ancient way by burning out the hollow.

The men probably made most of the bark and wooden dishes[1] and carved the spoons and paddles while the women made the baskets and sieves.

Hennepin writing on this subject remarks: " When the Savages are about to make Wooden Dishes, Porringers or Spoons, they form the Wood to their purpose with their Stone Hatchets, make it hollow with their Coles out of the Fire and scrape them afterward with Beavers Teeth for to polish them.[2]

---

[1] *See* Jesuit Relations, 23:55, 13:265; Lawson. Carolina, p. 208.
[2] Hennepin. Voyage, p. 103.

Large kettle, Gano^n'djowanĕ'.   Anciently large clay vessels were used. Later brass or copper kettles obtained from the whites were used. The use of clay vessels was early noticed by travelers[1] among the Indians of eastern North America. There are several good descriptions of the methods of pottery making, references to the use of the vessels for cooking and several illustrations of them [*see* fig. 15]. It seems most probable from these early accounts and illustrations that the clay kettles were placed directly over the fire, though perhaps supported by three or four stones properly arranged. Schoolcraft, however, illustrates one suspended over the fire. The writer once found a clay vessel in a fire pit with the remains of the fire about it and four or five pieces of angular shale at the bottom as a supporting base. There are several illustrations depicting this method in old works.

The coming of the traders with brass kettles was an event in the history of Indian cooking. It enlarged their capacity for cooking food in quantities. As brass kettles became common with them the smaller clay vessels passed out of use and were made but rarely. In this way the art gradually became forgotten.

Among the Seneca the writer found several persons who remembered hearing in their youth how the vessels were made. They asserted that clay was thus occasionally employed up to the middle of the last century. The Seneca seem to have conserved the art[2] at any rate for some time after their settlement at Tonawanda, Allegany and Cattaraugus.

The use of brass kettles among the Iroquois is still found, some of the more conservative seeming to prefer them [*see* pl. 10], but the majority now use iron or the more modern enameled ware pots.

Wooden mortar, Ga''niga''ta.[3]   The corn mortar was made of the wood of the trunk of a niiu''gägwasä, *pepperidge tree* or ogo'wä,

---

[1] These vessels are so strong that they do not crack when on the fire without water inside, as ours do, but at the same time they can not stand continued moisture and cold water long without becoming fragile and breaking at any slight knocks that any one may give them but otherwise they are very durable." Sagard. Histoire du Canada. 1638. Tross ed. Paris 1866. p. 260.

[2] *Cf* Harrington. Last of the Iroquois Potters. N. Y. State Mus. Rep't of Director. 1908.

[3] Ga'ni'ga' in Mohawk.

Sebastien Cramoisy in his relations (1634–36) said " . . . we have learned by experience that our sagamites are better pounded in a wooden mortar in the fashion of the Savages than ground within the mill. I believe it is because the mill makes the flour too fine." [*See* Jesuit Relations. Thwaite's ed. v. 8]

Plate 10

Interior of the Canadian Seneca ceremonial cook house, Grand River Reservation. Note the large brass kettle. From a photograph by the author

Plate 11

Iroquois corn mortar and pestle. The mortar is 25 inches high.
(Museum collection)

black oak. To conform to the proportions specified by custom the log was reduced to a diameter of 20 inches and then a section 22 inches long was cut or sawed off. A fire was built in the center of the end naturally uppermost and when it had eaten its way into the block for half an inch or thereabouts, the charcoal was carefully scraped out to give a fresh surface to a new fire which ate its way still deeper. The process was repeated until the bowlike hollow was of the desired depth, generally about 12 inches.[1] In this hollow was placed the corn to be pulverized. The relative values of mortars depended on their freedom from cracking and the grinding quality of the wood.

The use of the mortar[2] and pestle is shown in plates 11, 12 and 20. In the same illustrations is shown the corn strung or braided for convenience in handling, after the old Indian style now universally adopted by farmers.

The wooden mortar and pestle are found among most of the eastern Indians. The styles and shapes differed greatly. The Cherokee, for example, had a shallow saucerlike depression in the top of their mortars and a socket in the center. Their pestles were bulbous at the top but the grinding end was small and of a size designed to fit the socket loosely. As the meal was pounded it rose to the top and settled around the " saucer " top where it could easily be swept or scooped into a receptacle. Cherokee mortars like the Iroquois were made upright. The Pottawatomie, Chippewa and some others had horizontal mortars, that is the cavity was made in the side of the mortar log. The Seminole not content with one cavity made three or four in the side of a fallen tree. The Nanticoke made their mortars vase-shaped with a supporting base and the Choctaw chopped their mortar vases to a point to hold them stationary. Dr Speck found an odd mortar among the Connecticut Mohegan. It had been carved so as to resemble somewhat an hour glass. He was not able

---

[1] Adair describes the process as follows, ". . . cautiously burned a large log to a proper level and length, placed fire a-top, and with mortar [clay] around it, in order to give the utensil proper form, and when the fire was extinguished or occasion required, they chopped the inside with their stone instruments, patiently continuing the slow process till they finished the machine to the intended purpose." Adair, p. 416. Lond. 1725. *Cf.* DePratz. Paris 1724, 2:177.

[2] " The Indians always used mortars instead of mills and had them with almost every other convenience when first opened to trade." Adair, p.416.
" They pound it in a hollow tree." De Vries. Second Voyage. Hoorn 1655, p. 107. N. Y. Hist. Soc. Col. Ser. 2, v. 3, pt 1.

to obtain it because the tribe held it as communal property and looked upon it with a feeling of veneration.   The pestles differ as much as the mortars, some being mere clublike sticks.

Pestle, Hĕtge'oʻ or He'tgĕn"khă'[1]   The Seneca words mean *upper part* and are derived from hetgää'gwa, meaning *upper*.   The pestle is generally of hard maple wood about 48 inches long.   It is shaped the same on both ends and either may be used for pounding, although one end is generally chosen and always used thereafter.   The other end serves as a weight that adds to the power of the arm in making the stroke.   The mortar and pestle are used in pulverizing corn for soups, hominy, puddings and bread, and are by far the most important utensils used in preparing corn foods made from meal.

Stone mortar and pestle, Yeīstonniă"tă'. Up to within the time of the Civil War it was a common thing for the Seneca, as well as others of the Iroquois, to use stone mortars and pestles or rather mullers.   Some of these mortars were so small that they could easily be carried in a basket without inconvenience.   Corn could be cracked for soup by a single blow or by rubbing once or twice it could be re-

Fig. 5   Seneca stone mortar and muller.   The mortar is 8 inches in length

duced to meal.   Many of the older people remember these "stone mills" by which their odjis'toⁿnondä', *cracked corn hominy* was made[2] [*see* fig. 5]

M. R. Harrington found one of these mortars still in use by the Oneida in Madison county and described it in the American *Anthropologist.*[3]

---

[1] Ga'ni'ga' in Mohawk.

[2] *Cf.* Jesuit Relations, 1716–27, v. 67:213.   They crush the corn between two stones reducing it to a meal; afterward they make of it a porridge which they sometimes season with fat or with dried fish.

[3] New Ser. v. 10, no. 4.   1908.   p. 579.

Plate 12

Feast makers at the New York Seneca midwinter festival, February 1909. The costumes and other articles except the corn mortar are now in the State Museum collections.

Plate 13

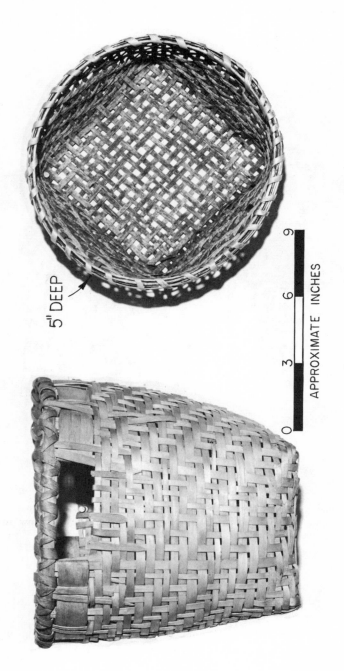

5" DEEP

APPROXIMATE INCHES

0   3   6   9

Hulling and hominy baskets.   Illustrations are one fifth actual size.   A. C. Parker, collector, 1908

Mullers and mealing slabs are commonly found on Iroquois village sites and sometimes may be picked up near log cabin sites on the present reservations. The Iroquois probably did not use the long cylindrical pestles to any great extent, as did the New York Algonquins as late as the Revolutionary War.

Mr Harrington found one of these cylindrical pestles among the descendants of the Shinnecock at Southampton, Long Island, together with a small wooden mortar. The Minisink Historical Society has one which was given an early settler by one of the Minsis before the Revolutionary War.

Hulling basket, Yegai"toätă'.[1] The Seneca word for hulling basket means *it washes corn*. This basket is woven with tight sides

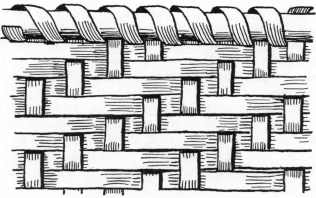

Fig. 6   Technic of the hulling basket

and a coarse sievelike bottom. It is about 18 inches deep and as many broad at the top tapering down to 12 inches at the bottom. In this basket is put squaw or hominy corn after it has been boiled in weak lye to loosen the hulls and outer skin. The basket of corn is then soused up and down in a large tub of water until all the hulls are free and have floated off in the many rinse waters.

The details of weaving the hulling basket are shown in figure 6 and the basket itself in plate 13. Hulling baskets are made in four styles; without handles of any sort; with handles made by openings in the body of the basket just below the rim; by raised loop handles made by fastening pieces of bent wood through the rim and into the body of the basket; and by a raised handle that arches from side to side. For the various styles see figure 7. This type of basket is

---

[1] Yegahreda^nda'kwa' in Mohawk

widely found among the eastern Indians although the Iroquois basket seems to have been higher.

The hominy sifter is woven in the same manner and the State Museum has specimens from the Cherokee and Shawnee which are

Fig. 7   Various forms of hulling baskets

similar in all details to the Iroquois baskets. Both of these peoples of course have been in contact with the Iroquois at different periods. The Delaware sifting and washing baskets were often made of shreds of bark but the Iroquois preferred the inner splints of the black ash.

Hominy sifter, Onïius'tawanĕs.[1]   The Seneca term means *coarse kernels*. This basket is of the same weave as the hulling basket. It is a foot square at the top and tapers down to 10 inches at the bottom. The bottom is sievelike, the openings being about $\frac{3}{16}$ inch square. The hominy corn cracked in the mortar is sifted through this basket and the coarser grains that remain are thrown back in the mortar to be repounded and resifted until all are of the requisite size.

Meal sifter,[2] Niu'nyoⁿ'sthasā'.[3] The Indian word is derived from niwa'a, *small*, and oniius'tă' *kernels*. In size and shape this basket is like the hominy sifter. The splints of which it is woven, however, are very fine, being about $\frac{1}{16}$ inch wide. Except for decorative purposes, no baskets were ever woven finer. The niu'nyoⁿs'thasā' was used for sifting corn meal for bread puddings. Sometimes it was used to sift other things, such as maple sugar, salt, seeds etc. So much labor was required to make one of these meal sifters that many of the Iroquois ceased to weave them when cheap wire sieves could be obtained, the price of the meal sieve basket being as high as $1 [*see* fig. 8].

----

[1] Yunoⁿ'owa'nĕs in Mohawk.

[2] " They have little baskets which they call *notassen,* and which are made of a kind of hemp the same as fig frails, which they make to serve as sieves." De Vries, p. 187.

[3] Niga'te'sera, flour sieve, in Mohawk.

Plate 14

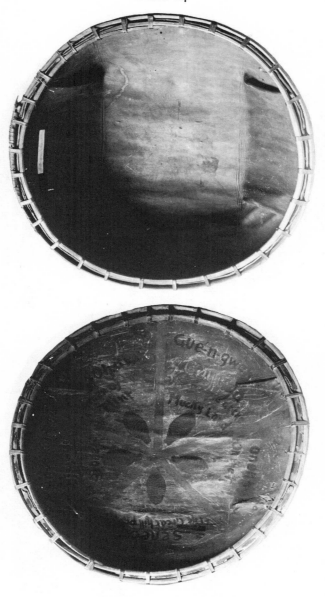

1 Seneca bark bowl. 2 Mohawk feast bowl used at the Six Nations annual meetings. The beaver tail symbols refer to a section in the Iroquois Constitution and symbolize peace and plenty. Illustrations are one sixth actual size. Coverse collection

Plate 15

Iroquois bread and eating bowls

Metallic meal sifters, now sometimes used, are regarded as inferior for sifting the Indian prepared meal because they give a metallic

Fig. 8 Meal sifter. Specimen is 12 inches in diameter and 4 inches deep. The mesh is $\frac{1}{16}$ inch.

taste to the food. It is said that the basket sieve makes lighter flour.

Ash sifter, Ogä'yeonto'.[1] The ash sifter was a small basket about 6 inches square at the top, 5 inches square or less at the bottom and about 3 inches deep. It was woven like the hominy sifter, the sieve bottom having somewhat smaller openings.

Ash sifters are rare in collections illustrating the series of baskets used in the preparation of corn for food. One in the State Museum is very old and was collected by Morgan at Tonawanda in 1851.

Bark bread bowl, Gŭsnongäoñ'wà'.[2] This dish is made from bark peeled in the spring or the early summer time, bent into the required shape and bound around the edges with a hoop of ash sewed on with a cord of inner elm or basswood bark. The usual dimen-

---

[1] Yonganrawakto' is the Mohawk form.
[2] Ga"sna'gahoñ'wa' in Mohawk.

sions are from 1 to 2 feet in diameter and from 4 to 9 inches deep. Some bowls are elliptical in shape. These bark bowls were used for mixing the corn meal into loaves previous to boiling and afterward for holding the finished loaf.

The writer has seen these bark bowls used for cooking vessels, heated stones being thrown into the liquid within it. The bark vessel can also be put over an outdoor earthen or stone fireplace and water heated if the flames are kept away from the rim. Bark bowls are still used in some parts of the Seneca reservations as dish pans, sap tubs, wash pans, etc. Bark dishes are easily made and their first use may be referred to very early times. Two of these bowls are shown in plate 14. Morgan collected a series of bark vessels for the State Museum in 1854 and some of the specimens are still on exhibition.

Wooden bread bowl, Owĕⁿgä'gä'oñ'wä'.[1] Sometimes instead of a bark dish a wooden one was used for a bread bowl. It was of about the same relative size and carved from pine or maple. The form naturally differed somewhat from the bark bowls, but in general outline followed them. Some of these bowls are carved from maple knots, or knots from other trees. Usually, however, they were carved from softer wood.

Wide paddle, Gatgŭn'yasshuwa'nĕ.[2] The wide paddle was used for lifting corn bread from the kettle in which it was boiled. Some of these paddles are beautifully carved and ornamented. The wide bread paddle took two forms, the round blade and the rectangular bladed paddle [*see* pl. 16]. A feature which distinguishes a lifting from a stirring paddle is the hole made in the middle of the blade. The holes are either round or heart-shaped.

Narrow paddle, Nigat'gwünyashäa'.[3] This paddle was used for stirring boiling soups and hulled corn.

Both wide and narrow paddles were carved from some hard wood, preferably some variety of maple. Some are decorated with carvings of phallic symbols. Such designs are regarded as sacred, in the Iroquois religion, and are never looked upon with levity. The carving of paddles gave opportunity for the carver to display his best genius. Chains were carved from the solid wood of the paddle handle and balls cut in barred receptacles [*see* pl. 16, fig. 3]. Even some of the plainer forms had decorations made by carving a series of small triangles arranged in figures on the handle.

---

[1] Oyĕn'de'ⁿgaonⁿwa' in Mohawk.
[2] Gagawe"tserhowanĕ' in Mohawk.
[3] Nigagawĕ"tsĕlha in Mohawk.

Within recent years this work of making and decorating these kitchen utensils has been the work of the men. No doubt they thought that a fine paddle would furnish a proper incentive for the making of a good soup.

Great dipping spoons, Ato'gwassho^{n}wa'ne'.[1] For dipping hulled corn soup, or in fact any other soup from a kettle, a large dipping spoon was generally used when there was one at hand. In form it was like the common eating spoon used by the Iroquois but very much larger, the bowl being about a foot in diameter. At present these large spoons are very rare. One specimen that the writer obtained for the American Museum of Natural History is said to have been used for years in council meetings on the Genesee Reservation, especially at the Green Corn Festivals. There are several large dipping spoons in the State Museum, but they are now not to be found in use on the New York Indian reservations. The specimen shown in the illustration, figure 1, plate 17, has a shorter handle than most.

The great dipping spoons were used for apportioning out the contents of the great feast cauldrons. The activity of collectors and the greater convenience of civilized articles has brought the tin dipper into greater prominence.

Deer jaw scraper, Yigăssho^n'gäya"to'.[2]. This implement is a very rare one. It is simply one of the rami of a deer's lower jaw and

Fig. 9　Deer jaw scraper for green corn.　Specimen is about 8 inches long,

is complete without trimming or finishing in any way. The jaw was held by the anterior toothless portion and with the sharp back teeth the green corn was scraped from the cob. The name of the implement, Yigăssho^n'gäya"to', is derived from ogo^n'sä, *green corn,* and yigowe^n'to', *it scrapes.*

The Seneca housewife when she uses the jaw scraper, with characteristic humor, says, " I am letting the deer chew the corn first for me."

---

[1] Wadogwa'tserhowănĕ' in Mohawk.

[2] Yĕ^{n}nos'stogä^{n}yatha' in Mohawk.

Another method of bruising green corn on the cob was to place a flat grinding stone in a large wooden or bark bowl, hold the ear on the stone with one hand and mash the unripe kernels with a milling stone held in the other hand. The bruised corn was then brushed from the mortar stone and the kernels that yet adhered to the cob, scraped off. When enough material had been thus prepared the lower stone was removed from the bowl and the mashed corn removed for cooking.

Dried corn was milled much in the same way. A handful of the corn was placed on the millstone and pulverized with the miller. The cracked corn would fall into the bowl and be pounded again and again until enough hominy or meal was obtained. The Seneca abandoned this method about 50 years ago, although a few have used it in recent times when a wooden mortar was not accessible.

The writer collected a deer jaw scraper in 1903 for the American Museum of Natural History and believes his description and specimen the first on record. Mr Harrington later collected and described the deer jaw scraper in Canada, corroborating the writer's data.[1]

Sagard in his *Voyages to the Hurons* describes another jaw method of removing green corn from the cob but says the jaws were those of the old women, the maidens and children who prepared the mass. He remarks that he had no liking for the food.

Eating bowl, Gă'oñ'wă'. Eating bowls[2] were made from bark or wood and were of various shapes.

Feast bowls oftentimes were of large size and were ornamented in various ways to distinguish them from ordinary dishes. There are two interesting specimens of feast bowls in the State collections. Both are Mohawk bowls from Grand River, Can. One has a handle styled after a beaver-tail, a beaver's tail being the symbol of a feast. The other bowl is made of elm bark. It was used at one of the Five Nation's councils some 10 years ago. The interior is divided into five sections by painted lines of yellow radiating from the center. At the angles of the radiating division lines are beaver tails, five in all. Upon the inner raised sides of the bowl is painted in red the names of the five nations and in black beneath the modern council names: Ga-ne-a-ga-o-no, Mohawk, Owner of the Flint; Gue-gweh-o-no, Onondaga, On the Hill; Nun-da-wah-o-no, Seneca, The

---

[1] *See also* Parker, A. C.   N. Y. State Mus. Bul. 117, p. 544.
[2] "Their dishes are wooden platters of sweet timber." Raleigh, in Hakluyt's Voyages. Lond. 1600. 3:304.

Plate 16

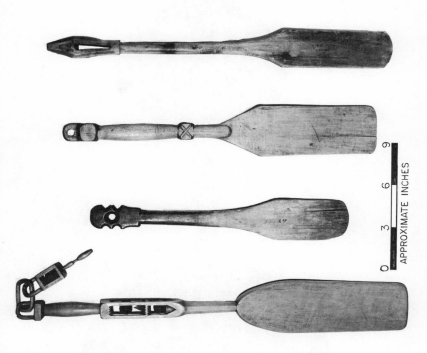

APPROXIMATE INCHES

Iroquois soup and bread paddles and turners. State Museum collection

Plate 17

1 Seneca feast dipping spoon. 2 Mohawk beaver tail national feast bowl.
Illustrations are about one fifth actual size. Mrs H. M. Converse collection
in State Museum

Great Hill People; O-na-ote-kah-o-no, Oneida, The People of the Stone. The label reads as follows:

(CANADIAN) MOHAWK BREAD BOWL.

This decoration is a fac-simile of the old bowl taken by the Mohawks when they left the League and departed with Brant.

5 yellow lines — The sun's path guarding the 5 nations. 5 Beaver tails — the beaver tail soup symbol. At the 5 Fire councils each Fire (or nation) was compelled to dip his soup from its own national division of the bowl. The dipping of the spoon into each portion allotted to its Fire signified union and fidelity. This bowl, obtained in Canada, was decorated by a Seneca Indian Artist on the Cattaraugus Reservation, June 12, 1899.

Harriet Maxwell Converse
Cattaraugus Reservation, N. Y.
June 15, 1899.

Ordinary eating bowls were smaller than feast bowls and were often carved with great nicety from maple, oak or pepperidge knots. After carving and polishing the bowls were dyed in a solution made from hemlock roots. Continual scouring soon reduced the bowl to a high polish and the grease which it absorbed gave it an attractive luster which contributed in a large measure to preserve the wood. Bowls which have been in the State Museum for 50 years still yield grease if scraped with a penknife.

Eating bowls are usually round but many of the older forms have suggestions of handles oppositely placed. Some of these handles go beyond mere suggestions and take the form of a bird's head and tail or two facing human effigies.[1] Bowls are shown in plates 14 and 15.

Wooden spoons, Atog'washä.[2] Great care was exercised in carving wooden spoons. As a rule, each individual had his own

Fig. 10 Wooden spoon from bottom of Black lake. Collected by E. R. Burmaster 1910. Specimen is 15 inches in length.

spoon which he recognized by the animal or bird carved on the handle. In olden times, the dream animal or clan totem was usually carved upon the handle, but specimens of later times nearly always

---

[1] *See* Harrington. Some Unusual Iroquois Specimens. Am. Anthropologist. new ser. 11 :85.

[2] Niwadonkwatserha, in Mohawk.

have the conventionalized forms of birds carved upon them.   In rare instances the figure was carved from a separate piece of wood and attached to the spoon handle with a peg.

The wood chosen for spoons was usually curly maple knots, although knots of other woods were valued and often used.   The Iroquois preferred to have their spoons of a dark color and as the "spoon wood" was white or yellow, they used dyes to darken them.   Hemlock bark or roots were boiled in water until the liquid was of the proper shade, which was dark red, and then the spoon

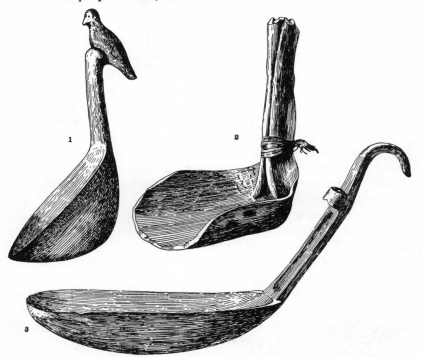

Fig. 11   Types of Seneca and Onondaga eating spoons.   1, wooden spoon; 2, bark ladle; 3, buffalo horn spoon.   Number 3 was collected by E. R. Burmaster, 1910, from the Alec John family who had preserved it as an heirloom for many years.

was plunged in and boiled with the dye until it had become thoroughly saturated with the dye and had partaken of the desired color.   By use and time the spoon became almost as black as ebony and took a high polish.

Spoons were sometimes shaped from elm bark but these were not durable. They were scoops rather than ladles or spoons.

The Iroquois did not readily abandon the use of wooden spoons and in some districts they are still used.   The Indians say that food

Plate 18

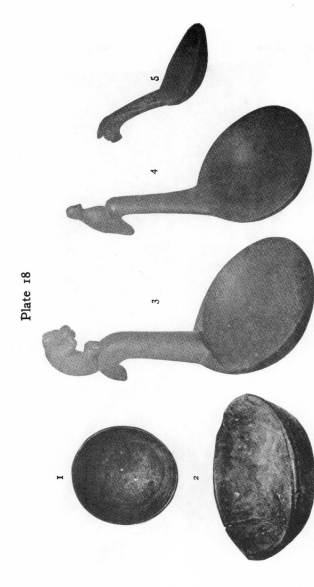

1 Onondaga salt bowl; 2 Seneca eating bowl; 3 Seneca spoon; 4 Onondaga spoon; 5 Delaware child's spoon

Plate 19

Elm bark planting baskets. 1 Seneca double-pocket basket, Morgan collection. 2 Delaware planting basket, collected by M. R. Harrington for the State Museum. Illustrations are one fourth size of specimens.

tastes much better when eaten from one and those who have not used them for some years express a longing to employ them again, recalling with evident pleasure the days when they ate from an " atog'washä." [1]

The favorite decorations for the tops of the handles were ducks, pigeons and sleeping swans. The tails of the birds projecting backward afforded a good hold for the hand and at the same time acted as a hook that prevented the spoon from slipping into the bowl when it was rested within it [see pl. 18].

The shape of the wooden spoon bowl is significant and seems to suggest that it was copied from the form of a clam shell or from a gourd spoon, these forms perhaps being the prototypes. Various types of spoons are shown in figure 11 and plate 18.

Husk salt bottle, Ojike′ta′hdä′wa. While not employed directly as a utensil for preparing corn foods, the husk salt bottle was used as a receptacle for the seasoning substances used for giving an added flavor to soups, bread etc. made from corn. The bottle was made of corn husk ingeniously woven. The stopper was a section of a corncob. Corn husk bottles sometimes were woven so tightly, it is said that they would hold water. On the other hand the bottles were valued for their property of keeping the salt dry, the outer husk absorbing and holding the moisture before it reached the salt within [see fig. 12].

The Iroquois have used these salt bottles within the last 10 years but only a few are now to be found.

The Iroquois say that they have not always used salt in the quantities which they now do and say that it has a debilitating effect upon them.

Fig. 12 Husk salt bottle. Cut is
½ size of specimen.

Parched corn sieve, Yŭndĕshoyondagwathä. This utensil was first described by Morgan[2] who collected a single specimen for the

---

[1] Beverly in describing the eating customs of the Virginia Indians, says, " The Spoons which they eat with do generally hold half a pint; and they laugh at the English for using small ones, which they must be forced to carry so often to their Mouths, and their Arms are in Danger of being tir'd before their Belly."

[2] See Morgan. Fabrics of the Iroquois. State Cabinet of Nat. Hist. Fifth An. Rep't 1852. p. 91.

State Museum in 1850. It consists of strips of wooden splints a little more than an ⅛ inch wide laid longitudinally, bound together with basswood cords and fastened tightly at either end making a canoe-shaped basket. It was used for sifting the ashes from parched corn and for sifting out the unburst kernels from pop corn. The writer has not been able to collect another old specimen of this basket and was told that the hominy sieve is now used instead.

The corn sieve is an interesting survival of a form of basket (the melon basket) now obsolete among the Canadian and New York Iroquois.[1] It has been preserved, however, among the Cherokee and is common among other southern tribes. Morgan's figure in the Fifth Museum Report is a poor illustration of the specimen and has confused several writers who have attempted to copy it. A better drawing is shown in the accompanying cut, figure 13.

Fig. 13   Popcorn sieve.   Morgan specimen.   This type is a survival of the melon basket now obsolete among the Iroquois except perhaps the Oneida. Specimen is 20 inches long.

Planting and harvesting baskets

Planting basket, Yŭndŭshinun'dakhwă'.[2] This is the small basket used for containing the seed corn for planting. The basket is generally tied to the waist so as to leave both hands free for dropping the seed and covering it with the hoe.

One planting basket in the museum collection is made of bark doubled in such a maner as to leave pockets on either side and a handle in the middle [see fig. 1, pl. 19].

Carrying basket, Ye'nīstĕⁿnĕk'wistă' or Yŭntge"dastha.[3] This basket is generally tied by a carrying strap, gŭsha'ā, to the head or chest and the ears of corn thrown over the shoulders into it as they were picked. The use of this basket is shown in plate 2, fig. 1.

---

[1] Harrington collected some interesting forms from the Oneida, two of which were acquired by the State Museum.

[2] Yuⁿterhaha'wida"kwa' in Mohawk.

[3] Yoⁿda"terhagehtslakwa in Mohawk.

VIII COOKING AND EATING CUSTOMS

1 **Fire making.** The precolonial method of producing fire was of course by friction and there were a number of ways for this

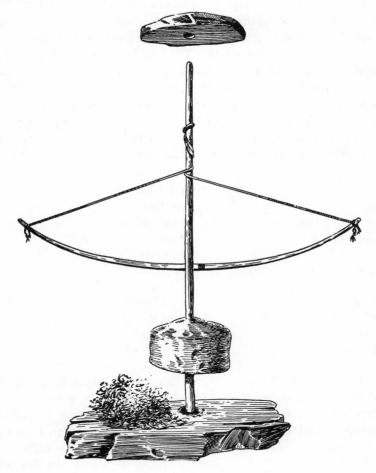

Fig. 14 Iroquois pump drill used for producing fire by friction. Collected by L. H. Morgan, 1850. Specimen is 18 inches high.

purpose. The most characteristic contrivance was the pump drill.[1] Morgan figured a pump drill in his report[2] to the Regents of the University. A pump drill is simply a weighted spindle of resinous

[1] Mason. Origin of Inventions, p. 88.
[2] N. Y. State Cab. Nat. Hist. Third An. Rep't. Albany 1851. p. 88.

wood to the top of which is fastened a very slack bow string, the bow hanging at right angles to the weight. By twisting up the string and then quickly pressing down on the bow a spinning motion is imparted to the spindle which immediately as the string unwinds, winds it up again in an opposite direction. The bow is then quickly pressed downward again and so continuously. The top of the spindle is inserted in a greased socket and the foot in a notch in a piece of very dry tinder wood. The rapid twirling of the spindle creates friction which as it increases ignites the powdered wood. A piece of inflammable tow is placed near this dust which suddenly ignites in the socket and fires the tow which is quickly transferred to a pile of kindling. Pump drills of course are not characteristically Iroquois, though the Iroquois used this means of producing fire by friction more generally than other methods [*see* fig. 14].[1]

TERMINOLOGY OF FIRE

Fire	ode'ka'
Match (it makes fire)	yiondĕkada"kwa'
I make a fire	eñgade'gat
Fire wood	oyän'dă'
Charcoal	odjä^n'stă'
Ashes	o'gä"ä'
Smoke (in house)	odiä"gwä'
Smoke (out of doors)	odiä"gweot
Flame	o'do^n'kot
Bake or broil	waen'dasko^{n}dĕ

For cooking food anciently the fires were generally made in sunken pits, variously called fire pits, pots or sunken ovens.

Pots of clay were probably placed only in shallow saucerlike depressions and held up by stones. The writer discovered such a pot at Ripley in 1906. It stood upright in a pit and was supported by some chunks of stone. Charcoal lay about it as if the fire had been hastily smothered. Schoolcraft pictures a clay pot suspended from a tripod, but most explorers picture the position of the clay vessel as above described.

Pits often were heated to a good temperature, the embers raked aside and corn, squashes or other foods thrown in, covered with

---

[1] *See* Morgan League, p. 381.

cold ashes and allowed to bake by the heat that remained in the ground. Small pits were thus made in clay banks and beans and other vegetables boiled to perfection. The remains of these pit ovens are found by all field archeologists who have worked in New York.[1]

2 **Meals and hospitality.** The Iroquois in precolonial and even during early colonial times had but one regular meal each day. This was called sĕdétcinegwa, *morning meal,* and was eaten between 9 and 11 o'clock. Few of the eastern Indians had more than two regular meals each day, but this did not prevent any one from eating as many times and as much as he liked for food was always ready in every house at all times.[2]

The food for the day was usually cooked in the morning and kept warm all day. For special occasions, however, a meal could be cooked at any time, but as a rule an Iroquois household did not

Fig. 15 Drawing of an Indian and his wife at dinner, from Beverly's *Virginia.* The numbers refer to Beverly's description which is as follows; "1. Is their Pot boiling with Hominy and Fish in it. 2. Is a Bowl of Corn, which they gather up in their Fingers, to feed themselves. 3. The Tomahawk which he lays by at Dinner. 4. His Pocket, which is likewise stript off, that he may be at full liberty. 5. A Fish. 6. A Heap of roasting Ears, both ready for dressing. 7. A Gourd of Water. 8. A Cockle-Shell, which they sometimes use instead of a Spoon. 9. The Mat they sit on."

expect a family meal except in the morning. As every one had four or five hours exercise before this meal it was thoroughly enjoyed.

---

[1] *Cf.* Harrington. Mohawk Strongholds. Manuscript in N. Y. State Museum.

[2] *Cf.* Heckewelder, p. 193; Morgan. House Life, p. 99.

Large eaters were not looked upon with favor, but every one was supposed to satisfy his hunger.

The housewife announced that a meal was ready by exclaiming Hâu! Sĕdek'onĭ, and the guest when he had finished the meal always exclaimed with emphasis " Niawĕⁿ' " meaning, *thanks are given.* This was supposed to be addressed to the Creator. As a response the host or hostess, the housewife or some member of the family would say " Niu' " meaning *it is well.* Neglect to use these words was supposed to indicate that the goddess of the harvest and the growth spirits or " the bounty of Providence " was not appreciated and that the eater was indifferent.

In apportioning a meal the housewife dipped the food from the kettle or took it from its receptacle and placed it in bark and wooden dishes, which she handed the men. They either sat on the floor or ground or stood along the wall as was most convenient. The women and children were then served. This old time custom still has its survival in the modern eating habits of the more primitive Iroquois. There are now tables and chairs and three regular meals, to be sure, but the women serve the men first and then, when the men have gone from the room, arrange the meal for themselves.

Regular meals two and three times a day did not come until the communal customs of the Iroquois had given way to the usages of modern civilization. Even then, as Morgan observes,[1] one of the difficulties was to change the old usage and accustom themselves to eating together. It came about, as this author says, with the abandonment of the communal houses and the establishment of single family houses where the food for the household was secured by the effort of the family alone.

Under the old régime food was kept ready for any one who might call for it at any time. The single meal of the late morning did not prevent any one from eating as many times as he pleased.

Springing from the law of communism came the law of common hospitality. Any one from anywhere could enter any house at any time if occupants were within, and be served with food. Indeed it was the duty of the housewife to offer food to every one that entered her door. If hungry the guest ate his fill but if he had already eaten he tasted the food as a compliment to the giver. A refusal to do this would have been an outright insult. There was never need for any one to go hungry or destitute, the unfortunate and

[1] Morgan. House Life, p. 99.

the lazy could avail themselves of the stores of the more fortunate and the more energetic. Neither begging nor laziness were encouraged, however, and the slightest indication of an imposition was rebuked in a stern manner.

Heckewelder explains this law of hospitality in a forcible manner. "They think that he (the Great Spirit), made the earth and all that it contains," he writes,[1] "that when he stocked the country that he gave them with plenty of game, it was not for the benefit of the few, but for all." This idea that the Creator gave of his bounty for the good of the entire body of people was one of the fundamental laws of the Iroquois. As air and rain were common so was everything else to be. Heckewelder expresses this when he continues, "Everything was given in common to the sons of men. Whatever liveth on land, whatsoever groweth out of the earth, and all that is in the rivers and waters flowing through the same, was given jointly to all, and every one is entitled to his share. From this principle hospitality flows as from its source. With them it was not a virtue but a strict duty; hence they are never in search of excuses to avoid giving, but freely supply their neighbors' wants from the stock prepared for their own use. They give and are hospitable to all without exception and will always share with each other and often with the stranger to the last morsel. They would rather lie down themselves on an empty stomach than have it laid to their charge that they had neglected their duty by not satisfying the wants of the stranger, the sick or the needy. The stranger has a claim to their hospitality, partly on account of his being at a distance from his family and friends, and partly because he has honored them with his visit and ought to leave them with a good impression on his mind; the sick and the poor because they have a right to be helped out of the common stock, for if the meat they are served with was taken from the woods it was common to all before the hunter took it; if corn and vegetables, it had grown out of the common ground, yet not by the power of men but by that of the Great Spirit."

When distinguished guests came into a community a great feast was prepared for them. Various French, Dutch and English writers who visited the Iroquois during the colonial period have written of these feasts and some of them describe the feasts in a vivid way. Sometimes the food was unpalatable to European

---

[1] Heckewelder. Indian Nations, p. 101.

taste and sometimes howsoever unpalatable it was eaten with great gusto, so sharp a sauce does hunger give.

John Bartram, who made a trip from Philadelphia to Onondaga in the middle of the 18th century, with Conrad Weiser, Lewis Evans and Shickalmy, records in his *Observations:*[1]

We lodged within 50 yards of a hunting cabin where there were two men, a squaw and a child. The men came to our fire, made us a present of some venison and invited Mr Weiser, Shickalmy and his son to a feast at their cabin. It is incumbent on those who partake of a feast of this sort to eat all that comes to their share or burn it. Now Weiser being a traveler was entitled to a double share, but being not very well, was forced to take the benefit of a liberty indulged him of eating by proxy, and he called me. But both being unable to cope with it, Evans came to our assistance notwithstanding which we were hard set to get down the neck and throat, for these were allotted to us. And now we had experienced the utmost bounds of their indulgence, for Lewis, ignorant of the ceremony of throwing a bone to the dog, though hungry dogs are generally nimble, the Indian, more nimble, laid hold of it first and committed it to the fire, religiously covering it over with hot ashes. This seemed to be a kind of offering, perhaps first fruits to the Almighty Power to crave future success in the approaching hunting season.

Instances of the hospitality of the Iroquois toward the whites and Indians could be cited at great length,[2] with but one result, that of confirming the statement that hospitality was an established usage. The Indians were often greatly surprised to find that on their visits to white settlements they were not accorded the same privilege, and thought the whites rude and uncivil people. " They are not even familiar with the common rules of civility which our mothers teach us in infancy," said one Indian in expressing his surprise.

The Iroquois were not great eaters, that is to say, they seldom gorged themselves with food at their private meals or at feasts, except perhaps for ceremonial reasons. To do so ordinarily would be a religious offense and destroy the capacity to withstand hunger. Children were trained to eat frugally and taught that overeating was far worse than undereating. They were warned that gluttons would be caught by a monster known as Sago′dăkwŭs who would humiliate them in a most terrible manner if he found that they were gourmands.

---

[1] Bartram. Observations. Lond. 1751. p. 24.
[2] *See* Morgan. House Life, p. 45–62.

The large appetites of white men who visited them was often a matter of surprise to the Indians who entertained them. Morgan[1] commenting on this says that a white man consumed and wasted five times as much as an Indian required. In a footnote[2] he quotes Robertson as writing that the appetite of the Spaniards appeared insatiably voracious; and that they affirmed that one Spaniard devoured more food in a day than was sufficient for 10 Americans (Indians).

The food and eating customs of the eastern Indians are described by various early writers with some conflict of opinion, but in general their system of free hospitality has the commendation of the majority of writers.[3]

There were and still are among the Iroquois, innumerable ways of combining foods and several ways of cooking each variety. Nearly all the early travelers expressed themselves as impressed with the number of ways of preparing corn and enumerate from 20 to 40 methods, though some are not so explicit.[4]

TERMINOLOGY

Food	gŭk'wa'
Breakfast (early morning meal)	sĕde'tciane'gwa
Midday meal	hä'de'wĕnishä
Sunset meal	hegä''gwaane'gwa'
Appetite	yeoⁿkwan'owas
A glutton	ha'kowane'
(Come thou) eat (imper.)	sedĕko'ni
I eat	aga'dekoni
You eat	eⁿsa'dĕkoni
Cook (she cooks)	yekoⁿ'nis
" (he cooks)	ha'koⁿ'nis
Hanging crane	eⁿsä''ĕnondăt
Kettle hook	adŭs'ha
Oven	yontä'gonda'gwa'ge

---

[1] Morgan. House Life of the American Aborigines, p. 60.

[2] *Ibid.* p. 61.

[3] *See* Lahontan, 2:11; Van der Donck. N. Y. Hist. Soc. Cols. v. 1, ser. 2, 192; Jesuit Relations, 67:141; Adair, p. 412; Bartram. Observations, p. 16, 59, 63; Smith. Virginia. Richmond ed. 1:83, 84; Heckewelder, p. 193; Morgan. House Life, 45 et seq.; Robertson. History of America, p. 178. N. Y. 1856.

[4] "Forty-two ways," Dumont. Memoirs sur La Louisiane. Paris 1753. 1:33–34. *Cf.* Loskiel, p. 67; Adair, p. 409; "40 methods," Boyle, Report for 1898; *cf.* Jesuit Relations, 10:103, "twenty ways."

IX FOODS PREPARED FROM CORN

Leaf bread tamales, oniä"tci'dǎ'. This is prepared from green corn. The kernels are cut or scraped from the cob and beaten to a milky paste in a mortar. The corn used for leaf cake tamales should be too hard for green corn good for boiling and eating on the cob. The paste will then be of the proper consistency. The paste is patted into shape and laid in a strip on one end of a broad corn leaf, the free half being doubled over the paste. Other leaves are folded over the first, the ends all projecting uniformly from one end for tying. The oniä"tci'dǎ' was then tied three times laterally and once transversely and dropped into boiling water. When cooked — cooking requires about 45 minutes — the wrappings are removed and the cake is eaten with sunflower or bear oil, though in these modern days bacon grease or butter are more in vogue. Oftentimes cooked beans are mixed with the mass before wrapping in the leaves. These impart their flavor and give variety.

Leaf cakes may be dried for winter's use if no beans have been used with the corn. In wrapping the leaf bread a bulbous shaped bundle is made resembling a large braid of hair doubled and tied, hence the name oniä"tci'dǎ', derived from yēnyǎ'tci'dot, *doubled braid of woman's hair.*

Heckewelder[1] describes this bread but says it is too sweet although the Indians consider it a delicate morsel. He says the mashed green corn is put in the corn blades with ladles.

Adair[2] in describing it remarks, " This sort of bread is very tempting to the taste, and reckoned most delicious by their strong palates."

David DeVries[3] writing of the dish says, " They make flat cakes of meal mixed with water, as large as a farthing cake in this country, and bake them in the ashes, first wrapping a vine or maize leaf around them.

Sagard in describing leaf cakes says that the Huron called it Andataroni. He describes the process of preparing it substantially as given above. He mentions that berries and beans are often added.[4]

---

[1] Heckewelder, p. 195.
[2] Adair. North American Indians.
[3] Second Voyage. N. Y. Hist. Soc. Col. Ser. 2. v. 3, pt 1, p. 107. *Cf.* Vincent. History of Delaware. Phila. 1870. p. 74.
[4] Grand Voyage. Tross ed. p. 96.

These early citations are interesting because they prove how persistently the Iroquois have clung to the dishes of their ancestors.

Baked green corn,[1] **Ogon'sä'.** When the milk has set, Tuscarora and sweet corn is scraped from the cob and beaten to a paste in a mortar. This should be done just before the evening meal. After the housework is finished the housewife lines a large kettle with basswood leaves three deep. The corn paste is then dumped in up to two thirds the depth of the vessel. The top is smoothed down and covered by three layers of leaves. Cold ashes to a finger's depth are now thrown over the leaves and smoothed down. A small fire is built under the kettle which hangs suspended from a crane or tripod. Glowing charcoal is placed on the ashes at the top. The small fire is kept brisk and the coals at the top renewed three times. The cook may now retire for the night if her kettle hangs in a shielded place or in a fire pit. In the morning the ashes and top leaves are carefully removed and the baked corn dumped out. The odor of this steaming ogon'sä' is most appetizing and it is eaten greedily with grease or butter. For winter's use the caked mass is sliced and dried in the sun all day, taken in at night to prevent dew from spoiling it and dogs or night prowlers from taking too much of it, and set out again in the morning to allow the sun to complete the drying. The ogon'sä' is then ready to be stored away for the winter. When ready for use the winter's store of ogon'sä' was taken from storage and a sufficient quantity for a meal thrown in cold water and immediately put on the stove. Boiling for a little more than a half hour produces a delicious dish. Ogon'sä' was one of the favorite foods of the Iroquois and remains so to this day. An Onondaga or Seneca can hardly mention the name without showing that it brings memories of the pleasant repasts that it has afforded.

In recent years the corn paste is prepared with a potato masher in a chopping bowl, or by running the corn as cut from the cob through a food chopper. Baking is done in shallow dripping pans in the oven. The food so prepared, however, lacks a deliciousness that makes the older method still popular.

Boiled green corn, O'kni'staga[n]**'o'.**[2] This is simply the green corn on the cob with which we are all familiar. Tuscarora corn as well as sweet corn, however, was used with equal favor. It was

---

[1] This is the ble'-grillé of the French.
[2] Ganossto'ho[n] is the Mohawk equivalent.

eaten on the cob or scraped off and eaten in dishes. Sometimes the kernels were cut from the cob and boiled as a soup.

The Seneca name means delicious corn food, from o'nius'ta, *corn,* and oga$^{n'}$o^n, *delicious food.*

Fried green corn, Gagoñ's'ä ge''dä. This dish was prepared by scraping the green corn, in the milk, from the cob, mashing it in a mortar and either patting it into cakes or tossing it in a basket to make a loose light mass. The corn was then ready for frying. The older Indians say that the frying could be done in a clay kettle and that corn so prepared was especially good if cooked in bear oil.[1]

Succotash, Ogon'sä' ganon'dä.[2]   Iroquois succotash was prepared much as is the modern form made by white people. The green corn cut or scraped from the cob was thrown in a pot of beans which had nearly been cooked and the mass cooked together until both ingredients were done. A sufficient quantity of salt and grease or oil was added for seasoning and flavor. The favorite corn for this dish was Tuscarora or sweet corn.

Baked cob-corn in the husk, Wades'kondŭk o'nis'ta. This was a popular way of preparing green corn on the cob. The ashes from the camp or hearth fire were brushed aside and a row of unhusked ears laid in the hot stones or ground. These were then covered with cold ashes. Embers were now heaped over and a hot fire built and continued until the corn beneath was thought sufficiently baked. Corn baked in this manner has a fine flavor and never becomes scorched.

Baked scraped corn, Ogo$^{n'}$sä' ohon'stä'.[3] The green corn is scraped from the cob with a deer's jaw or knife, pounded in a mortar or mashed in a wooden bowl with a stone, patted into cakes, sprinkled with dry meal and baked in small dishes. For baking in the ashes the cakes are wrapped in husk and covered with ashes. Embers are heaped over and a brisk fire built, this being kept going until the cakes were considered baked.

Carver, the British traveler, in writing of his experiences among the aboriginal Americans, says of this dish ". . . better flavored bread I never ate in this country." In describing the preparation

----

[1] Carr, quoting Carver's *Travels* (London 1778), notes, " We . . . cook our vegetables by themselves though formerly this was not the case for according to an old writer (Carver), when made with bear oil 'the fat moistens the pulse and renders it beyond comparison delicious.'"

[2] Onon'darha is the Mohawk name for succotash.

[3] O'gaserho'da is the Mohawk name.

Plate 20

Cayuga woman pounding Tuscarora corn. Photograph by W. N. Fenton, 1939.

Plate 21

Corn is roasted on a frame or pole placed over a pit filled with glowing
embers. The roasted corn is used for parched meal.

of these cakes he said that they were ". . . made without the addition of any liquid by the milk that flows from them; and when it is effected they parcel it out into cakes and enclosing them with leaves place them in the hot embers where they soon bake."

Cracked undried corn, Odjis'tĕnondä. The ripened but not dry corn was shelled from the cob and smashed kernel by kernel on a flat stone, a muller being used as a crusher. The crushed corn was mixed with new harvested beans and boiled for nearly three hours. Salt was used as a seasoning and deer or bear meat mixed with the mass if desired (*see* fig. 5).

Boiled corn bread, Gagai'tĕⁿtâⁿ'ä''kwă'.[1] For bread, purple, calico and the two hominy corns were used. After the corn was shelled it was boiled for from 15 to 30 minutes in a weak lye made of hard wood ashes and water. The lye solution, in order to be of the proper consistency must be strong enough to bite the tongue when tasted. When the hulls and outer skins had been loosened, looking white and swelled, the corn was put in a hulling basket, taken to a brook or large tub, where it was thoroughly rinsed to free the kernels of any trace of lye and to wash off the loosened hulls and skins. The corn was then drained, thrown in a mortar and pulverized with a pestle. The granules were sifted through the meal sieve to make the meal fine and light. After this process the meal was mixed with boiling water and quickly molded into a flattened cake about 8 inches in diameter and 3 inches thick. The cake was then plunged into boiling water and cooked for nearly an hour. The object of mixing the meal with boiling water was to coagulate the starch and make the meal stick together. After the meal is mixed with the hot water and molded, the hands are plunged in cold water and rubbed over the loaf to give it a smooth glossy surface. When the loaf floats it is considered properly cooked. Sometimes the molded loaf is baked instead of boiled, specially for journeys. The loaf is buried in hot ashes and a roaring fire built over it until it is baked thoroughly. When it is to be eaten the ashes are washed off and slices cut from the loaf. The baked loaf if not wet will not become moldy like boiled bread and this is the approved form for hunting and war parties.

---

[1] Ganoⁿ'stoharhe ganada'rhoⁿ, in Mohawk.

In the course of boiling some of the meal on the outside of the cake comes off, together with a quantity of starch and gluten, and mixes with the water. When the bread is sufficiently cooked this liquid is poured out in bowls and drunk as a tea. The Iroquois considered this gruel a great delicacy.

Fig. 16   Bark tray containing boiled bread, dried.   Specimens ⅓ actual size.   Seneca specimens collected 1908

Corn bread is fairly hard but readily crumbles when masticated. It is not dry, but moist and mealy. Before eating the cake it is sliced and spread with tallow or butter, bear or deer oil. It is a delicious food and considered highly nutritious. Often cooked cranberry beans or berries were mixed with the meal before boiling. These added to the flavor as well as nourishment.[1]

One of the best descriptions of boiled bread has been left us by Adair[2] who writes:

They have another sort of boiled bread which is mixed with beans or potatoes; they put on the soft corn till it begins to boil and pound it sufficiently fine; — their invention does not reach the use of any kind of milk. When the flour is stirred, and dried by the heat of the sun or fire, they sift it with sieves of different sizes, curiously made of the coarser or finer cane splinters. The thin cakes mixt with bear's oil, were formerly baked on thin broad stones placed over a fire, or on broad earthen bottoms fit for such a use, but now they use kettles. When they intend to bake great loaves, they make a strong

[1] " Some of the loaves were baked with nuts and dry blue berries and grains of the sunflower." *Van Curler's Diary, p.* 91.

[2] Adair. History of the American Indians. Lond. 1775. p. 407. *See also* Boyle. Ontario Arch. Rep't 1898. p. 188.

blazing fire, with short dry split wood on the hearth. When it is burnt down to coals they carefully rake them off to each side, and sweep away the remaining ashes; then they put their well kneaded broad loaf, first steeped in hot water, over the hearth, and an earthen basin above it, with the embers of coals atop. This method of baking is as clean and efficacious as could possibly be done in any oven; when they take it off they wash the loaf with warm water, and it soon becomes firm and very white. It is likewise very wholesome, and well tasted to any except the palate of an epicure.

Lafitau had no such pleasant impressions of the bread which would seem to bring him under the class of epicures. As a matter of fact white people of today regard the Iroquois boiled bread as a " well tasted " food, though a trifle heavy. The writer during his school days on the reservation often " swapped " his lunch of civilized viands with other Indian boys who were lucky enough to have half a loaf of boiled bread and a chunk of maple sugar or perhaps a leaf cake.

Beverly[1] describes the baking of corn bread in his *History of Virginia* and says that the Indians first covered the loaf with leaves and then with warm ashes over which were heaped the hot coals. The ash baked corn bread of the Indians has survived in the South as hoe cake, ash cake and " old fashioned " journey or Johnny cake.

Corn soup liquor, O'niyustagï'. The liquor in which the corn bread was boiled was carefully drained off and kept in jars or pots as a drink. It is said that the Indians were not fond of drinking water and preferred various beverages prepared from herbs or corn. One writer[2] in discussing this subject says: " Though in most of the Indian nations the water is good, because of their high situation, yet the traders very seldom drink any of it at home; for the women beat in mortars their flinty corn till all the husks are taken off, which having well sifted and fanned, they boil in large earthen pots; then straining off the thinnest part into a pot they mix it with cold water till it is sufficiently liquid for drinking; and when cold it is both pleasant and very nourishing; and is much liked even by genteel strangers."

Wedding bread, Gonniä''tä' oä'kwa. Corn was prepared in the same manner as for bread but was wrapped in two balls with a short connecting neck like a handleless dumbbell wrapped in corn

---

[1] Beverly. Virginia, p. 151.
[2] Adair, p. 416.

husk and tied in the middle. It was then ready for boiling. To complete the cooking required about one hour.

Twenty-four of these cakes were taken by the girl's maternal grandmother (by blood or by clan appointment, if the maternal grandmother was dead) to the door of the maternal grandmother of an eligible male. The recipient, who had previously conferred with the donor, if she favors the alliance suggested by the gift, tastes the bread and notifies her daughter that her (the daughter's) son is desired to unite with a certain young woman in marriage by the grandmother of that young woman. The mother of the boy must submit to her mother's wish if she can offer no substantial objection. The boy's grandmother then makes 24 wedding cakes[1] and carries them to the girl's grandmother who then notifies her daughter that the girl must marry a certain man. If the suit is rejected at the first proposal the wedding cakes are left untouched and the humiliated donor must creep back and reclaim the cakes. My informant says the rejected cakes were never eaten, but probably reserved as ammunition with which to pelt the offending old dowager, who had given reasons to believe that the suit was smiled upon. The bounds of a cake recipe forbid further discussion.

Sagard found this bread among the Huron who, he says, called it Coinkia. He remarked that instead of being baked it was boiled. His description " deux balles jointes ensemble " makes the identity of the dish absolute.[2]

Early bread, Ganēoⁿtē″doⁿ.[3] Before the corn was thoroughly dry in the autumn it was plucked for making early bread. The unhulled corn was mixed with a little water in a mortar and beaten to a paste instead of a meal. Loaves were molded by the hands from the paste and boiled. This bread was considered a great delicacy and valued especially as a food for invalids.

Early corn pudding, Ganeoⁿtē″doⁿ odjis′kwa. The paste from the mortar, as described above, was sometimes drained, sifted and tossed into a wet meal. It was then thrown in boiling water and boiled down into a pudding.

---

[1] Morgan. League, p. 322; cf. Sagard, p. 94, 136.

[2] ". . . excepté le pain mis et accommodé comme deux balles iointes ensemble, enueloppé entre des fueilles de bled d'Inde, puis boüilly et cuit en l'eau, et non sous la cendre, lequel ils appellent d'vn nom particulier Coinkia." Sagard, Grand Voyage, p. 136, Paris 1682, see also Tross ed. p. 94.

[3] Ga'te′doⁿgana′darho, *pounded bread*, Mohawk form.

Dumplings, Oho^{n}'stă'. Moisten a mass of corn meal with boiling water and quickly mold it into cakes in the closed hand moistened in cold water. Drop the dumplings one by one into boiling water and boil for a half hour.

Dumplings were the favorite thing to cook with boiling meats, especially game birds.

To fish the dumplings from the pot every one had a sharpened stick or bone. The dumplings were speared and held on the stick to cool and nibbled with the meat as it was eaten. The sticks after use were wiped off and stuck between the logs or bark of the wall for future use.

Many of the sharpened splinters of bone now excavated from village and camp sites are probably nothing more than these primitive forks, or more properly food holders.

Oho^{n}stă' was one of the foods of which children were very fond, nor did grown people despise it as a bread with their meat.

Hominy, Onon'däät.[1] Hominy is prepared from flint corns. For a family of five persons, a quart of corn was thrown in a mortar and moistened with a ladleful (four tablespoonfuls) of water.[2] To make the pounding easier a teaspoonful of white ashes or soda is thrown in also. The pounding with the pestle proceeds slowly at first to loosen the hulls, this work being accelerated if ashes have been used. When the hulls begin to come off easily the pounding is quickened until the corn is broken up into coarse pieces. It is then ready for the first sifting, e^{n}yowo^{n}k'. A basket called a onïius'tawanĕs is used for this purpose. The hominy passes through and is placed in a bowl while the uncracked corn is thrown back into the mortar to be repounded. After the second sifting the uncracked kernels that remain are thrown out to the birds or chickens. The hominy is then ready for winnowing. The results of the two poundings are carefully mixed and then put in a tossing bowl or basket. The hominy is tossed with a peculiar motion the bowl being held at a slant. The lighter chit rises to the top while the heavier portion stays at the bottom. The hulls and chit are thrown out by hand or by the use of a fan made of a bird's wing, called onĕg'osta'. The process of winnowing is called waegai$^{\prime\prime}$tawāk.

---

[1] Onoñ'darha is the Mohawk word.

[2] Harrington says cold water. *See* Seneca Corn Foods. Amer. Anthropologist. New Ser. v. 10, no. 3, p. 587.

The coarse granular meal so prepared is now ready for cooking. One part of meal is put in eight parts of water and boiled for two hours. Pork or bear's meat and beans are cooked with the hominy[1] for flavoring. When cooked salt or sugar were added, according to taste.

Sagard[2] in his *Grand Voyage* refers several times to this dish as *Sagamite*. In one instance he calls it a " good sort of substance " and says that its sustaining qualities surprised him.

With the Dutch hominy was called by another name. In Van der Donck's *Description of New Netherlands,* we find that the pap or mush of the Indians is called sapaen (suppawn). It was the common food of all Indians, he says, without which no Indian would think he had a satisfactory meal.

Hulled corn, Onno''kwă'.[3] This favorite dish was made from some soft corn treated as corn used for bread. It was washed until free from skins and hulls and then put in cold water and boiled for four hours until the kernels had burst open and were tender. Small chunks of meat and fat were thrown in the boiling liquid and sometimes berries. Onno''kwă' is the favorite feast dish of the Iroquois. This dish is a most palatable one and appeals to all tastes. It is used at Indian social gatherings as white people use ice cream, that is, as a fitting food for festal occasions. It must be confessed that the Indian's food was the more solid and perhaps the more sensible. Several canning companies now put up hulled corn under the name of Entire Hominy and it may be purchased in many modern provision stores.

Dried corn soup, Onädoonondä.[4] For winter's use, green, white, sweet or squaw sweet corn was cut from the cob and dried before a fire, taking care that the drying was rapid enough to prevent the milk from souring. The dried corn when prepared for

---

[1] This is the sagamite of the French. *See* Jesuit Relations.

[2] " Le pain de Mais, et la sagamite qui en est faicte, est de sort bonne substance, et m'estonnois de ce qu'elle nourrit si bien qu'elle facit : car pour ne boire que de l'eau en ce pays-là, et ne manger que sort peu sonnent de ce pain, et encore plus rarement de la viande, n'vsans presque que des seuls Sagamités auec vn bien peu de poisson, on ne laisse pas de se bien porter, et estre en bon poinct, pourueu qu'on en ait suffisamment, comme on n'en manque point dans le pays ; mais seulement en de longs voyages, où l'on souffre souuent de grandes necessitez ", *Le Grand Voyage du pays des Hurons.* Paris 1632. p. 137 ; *Tross ed. Paris 1865.* p. 97.

[3] Gagarhedonton is the Mohawk form of the word.

[4] Ganahandat is the Mohawk word.

food was boiled until tender, three-quarters of an hour. This dried corn was sometimes roasted and pounded for pudding meal.

Nut and corn pottage, Oniä' degaiyĭst'o^n onä'o'khŭ'. This was prepared by mixing nut meal or nut milk, oniä''ge', with parched corn meal.

Heckewelder[1] describes the use of nut milk with corn in a fairly detailed way as follows:

> The Indians have a number of manners of preparing their corn. They make an excellent pottage of it, by boiling it with fresh or dried meat (the latter pounded), dried pumpkins, dry beans and chestnuts. They sometimes sweeten it with sugar or molasses from the sugar-maple tree. Another very good dish is prepared by boiling with their corn or maize, the washed kernels of shell bark or hickory nut. They pound the nuts in a block or mortar, pouring a little warm water on them, and gradually a little more as they become dry until, at last, there is a sufficient quantity of water so that by stirring up the pounded nuts the broken shells separate from the liquor, which from the pounded kernels assumes the appearance of milk. This being put into the kettle and mixed with the pottage gives it a rich and agreeable flavor. If the broken shells do not all freely separate by swimming on the top or sinking to the bottom, the liquor is strained through a clean cloth before it is put into the kettle.

Corn and pumpkin pudding, Oniŭ''sä' odjis'kwa.[2] This favorite pudding was made from parched or yellow corn meal mixed with sugar and boiled pumpkin or squash. It was often used instead of gago^{n}sä odjis'kwa.

Samp, Gwä'onondä' or O'ni'yustāgĕ'. In making samp the corn was treated with the same process as for corn bread except that it was not beaten so fine in a mortar. It was boiled in water and when cooked tasted like the soup of corn bread, but it did not have so delicate a flavor. Often berries or meat were mixed and cooked with samp. For samp any corn that would hull easily was used.

Adair after describing hominy says, " the thin of this is what my Lord Bacon calls Cream of Maize, and highly commends for an excellent sort of nourishment." This is the samp, or gwä'onondä.' of the Iroquois.

Corn pudding, O^{n}so^n'wä.[3] For o^{n}so^n'wä white corn was

---

[1] Heckewelder, John. History, Manners and Customs of the Indian Nations. Hist. Soc. Pa. 12:194.

[2] Onoo^{n}se'rhagowa odjis'kwa is the Mohawk name.

[3] Wadĕnosstatsaha''to', *burnt corn,* is the Mohawk name.

roasted brown and pounded slowly in a mortar and sifted until all the granules were uniform, the coarser ones being pounded and resifted until this end was achieved. The meal was then thrown in boiling water and cooked until tender.

Preserved in skin bags this meal was carried by hunters and either eaten raw with water, boiled as above or thrown in with boiling meat.[1]

Van der Donck, in his *Description of New Netherlands,* says:

When they intend to go a great distance on a hunting expedition . . . where they expect no food, they provide themselves severally with a small bag of parched corn meal which is so nutritious that they can subsist upon the same many days. A quarter of a pound of the meal is sufficient for a day's subsistence; for as it shrinks much in drying, it also swells out again with moisture. When they are hungry they take a handful of meal after which they take a drink of water, and then they are so well fed that they can travel a day. [*See* N. Y. Hist. Soc. Col. Ser. 2. 1 :193–94, 1841.]

Heckewelder describes this food as follows: " Their Psindamocan or Tassmanane, as they call it, is the most durable food made out of the Indian corn. The blue sweetish kind is the grain which they prefer for that purpose. They parch it in clean hot ashes until it bursts, it is then sifted and cleaned, and pounded in a mortar into a kind of flour, and when they wish to make it very good they mix some sugar with it. When wanted for use they take about a tablespoonful of this flour in their mouths, then stooping to the river or brook, drink water to it. If, however, they have a cup or other small vessel at hand they put the flour in it and mix it with water, in the proportion of one tablespoonful to a pint. At their camps they will put a small quantity in a kettle with water and let it boil down, and they will have a thick pottage. With this food, the traveler and warrior will set out on long journeys and expeditions, and, as a little of it will serve them for a day, they have not a heavy load of provisions to carry. Persons who are unacquainted with this diet ought to be careful not to take too much at a time, and not to suffer themselves to be tempted too far by its flavor; more

---

[1] " The Indians boil it till it becomes tender and eat it with fish or venison instead of bread; sometimes they bruise it in mortars and so boil it. The most usual way is to parch it in ashes, stirring it so artificially as to be very tender, without burning; this they sift and beat in mortars into a fine meal which they eat dry or mixed with water." Harris. Discoveries and Settlements. Pinkerton's Voyages. 12 :258.

Plate 22

1 Long House of the Canadian Onondaga, Grand River Reservation. It is here that the feasts and thanksgivings for the products of the fields are held by the Canadian Onondaga.

2 Cook house of the Canadian Seneca. The architecture of the building follows the lines of the bark house. Note the smoke hole in the roof.

Plate 23

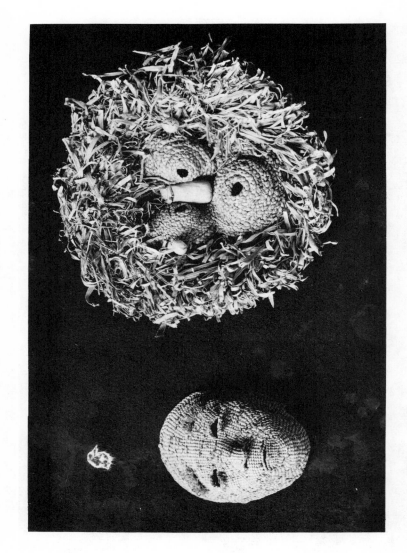

Masks made from shreds of braided husk, used by the Husk Face Company

than one or two spoonfuls at most at any one time or at one meal is dangerous; for it is apt to swell in the stomach or bowels, as when heated over a fire." :

A handful of the parched meal, 2 or 3 ounces, was considered a rather large meal if eaten out of hand and this quantity was even considered dangerous unless cooked in a pot.

Most of the old writers refer to this dish[2] and agree that it is a most sustaining food. Sugar was often mixed with the meal to give it flavor and dried cherries were sometimes pulverized with the parched corn. In this form the Mohawk call it O'hogwitz' orha.

Beverly[3] in describing traveling customs says, ". . . each man takes with him a Pint or Quart of Rockahomonie, that is, the finest Indian corn, parched and beaten to powder. When they find their Stomach empty, (and can not stay the tedious Cookery of other things) they put about a spoonful of this into their Mouths, and drink a Draught of Water upon it, which stays in their Stomachs. . ."

Roasted corn hominy, Odjis'tănondä'. The ripe corn was husked by the harvesters and stood " nose " upward against the top pole of a roasting pit. This pit was a long narrow trench a foot or more deep with Y-shaped sticks at either end as supporters for the top pole, which was placed horizontally in the crotches, after a fire of saplings and sticks had been reduced to a mass of glowing embers [see pl. 21]. The ears were then leaned at an angle against the pole, drawn out and roasted. Watchers turned them as they were parched sufficiently while other helpers gathered them up when done and shelled the kernels into a bark barrel.

The meal from this roasted corn was called odjis'tănondä'. If the parched corn was boiled it was called ona^{n}dä'ono^n'kwă'.

It should be noted that this dish is prepared from roasted green corn and not from ripe dried corn as is o^{n}so^n'wä.

Parched corn coffee, O'nīs'tagi'. Corn was well burnt and parched on the coals, scraped from the cob and thrown in a dish. Upon this boiling water was thrown and the dish or kettle placed over the fire again. To produce the burnt corn drink the boiling was continued for about five minutes.

---

[1] Heckewelder. History, Manners and Customs of the Indian Nations. Hist. Soc. Pa. 12:195.

[2] This is the Nocake or rockahominy of the New England Indians. *See* Williams. Key. Narragansett Club Reprint, 1 :40.

[3] History of Virginia, p. 155.

Roasted corn, Gani′stĕⁿ′dā. This was the husked ear of green corn baked in hot embers.

It is related that one of the old methods was to dig a long trench and place the ears across two slender green saplings and allow the heat of the hot coals to cook the corn. The ears could easily be turned over and the roasting made uniform (*see* pl. 21).

Sometimes a husked ear of corn was incased in clay and baked. This was called Oga′goäk′wa or gagoⁿdŭk. For roasting ears[1] singly a sharpened stick was shoved into the stem and the ear held in the embers.

If kernels of the corn prepared in this way were sufficiently dried and parched the entire ear or the shelled kernels were capable of long preservation. The writer has found roasted corn on the cob, several centuries old, buried in pits which evidently once had been bark lined cellarettes. Parched shelled kernels are commonly found in caches in Indian village or lodge sites.

Pop corn pudding, Watatoñ′gwŭs odjis′kwa. Corn was popped in a metal or clay kettle and then pulverized in a mortar and mixed with oil or syrup. The writer has often seen the modern Iroquois run their corn popped in a modern popper through a chopping machine and eat the light white meal with sugar and milk or cream.

Ceremonial foods

Bear's pudding, Niagwai″tätoⁿ odjis′kwa.[2] This was a ceremonial food prepared from yellow meal unseasoned and mixed with bits of fried meat. The meal was boiled into a pudding and the meat thrown in afterward. Bear dance pudding was only used as a ceremonial food in the Bear Society meetings or by members performing some of the rites.[3]

Buffalo dance pudding, Dĕgi′yagoⁿ odjis′kwa.[4] Squaw corn is pounded to a meal, boiled as a pudding and sweetened with maple or corn sugar. This pudding is harder than Bear dance pudding, its proper consistency being like the mud where the buffa-

---

[1] Beverly says, " They delight to feed on roasting ears, that is *Indian corn*, gathered green and milky, before it is grown to its full bigness." History of Virginia.

[2] O′kwa′rhi odjis′kwa is the Mohawk form.

[3] *See* Parker, A. C. Seneca Medicine Societies. Am. Anthropologist. New ser. v. XI, no. 2.

[4] Dege′lhiyagon odjis′kwa is the Mohawk form.

lces go when they dance off the flies. This pudding is used only by members of the Buffalo company, a " medicine " society.[1]

Ball players pudding, Gadjis′kwae′ odjis′kwa.[2] This is a charm pudding and made like false face pudding except that it is a little sweeter and contains more meat. A woman afflicted with rheumatism or some like disease prepares this pudding and presents it to a ball player, who, eating it, is supposed to charm away the disorder by his activity. He sets at defiance the spirits which have crippled the patient. If her case is very severe she bathes her limbs in sunflower oil and drinks it with the pudding.

False face pudding, Gago^n′să odjis′kwa.[3] This was a ceremonial pudding eaten at the False Face dances, at special private lodge feasts or in the ceremonies of healing the sick. It was composed of boiled parched corn meal mixed with maple sugar. Sunflower or bear oil was used with it in special cases. This pudding is considered a most delicious food and believed to be a very powerful factor for pleasing the masks. No one must make a disrespectful remark while eating this pudding as the mysterious faces were thought to be able to punish the offender by distorting their faces, and cases are cited to prove this assertion.

Unusual foods

Decayed corn, Utgī′onäo′. A corn food of which the Iroquois of today have no memory is described by Sagard who calls it *bledpuant*. To prepare this viand the ear of corn before it was fully mature was immersed in stagnant water and allowed to " ripen " for two or three months at the end of which time it was taken out and roasted or boiled with meat or fish. The odor of this putrid corn was so frightful that the good father either through imagination or from good cause relates that it clung to him for a number of days from simply touching it. Nevertheless he adds that the Indians sucked it as if it were sugar cane.[4]

It is safe to say that among the Iroquois no knowledge of this food remains. An Iroquois whom the writer interrogated said that

---

[1] *See* Parker, A. C. Seneca Medicine Societies. Am. Anthropologist. New ser. v. XI, no. 2.

[2] Dehajī′gwa′es odjis′kwa is the Mohawk form.

[3] Ago^n′hwarha odjis′kwa is the Mohawk name.

[4] Sagard. Le Grand Voyage du Pays Des Hurons, p. 97; Tross ed. 1865, p. 140; orig. ed. Paris 1632.

he could imagine that the Huron would eat such food but that he was sure that Iroquois never used anything so questionable.

Another writer mentions a variety of bread mixed with tobacco juice. He says: "When they were traveling or laying in wait for their enemies they took with them a kind of bread made of Indian corn and tobacco juice, which says Campanius was a very good thing to allay hunger and quench thirst in case they have nothing else at hand.[1]

X   USES OF THE CORN PLANT

1 **The stalk.** Stalk tubes, gŭshē"dă' or deyus'wände', were made for containing medicines. A section of the stalk was cut off at a joint, the pith removed, plugs were inserted at each end and the tube complete. Tubes were made from 2 to 8 inches long. Syrup, oshēstä', was extracted by boiling or evaporating the juice of young and green cornstalks. The top of the corn above the corn sheaths was cut, the stalk bruised and then thrown in a kettle and boiled, the juice was then strained off and evaporated. A metal polish, yestä'tedă'kwa, was made from the pith. The outer covering was stripped from a dry stalk and the pith used for rubbing copper and silver ornaments to a polish. Absorbent, ne"dĕskŭk, qualities of the dry pith were recognized and it was employed accordingly. A lotion, yago'găthă, of the juice of the green cornstalk and root was employed for cuts, bruises and sores. Fish line floats, hĕtgĕsho^niodyĕ', were made from sections of the dry stalk. Cornstalk war clubs and spears, gadji'wa, were used by boys in sham battles. Counter or jack straws, gasho'wēdă, were cut from the tassel stems and used with bean counters in games. Children were taught to count with these "straws."

2 **Uses of corn husks.** Single husks or strips pressed or folded together and dried were used to convey lights short distances, much as the rolled paper "lamp lighters" are used where matches are scarce. The Iroquois indeed now use husks for lighting lamps, calling them yedjistoñda"kwa. A larger quantity of dried husks was used in kindling a fire. Husks are shredded and used for pillow, cushion and mattress fillings, onion'nya'gago^n'shä'. For making "bride's bread" the corn pudding or grated green corn is wrapped in the green husk and baked or boiled as the case may require. Another use for the simple husks is as the water sprinklers

---

[1] Vincent. History of Delaware. Phil. 1870. p. 74–75.

used by the Otter company, Dowäändo^n', in their winter ceremony [*see* fig. 17]. In this instance the husks are pulled back over the stem and the cob broken midway as a handle. The sprinklers are called dionĕgo'gwŭtă'.

Fig. 17. Purification ceremony of the Society of Otters, a Seneca women's winter ceremony

Husks were sometimes braided in long strands and used for clothes lines, gäo^n''gä', in the houses. The loosely braided husks

from the strings of corn, ostĕⁿsĕⁿ'gäs'skĕⁿdoni, were used by the
" buffalo head " (Hade'yeoⁿ) announcers of the midwinter thanksgiving. A crown is arranged for the head and trailers tied to each
ankle. Braided in fine ropes, the husk was coiled up into the masks,
gatci'sha, used by the husk face (Gatci'sha'oäno') company [see
pl. 23]. The braided coils are sewn with thread. An outer binding
is fastened to the face, from which long shreds of the husk hang to
represent hair [see pl. 23, fig. 1].

Another variety of the husk mask is woven entirely and is not
sewed [see pl. 23, fig. 2]. These particular masks are used mostly
on the Allegany Reservation. Husk bottles, trays and baskets are
woven in the same manner as the woven mask as also are sandals
and moccasins although the latter are about obsolete now [see pl. 24].

Another interesting article manufactured from corn husk is the
lounging mat, onō'nya' gĕska'a or yiondyädĕⁿkwă'. This is made
of short lengths of the husk neatly rolled and folded at the ends,
into which other lengths were inserted and tied in place by a warp
of basswood cord. A specimen of this mat is shown in plate 25.
It was collected by the author in 1907 on the Tonawanda-Seneca
Reservation. It was claimed that it was the old form of the Iroquois sleeping and lounging mat. It can easily be rolled up and is
of no great weight. The writer is not aware of another specimen
in any museum. No great age is ascribed to the State Museum
specimen, the owner, Lyman Johnson, Gaiĕnt'wakĕ', claiming it had
been made in about 1900 by his mother.

Probably the corn husk article most familiar to white people surrounding Indian reservations is the husk door mat, gadji'shă'. This
mat is braided in such a manner that tufts of the husk are left protruding from the top of the braid. The braid then is coiled so as
to form an oval or round mat and the thick tufts of still husk
trimmed off evenly, and the flat braids sewed securely with threads
of husk. Mats of this kind are common on all the reservations.
The details of the foot mat are shown in plate 26.

Dolls, gayă''dă', are made by folding the husk in a pestlelike
form for the neck and body. Room is left for the head and neck
and the central core is pierced to allow a wisp of husk to be pulled
through to be braided into arms. The lower portion is pierced in
the same way and the husk for the legs pulled through. Husks are
rolled around the upper portion of the neck and the head is formed.

Plate 24

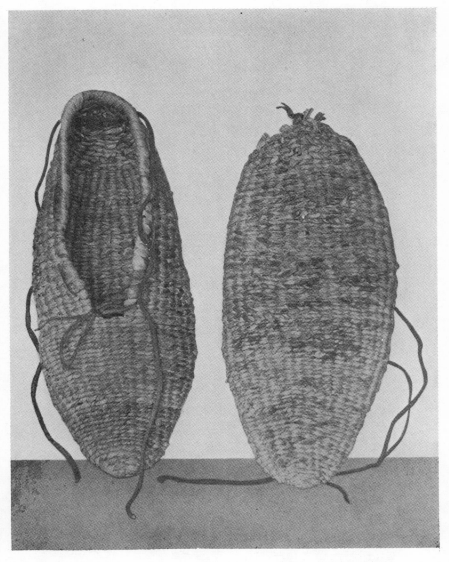

Seneca husk moccasins. Once common, these articles are now **obsolete among** the Iroquois. Collected by A. C. Parker, 1910

Plate 25

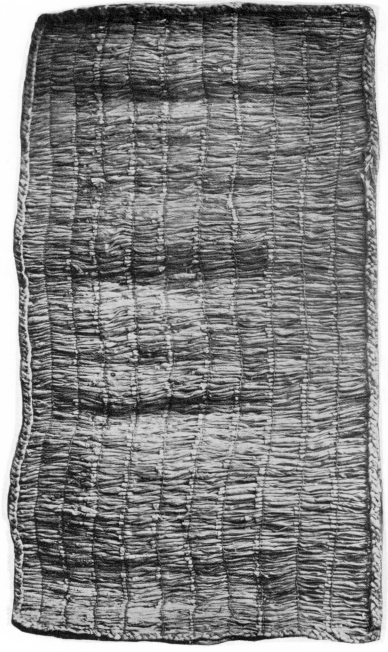

Husk bed mat. A rare Seneca specimen. Collected 1907 by A. C. Parker

Husks now are placed over the back of the neck and carried diagonally across the chest from either side. The same process is repeated from the front and the husk drawn diagonally across the back. This produces body and shoulders. The legs are then braided or neatly rolled into shape, wound spirally with twine and tied tightly at the ankle. The foot is then bent forward at right angles to the leg and wound into shape. The arms undergo a similar process but no attempt is made to simulate hands. The head and body are now ready for covering. For the head the wide husks are held upward against the top of the head and a string passed around them. The husks are then bent downward and the string tightened. This leaves a little circular opening at the top of the head. The head cover husks are drawn tightly over the form and tied at the neck, which is afterward wound neatly with a smooth husk. More diagonal pieces are placed over the shoulders fore and aft and drawn tightly down to the waist. A wide band is then drawn around the waist and tied. The doll is now ready for corn silk hair which may be sewn on, and its face may be painted on. These dolls are sometimes dressed in husk clothing but more often cloth or skin is used. Dolls are dressed as warriors and women and are given all the accessories, bows, tomahawks, baby-boards or paddles, as the sex may require.

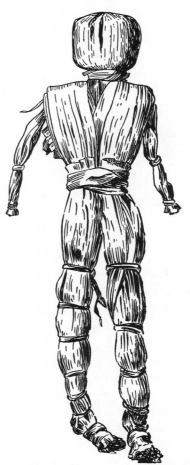

Fig. 18   Common type of the husk doll made by the Iroquois of New York and Canada.   Figure is half size.

Among the articles made from husks, moccasins are perhaps as uncommon as any. Morgan collected a pair for the State Museum in 1851, but the specimens are not now to be found. In 1910 the writer succeeded in getting two pairs on the Cattaraugus Reservation from a husk worker who spent some time in finding among the old women one who remembered the art. She was successful

in her inquiries and was able to make two pairs for the State Museum. They are most ingeniously woven but are as snug as any slipper ever made. The details of these moccasins are shown in plate 24.

Small baskets were woven from twisted corn husks. Trays, table mats and salt bottles were similarly made. The basket was commenced by tying two rolled husks together with another single husk inserted, and then starting two oppositely placed husks about them by the twining process as the width of the warp increased, as it radiated from the center others were inserted and the twining process repeated. When the desired size of the bottom was reached the warp was bent at right angle upward and the twining continued

Fig. 19   Doll made in obedience to a dream and cast aside to carry away some malady.   Specimen is actual size

until the hight wished had been achieved. The warp was then bent over along the top and braided, in a three strand plait. This stiffened and protected the top. Husk baskets are called onōnya' gaŭs'hä' (= husk basket).

Husk bottles for containing salt or ashes or other substances are called onō'nya' gŭs"heda' (= husk bottle) or yedji'kedä"kwă (= salt dish, from ye, feminine affix, and odjike"dä, salt, and iäkwă', meaning container, in compounding words). Salt bottles were tightly woven and some are said to be water tight. The Iroquois prize them, believing that the husk absorbs the moisture before it reaches the salt which is thereby kept dry.

Husk trays are used for containing small objects or food and are designed to be kept on a flat surface only. They are called o'dion'hä' iäkwă' (= crumb dish).

Baby hammocks, onō'nya' gaoⁿ'woⁿ', or gaoⁿ'yoñ, (onō'nya'

Plate 26

Husk foot mat, Seneca specimen

Plate 27

The feast of Mandamin, from an engraving by F. B. Mayer in Schoolcraft's *Indian Tribes*. This picture is reproduced as a suggeston as to the widespread veneration of the corn plant among the Indians of America.

Fig. 20   Corn husk basket. Collected by Lewis H. Morgan, 1850.
Specimen is 12 inches in diameter.

Fig. 21   Corn husk bottle and salt basket, about ⅔ actual size.
Collected 1908 by A. C. Parker. Seneca specimens.

+ gao$^{n'}$wo$^{n'}$ = boat, or gao$^{n'}$yoñ[1] = hanging boat). Hammocks are woven like the sleeping mat but they are shaped so that they will hang properly and hold a baby in safety. These hammocks are suspended over the beds of the parents where they can be swung and the babies easily cared for. Hammocks are now made by suspending a blanket or a quilt in the same manner. These modern contrivances are called iyōs'gashâ$^{n'}$ niä'do^n gao^{n}wo$^{n'}$, *blanket, it is made from boat*, (a hammock).

Husk pudding wrappings are called deyĕ''hodyĕ$^{n'}$yĭktă' (= a wrapping). Husks were braided for ropes and clothes lines, gäo$^{n''}$gä (= rope).

A woman unable to deliver the placenta is held over a pan in which a couple of handfuls of husks are burning. The smoke rises and exercises a medical function, it is thought, which facilitates the delivery. This was widely practised by the Iroquois as late as 1675, and now to some extent.

To stop "nose bleed" a small strand of husk is tied about the little finger. A wad of husk or kernel of corn was placed under the upper lip next to the gum and just over the middle incisors.

There are references to clothing of corn husk and Father Dablon in 1656 wrote of the brother of his host who arrayed himself to impersonate a satyr, "covering himself from head to foot with husks of Indian corn."

3 Uses of corn silk. Corn silk (when on stalk = odiot'; off = ogä") was used commonly for the hair of husk dolls. It was rarely used for adulterating tobacco. Another use of the dried corn silk was an adulterant for certain medicines. The dried silk was pulverized and kept in cornstalk bottles.

4 Uses of corn cobs. Cobs (Ono''gwĕ^{n}ä^n) were used for smoking meats and hides. A slow fire of cobs was built under the meat and then smothered so that the cobs merely smoldered and smoked. In smoking skins the skin was folded into a tentlike cone, suspended from a limb or crane and smoked on the underside from a small pit beneath, in which was a smoldering fire of cobs. The skin was then reversed and smoked. Cobs were not the only substances used for smoking.

---

[1] Gani'yōn = hanging, gaon'wo^n'= boat; gaonyoñ, hanging boat = hammock. The earlier form is gao'wo^n'niyoñ, hanging boat. *Cf.* Awĕ^n'o^n'niyoñ = hanging flower; Awĕ'o^n'= flower. Gano''djaniyoñ = hanging kettle, gano''dja = kettle + (ga)ni yoñ = hanging.

Plate 28

Interior of modern Mexican Indian kitchen, from a photograph by Prof. Marshall H. Saville. Note the clay pots, the scattered ears and cobs and the metates before the women

Plate 29

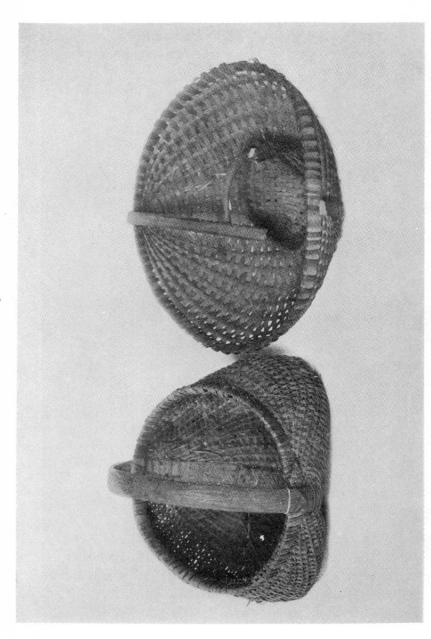

Types of melon baskets, used for gathering berries. 1 Cherokee specimen; 2, 3 Oneida specimens. Illustrations are about one quarter actual size. Collected for the State Museum by M. R. Harrington, 1910

Segments of cob are used for stoppers for husk salt bottles and for the openings in gourd rattles. Cobs were and still are used for hand and flesh scrubbing brushes, oyĕn'nyï'tä', and for pipe bowls. Cobs were " singed " and used as combs, ĕⁿyĕskĕⁿĕⁿwai', with which to clean pumpkin and squash seeds. Singed cobs were also used as back scratchers, yiontgĕⁿ''dătă'.

The ashes, o'gäⁿ', of the cob in quantities were used to make a lye, o'gäⁿ'gi', that induced vomiting. In small quantities cob ashes were used as a seasoning for food. " They killed stomach worms and prevented dyspepsia."

5 **Uses of the Caryopsis.** Besides their use as food, corn kernels were used as beads and decorations, as a medium for trade for the oil, for rattlers in gourds, and for sacrificial purposes.

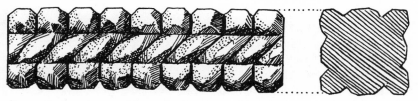

Fig. 22 Section of ceremonial cane showing the use of kernels of corn as a decorative motive

When used as decorations the various colored corns were soaked in water until soft and then strung, sometimes with beads alternating upon thread. Such strands could be used as necklaces and the writer has seen them strung as portieres. Oil, Onä'oⁿ ono", was extracted from the kernels and used for a rubbing oil and various poultices, oyĕⁿ'sä',[1] were made of corn meal. There are a number of references to the sacrifices to various spirits.

White Tuscarora corn kernels were parched on the stove and pulverized on a hot stone. The powder, onä'o ot'on'yoshä, was used as a compress on the navel of a baby from whom the dried navel chord (hoshet'dōt, masc., goshet'dot, fem.) had just been removed. It was thought to be a nonirritating absorbent and a valuable healing agent.

---

[1] Iroquois use poultices of boiled maize flour and apply them hot to the cheek. "I have found that this remedy has been very efficacious against a swelling," says Kalm, "as it lessens the pain, abates the swelling, opens a gathering if there be any, and procures a good discharge of pus." Kalm. Travels in North America, p. 514; Pinkerton. Voyages, p. 13.

In notifying people of the death feast an ear[1] or kernel of corn is given as a token. The person receiving it is bound to attend the ceremony.

The pulp of crushed green corn has been used effectively by the Iroquois as a substitute for deer's brains as a filler in tanning skins.

At the unveiling of the Mary Jemison monument in Letchworth Park on September 19, 1910, a Seneca girl threw handfuls of Tuscarora corn upon the grave and Mrs Thomas Kennedy, a Seneca and descendant of Mary Jemison, made a short address, saying that as the corn which Mary had so often planted sprang into life again, so it was hoped that her spirit would blossom in the heaven world.

6 **Uses of corn leaves.** Corn leaves, odio^n'să', newly torn from the stalk are used as wrappings for green corn tamales, or boiled cakes, oniă"tcidă' (= folded braid of hair). The green corn cut from the cob is thrown into a mortar and beaten into a paste and wrapped in corn leaves which are doubled over and tied three times laterally and once transversely.

In the *Jesuit Relations of* 1652–53, a Jesuit Father relates that his finger, the end of which has been cut off, was wrapped in a corn leaf to staunch the flow of blood.[2]

---

[1] Beauchamp.   Am. Folk Lore Jour.   11 :3.
[2] Jesuit Relations.   40 :153.

Part 2

NOTES ON CERTAIN FOOD PLANTS USED BY THE IROQUOIS

XI BEANS AND BEAN FOODS

Beans next to corn were regarded as a favorite food and quantities are still eaten. The Iroquois have 10 or more varieties of beans which they claim are ancient species which have long been cultivated. Some are said now to be cultivated only by the Iroquois.

The cornstalk bean,[1] oä''gēka, is thought by the Seneca to be the most ancient bean and perhaps the species which grew from the Earth-Mother's grave.

The bean is an indigenous American plant, at least it grew here in Precolumbian times. Explorers and early writers have left us many references to it and most agree that it is an American plant.

Varieties of Iroquois beans

Beans, osai''dă'

Bush beans	dega'gahă'
Wampum	o'tgo'ä osai''dă'
Purple kidney	awe'oñdagoⁿ
White kidney	o'sai''dăgän
Marrowfat	osai''dowanĕs
String	{ otgoⁿ'wasägaⁿoñ { odji'stanokwa
Cornstalk	oä''geka
Cranberry	hayuk'osai''dăt
Chestnut lima	onii'stă'
Hummingbird	djŭtowĕndoⁿ
White (small)	osai''dagä'n
Wild peas	owĕndo'ge'ä' osai''dă'
Bean vines	ooⁿ'să'
Poles	yoäno'dă'kwă'

Bean foods

Among the varieties of bean foods may be mentioned:

Bean soup, osai''dă'gĭ'. This was made in several ways: from string beans cooked in the pods, from shelled green beans and from dried beans. Often sugar was put in as a seasoning.

---

[1] *Cf.* N. Y. Hist. Soc. Proc. Ser. 2, 1 :189.

Fried cooked green beans (none"owi = *it is done*). The cooked green beans were fried in sunflower or bear oil and eaten with salt.

Mashed bean pudding (osai"dä' odjiis'kwa). Dried beans were put in a mortar and pounded coarsely, soaked in cold water and boiled down to a pudding with bear meat or vension.

Boiled beans (osai"dŭk odjis'kwa). These were mashed and mixed with sugar and grease.

Beans and squash " together " (Ganiŭ"sŭk osai"dä' kho). Cook cranberry beans with the pods and when beans are almost dry serve in the shell of a boiled squash. This dish is served at the Green Corn Thanksgiving ceremony and is called Onon'deikwawas, *cooked together food.*

Beans with corn (Gai'nondä). Green shelled beans were boiled with green sweet corn, meat or fat. The red beans were preferred.

XII SQUASHES AND OTHER VINE VEGETABLES

The squash plant is indigenous to America and was cultivated to a large extent by the Iroquois and other eastern stocks. The word *squash* is derived from the Algonquin *akuta squash* or *isquouter squash* (colonial spelling). Roger Williams[1] writing on the agriculture of the New England Indians says: "Askuta squash, their vine apples, which the English from them call squashes, are about the bigness of apples of several colours, a sweet light wholesome refreshing."

Van Curler in the same year wrote in his journal: " We had a good many pumpkins cooked and baked that they called anansira."

This was in December which of course shows the use of squashes in winter. Van Curler attests the hospitality of the Mohawk when he writes: "A woman came to meet us bringing us baked pumpkins to eat." [*See* Am. Hist. Soc. Trans. 1895. p. 91–92]

The squash was one of the principal foods of the Iroquois who even yet regard it as a favorite. The records of early travelers[2] abound in references to the uses of squashes and pumpkins. Some of them praised " pompions " for their goodness while others

---

[1] Williams. Key. 1643. p. 125. Narragansett Club Pub. *Cf.* Wood. New England Prospect. 1634: " In summer when their corn is spent Isquoter squashes is their best bread, a fruit like young Pompion."

[2] Heckewelder, p. 194–95; Jesuit Relations, 10:103.

affirmed that the " citrules " were hard tasteless things. Hunger and mood largely govern descriptions of food.

Lahontan[1] records that the *citruls* (pumpkins) of this country are sweet and of a different nature from those of Europe. ". . . and I am informed," he writes, " that the *American citruls* will not grow in *Europe*. They are as big as our *Melons;* and their Pulp is as yellow as Saffron. Commonly they are bak'd in Ovens, but the better way is to roast 'em under the Embers as the Savages do. Their Taste is much the same with that of the marmalade of Apples, only they are sweeter. One may eat as much of 'em as he pleases without fearing disorder."

Charles Hawley in his *Early Chapters of Cayuga History*[2] quotes Dr Shea's translation of de Casson's *Historie de Montreal* which gives the account of the journey of Trouvé and the Catholic fathers to Kenté. A part of the narrative reads:

Having arrived at Kenté we were regaled there as well as it was possible by the Indians of the place. It is true that the feast consisted only of some citrouilles (squashes) fricasseed with grease and which we found good; they are indeed excellent in this country and can not enter into comparison with those of Europe. It may even be said that it is wronging them to give them the name citrouilles. They are of a very great variety of shapes and scarcely one has any resemblance to those in France. They are some so hard as to require a hatchet if you wish to split them open before cooking. All have different names.

A favorite way of preserving pumpkins and squashes for winter use was to cut them into spirals[3] or thin sections and hang them on the drying racks to evaporate. Sometimes even now this method is used but the modern way among the Seneca and Onondaga at least is to cut off thin sections and string the pieces on cord. A string would hold about half a pumpkin or squash and be suspended perpendicularly to pegs back of the stove or near the fireplace.

Varieties of squashes

The Iroquois generally planted their squashes in the same hills with corn and some kinds of beans. Beside the land and labor saved by this custom there was a belief that these three vegetables were

---

[1] 1 :151.
[2] Early Chapters of Cayuga History. Auburn 1879.
[3] *Cf.* Adair, p. 408.

guarded by three inseparable spirit sisters and that the plants would not thrive apart in consequence.

Crook neck squash	onya'sa'
Hubbard squash	odaint'dowane'
Scalloped squash	onya'säo^n'we^n
Winter squash	gai'dowane'
Hard pumpkin	nyo'sowane'

Squash foods

Baked squash (wandenyo^{n}soñdŭk). Squashes were baked in ashes and the whole squash eaten, the shell and seeds included.

Boiled squash (Ganyu''sō). Squashes were split and cleaned and boiled in water salted to taste.

Boiled squash flower (ojaint'dŭk).[1] The infertile flowers of the squash were boiled with meat and the sauce used as a flavoring for meats and vegetables.

Melons

Cucumber	onios'kwäe'
Musk melons	wa'yais
Water melons	o nyut'sŭtgus

Other vine foods

"Husk tomatoes"	dji'wewa'yas

Melons were planted in patches in the woods cleared by burning, the leaf mold furnishing a good medium for growth. Those who planted melons in cleared woodland tracts set up poles upon which were painted the clan totems and the name signs of the owners. The totem sign signified that while, according to the communistic laws, the patch belonged, nominally, to the clan, and that any clansman might take the fruit if necessary, yet by virtue of the fact that the garden was cleared, planted and cultivated by the individual whose name was indicated, the individual claim and right should be recognized as actually prior, though not nominally.

Before the frost the melon vines that still had unripe fruit were often dug up without disturbing the roots, and replanted in a basket of sand to be taken to the lodge and kept under the beds or in small cellars. During the winter months, so several informants said, the melons would mature and were reserved for the sick.

---

[1] Bartram in his *Observations,* page 16, writes of "one kettle full of young squashes and their flowers boiled in water and a little meal mixed."

XIII LEAF AND STALK FOODS.[1]

Wild pea	*Lathyrus maritimus*	awĕndoʻgeʻa osaiʻʹdă'
Berry sprouts		wasēʺoikʹda' (= new sprouts)
Sumac sprouts	*Rhus glabra*	oʻtgoʺdă'
Wild asparagus	*Asparagus officinalis*	deoʹdaiʻho
Sorrel	*Oxalis* (var. sp.)	deyuʺyuʻdjis (= sour)
Yellowdock	*Rumex crispus*	iyeʻt (= she stands)
Mustard	*Brassica* (var. sp.)	djitgwäʹä niayawĕⁿoʺdä (= yellow blossom)
Dandelion	*Taraxacum officinale*	odjisshoⁿdă' (=yellow star)
Pokeberry plant[2]	*Phytolacca decandra*	oʺsheä onĕʺta' (= crimson leaves)
Milkweed	*Asclepisa syriaca*	onaosʹkäⁿ
Cowslips	*Caltha palustris*	ganoⁿʹnowʹs (=it wants)
Pigweed	*Chenopodium* (var. sp.)	gwisʹgwis ganĕʺdas
Burdock	*Arctium lappa*	onoⁿdowaʹnĕs (= big comb)

Berry and sumac sprouts newly grown and sorrel are eaten raw and esteemed an excellent alterative. In the spring new stalks of wild asparagus, peas, yellowdock, poke and milkweed are cooked as greens. The plants must be young and tender and not more than 6 to 10 inches high. All greens are supposed to be good for the liver, for the blood and as a remedy for rheumatism. Young dandelions, cowslips and mustard were cut at the ground and boiled as greens. Fat meat was generally cooked with greens.

XIV FUNGI AND LICHENS

Mushrooms	onĕⁿʹsă'
Puffballs	onĕⁿʹsă'waʹnĕʻ
Lichens	gŭstaot onĕʺta'

Mushrooms, puffballs and other edible fungi were esteemed as good materials for soup. The fungus is first peeled and then diced and thrown in boiling water, seasoned with salt and grease. Sometimes bits of meat are added. The Iroquois like edible fungi quite as well as meat.

---

[1] Adair, p. 415.
[2] *Ibid.* 412.

Puffballs were peeled and sliced and mushrooms peeled and fried entire in grease, sunflower or bear oil, though sometimes deer tallow was used.

Rale[1] mentions the use of tree fungi and says that they were " white as large mushrooms; these are cooked and reduced to a sort of porridge, but it is very far from having the flavor of porridge."

Lichens have been eaten but rarely within the memory of my oldest informants. Hunters when pressed by hunger, they remembered, had sometimes scraped the lichens from a tree or rock and boiled them with grease. In preparing them the lichens were first washed in a mixture of camp ashes and water to remove the bitterness. In times of great emergency, however, with hunger pressing, the cook did not stop to soak the lichens but cooked them as they were. The Jesuit Rale, in his letter to his brother mentions lichens and calls them " rock tripe." [2] When cooked, he says, they made a black and disagreeable porridge.

In Iceland for centuries lichens have been an important food and other peoples have not despised them. The nutritive value lies in the lichenin and starch which the plant contains.

XV FRUIT AND BERRYLIKE FOODS

The Iroquois considered fruits and berries a necessary part of everyday diet. Long before the Revolutionary War they had, in many places, extensive orchards of apples, peaches and plums. It is probable that at that period they cultivated fruit trees to a greater extent than any other native American people. The Iroquois loved the apple above other fruits, a fact which several writers mention.[3] General Sullivan in his famous raid against the hostile Iroquois cut down a single orchard of 1500 trees.[4]

A list of the principal fruits used by the Iroquois follows:

Apple	*Pyrus* (var. sp.)	⎧ ganyŭ″oyă ⎨ ⎩ oyă″odji′yă
Crab apples	*Pyrus coronaria*	djoik′dowa
Thorn apples	*Crataegus* (var. sp.)	ăwe′owek

---

[1] Jesuit Relations, 67 :223.

[2] Jesuit Relations, 67 :223.

[3] *See* Schoolcraft. Senate Document 24. Albany 1846. " The apple is the Indian's banana."

[4] History of New York during the Revolutionary War. New York 1879. II :334. Life of Brant. Albany 1865. v. II, ch. I.

Cherry, wild	*Prunus* (var. sp.)	oyă'gane gowa
Cherry, choke	*Prunus virginiana*	gane', or dyagyonyă'-täs
Peach[1]	*Prunus persico*	gai'däe' odji'yă'
Plum	*Prunus americana*	gä'e'
Grapes	*Vitis* (var. sp.)	oñiŭng'wisä'
Pawpaw	*Asimina triloba*	hadi'ot
Pear[1]	*Pyrus* (var. sp.)	odji'djo'gwa
Quince[1]	*Cydonia vulgaris*	odji'ju oyä''dji
Mandrake	*Podophyllum peltatum*	odä''onoshä'

Terminology

Tree	gē'it
Fruit skin	oä'wistă'
Fruit seeds or pits	oskä''e^n
Core	oä''dă'
Stem (also tree trunk)	oondă'
Cluster	wa'gwais'hänion

Apples were generally eaten raw but they were often boiled entire or cut up for sauce. The favorite way, however, was to bake them in ashes. The camp fire was brushed aside and the apples laid on a layer of hot gray ashes, covered with the same material, the hot embers raked over these and the fire rebuilt. Baked apples are called wada'gondŭk and the boiled sauce ganyaoyä' odji'skwa. The latter was eaten with roasted meats or bread.

Apples were stored in bark barrels and buried in winter pits with other vegetables. Apples were cut up in thin slices, strung on twine and dried. Even now it is a common thing to see apples strung up over the stove or hung on a pole at the top of the room in the houses of the more primitive Iroquois.

Cherries were dried for winter use and pulverized in a mortar and mixed with dried meat flour for soup.

Small fruits. Of the smaller fruits and berries the list which follows includes those most commonly used:

Blackberries	*Rubus* (var. sp.)	otgä'ashä'
Black raspberries	*R. occidentalis*	toñ'dâktho'
Red raspberries	*R. strigosus*	dagwä''dannĕ'

---

[1] Postcolumbian.

Blueberries	*Vaccinium* (var. sp.)	getdatge'a
Huckleberries	*Gaylussacia baccata*	oyādji''
Thimble	*Rubus odoratus*	
High cranberries	{ *(Vac. macrocarpon)*	onao^{n}shä''
	Viburnum opulus	ha·'nonŭndjŭk
Nannyberries	*V. lentago*	ga'në'să' wanunda
Mulberries	*Morus rubra*	odji'nowŏ^n'wadisiyas
		djo'yesshăyes
Strawberries	*Fragaria virginiana*	odjistondas'hä'
Elderberries	*Sambucus canadensis*	oniot'sŭtgŭs
Gooseberries	*Ribes* (var. sp.)	nŭ^n''gwussōt
Dewberries	*Rubus villosus*	ogau'o''gwă'
Wintergreen	*Gaultheria procum-*	djisdă''geä'
	bens	
Partridge vine	{	
Squaw vine	*Mitchella repens*	oshaistă''wayas
Oneberry	{	
June berries	{ *Amelanchier oblong-*	
	ifolia	hä'do^n
	A. canadensis	
Currants	*Ribes* (var. sp.)	djoägă''wayas
Sumac berries	*Rhus glabra*	o'tgo''dă'

Terminology

Bush	oi''ktă'
Berries	odji'yă'
Blossoms	awe'o^n
Briars	oi''kdaii'
Green fruit	ogä^n's'ä'
Seeds	oskä^n'a'
Berry time	o'wai'yai'
Berry picker	ha'yagwŭs
I pick berries	ga'yagwŭs

Berries when in season were eagerly gathered by the Iroquois and even today berries have not lost favor with them. They were eaten entire raw, crushed and mixed with sugar and water or mixed with various puddings. Blackberries, strawberries, elderberries and huckleberries seem to be the favorite varieties. For winter's use blackberries, black raspberries, huckleberries and blueberries are dried. Strawberries were also dried but required a great deal of care. These dried fruits were either soaked in sugared water and cooked

Plate 30

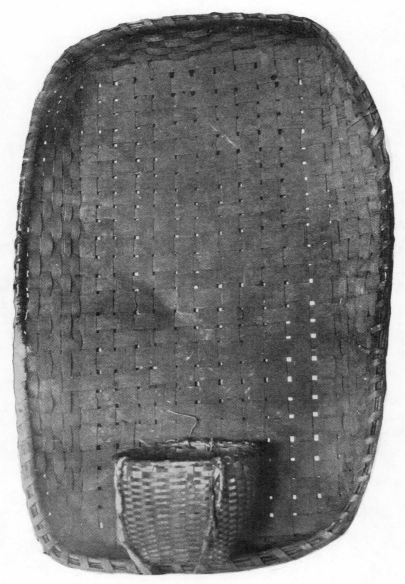

Seneca evaporating tray and berry picker's basket. The evaporating **tray** is used for green corn, pulpy fruits and berries. The tray is 40 inches **in** length. E. R. Burmaster, collector, 1910

Plate 31

Cache of charred acorns excavated by Harrington and Parker, 1903 (Peabody Museum of Archeology and Ethnology Expedition) on the Silverheels site, Brant township, Erie county, N. Y.

as a sauce or thrown in soups, puddings and breads or other foods. For making an expedition food berries were pounded with meat, parched corn and sugar. This food was eaten sparingly and washed down with quantities of water.

Dried blackberries are soaked in honey and water and used as a ceremonial food by the Bear Society in their rites.

Dried, and in modern times, preserved strawberries are mixed with water and maple sugar' and used as a refreshment by the Guardians of the Little Water Medicine[1] during their night song.

Strawberries are eagerly gathered in the spring and eaten by every one as a spring medicine. Handsome Lake, the prophet, commands their use for this purpose in his code, the Gai'wiiu.[2]

Juneberries were considered as a valuable blood remedy, which was given to mothers after childbirth to prevent afterpains and hemorrhages. The smaller branches of the Juneberry bush were broken up and steeped as a tea for the same purpose.

Cranberries were a favorite autumn food and were considered " good " for the blood and liver. Huckleberries were also valued for the same purpose.

Elderberries were eagerly gathered for sauce. They were considered a valuable remedial agent for fevered patients and convalescents.

Partridge berries were not generally eaten as food except perhaps by women. They were supposed to prevent severe labor pains and to facilitate easy delivery. There were other herbs also used for this purpose.

The drying of berries and small fruits in the late summer and autumn was and now to a certain extent is an important item in the domestic economy of the Iroquois.

Blackberries, black raspberries, huckleberries, elderberries and blueberries are easily dried entire if care is taken not to allow them to become damp during the process, which may spoil them. It is said that blackberries were best when dried on the stalk. The stalk or cluster stem was broken and allowed to hang on the bush where the sun could dry down the fruit with all its natural juices. The smaller pulpy berries were dried in shallow basket trays [see pl. 30]. The juicy berries such as strawberries and red raspberries were mashed

---

[1] Parker, A. C. Secret Medicine Societies of the Seneca. Am. Anthropologist. New ser. v. 11, no. 2.

[2] Translated by Parker & Bluesky. Manuscript in New York State Library.

in a wooden bowl and with as much juice as the mass would hold placed on basswood leaves on slabs of slate or other flat rocks. The juice that remained in the bowl was given to the children who even in those days loved to " lick out the bowl."

For winter's use the dried berries were soaked in cold water and then heated slowly, maple sugar being thrown in as a seasoning. The berries were then either eaten as a sauce or mixed with bread meal or onon'dā', hominy.

The gathering of the autumn berries was regarded more of a pastime than work. In fact, work with these people in many lines was made easier by its social character, and seemed more like a game where the thrill of it all kept the thought of fatigue away.

The work of berrying was left of course to the women and girls. They would go in groups to the places where patches of the vines and bushes grew and sing their folksongs as they gathered the fruit. Every one laughed or sang and picked as fast as their two hands could touch the berries. The picking baskets yiondasste''nondakwa‘ held about 5 quarts. They were suspended from the back of the neck and the chest, one fore, the other aft. The forward basket lay against the abdomen so that it was within easy reach. This being filled the berries were covered with sumac or basswood leaves held in place by two sticks, slung to the rear, the rear basket brought forward and filled. The two baskets were then carried to a larger basket holding about ½ bushel. One large basket and the two picking baskets full of berries constituted a load for a woman to carry.

Huckleberries were raked from the bushes with the fingers. Swamp huckleberries, bushes that grew along streams running through marshes, were bent over into a canoe and stripped of their berries which fell into large containing baskets. In picking mountain huckleberries or those which grew in snake infested places the moccasins were smeared with lard to frighten away the rattlers. The snakes, scenting the hog fat, would think that pigs were scouting for them.

This description of the berry-picking industry applies to a large extent to the Iroquois of the present day, especially the Seneca along the Cattaraugus, Allegany and Tonawanda.

The first fruit of the year is the wild strawberry and this the Iroquois takes as a symbol of the Creator's renewed promise of beneficence. Quantities are gathered and brought to the feast-makers at the Long House for the Strawberry Thanksgiving. This is an annual ceremony of importance though it lasts but a day.

The thrifty housewife examines the teeth of the June mullet which her husband has caught in the creeks to see if the base of its teeth is black. If so, it is an omen of a good blackberry year. A legend states that frost will never come when blackberries are in blossom in berry. Hă'tho, the frost spirit, once entered the lodge of O'swi'nodă', the summer spirit, but a boy entering and seeing the strange cold spirit in his father's house threw a pot of hot blackberry sauce in the frost spirit's face to his intense discomfort. Thereafter Hă"tho never ventured from his hiding place in the north from the time blackberries blossom until the fruit is mature. Blackberry juice makes a fine drink in the winter for it frightens away the cold. "Do not even bears eat berries all summer and defy the blasts of winter?" Blackberry roots are considered an effectual astringent and the tender new shoots as a fine blood remedy.

Thimble berries were eaten in the late summer as a diuretic. Dried for winter use they were valued for the same purpose. Sumac bobs were boiled in winter for a drink.

XVI FOOD NUTS OF THE IROQUOIS

Nuts formed an important part of the Iroquois diet. Great quantities were consumed during the nut season and quantities were stored for winter use. The nut season to the Iroquois was one of the happiest periods of the year[1] especially for the young people to whom fell the work of gathering most of the nuts. The women, however, often went in companies when serious business was meant, for with the failure of other crops, nuts formed an important food source. The nut season was called o'wadawisa'ho'n.

The favorite food nuts of the Iroquois were hickory and chestnuts though other nuts were valued: A list of the principal nuts used by the Iroquois follows:

Acorns	*Quercus* (sp)	ogowä''
Beechnuts	*Fagus grandifolia*	oskän'ä
Black walnuts	*Juglans nigra*	djonyot'gwak
Butternuts	*J. cinerea*	djonot'gwes
Chestnuts	*Castanea dentata*	onye"sta
Hickory, bitter	*Carya cordiformis*	onioⁿgwadjiwagĕⁿ
Hickory	*Carya ovata*	djistagä'oⁿ
Hazel	*Corylus americana*	oso'wishä'

[1] *See* Relation of 1670, ch. IX.

Terminology

Nut	onio"gwă'
Husk or shucks	goktdo^n'tso^n
Shells	oktdă"
I shuck them	o'gekdo^{n}tci'
Meats	oniä"
Burs	osi'gä'
I crack nuts	degadēnŭt'dyăk
Pitted nut stone	dyiodedă'kwĕ^n
Stone hammer	ye^{n}yĕ^n'dăkwă'
Entire outfit for cracking nuts	ge'ondeniya"dăktă'
Nut meal	onia"degai'to^n
Nut oil	onia"deyo^{n}no^{n}go
Nut milk	oniä'ono^n"gwă'
It is cracked	deganyo"dyă'go^n
Rancid meats	oniät'gä'
Good meats	ōnye'iu'
[1]Ripe meats	onie"stai'
Ripe (on tree)	o'wadawis'a'
Ripe (on ground)	odawis'sa^{n}o^n
It is not ripe	doodawis'sa'o^n
Nut time	o'wadawis'aho^n'
Roasted chestnut	wade'nyistdondŭk
Boiled	ganie"stok
Entire nut meat	[2]deyut'hage^n'o^n
I gather nuts	ogeniogwe'oek
They are gathering	hadinio'gwe'oek

Fresh nut meats were crushed in wooden bowls. The crushed meats were then thrown into a kettle of boiling water and the oil skimmed off. This oil was kept as a delicacy to be used with corn bread and puddings. Hickory and butternut oil was regarded especially palatable, the former being used for feeding infants. After the nut meats and oil were skimmed out the liquid was used as a drink. The crushed meats were often mixed with corn pudding or bread.

Chestnuts were boiled and the mealy interior used for puddings or the dried meats were pounded into a flour and mixed with bread meal to give the bread flavor.

---

[1] Means also boiled chestnut meats.
[2] Means *Spreads its legs*.

Acorns were boiled in lye and roasted[1] much as corn was to remove the bitterness, and after several washings pounded up in a mortar and mixed with meal or meat and made into soup or pudding. Children even now commonly eat raw acorns but their elders at present seldom use them for cooking. Their former employment remains only a memory.

The name hickory in its original uncorrupted form is derived from the name given by the Virginia Indians to a food or flavoring liquor prepared from a nut meat emulsion. John Smith in 1612 described this nut preparation as follows: "Then doe they dry them againe upon a mat over a hurdle. After they put it into a morter of wood and beat it very small: that done they mix it with water that the shells may sink to the bottome. This water will be coloured as milk; which they call *Pawcohiccora* and *keepe it for their use*."[2]

The original Lenape form of the word according to William Gerard[3] was patahikareo.

For cracking nuts cuplike depressions, the size of the nut were picked into small boulders or slabs of shale. The nut was placed in the depression and cracked or crushed with a suitable stone. These "nut stones" and hammers were used on the various reservations up to within a few years and there are many Indians in New York State who can remember having used them. These stones are to be found today near large old nut trees and the writer in his childhood days often hunted about for them in his grandfather's back fields and used them for the purpose previously mentioned. In the Cattaraugus valley where black walnut trees once were plentiful these nut stones are common. The Seneca call the pitted nut stone dyiodedä'kwĕⁿ. The hammer is called yĕⁿyĕⁿ'däkwä' and the entire nut cracking outfit deyondeniya''däktä'.

The Seneca say that in the early days dry butternut and hickory meats were pulverized and mixed with dried bear or deer meat pul-

---

[1] " . . . they search for — even acorns, which they value as highly as corn; after having dried these, they roast them in a kittle with ashes, in order to take away their bitterness. As for me, I eat them dry, and they take the place of bread." Rale. 1716–27. Jesuit Relations. 67:215; *cf. also* 1610, p. 243; Lawson, p. 178.

[2] Smith. Map of Virginia (1612) p. 12. *Cf.* Strachey. History of Travile into Virginia (1616); Norwood. Voyage to Virginia (1649), p. 37; Beverly. History of Virginia (1705). Bk 2, p. 16.

[3] Am. Anthropologist, New ser. v. 9, no. 1, Jan.-Mar. 1907. p. 92

verized in a mortar. This powder was thrown in a quantity of boiling water and used as a baby food.

The nursing bottle was a dried and greased bear-gut. The nipple was a bird's quill around which was tied the gut to give proper size. To clean these bottles they were untied at both ends, turned wrong side out, rinsed in warm water, thrown into cold water, shaken and hung in the smoke to dry.

Sunflower oil was used in quantities by the Iroquois, with whom it was a favorite food oil. It was prepared by bruising the ripe seed in a mortar, heating the mass for a half hour and then throwing it into boiling water until most of the oil had been separated from the pulp. The water was cooled and strained and then the oil skimmed off.

The use of this oil is mentioned elsewhere in this work.

XVII SAP AND BARK FOODS

The maple tree was one of the trees venerated by the Iroquois. It was in fact the goddess of trees and the only one to which a stated ceremony was dedicated and to which offerings were made. Pine, hemlock, elm and basswood of the forest trees were esteemed, but the maple was a special gift of the Creator and every spring at the foot of the largest maple tree in each village a ceremonial fire was built and a prayer chanted by the Keeper of the Maple Thanksgiving ceremony as he threw upon the embers pinches of sacred incense tobacco. The maple tree started the year. Its returning and rising sap to the Indian was the sign of the Creator's renewed covenant.

The Iroquois will ever remember the maple tree, but few now even remember the tradition of how it was, during the maple sap season, that the Laurentian Iroquois[1] struck their blow for freedom from Adirondack domination and fled into northern and central New York.[2]

Trees were probably tapped in early times by sawing a slanting gash into the trunk with a chert knife or saw. A flat stick was driven

---

[1] The Mohawk, the Oneida and Onondaga.

[2] One Mohawk tradition relates that the women flung hot maple sap into the faces of the Algonquin chiefs and thus helped their people in the fight for independence.

into the gash and the sap run down over it into bark tubs. For boiling the sap the Iroquois had in early times only their clay vessels but these were suitable receptacles though their capacity was small.

Fig. 23 Seneca sap basket or tub of elm bark, collected by L. H. Morgan. Specimen is 18 inches in length.

Maple sap was drunk as it came from the tree[1] and, fermented, was some times used as an intoxicant, the only record of such a thing which the writer has been able to find as used anciently by the Iroquois. When fermentation went too far a vinegar was produced which was highly esteemed. It was called wat'dă dyono^{n}ga'yotdjis.

The sugar syrup was sometimes poured into the empty shells of quail and duck eggs and these sugar eggs were valued by travelers.

One of the best early descriptions of maple sugar making has been left us by Lahontan whose description follows:

The maple-tree . . . yields a sap, which has a much pleasanter Taste than the best Limonade or Cherry Water, and makes the wholesomest Drink in the World. The Liquor is drawn by cutting the Tree two Inches deep into the Wood, the cut being run sloping to the Length of ten or twelve Inches. At the lower End of the Gash, a knife is thrust into the Tree slopingly so the Water running along the Cut or Gash, and falling upon the Knife that lies across the Channel, runs out upon the Knife, which has Vessels placed underneath to receive it. Some Trees will yield five or six Bottles of this Water

---

[1] Lahontan, 2:59.

a Day; and some Inhabitants of Canada, might draw twenty Hogsheads of it in one day, if they would thus cut and notch all the Mapples on their respective Plantations. The gash do's no harm to the tree. Of this Sap they make Sugar and Syrup, which is so valuable that there can't be a better Remedy for fortifying the Stomach.[1]

Bark was eaten by certain Indian tribes but seldom if ever by the Iroquois. Their ancient enemies and captors, the Adirondacks,[2] (in 'Seneca, *Hadi'ondas*, in Mohawk, *Adirhōn'daks*, meaning, *tree eaters*) ate bark in quantities. They were especially fond of the inside bark of the top of the pine especially in the spring when it was full of sweet sap.

The Iroquois in emergencies ate elm and basswood bark[3] and perhaps other barks but it was never a general article of diet. Sassafras bark and root as a carminative and aromatic was regarded with favor, as were several other spicy barks.

Maple	wat'dă'
Sap	owän'no^{n}gi'
Sugar	owän'no^n
Syrup	owän'no^{n}gi'
Boiling sap	goste''do^n
Saptime	o'gä'not
Sap runs	o'gä'not
He taps	ha'ge'o'tă
Sap spout	nio^n'geodă'kwa

XVIII FOOD ROOTS, Okdea

Root foods were not despised by the Iroquois but with few exceptions they were seldom used unless the scarcity of other foods made it necessary. It is difficult at this time to enumerate all the food roots used by the Iroquois since they have long since ceased to use wild roots and tubers as food, preferring, of course, cultivated

---

[1] Lahontan. New Voyages to America. Lond. 1735. 1:249.

[2] Tree Eaters, a people so called (living between 300 and 400 miles west into the land) from their only *Mihtuchquash,* that is trees: They are Men-eaters, they set no corne, but live on the *bark* of *Chestnut* and *Walnut* and other fine trees: They dry and eat this *bark* with the fat of beasts, and sometimes men . . ." Roger Williams. Key. Reprint R. I. Hist. Soc. Col. Providence 1827. vol. 1.

Rale mentions the use of green oak bark and "a kind of wood" which he was compelled to eat for want of anything better while among the Indians of the north St Lawrence valley. Jesuit Relations, 67:223.

[3] *See* Swetland. Captivity.

varieties. Even wild onions and artichokes are now seldom used. There is a dim recollection of food roots, however, and the writer succeeded in getting the list which follows:

Artichokes	*Helianthus tuberosus*	otwĕⁿ'ä'
Ground nuts	*Apios tuberosa*	yoandjagoⁿ'
Wild onions	*Allium canadense*	gahadagoⁿka'
Wild leek	*A. tricoccum*	o'no'saoⁿ
Yellow pond lily	*Nymphaea advena*	owäⁿ'osha'
Cat-tail	*Scirpus validus*	onoⁿ''gwĕⁿdă
Arrowhead	*Sagittaria latifolia*	ooⁿwa'ho'noⁿ'
Indian turnip	*Arisaema triphyllum*	gä'ọshä'
Milkweed	*Asclepias syriaea*	ono'skä'
Solomon's seal	{ *Polygonatum biflorum*	ga'ga'wiyas
	{ *P. commetatum*	(= crow eats it)
Potato	*Solanum tuberosum*	onon'oⁿ'dă'
Skunk cabbage	*Symplocarpus*	niagwai''igas
	foeditus	(= bear eats it)

Terminology

ENGLISH		SENECA
Root	okde'ä'	
I pull roots	o'gik'teodagok	
Root gatherer	hakde'ogwas	
Root eater	¹hakde'äs	

Artichokes were valued for their tasteful tubers which were edible raw as well as cooked. The boiled artichokes formed a dish which if properly seasoned with oil had some degree of palatability. Artichokes as food was early noted by explorers[2] and later writers mention their use. Champlain is the first writer to note their cultivation.[3] The Iroquois so far as it has been possible for the writer to

---

[1] Hak-de'-äs, from *h*, masculine affix; okde'ä', root; initial *o* changes to broad ă, terminal ä' is elided; iäs or ias, in compounds meaning *eater of*, loses initial *i* after *e* thus h-akde-äs, *he root eats.*

[2] On September 21, 1605, Champlain wrote of his explorations along the New England coast, ". . . We saw . . . very good roots which the savage cultivate, having a taste similar to that of chards." Elsewhere it was stated that these roots were Jerusalem artichokes. The Rev. Edmund F. Shafter commenting on this subject says that the Italians had procured these tubers for cultivation before Champlain's time, calling them girasole, corrupted and anglicized to Jerusalem.

[3] Champlain. Voyages. 11:112 footnote. Prince Soc. Bost. Pub. 1878.

inquire, never cultivated the plant but it frequently grew in their cornfields on flat lands along streams, and roots, raw or roasted, furnished food for the camp dinners of husking parties. Some women became especially fond of the tubers and were called otwäeⁿyas, *artichoke eaters,* a name which survives today among the Seneca.

Ground nuts, yoändjagoⁿ'oⁿ', were used in considerable quantities up to within the past 25 years. Their use early attracted the attention of explorers.[1] The ground nut was the favorite root food of a captive tribe, according to a tradition, and became the totem name of a clan.[2]

The plant grows on the rich alluvial bottom lands and the tubers which are strung along on the roots are easily dug and when boiled or roasted furnish a food which can be made palatable.

Several early writers mention the ground nuts used by the Indians, among them Peter Kalm, whose account follows:

Hopniss or hapniss was the Indian name of a wild plant which they ate at that time. The Sweedes still call it by that name and it grows in the meadows in good soil. The roots resemble potatoes, and were boiled by the Indians, who eat them instead of bread. Some of the Sweedes at that time likewise ate this root for want of bread. Some of the English still eat them instead of potatoes. Mr Bartram told me that the Indians who live further in the country not only eat these roots which are equal in goodness to potatoes, but likewise take the pease which lie in the pods of the plant, and prepare them like common pease.[3]

In the Paris Documents of 1666, is an account of the Iroquois who are there said to be divided into nine tribes the sixth of which was the Sconescheronon, or Potato People. A drawing is appended showing a string of potatoes as the tribe's totem. There is now only a dim recollection of this clan whose name and symbol was the ground nut rather than the potato.

Indian turnips,[4] gä'osha, at first though, scarcely seem an inviting food. The acrid repugnant taste of the fresh root leaves an impression not soon forgotten. The juice is an actual poison if used

---

[1] Ground nuts are probably what the French called " des chaplets, pource qu'elle est destingue par noends en forme de graeaes." Jesuit Relations 1634. p. 36.

[2] *See* Documentary History New York. 1:10.

[3] Kalm. Travels in North America. Lond. 1772. *See* Pinkerton. Voyages. Lond. 1812. 13:533.

[4] Synonyms: Jack-in-pulpit, wake-robin.

even in a small quantity and yet there seems to be good historical[1] evidence of the use of the root as food, not only by Indians but by white men as well. Harris has made a special study of this root and embodied a most interesting account of it in the Proceedings of the Rochester Academy, volume 1.

To prepare the roots they were sliced and dried and pulverized. Harris by inquiries among the old residents of the Genesee valley, found that the pioneers of that region had used the powdered roots of the Arum triphyllum as a substitute for flour and that they had obtained the receipt from the Seneca.[2]

Wild onions and leeks though often eaten raw with meat were a favorite substance for making soups. The onions were boiled and seasoned with oil. The writer was unable to find that onions were used as a flavoring for other soups or foods. The Iroquois seemed to like their onions in an unadulterated form.

The Iroquois have about forgotten the ancient use of yellow pond lily roots but a few old people were able to describe their use as food. The tuberous roots were gathered in the fall by treading them out with the toes and then scooping them up. When it is realized that the roots generally grew in 5 or 6 feet of water the difficulty of procuring them may be realized. A few Indians filched them from muskrat houses[3] but for superstitious reasons the practice never became general. Water animals were considered powerful magic agents and were thought to visit frightful vengeance when outraged. They might be killed for their meat or pelts but never robbed of their roots without special ceremonies.

---

[1] " Cos-cus-haw groweth in very muddy pools and moist ground. The juice is poison, and therefore heed must be taken before anything be made therewithal; either the roots must first be sliced and dried and then being pounded into a flour, will make good bread; or else while they are green they are to be pared, cut in pieces and stamped [pounded]; loaves of the same to be laid near or over the fire until sour, and then being well pounded again, bread or spoonmeat, very good in taste and very wholesome, may be made thereof." Thomas Hariot, Virginia 1585.
  " The chief food they have for food is called loc-ka-whough. It grows in the marshes . . . and is much of the greatness and taste of potatoes . . . Raw it is no better than poison, and being roasted, except it be tender and the heat abated, mixed with sorrel or meal, it will prick and torment the throat extremely; yet in summer they use this ordinarily for bread." Smith. Virginia. 1606. See Harris. Root Foods. Rochester Acad. Proc. I :III et seq. Cf. also Carver's Travels; Kalm, see Pinkerton. Voyages, 13 :534.
  [2] Harris. Root Foods. Roch. Acad. Proc. Rochester, 1891. I :113.
  [3] Harris, page 115, says it was the usual custom when hunting the little animals (muskrats) to search their houses for roots. This was probably the case only when the muskrats were killed.

The roots of the yellow pond lily are porous and somewhat sweet and glutinous. They were either boiled with meat or roasted. Early explorers frequently mentioned the use of these roots and left interesting descriptions. Few, however, agree as to their taste. Some say that they tasted like the liver of a sheep,[1] others that they tasted like licorice and still others possibly in the throes of starvation enthusiastically describe their fine flavor. Pond lily roots are one of the most widely known food roots on the continent and were eaten from eastern Canada to the Pacific coast.

The roots of the cat-tail were often used. Dried[2] and pulverized the roots made a sweet white flour useful for bread or pudding. Bruised and boiled fresh a syrupy gluten was obtained in which corn meal pudding was mixed.

My Abenaki informants told me that the juice from the bruised roots was eaten raw with bread within very recent years.

Arrowhead tubers[3] were esteemed as good if boiled. Sometimes they were eaten raw but in this state the bitter milky juice made them repugnant to any one but a starving person.

Kalm says that the Swedes of New Sweden called the root Katniss after the Indian name and that the Indians boiled the root or roasted it in ashes.[4]

The potato is a native American plant[5] but it seemed to have

---

[1] " The Indians eat the roots which are long aboiling. They taste like the liver of a sheep. The moose deer feed much upon them; at which time the Indians kill them when they have their heads under water." Josselyn. New England Rarities Discovered. London 1672. p. 105–238. Reprint Am. Antiq. Soc. Trans. v. IV. Bost. 1860. Cf. Pickering. Chronological History of Plants. Bost. 1879; Le Jeune. Relation 1633–34, p. 273.

[2] See Palmer, E. U. S. Dep't Agric. Rept. 1870. Washington 1871. p. 408.

[3] Ibid. p. 408.

[4] Pinkerton. Voyages, 13 :533.

[5] The potato was certainly indigenous. Sir Walter Raleigh, in his efforts to colonization, had it brought from Virginia, under the original name of openawg. But none of the North American tribes are known to have cultivated it. They dug it up, like other indigenous edible roots from the forest. But it has long been introduced into their villages and spread over the northern latitudes far beyond the present limit of zea maize. Its cultivation is so easy and so similar to that of the favorite corn, and its yield so great that it is remarkable it should not have received more general attention from all the tribes. Schoolcraft. Census of the Iroquois. 1845. p. 12–13. Senate Document 24, Albany 1846.

Hariot who came to Virginia with Raleigh in 1584 described potatoes as Openawk, " a kind of root of round form, some of the bigness of walnuts." In 1586 the openawk were carried back to England and later in 1597 were figured by Gerard under the name of Potato of Virginia. Cf. Harris, p. 109.

been cultivated but little before the colonial period. After and during that time however the Iroquois began to plant potatoes in increasing quantities until now as a food they are consumed in greater quantities than corn. To give the Indian method of preparing potatoes for food now would be merely to repeat what every modern cookbook gives. Their favorite recipes, however, were potato soup, boiled and baked potatoes. Distinctive flavoring was given by mixing in bear oil, sunflower oil and white ashes. Potatoes were sometimes dried and made into a flour.

The Seneca cultivated the potato long before the Revolutionary War. To them it was known as onon'nondä' while groundnuts were often called onon'nondä'oñ'wĕⁿ, original potatoes.

The root of Solomon's seal is said to have been used for food. The mature roots were gathered in the fall, dried, pounded and worked up into bread. Harris cites that a Seneca Indian in passing through Highland Park, Rochester, called the attention of his white companion John Nott to the plant saying it was once highly prized for its root.

The roots of skunk cabbage *Lymplocarpus foetidus* were also used being dried and pulverized. Harris says it was sometimes roasted or baked to extract its juice. The modern Seneca call it bear root.

The stalk of the milkweed rises from a tuberous root of considerable size. Western Indians it is said boil these roots for food. One writer[1] says that the Sioux gather the roots early in the morning while the dew is on the plant and prepare a crude sugar from them. He also states that the young seed pods are eaten after boiling them with buffalo meat and that the young stalks were used as white men use asparagus.

Wild rice was an important food of the Indians of the eastern portion of the continent, especially along the great lakes and the Mississippi valley. It was little used by the Iroquois however, although there are records of its employment. The Seneca some 40 years ago gathered a great quantity of it but the writer does not know of its use subsequently.

---

[1] Palmer, Dr E. U. S. Agric. Com'n Rep't 1870, p. 405.

LIST OF AUTHORITIES QUOTED

State Library number at extreme right

Adair, James. History of the American Indians. London 1775.
970.1   qAd.1

American Anthropologist. New ser.   Various issues;   *see* citations
572   O 8

American Antiquarian Society. Proceedings 1895.   Carr, Lucien.   Food of Certain American Indians and their Method of Preparation.
906   Am.3

American Historical Association. Transactions 1895.   Wilson, Gen. James Grant.   Journal of Arent Van Curler.

Bailey, L. H. The Evolution of Our Native Fruits.   New York 1898.
634   P 8a

Bartram, John. Observations on the Inhabitants, Climate, Soil, Rivers, Productions, Animals, in a Journey from Pennsylvania to Onondaga. Reprinted, Geneva 1895.   917.47   B 28r

——— Observations on the Creek and Cherokee Indians, 1789.   Reprinted in facsimile by the Am. Eth. Soc. 1909.

Beauchamp, W. M. Aboriginal Uses of Wood.   N. Y. State Mus. Bul. 89.   Albany 1905.

——— Corn Stories and Customs.   Jour. Am. Folk Lore, 2:195.

——— History of the New York Iroquois.   N. Y. State Mus. Bul. 78. 1905.

Beverly, Robert. The History of Virginia, Ed. 2.   London 1772.
975.5   B 46

Boyle, David. Reports.   Archeology of Ontario (Canada).   Submitted to Minister of Education.

Bozman, J. L. History of Maryland, from the First Settlement in 1633. Baltimore 1837.   975.2   B 71

Bradford. History of Plymouth Plantation.   Mass. Hist. Soc. Col. Ser. 4, v. III.   Boston 1856.   975.4   M38   v.33

Brown, P. A. History of Maize, v. 2.   Farmer's Cabinet Albany 1838.

Brown, D. J. History of Corn.   Am. Inst. Trans.   1846.

Burnaby, *Rev.* Andrew. Travels through the Middle Settlements in North America.   London 1798.

de Candolle, A. L. P. Origin of Cultivated Plants.   Appleton's Internat. Sci. Ser.   New York 1885.   581.6   o.5

Carr, Lucien. The Food of Certain American Indians and their Methods of Preparing It.   Am. Antiq. Soc. Proc.   1895.   New ser. v. 10, p. 1.
906   Am. 3   17

——— The Mounds of the Mississippi Valley Historically Considered; Memoirs of the Kentucky Geological Survey, 1883.   *Also* Smithsonian Rep't 1891.   506   K7   a 46

Cartier, Jacques. Bref Recit Voyages, 1535–36.   Tross ed.   Paris 1863.
973.18   C 24

Carver, Jonathan. Travels in the Interior Parts of North America. Phila. 1792.   917.3   C 25

Caswell, *Mrs* H. S. Our Life Among the Iroquois.   Boston 1892.

Champlain, Samuel de. Voyages of Samuel de Champlain. Reprint Prince Soc. Boston 1878.   917.1 C 351

Charlevolx, P. F. X. Hist. de la Nouvelle France. Paris 1774; trans. by Dr John G. Shea. New York 1900.   971 qC 382

Colden, Cadwallader. History of the Five Indian Nations. London 1767.

Cullen, Charles. History of Mexico. London 1787 (Translated from the Italian version by D. F. S. Clavigero).   972.01 qC 571

Creux. History of Canada.

Cyclopedia. Bailey's, Cyclopedia of American Agriculture.

De Laet, John. Description of New Netherlands. Col. N. Y. Hist. Soc. New York 1841.

De Vries, David. Journal Notes of Several Voyages. Hoorn 1655, Col. N. Y. Hist. Soc. 1841.

Gray, Asa. Manual of Botany. Ed. 6. New York 1889.   581.973 O 9

Greenhalgh. Documentary History of New York. v. 1.

Hakluyt. Collection of Voyages. London 1810.

Hariot, Thomas. Brief and True Report of a New Found Land in Virginia. Pinkerton's Voyages.

Harrington, M. R. Some Seneca Corn Foods and their Preparation. Reprinted from Am. Anthropologist. New ser. v. 10, no. 4. Lancaster 1908

——— Some Unusual Iroquois Specimens. Am. Anthropologist. Letters to author and manuscripts in N. Y. State Museum.

Harris, George H. Root Foods of the Seneca Indians. Reprinted from the Rochester Acad. of Sci. Proc. 1891. v. 1.   970.6 H 241

Heckewelder, John. History, Manners, and Customs of the Indian Nations. Rev. ed. Hist. Soc. Pa. 1876.   974.8 P 383

Hennepin, Louis. A New Discovery of a Vast Country in America. London 1698. Also edition of 1903 (Chicago). Edited by Reuben G. Thwaites.   917.3 H 396

American Folk Lore Journal. v. 18; W. M. Beauchamp. Corn Stories and Customs.   398 J 82

Kalm, Peter. Travels into North America. London 1772. *See* Pinkerton's Voyages.

Lahontan, A. L. de L. New Voyages to North America. London 1735.   917.1 L 131

Lafitau, Joseph F. Moeurs des Sauvages Ameriquains. Paris 1724.
                                                              970.1 qL 13

Lawson, John. History of Carolina. London 1714.   917.56 L 44

Lescarbot, Marc. History of New France. Champlain Soc. Pub. Toronto 1907.

Loskiel. Missions in America. London 1794.

Marchand, Henri. Translations of certain early French explorations: Manuscripts in Archeology section archives, N. Y. State Museum.

Megapolensis, Johannes. Mohawk Indians, (Korte Ontwerp van de Mahakanse Indianen of 1644). Antwerp 1651; J. B. Broadhead, translator, N. Y. Hist. Soc. Trans. Ser. 2, 1852. v. 3, pt 1.

Morgan, Louis H. Fabrics, Inventions, Implements and Utensils of the Iroquois. 5th Annual Report of the New York State Cabinet (Museum) 1852.

———— League of the Iroquois. Rochester 1851.

———— Report to the Regents of the University of the State of New York on the Articles Furnished the Indian Collection. Univ. State of N. Y. 3d Annual Rep't 1850.

———— Houses and House Life of the American Aborigines. Washington 1881.

N. Y. Historical Society. Collections, Ser. 2, v. 1, 2, 3. Proceedings. 1847, 1849.

N. Y. State Museum. Reports and bulletins, individually cited.

O'Callaghan, E. B. Documentary History of the State of New York. Albany 1849.

Ontario Archeological Rep't. Report for 1898; by David Boyle.

Palmer, Edward. Food Products of the North American Indians. U. S. Agric. Com'n Rep't 1870.

Parker, Arthur C. Erie Indian Village. N. Y. State Mus. Bul. 117. Albany 1907.

———— Secret Medicine Societies of the Seneca. Am. Anthropologist. New Ser. v. 11, no. 2.

———— Unpublished notes and manuscripts in N. Y. State Museum.

Pinkerton, John. Collection of Voyages and Travels. London 1812.
910.8 qP 65

Popular Science Monthly. What Is an Ear of Corn? Jan. 1906.
505 N 2

Prescott, William H. Conquest of Mexico. New York 1866.

Relations of the Jesuits. Jesuit Relations and Allied Documents. Burrowes Brothers ed. Edited by R. G. Thwaites. Cincinnati 1900.
971 T 42

Ruttenber, E. N. History of the Indian Tribes of Hudson's River. Albany 1872.
970.4 R 93

Sagard, Gabriel. Histoire du Canada, 1615. Tross ed. Paris 1866.
971 Sa. 1

———— Le grand Voyage Pays des Hurons. Tross ed. Paris 1865.
970.3 Sa 1

Salisbury, J. H. History and Chemical Investigation of Maize or Indian Corn. Reprinted from N. Y. State Agric. Soc. Trans. Albany 1849.

Sargent, Frederick L. Corn Plants, their Uses and Ways of Life. Boston 1899.
638 P 9

Schoolcraft, Henry. Census of the Iroquois. N. Y. State Senate Document 24. Albany 1846.

———— History of the Indian Tribes of the United States. Philadelphia 1857.

Seaver, James E. Life of Mary Jemison. Ed. by W. P. Letchworth. Ed. 6. New York 1898.

Shea, John G. Charlevoix, History of New France. New York 1900.
971 qC 382

Skinner, Alanson B. The Lenape Indians of Staten Island. Am. Mus. Nat. Hist. Anthropological Papers, v. 3. New York 1909.

———— Letters to Author.

Smith, *Capt*. John. General History of Virginia, New England and the Summer Isles. *See* Pinkerton's Voyages, v. 13.

Speck, Frank G. Personal Notes and Letters to Author.

Stites, Sara Henry. Economics of the Iroquois. Bryn Mawr Col. Monogr. v. 1, no. 3. Bryn Mawr 1905. 97 O.3 St. 5

Stone, William L. Life of Joseph Brant. v. 2. New 1838. 970.2 B 731

Sturtevant, E. L. Varieties of Maize. Am. Nat. 1884. p. 532.

Sullivan, *Gen*. John. Journals of Sullivan's Campaign. Secretary of State, Albany 1887.

Swetland, Luke. A Narrative of the Captivity of Luke Swetland, 1778–1779 among the Seneca Indians. Waterville, N. Y. 1875. 970.3 Sw. 4

Thomas, Cyrus. Mound Explorations of the Bureau of Ethnology. Bureau of Ethnology An. Rep't 1890. 572.97 qO1 v. 12

Thwaites, R. G. Hennepin's A New Discovery; ed. by R. G. Thwaites, Chicago 1903. 917.3 H 396

——— Compilation of Jesuit Relations.

Trumbull, Benjamin. History of Connecticut. Hartford 1797, Reprinted at New London 1898.

United States Dep't of Agriculture. Foods of the North American Indians. Dep't Agric. An. Rep't, 1870. 630.6 KO v. 22

United States Bureau of Ethnology. Handbook of American Indians. Bul. 30. 1907.

——— Annual Reports, *see* citations.

Van der Donck. New Netherlands. Amsterdam 1616; N. Y. Hist. Soc. Proc. Reprint Ser. 2. 1841. v. 1.

Williams, Roger. Key into the Language of the Indians. Reprint, R. I. Hist. Soc. Col. v. 1. Providence 1827.

Willoughby, Charles. Virginia Indians of the 17th Century. Am. Anthropologist. New ser. v. 9. Lancaster 1907.

Wilson, *Gen*. James Grant. Arent Van Curler and His Journals, 1634–35. Reprint Am. Hist. Soc. An. Rep't. 1895.

INDEX

Abbreviations, 7.
Acorns, 99, 101.
Adair, James, cited, 23, 30, 31, 32, 47, 65, 66, 70, 75, 91, 93, 110.
Alphabet and abbreviations, 6, 7.
American Anthropologist, cited, 110.
American Antiquarian Society, cited, 110.
American Folk Lore Journal, cited, 111.
American Historical Association, cited 110.
Apples, 94, 95.
Arrowhead, 105, 108.
Artichokes, 105.
Ash sifter, 51.
Asparagus, wild, 93.

Bailey, L. H., cited, 11, 110, 111.
Baked cob-corn in the husk, 68.
Baked green corn, 67.
Baked scraped corn, 68.
Ball players pudding, 79.
Bark bread bowl, 51–52.
Bark foods, 102–4.
Bark ladle, figure, 56.
Bartram, John, cited, 64, 65, 92, 110.
Baskets, 58.
Beads, corn kernels used as, 87.
Beans and bean foods, 20, 37, 38, 89–90, 91.
Bear root, 109.
Bear's pudding, 78.
Beatly, Lieut. Erkuries, quoted, 42.
Beauchamp, W. M., cited, 36, 38, 88, 110.
Beechnuts, 99.
Begnall, Capt. Richard, cited, 42.
Berries, list, 95–96.
Berry-picking industry, description, 98.
Berry sprouts, 93.
Berrylike foods, 94–99.

Beverly, Robert, cited, 11, 26, 29, 41, 57, 71, 77, 78, 101, 110.
Black raspberries, 95, 97.
Black walnuts, 99.
Blackberries, 95, 97, 99.
Blue corn, 42.
Blueberries, 96, 97.
Boiled corn bread, 69.
Boiled green corn, 67–68.
Bossee, cited, 24.
Bowl, eating, 54.
Boyle, David, cited, 65, 110.
Bozman, J. L., cited, 110.
Bradford, cited, 14, 110.
Brant, cited, 94.
Brass kettles, 46.
Bread, boiled, 69; figure, 70; leaf bread, 66.
Bread bowl, 55; bark, 51–52; wooden, 52.
Bread paddle, 52.
Brodhead, Daniel, quoted, 19.
Brown, D. J., cited, 9, 110.
Brown, P. A., cited, 9, 110.
Buffalo dance pudding, 78.
Burdock, 93.
Burnaby, Rev. Andrew, cited, 110.
Burrowes, Maj. John, journal, 19.
Butternuts, 99, 101.

Camerarius, cited, 10.
Candolle, A. L. P. de, cited, 9, 10, 110.
Carr, Lucien, cited, 5, 17, 21, 22, 68, 110.
Carrying basket, 58.
Cartier, Jacques, cited, 15, 34, 42, 110.
Carver, Jonathan, cited, 68, 107, 110.
Caryopsis, uses of, 87–88.
Caswell, Mrs H. S., cited, 110.
Cat-tail, 105, 108.
Ceremonial allusions to corn, 36–40.
Ceremonial foods, 78–79.
Champlain, Samuel de, cited, 17, 24, 34, 36, 105, 111.

115

BOOK TWO

The Code of Handsome Lake,
the Seneca Prophet

Contents

Plate I

Photo 1900 by A. C. Parker

The old log Long House on the Cattaraugus reservation formerly situated on the Buffalo "Plank road"

The Code of Handsome Lake, the Seneca Prophet

ARTHUR C. PARKER

INTRODUCTION

HANDSOME LAKE'S RELIGION

The Gai'wiio' is the record of the teachings of Handsome Lake, the Seneca prophet, and purports to be an exact exposition of the precepts that he taught during a term of sixteen years, ending with his death in 1815. It is the basis of the so-called " new religion " of the Six Nations and is preached or recited at all the annual midwinter festivals on the various Iroquois reservations in New York and Ontario that have adherents. These reservations are Onondaga, Tonawanda, Cattaraugus and Allegany in New York and Grand River and Muncytown in Ontario.

There are six authorized " holders " of the Gai'wiio'[1] among whom are John Gibson (Ganio'dai'io') and Edward Cornplanter (Soson'dowă), Senecas, and Frank Logan (Adodār'ho), Onondaga. Chief Cornplanter is by far the most conservative though Chief Gibson seems to have the greater store of explanatory matter, often interpolating it during his exposition. Chief Logan is a devout adherent of his religion and watches the waning of his prophet's teachings with grave concern. His grief is like that of Hiawatha (Haiyoⁿ'wĕntha) and inclines him to leave Onondaga for a region where the prophet will not be jeered.

---

[1] Key to pronunciation of Indian words on page 139. See also Glossary, page 140.

The stated times for the proclaiming of the Gai'wiio' are at the Six Nations' meeting in September and at the midwinter thanksgiving in the moon Nĭsko'wŭknĭ, between January 15th and February 15th. At such times the Oñgwe"oñwekā or "faithful Indians" send for an expounder paying his traveling expenses and entertaining him during his stay. Usually reservations "exchange" preachers, Cornplanter going to Grand River or Onondaga and Chief Gibson to Cattaraugus or Allegany.

The time consumed in reciting the Gai'wiio' is always three days. At noon each day the expositor stops, for the sun is in midheaven and ready to descend. All sacred things must be done sĕdĕ'tciä, *early in the morning.* Before sunrise each morning of the preaching the preacher stands at the fireplace in the long house and sings a song known as the Sun Song. This is an obedience to a command of the prophet who promised that it should insure good weather for the day. "The wind always dies down when I sing that song," affirms Chief Cornplanter.

During the recital of the Gai'wiio' the preacher stands at the fireplace which serves as the altar. Sitting beside him is an assistant or some officer of the rites who holds a white wampum strand.[1] A select congregation sits on benches placed across the long house but the majority use the double row of seats around the walls. The women wear shawls over their heads and during affecting parts of the story hide their faces to conceal the tears. Some of the men, stirred to emotion, likewise are moved to tears but are unable to hide them. Such emotion once detected by the auditors sometimes becomes contagious and serves as the means of scores repledging their allegiance to the old religion. In 1909, for example, 136 Allegany Senecas promised Chief Cornplanter that they would stop drinking liquor and obey the commands of Handsome Lake. Visiting Canadian Oneida Indians at the Grand River ceremonies, as a result of such a "revival," petitioned for a visit of the Gai'wiio' preachers several years ago, saying that a portion of the Oneida of the Thames wished to return to the "old way." This some of them have done but they complain of the persecution of their Christian tribesmen who threatened to burn their council house. In other places the case seems different and the "prophet's cause" is not espoused with much enthusiasm by the younger element to whom the white man's world and thought present a greater appeal.

---

[1] The original Handsome Lake belt is still displayed at the religious council at Tonawanda. (See plate 15.)

Those who live in communities in which the prophet's word is still strong are drawn to the ceremonies and to the recitals because it is a part of their social system.

·Its great appeal to the older people is that it presents in their own language a system of moral precepts and exhortations that they can readily understand. The prophet, who is called *" our great teacher "* (sedwa'gowā'në'), was a man of their own blood, and the ground that he traversed was their ancestral domain. Patriotism and religious emotion mingle, and, when the story of the " great wrongs " is remembered, spur on a ready acceptance. The fraudulent treaty of Buffalo of 1838, for example, caused many of the Buffalo Senecas to move to the Cattaraugus reservation. Here they settled at Ganŭn'dasē' or Newtown, then a desolate wilderness. Their bitter wrongs made them hate white men and to resist all missionary efforts. Today there is no mission chapel at Newtown. All attempts have failed.[1] Whether future ones will readily succeed is conjectural. The Indian there clings to his prophet and heeds the word of his teacher. At Cold Spring on the Allegany is another center of the " old time people." On the Tonawanda reservation this element is chiefly centered " down below " at the long house. On the Onondaga reservation the long house stands in the middle of the Onondaga village and the Ganŭñg'sĭsnē'ha (long house people) are distributed all over the reservation but perhaps chiefly on Hemlock road. It is an odd sight, provoking strange thoughts, to stand at the tomb of the prophet near the council house and watch each day the hundreds of automobiles that fly by over the State road. The Tuscarora and St Regis Indians are all nominally Christians and they have no long houses.

The present form of the Gai'wiio' was determined by a council of its preachers some fifty years ago. They met at Cold Spring, the old home of Handsome Lake, and compared their versions. Several differences were found and each preacher thought his version the correct one. At length Chief John Jacket, a Cattaraugus Seneca, and a man well versed in the lore of his people, was chosen to settle forever the words and the form of the Gai'wiio'. This he did by writing it out in the Seneca language by the method taught by Rev. Asher Wright, the Presbyterian missionary. The preachers assembled again, this time, according to Cornplanter, at Cattaraugus where they memorized the parts in which they were faulty. The original text was written on letter paper and now is entirely de-

---

[1] See Caswell, Our Life Among the Iroquois. Boston, 1898.

stroyed. Chief Jacket gave it to Henry Stevens and Chief Stevens passed it on to Chief Cornplanter who after he had memorized the teachings became careless and lost the papers sheet by sheet. Fearing that the true form might become lost Chief Cornplanter in 1903 began to rewrite the Gai'wiio' in an old minute book of the Seneca Lacrosse Club. He had finished the historical introduction when the writer discovered what he had done. He was implored to finish it and give it to the State of New York for preservation. He was at first reluctant, fearing criticism, but after a council with the leading men he consented to do so. He became greatly interested in the progress of the translation and is eager for the time to arrive when all white men may have the privilege of reading the " wonderful message " of the great prophet.

The translation was made chiefly by William Bluesky, the native lay preacher of the Baptist church. It was a lesson in religious toleration to see the Christian preacher and the " Instructor of the Gai'wiio' " side by side working over the sections of the code, for beyond a few smiles at certain passages, in which Chief Cornplanter himself shared, Mr Bluesky never showed but that he reverenced every message and revelation of the four messengers.

HANDSOME LAKE

Handsome Lake, the Seneca prophet, was born in 1735 in the Seneca village of Conawagas (Gānoⁿ'wagĕs) on the Genesee river opposite the present town of Avon, Livingston county. He is described by Buffalo Tom Jemison as a middle-sized man, slim and unhealthy looking. He was a member of one of the *noble* (hoya'nĕ') families in which the title of Ganio'dai'io' or Ska'niadar'io' is vested, thus holding the most honored Seneca title. What his warrior name was is not known and neither is it known just when he received the name and title by which he later became known. It is known, however, that he belonged to the Turtle clan. Later he was "borrowed" by the Wolves and reared by them. His half brother was the celebrated Cornplanter.

The general story of his life may be gleaned from a perusal of his code, there being nothing of any consequence known of his life up to the time of his "vision." In 1794 his name appears on a treaty but whether he took active part in the debates that led up to it is not known. It is known from tradition and from his own story that he was a dissolute person and a miserable victim of the drink habit. The loss of the Genesee country caused him to go with his tribesmen to the Allegany river settlements: Here he became afflicted with a wasting disease that was aggravated by his continued use of the white man's fire water. For four years he lay a helpless invalid. His bare cabin scarcely afforded him shelter but later he was nursed by his married daughter who seems to have treated him with affection. His sickness afforded him much time for serious meditation and it is quite possible that some of his precepts are the result of this opportunity. His own condition could not fail to impress him with the folly of using alcoholic drink and the wild whoops of the drunken raftsmen continually reminded him of the "demon's" power over thought and action. In the foreword of his revelation he tells how he became as dead, and of the visitation of the "four beings" who revealed the will of the Creator.

After this first revelation he seemed to recover and immediately began to tell the story of his visions. His first efforts were to condemn the use of the "*first word*" or the white man's "onĕ'gă." He became a temperance reformer but his success came not from an appeal to reason but to religious instinct. The ravages of intemperance for a century had made serious inroads on the domestic and social life of his people. It had demoralized their national life and caused his brother chiefs to barter land for the means of a debauch. It threatened the extinction of his people. Such were the factors that induced the revelation.

He was a man past the prime of life, a man weakened by disease and drunkenness. Yet he assumed the rôle of teacher and prophet. In two years' time his efforts were conducive of so much reform that they attracted the attention of President Jefferson who caused Secretary of War Dearborn to write a letter commending the teachings of Handsome Lake. The Seneca construed this as a recognition of the prophet's right to teach and prophesy. The nature of the document is revealed in the following letter, a copy of which is in the possession of every religious chief of the Six Nations:

Brothers — The President is pleased with seeing you all in good health, after so long a journey, and he rejoices in his heart that one of your own people has been employed to make you sober, good and happy; and that he is so well disposed to give you good advice, and to set before you so good examples.

Brothers — If all the red people follow the advice of your friend and teacher, the Handsome Lake, and in future will be sober, honest, industrious and good, there can be no doubt but the Great Spirit will take care of you and make you happy.

This letter came as one of the results of Handsome Lake's visit in 1802, to Washington with a delegation of Seneca and Onondaga chiefs. The successful results of his two years' ministry became more fruitful as time went on. In 1809 a number of members of the Society of Friends visiting Onondaga left the following record of the effects of the prophet's teachings: "We were informed, not only by themselves, but by the interpreter, that they totally refrained from the use of ardent spirits for about nine years, and that none of the natives will touch it."

The success of Handsome Lake's teachings did much to crystallize the Iroquois as a distinct social group. The encroachments of civilization had demoralized the old order of things. The old beliefs, though still held, had no coherence. The ancient system had no longer definite organization and thus no specific hold.

The frauds which the Six Nations had suffered, the loss of land and of ancient seats had reduced them to poverty and disheartened them. The crushing blow of Sullivan's campaign was yet felt and the wounds then inflicted were fresh. The national order of the Confederacy was destroyed. Poverty, the sting of defeat, the loss of ancestral homes, the memory of broken promises and the hostility

Plate 2

So-son-do-wa or Edward Cornplanter, the Seneca teacher of Handsome
Lake's Code

Plate 3

The Newtown Long House, Cattaraugus Reservation. Photograph by W. N. Fenton, 1955

The Tonawanda Seneca Long House, near Akron, N.Y. Photograph by W. N. Fenton, 1933

of the white settlers all conspired to bring despair. There is not much energy in a despairing nation who see themselves hopeless and alone, the greedy eyes of their conquerors fastened on the few acres that remain to them. It was little wonder that the Indian sought forgetfulness in the trader's rum.

As a victim of such conditions, Handsome Lake stalked from the gloom holding up as a beacon of hope his divine message, the Gai'wiio'. He became in spite of his detractors a commanding figure. He created a new system, a thing to think about, a thing to discuss, a thing to believe. His message, whether false or true, was a creation of their own and afforded a nucleus about which they could cluster themselves and fasten their hopes. A few great leaders such as Red Jacket denounced him as an imposter but this only afforded the necessary resistant element. The angels then conveniently revealed that Red Jacket was a schemer and a seller of land and an unhappy wretch doomed to carry burdens of soil through eternity as a punishment for perfidy. This was enough to create a prejudice among the Indians and one that lasts to this day among all classes of the reservation Iroquois. A few others endeavored to expose the prophet but this action only created a large faction that stood strongly for him.

Whatever may be the merits of the prophet's teachings, they created a revolution in Iroquois religious life. With the spread of his doctrines the older religious system was overturned until today it is to be doubted that a single adherent remains. Handsome Lake's followers were few at first. He was despised, ridiculed and subject to bodily insults. Certain failures to live up to a preconceived idea of what a prophet should be caused a continual persecution. Cornplanter, his half brother, continually harassed him, as may be seen in the relation. Some of his failures, real or fancied, caused calumny to be heaped upon him and they are current today among those inclined to scoff. It is said that he learned his ideas of morality from his nephew, Henry Obail (Abeal), who had been at school in Philadelphia. Henry, it is said, took him up in the mountains and explained the Christain Bible to him, thus giving him the idea of devising the Gai'wiio'. Other tales are that he failed to find the great serpent in the bed of the Allegany river though he pretended to locate it and charge it with having spread disease among the people, and that he erected an idol on an island in the river, a thing which from more authentic accounts he did not do.

Previous to his residence at Tonawanda he had lived ten years at Cornplanter's town and two years at Cold Spring. At the latter place he made so many enemies that he resolved to leave with his followers. This was in about 1812. With him went his chief followers and his family, among them his grandson Sos'hēowă who later became his successor.

Sos'hēowă was born in 1774 in the old town of Ganowa'gĕs, the home of both Cornplanter and Handsome Lake. Lewis H. Morgan, who knew him well, describes him as "an eminently pure and virtuous man . . . devoted . . . to the duties of his office, as the spiritual guide and teacher of the Iroquois."

Morgan gives a full account of the recitation of Sosehawa at the mourning council at Tonawanda in 1848[1] and credits the translation to Sosehawa's grandson, Ely S. Parker (Ha-sa-no-an-da).[2]

During the prophet's four years' stay at Tonawanda he became many times discouraged, "reluctant to tell," and though the people gradually became more friendly, he seemed loath at times to proclaim his revelations. Some Christian Indians have explained this as caused by an uneasy conscience that came with greater knowledge of the white man's religion but there is no evidence of this. During this stay he was invited to visit the Onondaga and this he did, though according to his visions it necessitated the singing of his "third song," which meant that he should die. In a vision which he related he saw the four messengers who said "They have stretched out their hands pleading for you to come and they are your own people at Onondaga" (section 122).

When the word was given, Handsome Lake with a few chosen followers started to walk to Onondaga. His prediction of his own death, however, caused many more to join the party when it became definitely known he had started. The first camping spot mentioned is at the old village, Ganon'wa'gĕs. Here upon retiring he commanded the company to assemble "early in the morning." At the morning gathering he announced a vision. It had been of a pathway covered with grass. At the next camp, at Ganundasa'ga, his vision was of a woman speaking. On the borders of Onondaga he discovered that he had lost a favorite knife and went back to find it. He was evidently much depressed and approached Onondaga with a reluctance that almost betokened fear. Upon his arrival he

---

[1] Morgan, League, p. 233, Rochester, 1851.

[2] Later known as Dionī'hogä'wĕ, *Door Keeper,* a sachem of the Seneca. Parker was Morgan's collaborator in writing the League of the Iroquois.

Plate 4

A typical family of the Seneca branch of the " vanishing race "

Photos by M. R. Harrington

A typical family at Newtown, Cattaraugus reservation. These people are all followers of Handsome Lake.

Plate 5

Onondaga Long House, Onondaga Reservation, Nedrow, N.Y. Photograph by W. N. Fenton, ca. 1940

St. Regis Mohawk Long House, N.Y. Photograph by W. N. Fenton, 1939

was unable to address the people because of his distress, so that it was said, " Our meeting is only a gathering about the fireplace." A game of lacrosse was played to cheer him but he could only respond to the honor by saying: " I will soon go to my new home. Soon will I step into the new world for there is a plain pathway before me leading there." He repaired to his cabin at the foot of the hill, in sight of the council house and there after a most distressing illness " commenced his walk " over the path that had appeared before him. He was buried under the council house with impressive ceremonies and his tomb may still be seen though the house has been removed. A granite monument, erected by the Six Nations, marks his resting place.

Handsome Lake lived to see his people divided into two factions, one that clung to the old order and one that followed him. After his death the older order gradually faded out of existence, either coming over to the New Religion or embracing Christianity. Thus by the time of the Civil War in 1861 there were only the two elements, the Christians and the followers of Handsome Lake. They stand so arrayed today but with the " new religionists " gradually diminishing in number. The force of Handsome Lake's teaching, however, is still felt and affects in some way all the New York reservations, except perhaps St Regis.

Handsome Lake as the founder of a religious system occupied such a position that his followers place implicit confidence in that system whatever his personal weaknesses and failures may have been.

" He made mistakes," said Chief Cornplanter, " many mistakes, so it is reported, but he was only a man and men are liable to commit errors. Whatever he did and said of himself is of no consequence. What he did and said by the direction of the four messengers is everything — it is our religion. Ganiodaiio was weak in many points and sometimes afraid to do as the messengers told him. He was almost an unwilling servant. He made no divine claims, he did not pose as infallible nor even truly virtuous. He merely proclaimed the Gai'wiio' and that is what we follow, not him. We do not worship him, we worship one great Creator. We honor and revere our prophet and leader, we revere the four messengers who watch over us — but the Creator alone do we worship." Such is the argument of his followers.

PRESENT EFFECTS OF HANDSOME LAKE'S TEACHING

There is no record of Handsome Lake's visiting Tuscarora, Oneida or St Regis. The result is that these reservations contain only Indians who are nominally Christian. The Oneida are virtually citizens, the Tuscarora as capable of being so as any community of whites, and the St Regis progressive enough not only to use all their own lands but to rent from the whites. Their " Indianess " is largely gone. They have no Indian customs though they are affected by Indian folk-thought and exist as Indian communities, governing themselves and receiving annuities. Their material culture is now largely that of the whites about them and they are Indians only because they dwell in an Indian reservation, possess Indian blood and speak an Iroquois dialect.

In contrast to these reservations where the Indian has become " whitemanized " stand out the reservations of the Seneca and Onondaga. On the latter the folk-ways and the " Indian way of thinking " struggle with the white man's civilization for supremacy. The Indian of the old way is arrayed against the Indian of the new way. The conservative Indian calls his Christian brother a traitor to his race, a man ashamed of his ancestors, a man who condones all the wrongs the white man has done his people, and a man who is at best an imitator and a poor one. On the other hand the Christain Indian calls his " feather wearing " (Adïstowäe') brother, " a blind man in the wilderness," a nonprogressive, behind the times, a man hopelessly struggling against fate, a heathen and a pagan. Even so, the followers of Handsome Lake constitute an influential element and the other Indians are affected by their beliefs whether they are willing or not. As was remarked in the beginning, Handsome Lake crystallized as a social unit the people whom he taught and those who follow him today constitute a unit that holds itself at variance with the social and accepted economic systems of the white communities about them. They assert that they have a perfect right to use their own system. They argue that the white man's teachings are not consistent with his practice and thus only one of their schemes for deceiving them. They assert that they wish to remain Indians and have a right to be so and to believe their own prophet. They are largely instrumental in conserving the systems peculiarly Indian and though they are a minority they control a majority of the offices in the nations to which they belong. Among the Onondaga and Tonawanda Seneca they hold most of the offices. In connection with the Allegany and Cattaraugus Seneca I use the word control, advisedly, since there may be times when the majority of councilors may be of the Christian party. Even so, the " conservative " party controls enough to maintain the system that they deem right.

When their poverty is urged as an argument against their religion and social system they assert that the true follower of the prophet will be poor and suffer much in this world but that his condition in the " new world above the sky " will be in direct contrast. They therefore esteem poverty, lowly surroundings and sickness as a sure indication of a rich heavenly reward and point to the better material surroundings and wealth of their brethren of the white man's way as an evidence that the devil has bought them.

The writer of this sketch has no complaint against the simple folk who have long been his friends. For a greater portion of his lifetime he has mingled with them, lived in their homes and received many honors from them. He has attended their ceremonies, heard their instructors and learned much of the old-time lore. Never has he been more royally entertained than by them, never was hospitality so genuine, never was gratitude more earnest, never were friends more sincere. There is virtue in their hearts and a sincerity and frankness that is refreshing. If only there were no engulfing " new way " and no modern rush, no need for progress, there could scarcely be a better devised system than theirs. It was almost perfectly fitted for the conditions which it was designed to meet, but now the new way has surrounded them, everything which they have and use in the line of material things, save a few simple maize foods and their ceremonial paraphernalia, is the product of the white man's hand and brain. The social and economic and moral order all about them is the white man's, not theirs. How long can they oppose their way to the overwhelming forces of the modern world and exist? How long will they seek to meet these overwhelming forces with those their ancestors devised but devised not with a knowledge of what the future would require? My Indian friends will answer, " Of these things we know nothing; we know only that the Great Ruler will care for us as long as we are faithful." Asked about the clothes they wear, the houses they live in, the long house they worship in, they reply, "All these things may be made of the white man's material but they are outside things. Our religion is not one of paint or feathers; it is a thing of the heart." That is the answer; it is a thing of the heart — who can change it?

HOW THE WHITE RACE CAME TO AMERICA AND WHY THE GAIWIIO BECAME A NECESSITY

RELATED BY SO-SON-DO-WA

Now this happened a long time ago and across the great salt sea, odji'′ke'dāgi′ga, that stretches east. There is, so it seems, a world there and soil like ours. There in the great queen's country where swarmed many people — so many that they crowded upon one another and had no place for hunting — there lived a great queen. Among her servants was a young preacher of the queen's religion, so, it is said.

Now this happened. The great queen requested the preacher to clean some old volumes which she had concealed in a hidden chest. So he obeyed and when he had cleaned the last book, which was at the bottom of the chest, he opened it and looked about and listened, for truly he had no right to read the book and wanted no one to detect him. He read. It was a great book and told him many things which he never knew before. Therefore he was greatly worried. He read of a great man who had been a prophet and the son of the Great Ruler. He had been born on the earth and the white men to whom he preached killed him. Now moreover the prophet had promised to return and become the King. In three days he was to come and then in forty to start his kingdom. This did not happen as his followers had expected and so they despaired. Then said one chief follower, " Surely he will come again sometime, we must watch for him."

Then the young preacher became worried for he had discovered that his god was not on earth to see. He was angry moreover because his teachers had deceived him. So then he went to the chief of preachers and asked him how it was that he had deceived him. Then the chief preacher said, " Seek him out and you will find him for indeed we think he does live on earth." Even so, his heart was angry but he resolved to seek.

On the morning of the next day he looked out from the opening of his room and saw out in the river a beautiful island and he marveled that he had never seen it before. He continued to gaze and as he did he saw among the trees a castle of gold and he marveled that he had not seen the castle of gold before. Then he said, " So beautiful a castle on so beautiful an isle must indeed be the

Plate 6

Graves near the Onondaga Long House near Six Nations, P. O. Ontario. In the lower right corner the charred embers of the grave fire may be seen.

Sour Springs (Upper Cayuga) Long House, Six Nations Reserve, Canada. Photograph by W. N. Fenton, 1945

Plate 7

Seneca Long House on Six Nations reservation, Brant county, Ontario

abode of him whom I seek." Immediately he put on his clothes and went to the men who had taught him and they wondered and said, " Indeed it must be as you say." So then together they went to the river and when they came to the shore they saw that it was spanned by a bridge of shining gold. Then one of the great preachers fell down and read from his book a long prayer and arising he turned his back upon the island and fled for he was afraid to meet the lord. Then with the young man the other crossed the bridge and he knelt on the grass and he cried loud and groaned his prayer but when he arose to his feet he too fled and would not look again at the house — the castle of gold.

Then was the young man disgusted and boldly he strode toward the house to attend to the business which he had in mind. He did not cry or pray and neither did he fall to his knees for he was not afraid. He knocked at the door and a handsome smiling man welcomed him in and said, "Do not be afraid of me." Then the smiling man in the castle of gold said, " I have wanted a young man such as you for some time. You are wise and afraid of nobody. Those older men were fools and would not have listened to me (direct) though they might listen to some one whom I had instructed. Listen to me and most truly you shall be rich. Across the ocean that lies toward the sunset is another world and a great country and a people whom you have never seen. Those people are virtuous, they have no unnatural evil habits and they are honest. A great reward is yours if you will help me. Here are five things that men and women enjoy; take them to these people and make them as white men are. Then shall you be rich and powerful and you may become the chief of all great preachers here."

So then the young man took the bundle containing the *five things* and made the bargain. He left the island and looking back saw that the bridge had disappeared and before he had turned his head the castle had gone and then as he looked the island itself vanished.

Now then the young man wondered if indeed he had seen his lord for his mind had been so full of business that he had forgotten to ask. So he opened his bundle of five things and found a flask of rum, a pack of playing cards, a handful of coins, a violin and a decayed leg bone. Then he thought the things very strange and he wondered if indeed his lord would send such gifts to the people across the water of the salt lake; but he remembered his promise.

The young man looked about for a suitable man in whom to confide his secret and after some searching he found a man named Columbus and to him he confided the story. Then did Columbus secure some big canoes and raise up wings and he sailed away. He sailed many days and his warriors became angry and cried that the chief who led them was a deceiver. They planned to behead him but he heard of the plan and promised that on the next day he would discover the new country. The next morning came and then did Columbus discover America. Then the boats turned back and reported their find to the whole world. Then did great ships come, a good many. Then did they bring many bundles of the five things and spread the gifts to all the men of the great earth island.

Then did the invisible man of the river island laugh and then did he say, " These cards will make them gamble away their wealth and idle their time; this money will make them dishonest and covetous and they will forget their old laws; this fiddle will make them dance with their arms about their wives and bring about a time of tattling and idle gossip; this rum will turn their minds to foolishness and they will barter their country for baubles; then will this secret poison eat the life from their blood and crumble their bones." So said the invisible man and he was Hanïsse'ono, the evil one.

Now all this was done and when afterward he saw the havoc and the misery his work had done he said, " I think I have made an enormous mistake for I did not dream that these people would suffer so." Then did even the devil himself lament that his evil had been so great.

So after the swarms of white men came and misery was thrust upon the Ongwe-oweh the Creator was sorry for his own people whom he had molded from the soil of the earth of this Great Island, and he spoke to his four messengers and many times they tried to tell right men the revelations of the Creator but none would listen. Then they found our head man sick. Then they heard him speak to the sun and to the moon and they saw his sickness. Then they knew that he suffered because of the cunning evils that Hanïsse'ono had given the Ongwe-oweh. So then they knew that he was the one. He was the one who should hear and tell Gai'wiio'. But when Ganio'dai'io' spoke the evil being ceased his lament and sought to obstruct Gai'wiio', for he claimed to be master.

Plate 8

Long House of the Lower Cayuga, Grand River Reservation. It is here
that the feasts and thanksgivings for the products of the fields are held.

Onondaga Long House, Six Nations Reserve (New Building). Photograph by W. N. Fenton, ca. 1939

Plate 9

Tomb of Handsome Lake, near Onondaga council house

The Gai'wiio' came from Hodiänok'doo^n Hĕd'iohe', the Great Ruler, to the Hadiöyä''geono^n, the four messengers. From them it was transmitted to Ganio'dai'io', Handsome Lake who taught it to Skandyo^n''gwadï (Owen Blacksnake) and to his own grandson, Sos'heowă (James Johnson). Blacksnake taught it to Henry Stevens (Ganishando), who taught it to Soson'dowa, Edward Cornplanter. " So I know that I have the true words and I preach them," adds Cornplanter.

NOW THIS IS GAIWIIO

The beginning was in Yai"kni [May], early in the moon, in the year 1800.

It commences now.

A TIME OF TROUBLE

The place is[1] Ohi'io' [on the Allegany river], in Diono'sade'gĭ [Cornplanter village].

Now it is the harvest time, so he[2] said.

Now a party of people move. They go down in canoes the Allegany river. They plan to hunt throughout the autumn and the winter seasons.

Now they land at Ganowoñ'goⁿ [Warren, Pa.] and set up camp.

The weather changes and they move again. They go farther down the river. The ice melts opening up the stream and so they go still farther down. They land at Diondēgă [Pittsburgh]. It is a little village of white people [literally, " our younger brethren "[3]]. Here they barter their skins, dried meat and fresh game for strong drink. They put a barrel of it in their canoes. Now all the canoes are lashed together like a raft.

Now all the men become filled with strong drink (gonigä'nongi). They yell and sing like demented people. Those who are in the middle canoes do this.[4]

Now they are homeward bound.

Now when they come to where they had left their wives and children these embark to return home. They go up Cornplanter creek, Awe'gäoⁿ.

Now that the party is home the men revel in strong drink and are very quarrelsome. Because of this the families become frightened and move away for safety. So from many places in the bushlands camp fires send up their smoke.

Now the drunken men run yelling through the village and there is no one there except the drunken men. Now they are beastlike

---

[1] The present tense is always used by Chief Cornplanter.

[2] The narrator, Handsome Lake.

[3] The Seneca term is Honio"oⁿ', meaning "our younger brother."

[4] The intoxicated men were put in the middle canoes to prevent their jumping into the water. The more sober men paddled from the outer canoes. This debauchery was common among the Six Nations at the beginning of the 19th century.

Plate 10

From a drawing by Jesse Cornplanter

The "Time of Trouble" at Cornplanter's village. (See p. 20.)

Plate II

The sick man meditating. (See p. 21.)

From a drawing by Jesse Cornplanter

and run about without clothing and all have weapons to injure those whom they meet.

Now there are no doors left in the houses for they have all been kicked off. So, also, there are no fires in the village and have not been for many days. Now the men full of strong drink have trodden in the fireplaces. They alone track there and there are no fires and their footprints are in all the fireplaces.

Now the dogs yelp and cry in all the houses for they are hungry. So this is what happens.[1]

THE SICK MAN

And now furthermore a man becomes sick. Some strong power holds him.

Now as he lies in sickness he meditates and longs that he might rise again and walk upon the earth. So he implores the Great Ruler to give him strength that he may walk upon this earth again. And then he thinks how evil and loathsome he is before the Great Ruler. He thinks how he has been evil ever since he had strength in this world and done evil ever since he had been able to work. But notwithstanding, he asks that he may again walk.

So now this is what he sang: O'gi'we,[2] Ye'ondă'thă,[3] and Gone'owoⁿ.[4] Now while he sings he has strong drink with him.

Now it comes to his mind that perchance evil has arisen because of strong drink and he resolves to use it nevermore. Now he continually thinks of this every day and every hour. Yea, he continually thinks of this. Then a time comes and he craves drink again for he thinks that he can not recover his strength without it.

Now two ways he thinks: what once he did and whether he will ever recover.

THE TWO WAYS HE THINKS

Now he thinks of the things he sees in the daylight.

The sunlight comes in and he sees it and he says, "The Creator made this sunshine." So he thinks. Now when he thinks of the sunshine and of the Creator who made it he feels a new hope within him and he feels that he may again be on his feet in this world.

Now he had previously given up hope of life but now he begs to see the light of another day. He thinks thus for night is coming.

---

[1] See plate 10.
[2] The Death chant.
[3] The Women's song.
[4] The Harvest song, see p. 95.

So now he makes an invocation that he may be able to endure the night.

Now he lives through the night and sees another day. So then he prays that he may see the night and it is so. Because of these things he now believes that the Great Ruler has heard him and he gives him thanks.

Now the sick man's bed is beside the fire. At night he looks up through the chimney hole and sees the stars and he thanks the Great Ruler that he can see them for he knows that he, the Creator, has made them.[1]

Now it comes to him that because of these new thoughts he may obtain help to arise from his bed and walk again in this world. Then again he despairs that he will ever see the new day because of his great weakness. Then again he has confidence that he will see the new day, and so he lives and sees it.

For everything he sees he is thankful. He thinks of the Creator and thanks him for the things he sees. Now he hears the birds singing and he thanks the Great Ruler for their music.

So then he thinks that a thankful heart will help him.

Now this man has been sick four years but he feels that he will now recover.

And the name of the sick man is Ganio'dai'io'[2] a council chief [Hoya'ne].

THE STRANGE DEATH OF THE SICK MAN

Now at this time the daughter of the sick man and her husband are sitting outside the house in the shed and the sick man is within alone. The door is ajar. Now the daughter and her husband are cleaning beans for the planting. Suddenly they hear the sick man exclaim, " Niio'! "[3] Then they hear him rising in his bed and they think how he is but yellow skin and dried bones from four years of sickness in bed. Now they hear him walking over the floor toward the door. Then the daughter looks up and sees her father coming out of doors. He totters and she rises quickly to catch him but he falls dying. Now they lift him up and carry him back within the house and dress him for burial.

Now he is dead.

---

[1] See plate 11.

[2] Handsome Lake, one of the fifty hereditary sachems, or lords. Hoya'ne means, *perfect one* or *noble*, and is translated *lord* by the Canadian Six Nations. See Hale, Book of Rites, p. 31, footnote.

[3] Meaning, *So be it.*

THE PEOPLE GATHER ABOUT THE DEAD MAN

Then the daughter says to her husband, "Run quickly and notify his nephew, Tää'wŏnyăs,[1] that he who has lain so many years in bed has gone. Bid him come immediately."

So the husband runs to carry the message to Tää'wŏnyăs. And Tää'wŏnyăs says, "Truly so. Now hasten to Gaiänt'wakă,[2] the brother of the dead man and say that he who lay sick for so many years is dead. So now go and say this."

So the husband goes alone to where Gaiänt'wakă lives and when he has spoken the wife says, "Gaiänt'wakă is at the island planting." So he goes there and says, "Gaiänt'wakă your brother is dead. He who was sick for so many years is dead. Go at once to his bed."

Then Gaiänt'wakă answers, "Truly, but first I must finish covering this small patch of seed. Then when I hoe it over I will come."

Now he who notifies is Hătgwi'yot, the husband of the daughter of Ganio'dai'io'. So now he returns home.

Now everyone hearing of the death of the sick man goes to where he lies.

Now first comes Tää'wŏnyăs. He touches the dead man on every part of his body. Now he feels a warm spot on his chest and then Tää'wŏnyăs says, "Hold back your sadness, friends," for he had discovered the warm spot and because of this he tells the people that perhaps the dead man may revive. Now many people are weeping and the speaker sits down by his head.

Now after some time Gaiänt'wakă comes in and feels over the body of the dead and he too discovers the warm spot but says nothing but sits silently down at the feet of the dead man.

And for many hours no one speaks.

Now it is the early morning and the dew is drying. This is a time of trouble for he lies dead.

Now continually Tää'wŏnyăs feels over the body of the dead man. He notices that the warm spot is spreading. Now the time is noon and he feels the warm blood pulsing in his veins. Now his breath comes and now he opens his eyes.

---

[1] Meaning, Needle or Awl Breaker, one of the fifty sachems.

[2] Meaning, Planter, commonly called Cornplanter, the half brother of Handsome Lake. See p. 136.

THE DEAD MAN REVIVES

Now Tää'wŏnyăs is speaking. "Are you well? What think you? (Isegeⁿ' onĕnt'gayei' hĕnesni'goĕ')?"

Now the people notice that the man is moving his lips as if speaking but no words come. Now this is near the noon hour. Now all are silent while Tää'wŏnyăs asks again, "My uncle, are you feeling well? (onigĕnt'gaiye')."

Then comes the answer, "Yes I believe myself well." So these are the first words Ganio'dai'io' spoke ("Iwi" nai' o'nĕ't'gai'ye hĕ'' nekni'goĕⁿ)."

Now then he speaks again saying, "Never have I seen such wondrous visions! Now at first I heard some one speaking. Some one spoke and said, 'Come out awhile' and said this three times. Now since I saw no one speaking I thought that in my sickness I myself was speaking but I thought again and found that it was not my voice. So I called out boldly, 'Niio'!' and arose and went out and there standing in the clear swept space I saw three men clothed in fine clean raiment. Their cheeks were painted red and it seemed that they had been painted the day before. Only a few feathers were in their bonnets. All three were alike and all seemed middle aged. Never before have I seen such handsome commanding men and they had in one hand bows and arrows as canes. Now in their other hands were huckleberry bushes and the berries were of every color.

"Then said the beings, addressing me, 'He who created the world at the beginning employed us to come to earth. Our visit now is not the only one we have made. He commanded us saying "Go once more down upon the earth and [this time] visit him who thinks of me. He is grateful for my creations, moreover he wishes to rise from sickness and walk [in health] upon the earth. Go you and help him to recover."' Then said the messengers, 'Take these berries and eat of every color. They will give you strength and your people with us will help you rise.' So I took and ate the berries. Then said the beings, 'On the morrow we will have it that a fire will be in the bushes and a medicine steeped to give you strength. We will appoint Odjis'kwăthĕⁿ¹ and Gayänt'gogwŭs,² a man and his wife, to make the medicine. Now they are the best of all the medicine people. Early in the morning we will see them and at that time you will have the medicine for your use, and before noon the unused medicine will be cast away because you will

---

¹ Dry Pudding.   ² Dipped Tobacco.

have recovered. Now moreover before noon many people will gather at the council house. These people will be your relatives and will see you. They will have gathered the early strawberries[1] and made a strawberry feast, and moreover will have strawberry wine sweetened with sugar. Then will all drink the juice of the berry and thank the Creator for your recovery and moreover they severally will call upon you by your name as a relative according as you are.'

" Now when the day came I went as appointed and all the people saw me coming and it was as predicted."

THE MESSAGE OF THE FOUR BEINGS

" Now the messengers spoke to me and said that they would now tell me how things ought to be upon the earth. They said: 'Do not allow any one to say that you have had great fortune in being able to rise again. The favor of the four beings is not alone for you and the Creator is willing to help all mankind.'

" Now on that same day the Great Feather[2] and the Harvest dances were to be celebrated and at this time the beings told me that my relatives would restore me. 'Your feelings and spirits are low,' they said, 'and must be aroused. Then will you obtain power to recover.' Verily the servants of the Creator (Hadio^{n}yă"geono^n) said this. Now moreover they commanded that henceforth dances of this same kind should be held and thanksgiving offered whenever the strawberries were ripe. Furthermore they said that the juice of the berry must be drunk by the children and the aged and all the people. Truly all must drink of the berry juice, for they said that the sweet water of the berries was a medicine and that the early strawberries were a great medicine. So they bade me tell this story to my people when I move upon the earth again. Now they said, ' We shall continually reveal things unto you. We, the servants of him who made us, say that as he employed us to come unto you to reveal his will, so you must carry it to your people. Now we are they whom he created when he made the world and our duty is to watch over and care for mankind. Now there are four of us but the fourth is not here present. When we called you by name and you heard, he returned to tell the news.

---

[1] The earliest of the wild strawberries are thought to be of great medicinal value and are eagerly eaten as soon as ripe. So sacred a plant is the strawberry that it is thought to grow along the " heaven road." A person recovering from a severe illness says, " I almost ate strawberries."

[2] The Osto'wä'gō'wā, the chief religious dance. See Morgan, p. 279.

This will bring joy into the heaven-world of our Creator. So it is that the fourth is not with us but you shall see him at another time and when that time is at hand you shall know. Now furthermore we must remind you of the evil things that you have done and you must repent of all things that you believe to have been evil. You think that you have done wrong because of O'gi'wē, Ye'ondă'thă and Gone'owo[1] and because you partook of strong drink. Verily you must do as you think for whatsoever you think is evil is evil.' "

GANIODAIIO COMMANDED TO PROCLAIM THE GAIWIIO

" 'And now behold! Look through the valley between two hills. Look between the sunrise and the noon!'

" So I looked, and in the valley there was a deeper hollow from which smoke was arising and steam as if a hot place were beneath.

" Then spoke the messengers saying, ' What do you see?'

" I answered, ' I see a place in the valley from which smoke is arising and it is also steaming as a hot place were beneath.'

" Then said the beings, ' Truly you have spoken. It is the truth. In that place a man is buried. He lies between the two hills in the hollow in the valley ànd a great message is buried with him. Once we commanded that man to proclaim that message to the world but he refused to obey. So now he will never rise from that spot for he refused to obey. So now to you, therefore, we say, proclaim the message that we give you and tell it truly before all people.'

" ' Now the first thing has been finished and it remains for us to uncover all wickedness before you.' So they said."

---

[1] See notes, p. 21.

THE GREAT MESSAGE

SECTION I

· " Now the beings spoke saying, ' We must now relate our message. We will uncover the evil upon the earth and show how men spoil the laws the Great Ruler has made and thereby made him angry.'

" ' The Creator made man a living creature.'

" ' Four words tell a great story of wrong and the Creator is sad because of the trouble they bring, so go and tell your people.'

" ' The first word is One'ga'.[1] It seems that you never have known that this word stands for a great and monstrous evil and has reared a high mound of bones. Ga''nigoĕntdoⁿ'tha, you lose your minds and one'ga' causes it all. Alas, many are fond of it and are too fond of it. So now all must now say, " I will use it nevermore. As long as I live, as long as the number of my days is I will never use it again. I now stop." So must all say when they hear this message.' Now the beings, the servants of the Great Ruler, the messengers of him who created us, said this. Furthermore they said that the Creator made one'ga' and gave it to our younger brethren, the white man, as a medicine but they use it for evil for they drink it for other purposes than medicine and drink instead of work and idlers drink one'ga'. No, the Creator did not make it for you."

So they said and he said. Eniä'iehŭk!²

SECTION 2

" Now spoke the beings and said, ' We now speak of the second word. This makes the Creator angry. The word is Got'goⁿ'.³

---

¹ Whiskey or Rum.

² Eniä'iehŭk meaning, *It was that way.*

³ A certain number of the Seneca Iroquois still cling to the belief in witchcraft although they are loath to admit it to any one in whom they have not implicit confidence. While they assert that witchcraft was introduced among them by some Algonquin tribe which they had adopted, their early legends and traditions contain many allusions to witches and witchcraft. There are at least two distinct methods employed by witches to accomplish their ends. The first, it is claimed, is the older way and is the employment

Witches are people without their right minds. They make disease and spread sickness to make the living die. They cut short the numbered days, for the Creator has given each person a certain number of days in which to live in this world.

"'Now this must you do: When you have told this message and the witches hear it they will confess before all the people and will say, "I am doing this evil thing but now I cease it forever, as long as I live." Some witches are more evil and can not speak in public so these must come privately and confess to you, Handsome Lake, or a preacher of this Gai'wiio'. Now some are most evil and they must go far out upon an abandoned trail and there they must

---

of what is described by informants as analogous to "malific mental suggestion," either verbal or telepathic. Such witches were able to assume the form of ancient monsters, the nia''gwahē or *mammoth bear* being the favorite form. They had power of transforming people into beasts, of imprisoning them within trees without destroying the human nature or sensibilities of their victims. Many stories are related of how chivalrous young men fresh from the dream fast were able to release the unhappy prisoners from the spells that bound them.

The second and modern class of witches work their evil spells by introducing into the bodies of their victims by supernatural means a small needle-like splinter pointed on either end and having a central eye to which was tied the hair of the witch, a splinter of bone from the fibula of a deer, a worm or some like object. Instances where such things have been drawn from bewitched persons are commonly reported.

A witch can work fearlessly and successfully as long as she remains unknown to the victim and under some circumstances even when known. A "witched" person is often able to see as in a vision the witch wherever she goes and is likewise able to tell when she is about to approach the house. Witches fear the threat of an angry person to kill them. Such a threat if an earnest one is an effectual charm against further annoyance. To burn the object that a witch has introduced into one's body will torture the witch and kill her. Such objects are not often burned. If revenge is desired the victim, if sufficiently angry, can throw the object through space and injure the witch wherever he wishes. A person who successfully resists and destroys another witch's power may become a witch if so desired.

To torture a witch, force a confession and exact a promise of repentance, take a living bird, black in color (a hen is now usually employed) and carry it into the woods at midnight. Here build a fire and then split open the bird's body, extract its beating heart and hang it by its chords over a small fire to roast slowly. The witch will then exert every possible means to reach the spot and beg that the heart be taken from the fire before it is consumed. At such a time any promise may be exacted, for the witch is powerless. If the heart is consumed the witch will die of a "burnt heart." Witch poison may be extracted by putting fine sifted ashes on the afflicted part and staying

confess before the Creator alone.   This course may be taken by
witches of whom no one knows.

   " ' Now when they go they must say:

   " Our Creator, O listen to me!
   I am a miserable creature.
   I think that way
   So now I cease.
   Now this is appointed
   For all of my days,
   As long as I live here
   In this earth-world.
   I have spoken."

   " ' In this manner all must say and say truly, then the prayer will
be sufficient.' "

   So they said and he said.   Eniaiehuk.

SECTION 3

   " Now the beings spoke again saying, ' This is the third word.
It is a sad one and the Creator is very sad because of this third
word.   It seems that you have never known that a great pile of
human bodies lies dead because of this word, Ono'ityi'yende, the
nigă'hos'säă', the secret poisons in little bundles named Ḡawĕn-

---

in bed until the poison comes out.   The charm will then be found in the
ashes.   The spirits of great witches are able to return and possess another
witch.   A witch who has such a " friend " is especially favored, for in time
of need the spirit-witch will direct her to money, goods or food.   Witches
do not always injure people who have offended them but more often their
children or other near relatives.   This is done that the person they desire
to punish may see an innocent person suffer for their offense and so be
tortured the more.

   " Witch doctors " are of two classes: witches who are willing to pit their
powers against other witches; and medicine men who have made a special
study of the charms that will offset witch spells.   This class may also be
divided into two divisions, those who make a regular profession of dis-
pelling witch influences, of discovering the cause of mysterious ailments, of
extracting the object that causes the trouble and of identifying witches, and
those who by reason of some special service they have rendered some spirit
of nature have been rewarded with magical powers, great wisdom and im-
munity from malific influences.   This class renders its services gratuitously.
Small false faces worn on the person and frequent invocations of the
Thunder spirit with liberal offerings of sacred tobacco are potent charms
against witches.   The False Face company has an annual ceremony in which
witch spirits are expelled from the community.   The I"dos company (q. v.)
is said to be the survival of the older witch society introduced among the
Seneca by the Nanticoke.   Its members are reputed to possess magic powers.

nodŭs'hä (compelling charms[1]). Now the Creator who made us commands that they who do this evil, when they hear this message, must stop it immediately and do it nevermore while they live upon this earth-world. It matters not how much destruction they have wrought — let them repent and not fail for fear the Creator will not accept them as his own.' "

So they said and he said. Eniaiehuk.

SECTION 4

" ' Now another word. It is sad. It is the fourth word. It is the way Yondwi'nias swa'yas.[2]

" ' Now the Creator ordained that women should bear children.

" ' Now a certain young married woman had children and suffered much. Now she is with child again and her mother wishing to prevent further sufferings designs to administer a medicine to cut off the child and to prevent forever other children from coming.[3] So the mother makes the medicine and gives it. Now when she does this she forever cuts away her daughter's string of children. Now it is because of such things that the Creator is sad. He created life to live and he wishes such evils to cease. He wishes those who employ such medicines to cease such practices forevermore. Now they must stop when they hear this message. Go and tell your people.' "

So they said and he said. Eniaiehuk.

---

[1] Charms. Should a person die holding a secret, one may discover it by sleeping upon the ground with a handful of the grave dirt beneath his head. Then, *if all conditions are perfect,* the dead person will appear in three successive visions and reveal its mystery.

A young man, wishing to become a swift runner, may add to his powers by concealing in his belt a bone from the grave of some celebrated runner of the past. It is said that most famous runners of the League carried these charms.

A warrior who wishes to guard against sudden attack from behind may make an unfailing charm by cutting three slits in the back of his neck and rubbing into the wounds the oil extracted from the scalps of enemies. A peculiar soft white flesh will fill up the cuts and when completely healed will protrude. Should an enemy then approach these protruding scars will quiver and warn the warrior of danger.

The most effective charm for drawing riches is the tooth of a nia'gwahē.

[2] Meaning " she cuts it off by abortion."

[3] The Iroquois knew of such an herb. I find it mentioned by Dr Peter Wilson, the Cayuga, and it was pointed out to me at Onondaga in 1911. The Seneca and Onondaga belief is that every woman has a certain number of children predestined to them and that they are fastened on a stringlike runner like tubers, or like eggs within a bird.

SECTION 6

" ' Now another message.

" ' Go tell your people that the Great Ruler is sad because of
what people do.

" ' The Creator has made it so that the married should live
together and that children should grow from them.

" 'Now it often happens that it is only a little while when people
are married that the husband speaks evil of his wife because he
does not wish to care for her children. Now a man who does that
stirs up trouble with his wife and soon deserts her and his children.
Then he searches for another woman and when he has found her
he marries her. Then when he finds her with child he goes away
from her and leaves her alone. Again he looks for another woman
and when he has lived with her for a time and sees her growing
large, he deserts her, the third woman.

" ' Now this is true. We, the messengers, saw him leave the two
women and the Creator himself saw him desert the third and punished him. Now a sure torment in the after life is for him who
leaves two women with child but the Creator alone knows what the
punishment is for the man who leaves the third.' "

So they said and he said. Eniaiehuk.

SECTION 7

" ' Now another message.

" ' The Creator has ordered that man and wife should rear their
children well, love them and keep them in health. This is the
Creator's rule. We, the messengers, have seen both men and
women desert each other when children come. The woman discovers that the man, her husband, loves his child and she is very
jealous and spreads evil reports of him. She does this for an ex-
cuse before the world to leave him. Thus the messengers say that
the Creator desires men and women to cease such mischief.' "

So they said and he said. Eniaiehuk.

SECTION 8

" ' Now another message.

" ' Tell your people that the Creator has ordered regular marriage customs. When the young people are old enough to marry,
tell them so. When they marry they will live pleasantly. Now it
may happen that the girl's mother discovers that she is very happy

with her husband. Then she endeavors to make her daughter angry with her husband when he returns from a journey. But when the husband returns the young wife forgets the evil advice and greets him lovingly. Now the older woman, the mother, seeing this, speaks again hoping to stir up an ill feeling. Says the old woman, " My daughter, your spirits are dull, you are not bright. When I was young I was not so agreeable. I was harsh with my husband." Now the Creator is sad because of the tendency of old women to breed mischief. Such work must stop. Tell your people it must stop.' "

So they said and he said. Eniaiehuk.

SECTION 10

" ' Now another message to tell your people.

" ' The married often live well together for a while. Then a man becomes ugly in temper and abuses his wife. It seems to afford him pleasure. Now because of such things the Creator is very sad. So he bids us to tell you that such evils must stop. Neither man nor woman must strike each other.' So they said.

" Now furthermore they said, ' We will tell you what people must do. It is the way he calls best. Love one another and do not strive for another's undoing. Even as you desire good treatment, so render it. Treat your wife well and she will treat you well.' "

So they said and he said. Eniaiehuk.

SECTION 11

" ' Now another message to tell your people.

" ' This concerns short marriages.

" ' Now some live together peaceably and keep the family as should be. Then after a time the man resolves to go off on a hunting excursion in the woods for a certain number of days. So he goes, having agreed with his wife about it. All is well and he returns with a load of game. He feels well and thinks he is doing well in thus providing for his family. On his way homeward he meets some one who tells him that in his absence his wife has been living with another man. When he hears this report he feels sad and angry. He refuses to go to his home and turns from his path and goes to his relatives. Now whoever makes mischief of this kind does a great wrong before the Creator. So he bids his people to forever stop such evil practices.' "

So they said and he said. Eniaiehuk.

SECTION 12

" ' Now another message.

" ' Now this concerns both husband and wife. Now it may happen that a man and wife live together happily. At length the man thinks that he will go to another settlement to visit relatives there. His wife agrees and he goes. Now when he gets to the village he induces some agreeable woman to live with him saying he is single. Then after some time the man goes back to his own family. His wife treats him cordially as if no trouble had occurred. Now we, the messengers, say that the woman is good in the eyes of her Creator and has a place reserved for her in the heaven-world. Now the woman knew all that had been done in the other settlement but she thought it best to be peaceful and remain silent. And the Creator says that she is right and has her path toward the heaven-world, but he, the man, is on his way to the house of the Wicked One.' "

So they said and he said. Eniaiehuk.

SECTION 13

" ' Now another message.

" ' This concerns a certain thing that human creatures follow. It is concerning gakno'we'haat. Some men desire constant new experience, that is some men are always following yē'oⁿ'. Now it is a great evil for men to have such desires. This is a thing that the so sinful must confess. A man who desires to know gagwēgoⁿ yē'oⁿ'sho' will never be satisfied, for yē'oⁿ' will arise whom he can not know and he will fall flat. Now we, the messengers, say that all this is sinful and men must not follow such desires.' "

So they said and he said. Eniaiehuk.

SECTION 14

" ' Now another message.

" ' This is what your people do.

" ' An old woman punished her children [1] unjustly. The Creator is sad because of such things and bids us tell you that such practices must cease.' So they said.

---

[1] Handsome Lake was ever the lover and champion of children. There are many instances in the Gaiwiio relating to the care and rearing of children. The mode of punishment here referred to was one of long usage. Sometimes the mother would fill her mouth with water and blow it into the face of the little offender, repeating until obedience was enforced. Punishment by violence as by whipping or striking was discountenanced. The mother

" ' Now this is the way ordained by the Creator: Talk slowly and kindly to children and never punish them unjustly. When a child will not obey let the mother say, " Come to the water and I will immerse you." If after this warning the child is still obstinate she must take it to the water's edge and say, " Do you now obey? " and she must say so again and if at the third time there is no obedience then the child must be thrust in the water. But if the child cries for mercy it must have it and the woman must not throw it into the water. If she does she does evil.' "

So they said and he said. Eniaiehuk.

SECTION 15

" ' Now another message of things not right.

" ' Parents disregard the warnings of their children. When a child says, " Mother, I want you to stop wrongdoing," the child speaks straight words and the Creator says that the child speaks right words and the mother must obey. Furthermore the Creator proclaims that such words from a child are wonderful and that the mother who disregards them takes the wicked part. The mother may reply, " Daughter, stop your noise. I know better than you. I am the older and you are but a child. Think not that you can influence me by your speaking." Now when you tell this message to your people say that it is wrong to speak to children in such words.' "

So they said and he said. Eniaiehuk.

SECTION 16

" ' Now another message.

" ' Tell your people that the Creator is sad because of what they are doing.

" ' Some people live together well as man and wife and family, but the man of the family uses strong drink. Then when he comes home he lifts up his child to fondle it and he is drunk. Now we, the messengers of the Creator, say that this is not right for if a man filled with strong drink touches his child he burns its blood. Tell your people to heed this warning.' "

So they said and he said. Eniaiehuk.

---

who was intrusted with the care of children was accustomed to tell her children what was wrong and allow them by experience to know that her word was to be relied upon. A boy remained under the discipline of his mother until the age of sixteen when he was turned over to the training of his father. If the boy was unruly and without ambition the mother received the blame and was sometimes punished.

SECTION 17

"'Now another message.

"'Some people live together righteously as man and wife according as the Creator ordained, but they have no child. When this is so let this be the way: If the wife's sister has children, of these let the wife without issue take from one to three and rear them and thereby fulfil her duty to the Creator. Moreover when a woman takes children she must rear them well as if born of herself. We, the messengers, say that you must tell this to your people.'"

So they said and he said. Eniaiehuk.

SECTION 18

"'Now another message.

"'Tell your people that ofttimes when a woman hears that a child is born and goes to see it, she returns and says in many houses where she stops that its mother's husband is not its father. Now we say that it is exceedingly wrong to speak such evil of children. The Creator formed the children as they are; therefore, let the people stop their evil sayings.'"

So they said and he said. Eniaiehuk.

SECTION 19

"'Now another message.

"'Now the Creator of mankind ordained that people should live to an old age. He appointed that when a woman becomes old she should be without strength and unable to work.[1] Now the Creator says that it is a great wrong to be unkind to our grandmothers. The Creator forbids unkindness to the old. We, the messengers, say it. The Creator appointed this way: he designed that an old woman should be as a child again and when she becomes so the Creator wishes the grandchildren to help her, for only because she is, they are. Whosoever does right to the aged does right in the sight of the Creator.'"

So they said and he said. Eniaiehuk.

(So many words, Odi'waga''de, end of first day's preaching)

Recitation of the second day

SECTION 20

"'Now another message.

"'A way that was followed.

---

[1] The wisdom of the aged, especially upon ceremonial matters, was never questioned.

" ' Sometimes a mother is ready to feed her family. When she is ready to bid them sit down, she glances out and sees some one coming and straightway hides the food. A woman visitor comes in. Now after some conversation the visitor says she is unwell and goes out. Then the family commences to eat. And the Creator says that who follow such tricks must repent as soon as they hear this message, for such practices are most wicked.' "

" Now the messengers said this."

" ' Now the Creator made food for all creatures and it must be free for all. He ordained that people should live in communities. Now when visitors enter a lodge the woman must always say, " Sede'konĭ"," *come eat.* Now it is not right to refuse what is offered. The visitor must take two or three bites at least and say, " Niawĕⁿ'." Tell this to all your people.' "

So they said and he said. Eniaiehuk.

SECTION 21

" ' Now another message.

" ' Now this is right.

" ' When a woman hears children playing near her lodge she must call them in and ask them to eat. The Creator says that this is right for some children are of poor parents and have little to eat. The Creator loves poor children and whosoever feeds the poor and unfortunate does right before him.' "

So they said and he said. Eniaiehuk.

SECTION 22

" ' Now another message.

" ' When a woman sees an unfortunate girl who has neither parents nor settled home and calls her in and helps her repair her clothing, cleanse herself and comb her hair, she does right and has favor in the sight of her Creator. He loves the poor and the woman does right before him. So we, the messengers, say that you must tell your people to continue to do this good thing.' "

So they said and he said. Eniaiehuk.

SECTION 23

" ' Now another message.

" ' The Creator is sad because of the sins of the beings that he created.

" ' He ordained that mankind should live as social beings in communities.

" ' Now it may happen that a woman sets out to destroy good feelings between neighbors by telling go‘diodia′se (stories that augment by repetition). Now this woman goes to a house and says, " I love you and because I do I will tell you a secret. The woman in the next house speaks evil of you." Now heretofore the two women had been friends but upon hearing this story the woman becomes an enemy of her former friend. Then the evil story-teller goes to the woman whom she lied about and tells her the hard words that the other woman has spoken. Then is the liar happy having started a feud, and she hastens from house to house to tell of it. Now great troubles arise and soon a fight, and one woman causes it all. Therefore the Creator is very sad. Tell your people that such things must stop the moment this message is told.

" ' Now the Creator has ordained another way. He has ordained that human creatures should be kind one to the other and help each other. When a woman visits another house she must help at the work in progress and talk pleasantly. If she relates jokes they must always be upon herself. If she speaks harshly of others the woman of the house must say, " I remember the desires of our Creator. I can not hear what you say. I can not take that evil story." So the trouble is ended there. Now the Creator says that the woman is true who refuses to hear evil reports. She cuts off the evil at its beginning and it does not go from her. So she has won favor before the Creator.' "

So they said and he said. Eniaiehuk.

SECTION 24

" ' Now another message.

" ' The Creator who made you is sad.

" ' The Creator made every person with a different face.

" ' Now a man talks saying that he is far more handsome than other men. He boasts that he is exceedingly handsome and grand. But the Creator says all this is very wrong. The vain must repent and never boast again.' So they said.

" ' Now animals seem alike to you. A wild animal that you have once seen you can not easily say you have seen again. But people are different before you. Now when a man is handsome let him thank his Creator for his comliness.' So they said.

" ' Now furthermore a man says " I am the strongest man of all. There is no one who can throw me to the ground." A man who talks thus is a boaster before the people. Now the Creator says that such boasting is evil. The Creator endowed the man with strength and therefore he should not boast but thank the giver who is the Creator. So tell your people these things.' So they said.

" ' Now furthermore a man says, " I am the swiftest runner of the world. No one can outrun me." Now he regards himself as a mighty man and boasts before his people. Now the Creator says that such boasting is evil. The Creator endowed the man with his speed and he should offer thanks and not boast. So we, the messengers, say your people must cease their boasting.' " [1]

So they said and he said. Eniaiehuk.

SECTION 25

" ' Now another message.

" ' Three things that our younger brethren (the white people) do are right to follow.

" ' Now, the first. The white man works on a tract of cultivated ground and harvests food for his family. So if he should die they still have the ground for help. If any of your people have cultivated ground let them not be proud on that account. If one is proud there is sin within him but if there be no pride there is no sin.

" ' Now, the second thing. It is the way a white man builds a house. He builds one warm and fine appearing so if he dies the family has the house for help. Whoso among you does this does right, always providing there is no pride. If there is pride it is evil but if there is none, it is well.

" ' Now the third. The white man keeps horses and cattle. Now there is no evil in this for they are a help to his family. So if he dies his family has the stock for help. Now all this is right if there is no pride. No evil will follow this practice if the animals are well fed, treated kindly and not overworked. Tell this to your people.' "

So they said and he said. Eniaiehuk.

SECTION 26

" ' Now another message to tell your relatives.

" ' This concerns education. It is concerning studying in English schools.

" ' Now let the Council appoint twelve people to study, two from each nation of the six. So many white people are about you that you must study to know their ways.' "

So they said and he said. Eniaiehuk.

---

[1] A more complete catalog of the besetting sins of the Iroquois than set forth in the foregoing sections can not be found nor are they elsewhere more graphically described.

SECTION 27

" ' Now another message to tell your people.

" ' Now some men have much work and invite all their friends to come and aid them and they do so. Now this is a good plan and the Creator designed it. He ordained that men should help one another [1] (ādanidä′oshä′).' "

So they said and he said. Eniaiehuk.

SECTION 28

" ' Now another message of things not right.

" ' People do wrong in the world and the Creator looks at all things.

" ' A woman sees some green vegetables and they are not hers. She takes them wrongly. Now she is yenon′skwaswa′don, a thieving woman. Tell your people that petty thieving must cease.' So they said.

" ' Now the Creator gave Diohe″kon [2] for a living. When a woman sees a new crop and wishes to eat of it in her own house, she must ask the owner for a portion and offer payment. Then may the owner use her judgment and accept recompense or give the request freely.' " [3]

So they said and he said. Eniaiehuk.

SECTION 29

" ' Now another message for you to tell your people.

" ' It is not right for you to have so many dances [4] and dance songs.

" 'A man calls a dance in honor of some totem animal from which he desires favor or power. This is very wrong, for you do not know what injury it may work upon other people.

---

[1] The bee is a very popular institution among the Iroquois. See Museum Bulletin 144, p. 31.

[2] Meaning, " our life givers," the corn, beans and squashes. See Iroquois Uses of Maize, p. 36.

[3] One of the old methods of gardening was to clear a small patch in the woods by girdling the trees and planting in the mellow forest mold. The name and totem of the owner of the garden was painted on a post, signifying that the ground was private property. The clan totem gave permission to any hard-pressed clansman to take what he wished in emergency but only in such a case. These isolated gardens in the forests were objects of temptation sometimes, as the prophet intimates.

[4] The Seneca had thirty-three dances, ten of which were acquired from other tribes. See p. 81.

" ' Tell your people that these things must cease.   Tell them to repent and cease.' "

So they said and he said.   Eniaiehŭk.

" ' Now this shall be the way: They who belong to these totem animal societies[1] must throw tobacco and disband.'   So they said."
" Now in those days when the head men heard this message they said at once, in anger, ' We disband,' and they said this without holding a ceremony as the messenger had directed."[2]

Eniaiehŭk.

SECTION 30

" ' Now another message to tell your people.

" ' Four words the Creator has given for bringing happiness.   They

---

[1] Animal Societies and Totems.   The Seneca firmly believe that by using the proper formula the favor of various animals can be purchased.   The animal petitioned it is believed will make the person successful in any pursuit in which itself is proficient.   The charm-animal was sometimes revealed in a dream, sometimes by a diviner of mysteries and was often sought directly.   A warrior wishing to become a successful fisherman, for instance, might do any one of three things.   He might seek for a dream that would show him what animal would make him an expert fisher, he might consult a " clairvoyant " or he might go directly to a stream of water and selecting some animal petition its favor.

The patron of the fisheries was the otter and there is a special society of those who have the otter for a " friend."   The Society of Otters preserves the rites of invocation and the method of propitiation and also the method of healing afflicted members.

Other animals which are thought to be " great medicine " are the eagle, the bear, the buffalo and the mythical *nia'gwahē* or mammoth bear that was alternately a man and a beast.   To be ungrateful to these givers of luck is a sin that arouses the ire of the animal who will punish the offender by inflicting him with some strange sickness.   The offense may be one of neglect or altogether unintentional and unknown.   It is then the duty of the society to appease the offended animal by performing the rites on a grand scale that the individual has failed to do in the ordinary way.   The ordinary individual ceremony consisted simply of going to the bank of some clear stream, in the case of the Otters for instance, and after smoking sacred tobacco, casting the pulverized tobacco into the water at intervals during a thanksgiving and praise chant.   Then will the otters know that their human brothers are not ungrateful for the fortune they are receiving.

There were four societies, having as their genii the spirits of the bear, the birds (eagle), the buffalo and the otter, respectively, and taking their names from their guardian animal (Secret Medicine Societies of the Seneca, p. 113).

[2] This was done at the suggestion of Cornplanter who is accused of endeavoring to upset the plans and prophecies of Handsome Lake in many sly ways.

are amusements devised in the heaven world, the Osto'wägo'wa,[1] Gonĕ'owoⁿ', Adoⁿ'wĕⁿ and Ganäwĕⁿ'gowa.' "

So they said and he said. Eniaiehuk.

SECTION 31

" ' Now another message to tell your people.

" ' The Creator has sanctioned four dances for producing a joyful spirit and he has placed them in the keeping of Honon'diont[2] who have authority over them. The Creator has ordered that on certain times and occasions there should be thanksgiving ceremonies. At such times all must thank the Creator that they live. After that, let the chiefs thank him for the ground and the things on the ground and then upward to the sky and the heaven-world where he is. Let the children and old folk come and give thanks. Let the old women who can scarcely walk come. They may lean against the middle benches and after listening to three or four songs must say, " I thank the Great Ruler that I have seen this day." Then will the Creator call them right before him.

" ' It seems that you have never known that when Osto'wägo'wa was being celebrated that one of the four beings was in the midst of it, but it is so. Now when the time for dancing comes you must wash your faces and comb your hair, paint your face with red spots on either cheek, and with a thankful heart go to the ceremony. This preparation will be sufficient, therefore, do not let your style of dress hold you back.

" ' You have not previously been aware that when a Godi'ont is appointed that you have not appointed her. No, for the Great Ruler has chosen her. A road leads from the feet of every godi'ont and hodi'ont toward heaven. Truly this is so only of they who do right before the Creator.' "

So they said and he said. Eniaiehuk.

SECTION 32

" ' Now another message for your people.

" ' He who created us appointed that there should be chiefs, (hodi'ion'), and that they should do good for the people.' "

So they said and he said. Eniaiehuk.

---

[1] The Great Feather dance, the Harvest dance, the Sacred Song and the Peach Stone game.

[2] *Honon'diont, overseers* or *keepers of ceremonies,* more often women than men. The word means *They are mountains.* (Hodi'ont is mas. sing.; **Godi'ont, fem. sing.**).

SECTION 33

"'So now another.

"'Tell your relations this. The Creator has sanctioned a feast to a medicine animal on a great day.'"

So they said and he said. Eniaiehuk.

SECTION 34

"'Now another message to tell your people.

"'Now the messengers said that this thing was beyond the control of Indians.

"'At some future day the wild animals will become extinct. Now when that day comes the people will raise cattle and swine for feast food at the thanksgivings.'"[1]

So they said and he said. Eniaiehuk.

SECTION 35

"'Now another message to tell your people.

"'You have been ignorant of this thing.

"'When the Honondi'ont go about to notify the community of a meeting for the celebration of Osto'wägo'wa, or for hearing the Great Ruler's message, the evil spirit at the same time appoints and sends another man, an invisible one, in his tracks saying, "Do not go. It is of no use, no benefit comes to you; rather do your own work at home and stay away." Now it is the messenger of the evil spirit that argues thus. Now know you that the evil spirit will hinder you in all good things but you can outwit him by doing the things that he does not wish you to do. Go then to the meetings. Then will the evil messenger follow you to the Long House and when from the outside you have heard the songs he will say that such is sufficient and that you may now return. Do not heed him but enter and take your seat. Then will he argue again saying that it is sufficient to listen and not take a part because you would not appear well in shabby clothing. Heed him not. Now this spirit speaks to your minds and his face is between you all.'"

So they said and he said. Eniaiehuk.

SECTION 36

"'Now another message to tell your people.

"'This will happen.

"'We have told you to watch.

---

[1] Pork is now the principal ceremonial food.

" ' The Honon'diont will go out in fours for game for the feasts.
" ' You may think that they are fulfilling their duty to Gai'wiio'.
" ' The animals that fall must be thirty.
" ' But this will happen when Gai'wiio' is new. The Honon'diont
will kill twenty-nine and the twenty-ninth will be a cub bear. So
there will not be thirty.
" ' So this will be done when Gai'wiio' is new. It will be done at
Adekwe'oⁿge, the Green Corn thanksgiving ceremony.' "
So they said and he said. Eniaiehuk.

SECTION 37

" ' Now another message to tell your people.
" ' Now this is a thing to happen.
" ' Hereafter we shall have a new species of deer.[1] The Creator
will create somewhere a pair, male and female. The male deer will
be spotted with white and the female striped with white over her
back. This will be done and we say it.
" ' Now moreover the messengers command that these animals
shall never be killed.' "
So they said and he said. Eniaiehuk.

SECTION 38

" ' Now another message for your people.
" ' If all the world would repent the earth would become as new
again. Because of sin the under-world[2] is crumbling with decay.
The world is full of sin. Truly, this is so.' "
So they said and he said. Eniaiehuk.

---

[1] These deer are the sacred creations of the Great Ruler and as such no
" pale invader " is permitted to see them, though a few of the faithful have
at certain seasons seen them in the darkness fleeing from discovery. Cornplanter says these deer were killed by a jealous rival of the prophet while
he yet lived, so defying the new command.

[2] The under-world was thought to be a dark region beneath the surface
of the earth where were confined the creations of the evil-minded spirit. It
was a vast cave full of winding chambers, dark turbid rivers, bottomless
sloughs, hot springs and fetid odors, rapacious beasts, venomous serpents,
poisonous insects and noxious weeds. The door of the under-world was
guarded by the under-earth elves who had great difficulty in preventing the
white buffaloes from escaping. Frequently they did and then began a great
pursuit to kill or bring back the white buffaloes. At such a time the elves
would tell the sun of the calamity and he would paint his face red as a sign
to all the elves the world over that the chase was on. See Legend, Origin of
Death Dance.

SECTION 39

" ' Now another message to tell your people.

" ' We, the messengers of the Creator, are of the opinion that the world will continue for three generations longer (or three hundred years).[1]   Then will Gai'wiio' be fulfilled.' "

So they said and he said. Eniaiehuk.

SECTION 40

" ' Now another message to tell your people.

" 'The religious leaders and the chiefs must enforce obedience to the teachings of Gai'wiio'.' "

So they said and he said. Eniaiehuk.

SECTION 41

" ' Now another message to tell your people.

" ' This thing will happen when it is new.

" ' Truly men will repent and reform but it will happen that three certain ones will neither confess nor reform. Nothing will induce them to confess.

" ' There are grades of sin:[2] the sins of Hasan'owān'ĕ', the sins of Honon'diont and the sins of the ordinary people.

" ' Now when you are preaching repentance, Gaiänt'wakă will say that these men when they pass from this world are most vile. He will say, " Let us cast them into the water for they are not worthy to be dressed for the grave. The Creator will not receive them." Now no one will object to what Gaiänt'wakă says.' "

Now this thing did happen as predicted and when the messenger arose the first thing that he did was to spread the news and give the command that it must not be done.

" Now they said, ' The Creator will not give up hope of them until they pass from the earth. It is only then that they can lose their souls if they have not repented. So the Creator always hopes for repentance.' " [3]

So they said and he said. Eniaiehuk.

SECTION 42

" ' Now another message to tell your people.

---

[1] Handsome Lake taught that the world would end in the year 2100.

[2] The higher the position the greater the sin, is the prophet's rule.

[3] See p. 61, Idea of soul.

" ' Chiefs and high officers have spoken derisively of each other and quarreled.[1] What they have done must not be done again.' "

So they said and he said. Eniaiehuk.

SECTION 43

" 'Now another message to tell your people.

" ' Good food is turned into evil drink. Now some have said that there is no harm in partaking of fermented liquids.

" ' Then let this plan be followed: let men gather in two parties, one having a feast of food, apples and corn, and the other have cider and whiskey. Let the parties be equally divided and matched and let them commence their feasting at the same time. When the feast is finished you will see those who drank the fermented juices murder one of their own party but not so with those who ate food only.' "

So they said and he said. Eniaiehuk.

SECTION 44

" ' Now another message for your people.

" ' You have had the constant fear that the white race would exterminate you.[2] The Creator will care for his Oñgwe'oⁿwe (real people).' "

So they said and he said. Eniaiehuk.

SECTION 45

" ' Now another message for your people.

" ' Some of your relatives and descendants will say, " We lack an understanding of this religion," and this will be the cry of the

---

[1] Jealousy was the principal cause of the dissension that led to the decay of the League of the Iroquois.

[2] The Iroquois saw that the white race had encircled them and were drawing the lines ever tighter. They saw that they were in a position of great disadvantage, living as they did in the midst of a people against whom they had fought not only in their own wars but also as allies of the British. They saw how all other native tribes had been swept away with the advance of the invading race and thus no wonder they feared. Yet today (1912) they still exist unabsorbed and as a distinct people in the midst of the civilization of the Empire State under their own tribal laws and recognized nominally as nations. The story of how they have preserved themselves through three centuries of contact with an invading race that had little love for them and whose policy like their own in ancient times, is to absorb or exterminate, to accomplish a thing that no other aboriginal race has done, is well worth a place in history as one of its marvels. " Truly the Creator has cared for his red children ! "

people. But even we, the servants of the Creator, do not understand all things. Now some when they are turned to the right way will say, ". I will continue so for all of my days," but this will not be so for they surely will fall short in some things. This is why even we can not understand all things.' "

So they said. Eniaiehuk.

SECTION 46

" At the time of this prophecy I was in the Cold Spring village. It occurred at this time. The prophecy was then new.

" At that time a woman and her daughter administered a witch-powder[1] to a man and he lost his mind. He wandered off alone and died and thus a great crime was committed.

" Now at that time it was said among the head men, ' We will punish the women.' So it was the plan that each chief give the women one lash.

" Now I, Ganiodai'io' heard the resolution of the chiefs and was of the opinion that the women would easily survive such punishment, so, also, the chiefs believed it.

" Now all this happened when the head men sat in council, the four messengers being present.

" Now this thing must never happen again. Such councils never accomplish good. It is natural that foolish women should have done what these did.

" Now at the time of the lashing it was in my mind that they would surely live.

" So this must never happen again because the Creator has not privileged men to punish each other." Eniaiehuk. [See plate 12.]

SECTION 47

" So now another story.

" It happened that at a certain time a certain person did not honor Gai'wiio'. At a gathering where Gai'wiio' was being told this was done. It was at Cold Spring village.

"A man was standing in the doorway showing disrespect to the proceedings within. The prophet was speaking and as he said in closing ' It is finished,' the man in the doorway dainï''dădi. Now that was the last. The man did not go home to his dwelling and

---

[1] Witch-powders were used for various purposes but generally as poisons or love charms. Their use is condemned in section 3 and the punishment of those who use them in section 104.

Plate 12

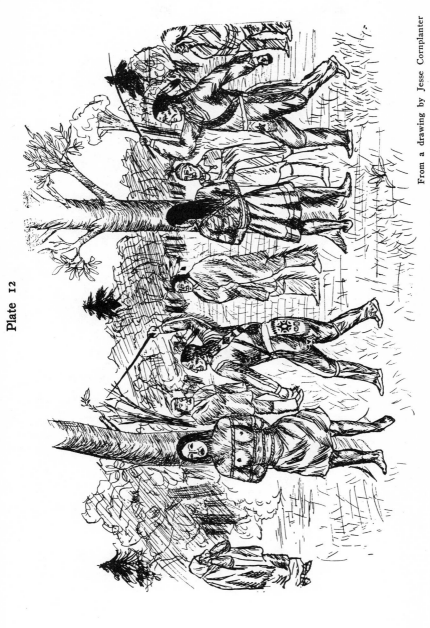

The whipping of the witches. (See section 46 of the code, p. 46.)

From a drawing by Jesse Cornplanter

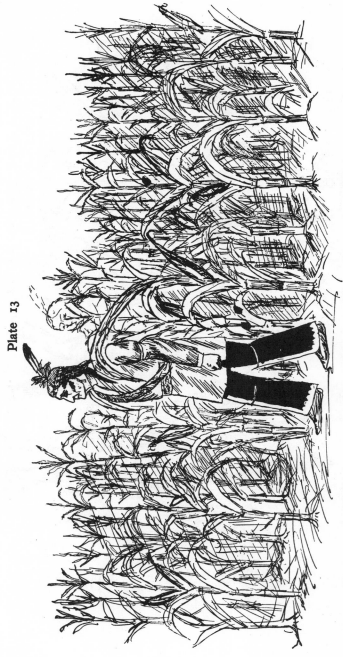

Plate 13

The Spirit of the Corn speaking to Handsome Lake, the Seneca prophet. (From a drawing by Jesse Cornplanter, a Seneca boy artist)

the next day it was rumored that he was missing. A search was made and on the other side of the Allegany in a swamp two days later the man was found. He was sitting above it. He had broken branches and arranged them in the form of a nest upon which he sat devouring snakes. He was not in his right mind. They took him from his nest (ho'non'gwae') and soon he died." Eniaiehuk.

SECTION 48

" Now another story.

1 " Now it was that when the people reviled me, the proclaimer of the prophecy, the impression came to me that it would be well to depart and go to Tonawanda. In that place I had relatives and friends and thought that my bones might find a resting place there. Thus I thought through the day.

" Then the messengers came to me and said ' We understand your thoughts. We will visit you more frequently and converse with you. Wherever you go take care not to be alone. Be cautious and move secretly.'

" Then the messengers told me that my life journey would be in three stages and when I entered the third I would enter into the eternity of the New World,[1] the land of our Creator. So they said." Eniaiehuk.

2 " The day was bright when I went into the planted field and alone I wandered in the planted field and it was the time of the second hoeing. Suddenly a damsel[2] appeared and threw her arms about my neck and as she clasped me she spoke saying, ' When you leave this earth for the new world above, it is our wish to follow you.' I looked for the damsel but saw only the long leaves of corn twining round my shoulders. And then I understood that it was the spirit of the corn who had spoken, she the sustainer of life. So I replied, ' O spirit of the corn, follow not me but abide still upon the earth and be strong and be faithful to your purpose. Ever endure and do not fail the children of women. It is not time for you to follow for Gai'wiio' is only in its beginning.' " Eniaiehuk.

SECTION 49

" ' Now another message to tell your people.

---

[1] The heaven described by Ganiodai'io' was called the New World because it had not been previously known. The generations before had not gone there, not having known the will of the Creator as revealed by the prophet.

[2] See plate 13, the Spirit of the Corn.

" ' There is a dispute in the heaven-world between two parties. It is a controversy about you, the children of earth. Two great beings are disputing — one is the Great Ruler, the Creator, and the other is the evil-minded spirit.

" ' You who are on earth do not know the things of heaven.

" ' Now the evil one said, " I am the ruler of the earth because when I command I speak but once and man obeys."

" ' Then answered the Great Ruler, " The earth is mine for I have created it and you have helped me in no part."

" ' Now the evil one answered, " I do not acknowledge that you have created the earth and that I helped in no part, but I say that when I say to men, ' Obey me,' they straightway obey, but they do not hear your voice."

" ' Then the Great Ruler replied, " Truly the children are my own for they have never done evil."

" ' And the evil one answering said, " Nay, the children are mine for when I bid one saying, ' Pick up that stick and strike your fellow,' they obey me quickly. Aye, the children are mine."

" ' Then was the Great Ruler very sad and he said, " Once more will I send my messengers and tell them my heart and they will tell my people and thus I will redeem my own."

" ' Then the evil one replied, " Even so it will not be long before men transgress your commands. I can destroy it with a word for they will do my bidding. Verily I delight in the name Hanïssē'ono. It is very true that they who love my name, though they be on the other side of the earth, will find me at their backs the moment they pronounce my name."

" ' Now at that time the Great Ruler spoke to the four messengers saying, " Go tell mankind that at present they must not call me Hawi'n'io', the Great Ruler, until a later time, for the Evil One calls himself the Ruler of Mankind. So now whosoever is turned into my way must say when he calls upon my name, Hodiänok'doon Hĕd'iohe', our Creator. So also whosoever speaks the name of the evil one must say, Segoewa'tha, The Tormentor. Then will the evil one know that you have discovered who he is, for it is he who will punish the wicked when they depart from this world.' "[1]

So they said and he said. Eniaiehuk.

---

[1] A typical example of Iroquois philosophy. The Iroquois were fond of devising stories of this character and many of them reveal the subtle reasoning powers of the Indian in a striking manner.

SECTION 50

" ' Now another message to tell your people.

1 " ' Now we are of the mind that the cold of winter will take life away. Many will be taken away because of the changing cold. Moreover some will freeze because they are filled with strong drink. Then again when the earth grows warm and the warm changes come, many will perish because of strong drink. Now the Creator never intended that variations of weather and season, warm and cold, should cause death.' "

2 " ' The Creator made the waters of the earth, the rivers and lakes. These too will cause death and some filled with strong drink will be swallowed up by the waters.' "

3 " 'And now more. The Creator made fire and this will also cause death and some filled with strong drink will be destroyed by the flames.' "

" ' Verily he has said and ordained that they who disobey Gai'wiio' should fall into hardships.' "

So they said and he said. Eniaiehuk.

SECTION 51

" ' Now another message to tell your people.

" ' The messengers have given the promise to the prophet that he will be able to judge diseases and prescribe remedies.[1] So also he will be able to see far down into the earth as far as runs the elm's root. Then if any trouble comes and anyone asks the help of the prophet, he must give it freely, but they who ask must give an offering of tobacco. Now there will be some in your care who will be taken from your hands for other treatment. No wrong will be done and you must bear no ill will. It is said that the events of all our days are foreknown, so when the time comes for you to exercise your power we will tell you and then you may judge the earth and cure diseases.' "

So they said and he said. Eniaiehuk.

SECTION 52

" ' Now another message for your people.

" Now when my relatives heard all this they said, ' This man must be a clairvoyant (hĕnne'yoⁿ').'[2]

---

[1] See p. 113, medicine men.

[2] Diviners of mysteries have always been prominent characters among the Indians. Their office was to tell their clients the proper medicine society

" The news spread and Gaiänt'wakă came as a messenger.[1] Now he came to Ganiodai'io' and said, ' Why, having the assurance of powers, do you not commence now. Come prophesy!' Now he had tobacco for an offering. Then he said, ' My daughter is very sick.'

" Now the diviner of mysteries did not respond to his entreaty and so Gaiänt'wakă went out but soon came running back. This second time he had the same request and plead more earnestly, but without avail.

" Then it was said that he would not respond to the cry of a brother and had no hearing for the voice of a brother.

"Again Gaiänt'wakă returned and urged his brother.

" Now the people said, ' Have we not something to say to you as well as the messengers of the Creator?'

" Then he answered and said, ' Truly the people say that I will not reason. Verily I am true to my words. Now I can do nothing but try but I have not yet the permission of the messengers.'

" Now he went into a deep sleep and when he awoke he told his vision. Now he said that O'gi'we[2] should be sung for the sick woman.

" Now it is said that at that time the first song was in order but every part of the song was silent.

" Now a rumor spread that after all it was not wrong to continue the ceremonial dances once forbidden. So many were sick because they had not observed the commanded method of closing the societies."

This was so when Gai'wiio' was new. Eniaiehuk.

SECTION 53

" ' Now another message.

" The four messengers arose from a sitting of the prophecy.

" Now he said that certain songs and parts of songs are not known and some societies are new and their powers untried. So

that would be most efficacious in curing the sick, to discover the whereabouts of lost children or articles, to discover what witch was working her spells, and to tell fortunes, as well as to interpret dreams.

[1] Cornplanter again endeavored to get his brother into disfavor with the four messengers by forcing him to exercise his powers prematurely. For this reason the followers of Handsome Lake to this day regard Cornplanter as a malicious character who ever tried to upset the Gai'wiio'.

[2] The death chant, a ceremony belonging to the O'gi'weono' or Society of Chanters. See the legend *Origin of the Death Dance.*

make a feast and throw tobacco instead of singing. But the chiefs said that that plan should be laid aside and notwithstanding, the songs should be sung as far as possible.

"Now the messengers said that they should secure provisions enough for the feast and be sure. Some have planned to have strong drink used at the feast but this must not be tolerated. Only food must be used."[1]

So they said and he said. Eniaiehuk.

SECTION 54

"Now I will relate another.

"There is a certain ceremony in the midwinter.[2] It is said that it is most important to uphold the customs of midwinter and that any one having a part should fulfil it. It is said that to fulfil the customs they must go about the neighborhood holding dances. It is said that the Creator has sanctioned certain dances for thanksgiving."

"Now the messengers said that Ganio'dai'io' must sing[3] early in the morning on three mornings and give the cheer-cries of the Gai'wiio'."

So they said and he said. Eniaiehuk.

SECTION 55

"'Now another message.

"'It is said that all your relatives and friends must be told.

"'It is said that when these rites are performed one person is to be selected to offer thanks[4] to the Creator. Now when thanks are rendered begin with the things upon the ground and thank upward to the things in the new world above. Afterward any one so inclined may arise and thank the Creator in the manner he thinks best.'"

So it is said. Eniaiehuk.

---

[1] It is related that at one period whiskey had so far debauched the Indians that their once sacred ceremonies, like those of the early Christians at Corinth, were made the excuses of the grossest licentiousness and drunken revelry. Whiskey had entirely supplanted the feast foods.

[2] See the Burning of the White Dog, p. 85.

[3] This song is still sung by the preacher of the Gai'wiio'. The preacher stands at the door of the Long House on three successive mornings of the new year's season and greets the sunrise with his song. It is said to be a charm against high winds and the faithful claim that Gao', the spirit of the wind, holds back his fury when the song floats over the settlement.

[4] See The Goneowo ceremony, p. 95.

SECTION 56

" ' Now another message.

" This happened when Gai'wiio‘ was new. It was the time when he dwelt at Dionoⁿ''sodegĕ‘.[1]

"A father and son appeared in Dionoⁿ''sodegĕ‘. Now the name of the son was Gani'seoñ. They were on a hunting journey and came from Gadäges'käoⁿ[2] with a horse and cart. Now they tarried in Dionoⁿ''sodegĕ‘ for several nights before again taking up their journey.

" It was during the hunting season that the news spread that some one had returned from the hunting grounds without a companion. It was the young man who had returned. So they questioned him and asked where his father was. He answered, ' My father is lost. I went about searching for my father a number of days. I walked and searched and signalled with gun discharges hoping to find him. I could not find him and became weary waiting for his return.' So he said."

" Now Gaiänt'wakă when he heard this said, ' It is apparent to me that the young man has spoken the untruth.' So then they all went to the diviner of mysteries and Gaiänt'wakă spoke to him saying, ' It is my opinion that the boy has murdered his own father.' And the prophet answering said, ' They have not yet given me the power to see things but this will I do. Bring a bullet, a knife, and a hatchet that the boy may look upon these things when I speak and perhaps the truth will come (see plate 14). One of these things will move though not touched and he shall be the witness.' So the head men did as bidden and placed the objects as directed. In the middle of the floor they spread a blanket and put the articles upon it. Then they gathered around it and watched, and as they watched he spoke and the bullet moved. Thus it happened. Then spoke Ganio‘dai'io‘, ' This brings the confirmation of the rumor. Truly the youth has murdered his father, and furthermore I say that the crime was committed between Gānos'[3] and Hanĕnk'gaek.[4] On the south side of a mountain, where half way up an elm is broken, leaning over on the downhill side to the west lies the body buried in the leaves of the top branches. He, the father, is buried in the leaves.' So he said when he spoke. The

---

[1] Cornplanter village.
[2] Cattaraugus village, the principal town of the Cattaraugus region.
[3] Franklin, Pa.
[4] Oil City, Pa.

Plate 14

The discovery of the murderer, section 56. (See p. 52.)

From a drawing by Jesse Cornplanter

Plate 15

From a drawing by Jesse Cornplanter

Handsome Lake preaching at Tonawanda

chiefs and head-men appointed a delegation to see if all he had said were true. So they went as they had been told and found the body of the father and brought it back with them." Eniaiehuk.

SECTION 57

" ' Now another message to tell your people.

" ' You may ask three questions concerning three privileges when you go among your relatives at the ceremony of Nïsko'wŭknï[1] and ask what one is fitted for them.

" ' Who among you likes best to call upon the afflicted? Who among you loves to commune alone in the forests? Who among you is most anxious concerning religious conditions? ' "

So they asked him. Eniaiehuk.

SECTION 58

" ' Now another message.

" ' Now this matter will devolve upon you.

" ' The people will assemble in council and ask, " Who among us is able to say, ' I compel you to assemble? ' "

" ' Now when the question is set forth each person must make reply. The chiefs must demand it.'

" Now it happened that he fulfilled the requirements and all the people assembled and with one accord acclaimed that Ganio'dai'io' should lead them and that they should never murmur.

" Now that the people had done, he was patient to learn the result.

" The council adjourned and the messengers came and questioned him saying, ' How did you understand your people? '

" He answered, ' The majority consented that I should lead them.'[2]

" Then the messengers replied, ' Truly the greater number will follow you.' "

So they said and he said. Eniaiehuk.

SECTION 59

" ' Now another message.

" ' It is this: We, the messengers of our Creator, see strong drink used during the season when corn is planted. Now let those

---

[1] February, the moon of the midwinter, the time of thanksgiving.

[2] Because the people of this council elected that Handsome Lake should have authority over them he is ever after called Sēdwāgo'wănĕ, or chief leader, or our great teacher.

who use this evil drink know that it consumes the elements of life
They must repent.' "

So they said and he said.   Eniaiehuk.

SECTION 60

" ' Now another message.

" ' It is a custom for thanksgiving to be made over the hills of
planted corn.[1]   Let the head one of the family make an invocation
over the planted hills that the corn may continue to support life.
Now this will be a right thing and whosoever asks the help of the
Creator will receive it.' "

So they said and he said. . Eniaiehuk.

SECTION 61.

" ' So now another.

" ' Now it is understood that Dio'he'′ko^n (the corn, bean and
squash spirits), have a secret medicine, o'sagan′dă' and o'sdĭs′dani.
So soak your seed corn in these two medicines before you plant
your fields.   The medicines grow on the flat lands near streams.' "

So they said and he said.   Eniaiehuk.

SECTION 62

" ' Now another message.

" ' Now there are some who have boasted that they could drink
all the strong drink in the world.   Now we, the messengers, say
that they who thus idly boast will never live to accomplish what
they boast.   White men will ever distil the evil liquor.' "[2]

So they said and he said.   Eniaiehuk.

SECTION 63

" ' Now another message.

" ' Tell your friends and relatives that there will be two divisions

---

[1] The ceremony of invoking the Creator over the hills of corn was an old
one and like many other old customs was indorsed by the prophet.   This
custom is still continued among some of the Iroquois.   " When the leaf of
the dogwood is the size of a squirrel's ear, the planting season has come.
Before the dawn of the first day of the planting a virgin girl is sent to the
fields where she scatters a few grains of corn to the earth as she invokes
the assistance of the spirit of the corn for the harvest."

[2] This section with others of similar import brings out the prophet's intense
dislike of idle boasting.

óf mind[1] among the chiefs and head-men and among the people. Nevermore will your race be united.' "

So they said and he said.   Eniaiehuk.

SECTION 64

" ' Now another message.

" Now the messengers commanded him to give attention and he did. Then he saw a great assembly and the assembly was singing:

> ' The whole earth is here assembled,
> The whole world may come to us.
> We are ready.'

" Then said the messengers, ' What did you see when you gave attention? '

" He answered, ' I saw a great gathering of beings and the gathering was singing and the words of the song were:

> ' The whole earth is here assembled,
> The whole world may come to us.
> We are ready.'

" Then said the messengers, ' It is very true. The beings that you saw resemble human creatures. It is true that they are singing. Now the assembly is a gathered host of medicines for healing. Now let this be your ceremony when you wish to employ the medicine in a plant: First offer tobacco. Then tell the plant in gentle words what you desire of it and pluck it from the roots. It is said in the upper world that it is not right to take a plant for medicine without first talking to it. Let not one ever be taken without first speaking.' "[2]

So they said and he said.   Eniaiehuk.

---

[1] This seemingly obscure section is cleared of its mystery when the preacher explains that the divisions of mind refer to the Gaiwios'tŭk or Christian and Oñgwe'oⁿwekā' or Indian parties. " Dewadia'ke' gani'goï', *broken in twain, the unity of purpose,*" is Chief Cornplanter's term.

[2] The ceremony of gathering herbs. When a Seneca wishes to gather medicinal herbs, he goes into the woods where they grow and builds a small fire. When there is a quantity of glowing embers he stands before it and as he speaks at intervals casts a pinch of tobacco on the coals. He speaks to the spirits of the medicines telling them that he desires their healing virtues to cure his people of their afflictions.

"You have said that you are ready to heal the earth," chants the gatherer of herbs, " so now I claim you for my medicine. Give me of your healing virtues to purge and cleanse and cure. I will not destroy you but plant your seed that you may come again and yield fourfold more. Spirits of the herbs, I do not take your lives without purpose but to make you the agent of heal-

SECTION 65

" ' Now another message.

" 'It has been a custom when a person knows of a healing herb
to ask payment for giving it to a patient. Now we say that this is
not right. It is not right to demand compensation for treating the
sick. If such is done it adds greater afflictions to the sick one.
The Creator has given different people knowledge of different
things and it is the Creator's desire that men should employ their
knowledge to help one another, especially those who are afflicted.
Now moreover the person helped out ought only to give tobacco for
an offering.' "

So they said and he said.   Eniaiehuk.

SECTION 66

" ' Now another message.

" ' Now it is said that your fathers of old never reached the true
lands of our Creator nor did they ever enter the house of the
tormentor, Ganos'ge'.[1] It is said that in some matters they did the
will of the Creator and that in others they did not. They did both
good and bad and none was either good or bad. They are therefore in a place separate and unknown to us, we think, enjoying
themselves.' "

So they said and he said.   Eniaiehuk.

SECTION 67

" ' Now another message.

" 'Now it is said that your people must change certain customs.
It has been the custom to mourn at each recurring anniversary of
the death of a friend or relative.[2] It is said that while you are

---

ing, for we are very sick. You have said that all the world might come to
you, so I have come. I give you thanks for your benefits and thank the
Creator for your gift."

When the last puff of tobacco smoke had arisen the gatherer of herbs
begins his work. He digs the plant from the roots and breaking off the seed
stalks drops the pods into the hole and gently covers them over with fertile
leaf mold.

" The plant will come again," he says, " and I have not destroyed life
but helped increase it. So the plant is willing to lend me of its virtue."
Gahadondeh, (Woodland Border), Seneca.

[1] The evil spirit has no domain except his house. A land in which the
condemned spirit might roam would not be so terrible but eternal confinement within a house was considered a horrible fate by the liberty-loving
Iroquois.

[2] See Funeral and Mourning Customs, p. 107.

upon the earth you do not realize the harm that this works upon the departed.

"'Now moreover it is said that when an infant is born upon the earth with which the parents are dissatisfied, it knows and says, "I will return to my home above the earth.'"

"Now it is said that our grief adds to the sorrows of the dead. It is said that it is not possible to grieve always. Ten days shall be the time for mourning and when our friends depart we must lay grief aside. When you, the beings of earth, lose one of your number you must bury your grief in their grave. Some will die today and some tomorrow for the number of our days is known in the sky-world. So hereafter do not grieve. Now it is said that when the ten days have elapsed to prepare a feast and the soul of the dead will return and partake of it with you. It is said moreover that you can journey with the dead only as far as the grave. It is said that when you follow a body to the grave you must have prepared for that journey as if to travel afar. Put on your finest clothing for every human creature is on its journey graveward. It is said that the bodies of the dead have intelligence and know what transpires about them.[1] It is true.'"

So they said and he said. Eniaiehuk.

SECTION 68

"Now it is said that when Ganio'dai'io' was at Tonawanda spreading Gai'wiio' it happened that a certain man named Segwai"doⁿgwi said, 'I will also send a message to the four messengers and ask whether I am right in my belief in repentance and right doing.' So he sent his message upward in tobacco smoke."

Now when the messengers arose from a council with Ganio'dai'io' he reported what they had told him. "It is a hard matter for he, the questioner, is two-minded." So he said.

Then Segwai"doⁿgwi said, "Now this will I do: I will give a string of wampum, ot'go'ä, to the chiefs for a proof of my repentance, for though I have been thinking, yet I can not discover that I am two-minded."

Now when Gai'wiiostŭk (the Christian religion) came this man was the first to accept its teaching. When the chiefs heard of it they went to him and offered to return his wampum.

Then said the man, "I will not turn back because it is for the good of all that I have this religion."

---

[1] See, The death feast, p. 110.

Now all the chiefs and head-men could not persuade him to return to the right way.

So it is said.   Eniaiehuk.

SECTION 69

" Now another message.

" Now it is said that you must relate what the messengers say about the coming end of the earth.   Relate how all those who refuse to believe in Gai'wiio' will suffer hardships.[1]   Now when the earth is about to end the chiefs and head-men will disagree and that will be a sign.   So also, the Honon'doint will disagree.   Then will the relations know the truth."

So they said and he said.   Eniaiehuk.

SECTION 70

" Now another message.

" Now we say that you must tell your friends and relatives that there will be a time when all the earth will withhold its sustaining foods.   Then will come the end of the world and those who refuse to believe in Gai'wiio' will suffer great hardships."

So they said and he said.   Eniaiehuk.

SECTION 71

" Now another message.

" Now we think that a time will come when a great plague will kill many people and no one will know its cause.   Then will you know that the end is near and those who do not believe will suffer great hardships."

So they said and he said.   Eniaiehuk.

SECTION 72

" Now another message.

" Now we think that a time will come when a woman will be seen performing her witch spells in the daylight.   Then will you know that the end is near.   She will run through the neighborhood boasting how many she has slain by her sorcery.   Then will you see how she who refused to believe in Gai'wiio' will suffer punishment."

So they said and he said.   Eniaiehuk.

SECTION 73

" Now another message.

" In that time you will hear many rumors of men who say, ' I have spoken with the Creator.'   So also will you see many wonders

---

[1] See Introduction, p. 26.

but they will not endure for they will be the work of the evil spirit.

"Verily we say that there will be none other than you who will receive a message from the Creator through us. This truth will be proclaimed when the end comes."

So they said and he said. Eniaiehuk.

SECTION 74

"Now another message.

"In that time every poisonous creature will appear. These creatures the Creator has imprisoned in the underworld and they are the creations of the evil-minded spirit. Now it is our opinion that when they are released many people will be captured and poisoned by them. Men will see these hardships when they fail to believe in Gai'wiio'."

So they said and he said. Eniaiehuk.

SECTION 75

"Now another message.

"Now there will be some who will enter into a sleep. When they lie down they will be in health and as they sleep the Creator will withdraw their lives for they are true. To the faithful this will happen." [1]

So they said and he said. Eniaiehuk.

SECTION 76

"Now another message.

"Now we think that the Creator will stop the earth and heavens. All the powers of nature will he suspend. Now they will see this who refuse to believe in Gai'wiio'."

So they said and he said. Eniaiehuk.

SECTION 77

"Now another message.

"Now we think that when the end comes the earth will be destroyed by fire and not one upon it will escape for all the earth will be enveloped in flames and all those who refuse to believe in Gai'wiio' will be in it."

So they said and he said. Eniaiehuk.

---

[1] Because Handsome Lake did not die in this manner some of his half believing followers at Onondaga repudiated his teaching.

Recitation of the third day

NOW AT TONAWANDA

SECTION 78

" Now another message. Tell it to those at Tonawanda.

" Now they said to him, ' Watch a certain place.' So he did and he saw a certain person holding meat in his hands. The man was rejoicing and was well clothed and fed and his name was Tă'dondä'ieha', and he recognized him."

" Then said they to him, ' How is it?'

" He answered, ' I recognized Tă'dondä'ieha' and he held meat in his hands.' So answered he who talked religiously."

" Then the messengers answered, ' Truly you saw a man with meat enjoying himself. He was joyous because he was a prosperous and successful hunter and gave game as presents to his neighbors. So his neighbors were grateful and thanked him. Now the man you saw has departed from the earth. In his earth-life he cleansed himself each day, visited and enjoyed himself in his best clothing. He was ever good to his fellow-beings and so he is blessed and will receive the reward reserved for him by his Creator."

So they said and he said. Eniaiehuk.

SECTION 79

" Now another message.

" This will happen.

" You will sing three times and the third time you sing you will step into oyă'dedion'diade', the other world.[1] That you go there will be the earnest wish of all who have heard your message."

So they said and he said. Eniaiehuk.

SECTION 80

" Now another message.

" Every person has a song to sing when the time comes to leave the earth. When a person is departing he must sing that song

---

[1] It was customary for the friends and relatives to address the body of the dead and give expression to one's desires, etc. The soul when it reached the heaven-world would then tell the Great Ruler who would attend to the wishes expressed.

and continue to sing on his journey to the other world.[1] They will do this who have repented and who believe in Gai'wiio'."

So they said and he said. Eniaiehuk.

SECTION 81

"Now another message.

"Now the messengers said, 'Look you back in a vision to Cornplanter village and the place where the creek empties into the river.' So he looked and saw a large number of canoes gathered there. Many people were assembled and there were barrels of strong drink at the place. The people were making much noise. Now moreover there was a man there, hopping from canoe to canoe and singing Dji'hayā, the song of the evil-minded spirit. Now the words that he sang were these:

'More happy am I in my own house,
Far more happy there than here.'

"Yet the man seemed to be greatly enjoying himself.

"Then said the messengers, 'You have been observing, now what did you see?'

He answered, 'I saw a man hopping from canoe to canoe singing the song of the evil-minded one. He said that his house was more happy a place than that where he was. The people about I should judge were filled with strong drink.' So he said in answer to the messengers.

_____

[1] Ideas of the soul. The following ideas of the human soul were anciently held by the Iroquois and their influence on the teachings of Handsome Lake's teachings will be noted upon reading the Gai'wiio':

Every soul has a path to its destiny after death.

Every soul retains its personal identity whatever form it may inhabit.

Soul differs from life.

When the soul leaves the body life does not necessarily.

When life leaves the body the soul generally does, though not always immediately but may linger for ten days.

The soul may pass from a living body and enter any object or go to any place to acquire wisdom and returning reveal it to the person in dreams or visions.

Should a person refuse persistently to heed these warning visions the soul is liable to desert him, leaving the person simply a creature without power to resist or understand the influence of the various spirits good or bad.

Thinking that by some oversight or evil doing that he may lose his soul the Indian often offers sacrifice to his evil spirit. This is to satisfy his evil spirit with other things than wrong doing and thereby not offend his good spirit.

" Then answered the messengers, ' What you say is true. The man was the punisher and his delight is to see people filled with strong drink.' "

So they said and he said. Eniaiehuk.

THE JOURNEY OVER THE GREAT SKY-ROAD

SECTION 82

" ' Now another message.

" ' Now it is the time for our departure. We shall now go on a journey and then you shall see the coming of the fourth messenger, the journey of our friends and the works of the living of earth. More, you will see the house of the punisher and the lands of our Creator.' "

So they said. Eniaiehuk.

SECTION 83

" ' Now another message.

" Suddenly as they looked, a road slowly descended from the south sky[1] and came to where they were standing. Now thereon he saw the four tracks of the human race going in one direction. The footprints were all of different sizes from small to great. Now moreover a more brilliant light than the light of earth appeared."

So they said. Eniaiehuk.

SECTION 84

" ' Now they said unto him, ' We will tarry here a while in order that you may see.'

" Now as he watched and believed, he saw a large woman sitting there. Now the woman was grasping frantically at all things within her reach, and it seemed that she could not stand because of her great size. That was what he saw.

" Then they said to him, ' What did you see ? '

" He answered, ' It is hard to say. I saw a woman sitting and she was large of size and snatching at everything about her. I am of the opinion that she can not rise.' So he answered when he spoke.

" Then the messengers answered, ' It is true. That which you saw was the evil of stinginess. She can not stand and thus she will

---

[1] The great sky-road of the Gai'wiio' is the milky way. The souls of the dead are supposed to journey over the broad band and divide at the forks. The multitude of stars are thought to be the footprints of the dead.

remain forever. Thus it will be with those who forsake religious teachings and think more of the things of earth than of the new world above. (Having glutted themselves with the things of earth they are unable to stand upon the heaven road.)' " [1]

So they said and he said. Eniaiehuk.

SECTION 85

" Now they said, ' We shall proceed.' Now the farther they went the more brilliant the light became. They had not gone far when the four messengers said, ' Now we will stop again. Look attentively at what you see.'

" So he looked and saw three groups of people and each group was of a different size. The first was large, the second small and the third still smaller.

" Then the messengers asked him, ' What do you see? '

" He answered, ' I saw three groups, the first a large group, the second half as large as the first and the third still smaller.' That is what he said when he answered.

" Then they replied, ' Truly you have seen. The groups represent the people of earth. The first group you saw was composed of those who have not repented; the second group was inclined half way, and the third group, the smallest one, was composed of those who have repented. They are protected by the true belief in Gai'wiio'.' "

So they said and he said. Eniaiehuk.

SECTION 86

" So they proceeded a short distance and again came to a halt. Then the messengers pointed out a spot and bade him watch attentively. Then he saw a house strongly built and within it he saw three different things. The first was a pair of handcuffs, the second a whip and the third a hang-rope."

" Then asked the messengers, ' What did you see? '

" He answered, ' The house I saw was strongly built and within the house I saw three different things. The first was a pair of handcuffs, the second a whip and the third a hangman's rope.' So he answered.

---

[1] Those who gain great riches and lack humility can not stand upon the sky-road nor can they walk. The poor and meek only can travel skyward and not even the poor unless their ways have been humble and marked with virtue. Thus it is said, " It is better to be poor on earth and rich in the sky-world than to have earth riches and no heaven."

" Then they replied, ' Truly it is a strongly built house. It is a prison. Now it is true that three things are there for punishment. How hard it is for a transgressor to see that he should be punished; yet it is the cry of the people that the laws of the white man are better than the teachings of Gai'wiio'. This frightens even the Great Spirit for he knows the punishment of those who say such things.' "

So they said and he said. Eniaiehuk.

SECTION 87

" So they proceeded and it was not long before they said, ' We must stop here.' Then they pointed in a certain direction and commanded him to watch. So he watched and as he did he saw a house with a spire and a path leading into the house and none out. There was no door, neither were there any windows in the house. Within was a great noise, wailing and crying, and the house was hot.

" Then the messengers asked him what he saw.

" He answered, ' I saw a house with a spire and a path leading to the house. There was no door, neither were there any windows in the house. Within was a great noise, wailing and crying, and the house was hot.'

" Then they replied, ' You have truly seen. It is a hard matter for Indians to embrace these conditions, that is, to embrace the belief of Bible believers.' "

So they said and he said. Eniaiehuk.

SECTION 88

" So they proceeded and had not gone far when the messengers said, ' Look downward upon the Buffalo Creek reservation.'

" Se he looked and the place seemed honeycombed and covered with a net.

" Then the messengers asked him what he saw.

" He answered, ' I saw the Buffalo Creek reservation and it seemed honeycombed like ice and covered with a net.' So he replied.

" Then the messengers said, ' Truly! We think that this reservation will fall.' Now they said moreover that it was the duty of the chiefs to preserve it but it should be hard for some should take an upper hand.' "

So they said and he said. Eniaiehuk.

SECTION 89

" So they proceeded a little ways farther and soon they said, ' We will stop here.' Then they pointed out a certain spot and said, ' Watch! Look upon the eastern heavens and observe! '

" So he looked and saw two immense drops (or balls of liquid) hanging, one red and one yellow. It seemed that they were suspended only for an instant and would momentarily fall.

" Then the messengers asked, ' What did you see there? '

" He answered, ' I saw two drops, one red and one yellow, suspended as if about to fall.'

" Then the messengers replied, ' Truly you have spoken. It is so. Should one of those drops fall it would bring great calamity upon the earth. Many people would leave the earth should one drop but we are doing our utmost to prevent such an event.' "

So they said and he said. Eniaiehuk.

SECTION 90

" So they proceeded but had not gone a long distance before they said, ' We will stop and watch a certain place. Now listen to the earth.'

" So he listened and as well as he could understand he thought that he heard wailing and mourning. The sounds seemed to be the crying of children.

" Then the messengers asked, ' What did you observe? '

" He answered, ' I thought that I heard the wailing of the aged and the crying of children.'

" Then the messengers replied, ' It is true. What you have heard is the substance of life going back to the Creator. When this time comes there will be great misery upon the earth.' "

So they said and he said. Eniaiehuk.

SECTION 91

" So they proceeded a little ways farther and in a short time they reached a certain spot and stopped.

" Then said the messengers, ' Look toward the setting sun.'

" So he looked and saw. Now as he looked he seemed to see a man pacing to and fro. He seemed to be a white man and in his hand he seemed to have a bayonet with which he prodded the ground. Now moreover he seemed very angry.

" Then said the messengers, ' What did you see? '

" He answered, ' I saw what seemed to be a man pacing to and fro. He seemed to be a white man and in his hand he seemed to have a bayonet with which he prodded the ground, and, moreover, it seemed that he was angry.' So he said when he answered.

" Then the messengers said, ' It is true. He is a white man and in a temper. It is true. Indians must not help him and the head-men must honestly strive to prevent their followers from helping him.' " [1]

So they said and he said. Eniaiehuk.

SECTION 92

" So they proceeded on their journey and had not gone far when they stopped.

" Then the messengers said, ' Watch attentively.' Then they pointed out to him a certain spot midway between the earth and the clouds. So he watched there. Now this is true. He saw a house suspended there and on the veranda with a railing about it, a man walked and with him was a penny dog (kwĕn'nĭs dji''yä). Now moreover the man was rejoicing and he was a white man.

" Then said the messengers, ' What did you see? '

" He answered, ' I saw a house suspended in the air and on the porch with a railing about it a man was walking and with him was a penny dog. Now moreover the man was a white man.'

" Then the messengers said, ' Truly you have seen. It is said that the man is the first and oldest president of the United States. Now he enjoys himself and he is the only white man so near the new world of our Creator. Now it is said that there was once a time when the Thirteen Fires and the King[2] were in trouble. The Thirteen Fires were victorious and this man won the victory from the king. Said the king, " You have overpowered me, so now I release everything that was in my control, even these Iroquois who were my helpers. It rests with you what shall be done with them. Let them be to you a thing for a sacrifice." Then said the president, " I shall let them live and go back to the places that are theirs for they are an independent people." So it is said. Now this man did a great work. He has ordered things that we may enjoy ourselves, as long as the sun shines and waters run. This is the doing of our Great Creator.' "[3]

So they said and he said. Eniaiehuk.

---

[1] This section refers to the " war in the west," probably General Harrison's campaign against Tecumseh in 1811. Red Jacket and all the principal chiefs were anxious to preserve peace and did all within their power to prevent their young warriors from enlisting on either side but were not entirely successful. The issue was of such moment that the prophet deemed it wise to reveal the will of the four messengers in the matter.

[2] The word here is feminine and should be translated queen but this would manifestly not be in accord with truth. The error was made by Chief John Jacket who wrote out the Gai'wiio' in Seneca in 1860, during the reign of Queen Victoria.

[3] See Washington and the Iroquois, p. 137.

The women's dance

Plate 17

The Seneca buffalo dance

From a drawing by Jesse Cornplanter

SECTION 93

" So then they proceeded on their journey but had not gone far when they stopped.

" Then the messengers said, ' Watch,' and pointed to a certain spot toward the setting sun.

" So he. watched and saw a large object revolving. It was white and moving slowly.

" Then said the four messengers, ' What did you see? '

" He answered, ' I saw a large object revolving. It was white and moving slowly.'

" Then said the messengers, ' It is true. The thing is that which regulates the air over the earth. It is that which we call the Odā'eo (the veil over all). It is said that it would bring great calamity should it revolve too fast. Should it turn faster it would injure mankind. Now we are the regulators and watchers of the veil over all.' "

So they said and he said. Eniaiehuk.

SECTION 94

" So they proceeded on their journey and it happened that a vision appeared unto them. They seemed to be advancing toward an approaching man. Soon they met him and passed. Now when they were a distance apart they turned and he was facing them. So they greeted each other. Then said the man, ' Sedwāgo'wanĕ, I must ask you a question. Did you never hear your grandfathers say that once there was a certain man upon the earth across the great waters who was slain by his own people? ' That was what he said when he spoke.

" Then answered Sedwāgo'wanĕ, ' It is true. I have heard my grandparents say this.'

" Then answered the man, ' I am he.' (Segaⁿ'hedŭs, *He who resurrects*). And he turned his palms upward and they were scarred and his feet were likewise and his breast was pierced by a spear wound. It appeared that his hands and his feet were torn by iron nails.

"All this was true. It could be seen and blood was fresh upon him.

" Then said the man, ' They slew me because of their independence and unbelief. So I have gone home to shut the doors of heaven that they may not see me again until the earth passes away. Then will all the people cry to me for succor, and when I come it will be in this wise: my face will be sober and I shall turn it to my people. Now let me ask how your people receive your teachings.'

" He answered, ' It is my opinion that half my people are inclined to believe in me.'

" Then answered he, ' You are more successful than I for some believe in you but none in me. I am inclined to believe that in the end it will also be so with you. Now it is rumored that you are but a talker with spirits (djïs'gäⁿdătăha' [1]). Now it is true that I am a spirit and the one of him who was murdered. Now tell your people that they will become lost when they follow the ways of the white man.' "

So that is what he said. Eniaiehuk.

SECTION 95

" So they proceeded on their journey and had not gone far when they came to a halt.

" Then the messengers pointed out a certain spot and said, ' Watch attentively,' and beheld a man carrying loads of dirt and depositing them in a certain spot. He carried the earth in a wheelbarrow and his task was a hard one. Then he knew that the name of the man was Sagoyewat'ha, a chief.

" Then asked the messengers, 'What did you see?'

" He answered, ' I beheld a man carrying dirt in a wheelbarrow and that man had a laborious task. His name was Sagoyewat'ha, a chief.'

" Then answered the messengers, ' You have spoken truly. Sagoyewat'ha is the name of the man who carries the dirt. It is true that his work is laborious and this is for a punishment for he was the one who first gave his consent to the sale of Indian reservations. It is said that there is hardship for those who part with their lands for money or trade. So now you have seen the doom of those who repent not. Their eternity will be one of punishment.' "[2]

So they said and he said. Eniaiehuk.

---

[1] See Spiritism, p. 126.

[2] The followers of the Gai'wiio' to this day mention the name of Red Jacket with contempt. While they acknowledge his mental superiority they have no other admiration for him. He was ever the enemy of Cornplanter and Ganiodaiio with whom he had frequent collision and recognized the sachem-prophet only as an impostor. The teachings of Ganiodaiio have done much to prejudice the Iroquois against Red Jacket.

SECTION 96

" Now again they took up their journey and had not traveled far when they saw a crowd on both sides of the road. And when they came to where it was they saw that they were at the forks of the road. One road, on the right, was a narrow one and the tracks upon it were mostly those of children and all were pointed in one direction. Few adults had their tracks on this road, the road rough and wide. Now as they watched they saw a woman approaching the forks of the road from behind them. She came to where the road divided and as she halted before the roads a man who stood to the left shouted, ' To this side.' (Now the road of the wicked is owa'ĕtgä^n, a rough road.) Then the man on the right said, ' Not so. This woman has done her whole duty. She has truly repented.' Then answered the man on the left, ' You are wrong, for her repentance has been of short duration and so of slight effect. But the man on the right replied, ' Truly in her earth-life she repented and was faithful to her promises. This is all that is required and she will walk upon the narrow road.'

" Now one of the messengers turned to him and said, ' The woman has lived a repented life for three days and has entered into the happy eternity. It was not an easy matter for her to do so of herself, but we, the messengers, have plead before the Creator and he has heard us. Three times we assist every one who believes to continue in the faith of the Gai'wiio'. At this division in the great road we guide the spirits of the earth into Tain'tciadĕ (heaven land). At the forks of the road the spirits of the dead are divided. The narrow road leads to the pleasant lands of the Creator and the wide and rough road leads to the great lodge of the punisher.' "

So they said and he said. Eniaiehuk.

SECTION 97

" So now another.

" ' Verily you have seen the breast of a man hanging here by the road and in the center of that breast you saw a bullet hole.[1] Now we have caused this thing to be placed there. All will see it and he will see it who did the wrong when he comes upon the great road and know that he must turn aside and enter upon a journey over the wide and rough road.' "

So they said and he said. Eniaiehuk.

---

[1] See section 56.

SECTION 98

" Now again they told him that they would take up their journey and as they went they drew near to the house of the punisher. As they went over the broad road they walked well on the sides for the path was very stony. Now, strange, this was true; some great force seemed pushing them onward toward the house of the punisher.[1] Soon they began to inhale heated air and soon they heard the far away echoes of mournful cries borne on the blasts of the hot wind. At times the air was suffocating and the cries of the doomed were distressing."

So he said. Eniaiehuk.

SECTION 99

" Now they approached a great lodge. It seemed constructed of iron that had been highly heated and allowed to cool. Within the building hot vapor was rising from the fire pits.

" Now the messengers spoke saying, ' Let us tarry here a while.' Then one of the beings took from his bosom a crystal and pointed it at the lodge. He approached holding the glass at arm's length and as he came near the lodge arose to the height of the man so powerful was the crystal." Eniaiehuk.

SECTION 100

" Now they saw and then everyone knew that the house was very long and extended far out of the eye's reach. Now this is true. When a certain woman within saw the four and him drawing near she stretched out her arms and cried for help. Then answered the four, ' It is beyond our power to alter your condition now. Our work was with you on earth. Too late.' "

So they said and he said. Eniaiehuk.

SECTION 101

" Now as they looked they saw a being walking about as if he were the master of the lodge. He seemed continually distorting himself. At times horns shot out from his forehead, at times a cloven foot appeared and at times a tail was visible.[2]

---

[1] The prophet here alludes to the ease with which one may glide over the broad road. " It is no work to sin," says the preacher, " for the devil furnishes the legs for you."

[2] The prophet has very evidently borrowed his devil from transatlantic sources.

" Then said the four messengers to Ganiodai'io', ' That being is the punisher. It is he who torments those who have refused the words of Gai'wiio' when they heard them on the earth.' "

So they said. Eniaiehuk.

SECTION 102

" In a loud voice the punisher cried to a certain person saying, ' Come hither.' The punisher held a drinking vessel in his hand and within it was molten metal and thrusting it in the hands of the man he had called he said, ' Now warm yourself again as was your custom while on the earth for you loved hot drink.' Now the man pleaded but the punisher compelled him to swallow the molten metal. Then the man screamed in a loud voice and fell prone upon the ground with vapor steaming from his throat. Now he cried no more.

" Then said the four messengers, ' You have seen the manner of punishing those who persist in taking the fiery drink.' "

So they said. Eniaiehuk.

SECTION 103

" Now as they looked the master of the house spoke saying, ' Come.' Now the master knew the name of every one within the house. And straightway a woman came to where he stood. Then he grabbed her and forced her body into a great cauldron filled with a boiling liquid. Frequently he looked down into the cauldron to see if the woman had come again to the top. Suddenly she shot to the surface crying in a strange voice like some unknown animal and then sank down again. Soon again she appeared and cried, ' O, it is too hot! I should have an interval in which to cool myself!' Answered the punisher, ' Thou are not one-minded,' and jerking her out he flung her on one side. But the woman screeched in agony, ' O, it is too cold!' and her complaint was continuous and she moaned, ' It is too cold!' Then the punisher thrust her back into the boiling cauldron and immediately her bones rattled to the bottom. Such was the punishment given by the keeper of the house of torment.

" Then spoke the four messengers and said, ' This is the punishment given those who practice witchcraft. The woman whom you saw will suffer two deaths in this place and when her body is reduced to dust the punisher will gather them up again and conjure the dust back into a living body and continue his sport until finally

he has become weary when he will blow her ashes to destruction.
Such things happen to those who will not believe in Gai'wiio'.' "
So they said and he said. Eniaiehuk.

SECTION 104

" Now he saw a certain nude woman coming out from a crowd
and in all the hair of her body were writhing serpents. Her cheeks
were parched to the bone where she had been wont to color them
and likewise where her hair was parted there was no flesh. Now
she was greatly ashamed but she could not cover her nakedness. So
in this condition he saw her.

" Then said the four messengers, ' Saw thou that woman? In
life she was wont to give on'oityi'yĕnde, [secret powders] to men
to attract them to her. So you have seen the punishment meted
out to those who do this and do not repent.' "
So they said. Eniaiehuk.

SECTION 105

" Now they revealed another.

" Now the master of the house looked about and saw another
person. So he said, ' Come here, my nephew, I wish to see you flog
your wife as was your custom on the earth.' The punisher then
pointed out the image of a woman heated hot with fire and commanded the man to beat the image. Then the man pleaded with
moans to be released from the command but the punisher forced
him to strike the image with his bare hands, and the man fell in
agony prostrate upon the floor screaming. So he saw.

" Then said the four messengers, ' You have seen the punishment given to the man who beat his wife. Thus it will be with all
who fail to repent and fail to believe in Gai'wiio'. Now such was the
evil that this man did to grieve his Creator.' "
So they said and he said. Eniaiehuk.

SECTION 106

" Now they revealed another.

" The master of the house called out the names of two persons,
saying, ' Come here, my nephews,'[1] and straightway they stood
before him. Then said he, ' Commence an argument, you two, for
you are the man and wife who in your earth-life were wont to

---

[1] The Seneca term means, " my sister's children," thus both nephews and
nieces.

Plate 18

From a drawing by Jesse Cornplanter

The death chant and march at the Newtown Long House

Plate 19

The Spirit of the Hurricane

From a drawing by Jesse Cornplanter

quarrel continually, so quarrel again!' Then when he saw that the people were reluctant he compelled them to argue. Then they disputed until their eyes bulged from their heads, their tongues lolled out and flames of fire shot from ganä'shoo'. So this was what he saw.

"Then said the messengers, 'This is the punish nent reserved for those who quarrel without ceasing and fail to repent.'"

So they said. Eniaiehuk.

SECTION 107

"Now they showed him another:

"Now the punisher called out a certain woman's name saying, 'Come to me, my niece,' and straightway she came. Then said he, 'It was once your delight gaknowe'haat.' As he said this he lifted up an object from a pile and thrust it within her. Now the object was like ha'ji'no' gänää'', and it was red hot. Then she cried aloud in agony and she fell with steam issuing from her body. Now there were three piles of gä'nää', the first white, the second red and the third black and all were gä'nää'.' So this was what he saw.

"Then the messengers said, 'You have seen the punishment of the immoral woman.'"

So they said. Eniaiehuk.

SECTION 108

"Now they showed him another.

"Now the punisher called out in a loud voice saying, 'My nephew, come hither,' and the man stood before him. 'Now, nephew, play your violin as was once your delight.' The punisher handed the man a bar of hot iron and forced him to rub it upon his arm. So he played and the cords of his arm were the strings of the instrument and made the music. So in great agony he cried and screamed until he fell.[1]

"Then said the four messengers, 'You have seen the punishment of the man who failed to repent.'"

So they said. Eniaiehuk.

SECTION 109

"Now they revealed another.

"Now the punisher called out in a loud voice and commanded two persons to appear before him. Now when they stood before

---

[1] The pagan Indians detest the "fiddle" and "fiddle dances" as things of great evil and assert that they produce as much wickedness as drunkenness.

him he handed them what seemed a pack of red hot iron cards. Then he forced the two to sit down facing each other and compelled them to shuffle the cards and as they did flames spurted out from between them. So they cried out in great agony, sucked their fingers in their mouths, handled the cards again until their flesh was eaten away and the meat fell off. So this is what he saw.

" Then the messengers said, ' This is the punishment meted out to those who handle cards and repent not.' "

So they said. Eniaiehuk.

SECTION 110

" Verily he saw those who were upon the earth and those who were alive and he saw the wicked in the house of torment. He saw Gowonoⁿ'gowa [she great talker], Găkon'go' [she-glutton animal], Gănonjoni'yon [hanging kettle] and Hano'ēs [head-eater]. Verily he saw these four persons.

" Then said the four messengers, ' These four have committed the great sin and can not be forgiven.' "

So they said. Eniaiehuk.

SECTION 111

" Then said the messengers, ' We will proceed on our journey. It would be a hard thing should we tarry too long and meet the Creator on the road before we reach his pleasant lands. If we should meet him you should be compelled to stay here forever.' "[1]

So they said. Eniaiehuk.

SECTION 112

" Then they went out upon the narrow road and had not gone far upon it when a far more brilliant light appeared. It was then that they smelled the fragrant odors of the flowers along the road. Delicious looking fruits were growing on the wayside and every kind of bird flew in the air above them. The most marvelous and beautiful things were on every hand. And all these things were on the heaven road." Eniaiehuk.

SECTION 113

" So they continued on their journey and after a short time they came to a halt. Then spoke the messengers, ' This place is called, " the spring " and it is a place for rest.' Then behold he saw the spring and he thought that he had never seen so beautiful and

---

[1] See legend, Two brothers who went to the sky, p. 132.

clear a fount of water. Then said the four, ' This is a place of refreshment.' One of the four drew a bottle from his bosom, so it
seemed and it was, and dipped it in the spring. Then he said, ' You
must partake first,' and so he took it, but when he looked at it he
thought it was not enough. So he said, ' I think that this is not
sufficient.' And when he had said this the messengers looked at
one another and smiled and one said, ' Truly it is enough. If it
lacks, there is still the spring and the vessel may be refilled. So all
took and drank and all the drink that all wished was in the bottle.
Then said the messengers, ' This is a place of meeting. Now we
will go on our journey.' " [There are also said to have been two
other meeting places, Diogē''djaie, Grassy Place, and Dion'dot, The
Tree.]

So they said. Eniaiehuk.

SECTION 114

" So then they proceeded on their journey and had gone but a
short way when they saw someone coming toward them and it was
not long before they met. Then he saw it was a dog and when they
met, the dog began to wag its tail and sprang upon him. Then he
recognized the animal as his own dog and it appeared just as it had
when he had decorated it for the sacrifice in the Hadidji'yontwŭs
[New Year's ceremony]. Then said the four, ' This thing attests to
the value of our thankoffering to the Creator.' "[1]

So they said. Eniaiehuk.

SECTION 115

" So they took up their journey again and in a short time came
to a halt. In the distance before them a man appeared to be coming
and soon he came nearer. Then he saw that the man was guiding
two others, one on either side of him. Now as he looked he saw
that one was the daughter of Gaiänt'wakă and it appeared that she
was a large child. With her was his (Ganio'dai'io') own son, an
infant, and they greeted one another, the son and the daughter.
Now one could see that they were not strangers for they were
friendly. Now moreover a fourth person was leading them all."
Eniaiehuk.

SECTION 116

" Now that person spoke and said, ' I brought them with me to
testify to the truth that those of the lower world when they pass
away come hither.'

---

[1] See p. 85, Sacrifice of the white dog.

" Then spoke the daughter of Gaiän'twakă, ' I send a message.
It is this: It grieves me to know that my brothers on the earth disagree with my father. Bid them cease their disagreement.' So
she said."
Eniaiehuk.

SECTION 117

" So they took up their journey again and in a short time came
to a halt. There was a more brilliant light and as they stood suddenly they heard the echo of a commanding voice calling the people
together for the performance of the great feather dance.

" Then asked the four messengers, ' What think you has happened? '

" He answered, ' I heard the commanding voice of Joi'ise calling
the people to celebrate the great feather dance.'

" Then replied the four messengers, ' Verily, Joi'ise, your friend
is he who calls. He it was who was faithful and good and when
he passed away in the lands of the Creator he continued as on the
earth [to be a leader].' "
So they said. Eniaiehuk.

SECTION 118

" So they took up their journey again and after a ways the four
messengers said, ' We have arrived at the point where you must
return. Here there is a house prepared for your eternal abode but
should you now enter a room you could never go back to the earth-
world.' "
So they said. Eniaiehuk.

SECTION 119

" Now when he arrived in Tonawanda having come from
Dionon''sădegĕ he was reluctant in performing his religious duties."

SECTION 120

" Now he was at Cornplanter ten years, at Cold Spring two years
and at Tonawanda four years. From there he went to Ganonktiyuk'gegäo, Onondaga, and there fell our head man."

SECTION 121

" Now it happened that while he still abode at Tonawanda an invitation was extended by the people of Onondaga asking him to
come and preach Gai'wiio' to the chiefs and head men there."

SECTION 122

" Now it happened that the four messengers appeared to him when the invitation was extended, they the four speakers and messengers of the Great Spirit of the worlds.

" Now the first words that they spoke were these, ' They have stretched out their hands pleading for you to come and they are your own people at Onondaga. Let this be the way, prepare yourself and cleanse your body with medicine.[1] It is necessary moreover for you to secrete yourself in some hidden spot and await our call to start.' "

So they said. Eniaiehuk.

SECTION 123

" Now there will be another and his name will be the New Voice, Hawĕnose".

" So now it was that Ganio'dai'io' was bidden the third time to sing his song and this the messengers said would be the last.

" Now then he said, ' There is nothing to incumber me from fulfilling my call.' "

So said our head man. Eniaiehuk.

SECTION 124

" Thus it happened in the past and it is the truth.

" ' I must now take up my final journey to the new world,' he thought, and he was greatly troubled and longed for the home of his childhood and pined to return.

---

[1] Purification. The herb used most extensively by the Iroquois for " purification" was witch hopple, the bark of which was used both as an emetic and a purgative. For an emetic the bark was peeled upward and for a purgative downward.

Early in the spring during the spell of warm days the people would take their kettles, jars of soup and deerskins and go alone into the woods for their ceremony of purification. Here they would scrape the bark, build a fire and make a strong infusion of the witch hopple bark. The drink was taken in large quantities and then the Indian would sit wrapped in his deerskin to await the results. From sunrise to sunset the drink would be taken until the alimentary tract was completely emptied. Toward sundown a little soup would be sipped to ward off excessive weakness, and give strength to return home. The next morning sweat baths were often taken, though not always, and then solid food was eaten. This process was thought to purify the body and without doubt did much to do so. Besides the customary spring purification others were sometimes ordered for disease and for preparations for ordeals, tests and ceremonial purposes. The process was again repeated in the autumn.

" Then came the four messengers to him and said, ' The children will comfort you in your distress for they are without sin. They will elect a certain one from among them to plead that you continue to abide among them.' "

So they said. Eniaiehuk.

" Now it happened that it came to pass that all the children assembled and their spokesman did his utmost to exact a promise from Ganio'dai'io'. So great was his grief that after he had spoken a short time he could no longer plead. Then another boy was appointed by the children, a boy not bashful but rough and bold. So he, too, endeavored to persuade Ganio'dai'io', but it was a difficult task for him and he could scarcely speak, but he did. Then Ganio'dai'io' made an answer to the children. He rose and exhorted them to ever be faithful and a great multitude heard him and wept." Eniaiehuk.

SECTION 125

" Now at this time there was a man and his name was New Voice, a chief of equal rank with Cornplanter. Now this man urged Ganio'dai'io' to accept the invitation of his friends and relatives of Onondaga. He said, ' It is as if they were stretching forth their necks to see you coming. Now I am going forth to a gathering of chiefs at Buffalo on the long strip that is the fireplace of the Six Nations,[1] the great meeting place of human creatures. I will go so that I may believe that you are on your journey and I will ride away as fast as my horse can go.' So he said."

SECTION 126

" Now then Ganio'dai'io' started on his journey and a large number followed him that they might hear him speak. They had no conveyances but traveled afoot.

" Now when they came to their camping spot at Ganowa'gĕs,[2] he said to them in a commanding voice, 'Assemble early in the morning.' Now when they did he offered thanks and afterward he said, ' I have had a dream, a wondrous vision. I seemed to see a pathway, a trail overgrown and covered with grass so that it appeared not to have been traveled in a long time.' Now no one spoke but

---

[1] At this time there was an Onondaga village on the Buffalo Creek tract. It became therefore a legal meeting place for the Six Nations. The Canadian refugees often returned to council there.

[2] The site of the village opposite the present Avon, N. Y.

when all had heard and he had finished they dispersed and they continued on their journey."

SECTION 127

" Now their next camping spot was near Ganŭndase"ge'.[1]

" Now when they had all come up to the spot he called out in a commanding voice, ' Come hither and give thanks.' Now when the ceremony was over he said, ' I heard in a dream a certain woman speaking but I am not able to say whether she was of Onondaga or of Tonawanda from whence we came.' So this was what he said when he related his dream. Then all the company dispersed." Eniaiehuk.

SECTION 128

" So they proceeded on their journey.

" Now it happened that when they were near the reservation line he said, ' Let us refresh ourselves before going farther.' So they sat down and ate and then they continued on their journey."

" Now it happened that when they were over the reservation line that he said, ' I have forgotten my knife. I may have left it where we stopped and ate last. I can not lose that knife for it is one that I prize above many things. Therefore I must return and find it.'

" The preacher went back alone and there was no one to go with him. Now he became very ill and it was with great difficulty that he returned. The others had all gone on to the council but he was not able to get to it for he was very sick and in great distress. So when he did not come it was said, ' Our meeting is only a gathering about the fireplace.' " Eniaiehuk.

SECTION 129

" Now it happened that they all wished to comfort him. So for his pleasure they started a game of lacrosse[2] and played the game well. It was a bright and beautiful day and they brought him out so that he might see the play. Soon he desired to be taken back into the house." Eniaiehuk.

SECTION 130

" Now shortly after he said a few words. To the numbers gathered about him to hear his message he said, ' I will soon go to

---

[1] The Seneca village near the present site of Geneva, N. Y.

[2] Games were often played to cheer and cure the sick. Special foods were given the players.

my new home.[1]   Soon I will step into the new world for there is a plain pathway before me leading there.   Whoever follows my teachings will follow in my footsteps and I will look back upon him with outstretched arms inviting him into the new world of our Creator. Alas, I fear that a pall of smoke will obscure the eyes of many from the truth of Gai'wiio' but I pray that when I am gone that all may do what I have taught.'

" This is what he said.   This is what Ganio'dai'io', our head man, said to his people."   Eniaiehuk.

[Then the preacher says:]   " Relatives and friends: His term of ministry was sixteen years.   So preached our head man, Ganio'-dai'io'.

" Let this be our thanks to you and to the four messengers also. I give thanks to them for they are the messengers of our Creator. So, also, I give thanks to him whom we call Sĕdwāgowănĕ, our great teacher.   So, also, I give thanks to our great Creator.

" So have I said, I, Sosondowa (Great Night), the preacher."

[Signed]   EDWARD CORNPLANTER, *Sosondowa*

---

[1] Handsome Lake died August 10, 1815, at Onondaga.   His last moments were spent in a small cabin near the creek that runs into Onondaga creek at the foot of the terrace.   Three persons attended him and swore to keep all details secret.   He is said to have died before his nephew, Henry Obeal, could reach him.

PART 2

FIELD NOTES ON THE RITES AND CEREMONIES OF THE GANIO'DAI'IO' RELIGION [1]

GÄNÄ'YASTA'

The midwinter festival of the Iroquois, commonly called Indian New Year.

On the third day of what the Seneca term Niskowŭkni ne'' Sadē'goshä or the moon of midwinter, a council of head men is called and officers elected to officiate at the Gänä'yasta' or midwinter thanksgiving ceremony to be held two days later. Officers are chosen from each of the two brotherhoods [2] of clans.

On the first day of the ceremony officers called Ondeyä, dressed in buffalo skins, meet and lay out a route of houses which each pair of Ondeyä is to visit. This settled, they draw the buffalo heads over their heads and start out.

There are three excursions of Ondeyä from their lodges, one at about 9 a. m., one at about 12 m. and one at about 3 p. m. Two Ondeyä, carrying corn pounders painted with red stripes, knock at the door of a house and entering intone:

Hail, nephews. Now also the cousins with you. Now also you see the big heads.

> Ye hē! Gwäwandĕ!
> Onen''dĭq wodewĕ'noyē ne' nē'sēso gwäwandĕ!
> Onen''dĭq īswāgēn' noĭwane'!

This is repeated and the Ondeyä depart.

At noon the Ondeyä repair to their meeting place and emerging again go over the same route. Their message as they enter a lodge at this time is.

Hail. Be clean! Do not be confused, O nephews. Do not tread upon things, nephews, cousins, when you move.

> Yĕhe! Jokwehon! sänon'di gwä'wandĭ! dänondodädĕ,
> gwä'wandĭ nenc'sēso nänondo''yäno'!

At 3 p. m., returning to the same lodge, the message is:

> Yĕhē! Oisendase' susniun'nano ne'' swaisĕ'' dŭgayio' sändo.'
> One'' dĭq ĭtchigaine'son nongwŭk'sado' nenwande' sä'non dĭq
> ĭtch'nonadoktĕ' ongwŭkädo'. One'' dĭq nĕkho'' non'jiyē.

---

[1] Taken at Newtown, Cattaraugus reservation, January 1905, by A. C. Parker.

[2] See Phratries. [81]

After one has intoned this message or announcement the other pokes up the ashes with a basswood paddle and sings a song.

The first day is spent in this way, formal announcements being given by the officers.

On the morning of the second day all the lodges are visited by officers called Hadēiyäyoʻ. Later, say 9 a. m., clan officers, known as Hanä'sishě, begin their round of visits. Two men and two women are chosen from the phratries and going in couples to the various houses conduct a thanks or praise service. The burden of their words is a thanksgiving to God for the blessings that have been received by that house during the past year.

When this ceremony is over these officers throw up a paddle (Wadigusä'wea) signifying that the ceremony is over. At this time a chief makes a long thanksgiving speech in the council house.

At noon the " big feather " dancers visit every lodge and dance the sacred dance. Two women at least must participate. On entering a lodge the leader of the feather dancers must say:

> Onĕn"dĭq'   hodo"issoin'yŭnde   sedwā'ă'wŭk   gäon'ya'ge'
> honoñ'geʻ. Nēkho"nai' hodo'isshongonoindi neʻ' häwonn'.
> Hodawisa'sēʻ Osto'wägowă.
>   Onĕn"dĭq'dji'wŭsnowät   nĕ"   gissän   äyĕnoñgwēʻ   Osto'-
> wägowă.   Gagwēgon,'   onĕn"   dĭq,' djiwŭsnowät heniyonʻ
> swao'iwayandon'!
> Da'neho"!

At about 2 p. m. public dances begin in the " long house."

The Society of Bears, which during the early afternoon had been holding a session in the house of some member, enter the long house and dance publicly. The same is true of the False Face Company.

Other dances are the Pigeon song dance (Tcä'kowa) and the Gädä'ciot. The only dance in which physical contact is permitted is the Yĕndonĭssontăʻ or " dance of the beans." Dancers hold each other's hands as they circle around the singers. This is to represent the bean vine as it clings to a sapling or corn stalk.

On the morning of the third day the priest arises before daylight and standing at the door of the council house begins his song of thanks. The song is sung until dawn appears and then the priest ceases. Should a fierce wind be blowing it is believed that when the words of the song float upward the Great Spirit will say, " Cease your movements, Oh wind, I am listening to the song of my children."

The first verse is as follows:

Onĕⁿ'' dǐq' okno'wi, Onĕⁿ'' dǐq,' dasĕnni''dottondē
Găo'yä gütci'ja'! Yoändjă'gĕ igĕⁿ's
Onĕⁿ'' dǐq' o'gai'wayi' onĕ''
Dĕawĕn'nissĕ no'gowĕs
Dĕowiono'gowes
Saiwisa'honio'
Onĕⁿ'' dǐq' wadi'wayēïs.

The song begins with the singer's face to the west; he turns and sings in all directions, that all may hear his voice.

A legend relates that this song originated ages ago. An old woman is said to have been with child and before her son was born, from the heavens came this song.

Only one or two Indians sing this now, no others being able for some reason. After the song the priest calls upon the Great Spirit in these words:

Ye, ye-e, yēē!
Dane''agwa none''neⁿgä' nē'wa
Onĕⁿ'' dǐq dasa''tondat' gäogĕ'gĕ'
tci'ja', etc., etc.

At about 9 a. m. another officer of religion enters the long house and sings the Ganio'dai'io' song:

Fig. 1 Prayer rattle made from a dried squash. Allegany Seneca specimen.

Translation:

I love my world, I love my time, I love my growing children, I love my old people, I love my ceremonies.

At noon various societies and companies which have been holding sessions in private lodges adjourn to the council house to engage in public ceremonies. The great feather dance is celebrated at noon. Afterward nearly all the common dances are given, among which is the woman's football game and dance.

The morning of the third day is greeted as the previous day, by the song and prayer of the priest.

At 9 a. m. of the fourth day the Gonio'dai'io' song is chanted again.   Meanwhile the company of harvest dancers hold their dances at private houses going to the long house (ganon'sŭsgen') at noon.   Soon after the Bird Society or Gane"gwäē enters the council house and begins its dance.   Two dancers are chosen from each phratry, as are also two speakers.   The evening is devoted to the Trotting, Fish, Pigeon, Bear, False Face, Buffalo and other dances.   At 10 p. m. the ceremonies cease.

On the fifth day the dawn ceremony is repeated and at 9 a. m. the Ganio'dai'io' song is sung.   Societies hold meetings in their own lodges.

At about 1 p. m. a company of women dancers visit each house, dance and sing and return to the long house.   False Face beggars also roam from lodge to lodge in search of sacred tobacco.   In the afternoon and evening various dances are held in the long house. At about 11 p. m. the Husk Face Company enters the long house and engages in their public ceremony.   After this dance the people are dismissed by a chief.

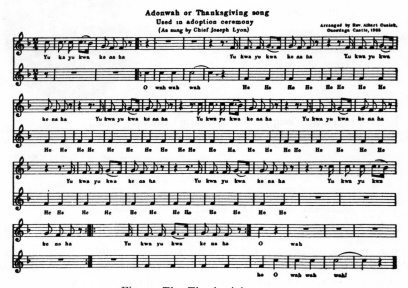

Fig. 2   The Thanksgiving song

The morning of the sixth day is devoted to the dog sacrifice and the tobacco offering.   Afterward the Ado"we' are sung.   This song may be translated: I am now going home, I step upon another world, I turn and extend my arms for a friend to lead me, I pray all may go where I go. Now the earth is smoky and none can see the other world [as I do].

On the seventh day the Honon'diont hold a morning dance and then proceed to cook the feast. Costumed feather dancers enter the long house and dance. The "wind is open for names," or opportunity is now given to bestow names. At this point if a boy is to be named the priest rises and says, " Hio'gĕnē", dji'wagä ne-e! "

" Hu", hu", hu"hu"-ä! " respond the people.

If a girl is to be named there is no ceremony other than the mere announcement of the name. A speech is now made by a chief bidding people make ready for the sacred bowl game.

Honon'diont visit each lodge exacting from every person stakes for the sacred gamble. Each phratry is to play against the other The Honon'diont then meet and match articles, value for value.

The night previous every person endeavors to have a prophetic dream, whereby they may know the result of this game. No one must cheat in this game for " it is God's."

The great feather dance is repeated and names bestowed on this day. At night the Husk Faces return and give a grand final dance.

The ninth day is the last one of the midwinter's ceremony. Early in the morning the priest gives a thanksgiving " sermon." At 5 p. m. occurs the dance in honor of the " three sisters," Diohē"ko, (these-we-live-on). Afterward the woman's dance is held, alternating with the following men's dances, Trotting, Pumpkin, Pigeon and Beans. The feast is then distributed and the people disperse.

THE WHITE DOG SACRIFICE[1]

A preliminary translation of the ceremonial prayer at the burning of the white dog at the Seneca Indian new year's ceremony (February).

Wotok waiiendakwa Gaiantguntgwaa

(wotok'waiïen'dakwa gaiäñt'guntgwä')

Gwa! Gwa! Gwa!
So now this is the appointed time!
Oh listen, you who dwell in the sky!

---

[1] Recorded February 1906, at Cattaraugus reservation.

Our words are straight —
Only these can we speak unto you,
Oh you from whom we are descended,
Oh you who dwell in the sky!
You look down upon us and know that we are all children.
Now we petition you as we burn this sacred tobacco!
Now we commence our invocation,
Now we speak of all that you have created.
Now [in the beginning] you did think that men-beings should inherit the blessings of your creations,
For you did say, " Earth was my birthplace! "
Now we have spoken in this incense [throws tobacco upon the flames].
Oh now inhale the smoke, so listen to our words.
Now we commence, we are all that remain upon the earth.
You behold the places that once were filled but now are empty;
We were unable to change it for you made the law.
Now you think that there should be two conditions of temperature upon the earth;
One you thought should be cold and one should be warm
And when the warm season came that Diohē"ko, our substance, should spring from the bosom of Earth, our mother.
Now we have harvested the Diohe"ko from whence our living is
For the warm season has gone and we have here assembled.
Now we have made inquiries among all the people and they remember their promises,
For they promised you that they should assemble again at Gaiwanos'kwa gowa'
On the fifth sun of the moon Nĭskowŭk'nĭ.
So all fulfilled the plan and gathered together in the moon Nĭs'a, even those here present,
Oh you who were born of Earth, yet dwell in the sky!
Now all have fulfilled the law, for you did plan that the rites should be perpetuated even forever.
Now we are commencing, Oh you who were born of Earth!
Upon the first day the Great Feather dance went through the village for your pleasure.
The honon'diont and their cousins did their full duty.
Now on the next day Ganēo' was celebrated; at midday they went through the village,

Plate 20

Sacrifice of the White Dog on the Grand River reservation of the Six
Nations, Canada

Plate 21

A corner of the I'dos lodge at Newtown, Cattaraugus reservation

And you did give us great joy because we performed this ceremony.
For you did think that Ganēo' should be celebrated upon the earth
    for thine own self.
Thus did we fulfil your desires, Oh you who were born of Earth,
    yet live in the sky!
Now on the next day Gagandot was played.
Truly we did fulfil your desires,
Oh you who were born of Earth, you who live in the sky!
You did see all that was done,
Oh you who were born of Earth, you who live in the sky!
In the beginning you thought that you would lay this sacred tobacco
    by man's side
That men should have an incense with which to send his words up
    to the sky,
With which to lift his words when the year ended.
Truly we have fulfilled your desires and here we have that basket
    of sacred tobacco,
Oh you who were born of Earth, you who dwell in the sky!
[Throws tobacco on the flames.]
So now the smoke arises!
Oh inhale the incense as you listen!
For now do we commence to speak of what you have created.
In the beginning you thought that there should be a world
Upon which men beings should travel
That you might say, " They are my descendants."
Now there is a shaft that reaches up to you, Ganeowi, the sacred
    song of the morning it is.
Now of your descendants as many as remain are gathered here.
Now you thought that there should be two sexes of men-beings,
That one should be the male and one should be the female,
And the function of the female should be the rearing of children.
Truly the females are fulfilling the design of their creation
For in their arms we see their children.
Truly it is in progress what you planned for them.
Now the smoke arises!
So now inhale this sacred incense!
Now we petition you that this thing should continue so henceforth,
And shall continue as long as the earth endures.
Now you thought that there should be a world
Upon which grasses of different kinds should grow

And that some should be medicinal,
And that some should yield fruits for a help to the men-beings
    who dwell upon the earth.
Thus did you think, O you who dwell in the sky!
Now it was ordered to be so when the warm season warmed the
    earth
And that it should be fulfilled them and that your descendants
    should see the return of things.
Now again the smoke arises
And the people speak through it to you,
Oh you who dwell in the sky!
Now we implore you that it may so occur again when the earth
    warms,
That your desires may be fulfilled and that your descendants may
    again see your creations.
Now again the smoke arises
And the people speak through it to you,
Oh you who dwell in the sky
Yet were born of Earth!

Now our sustenance you thought should be placed beside us,
And that men-beings should labor for their living.
These plans are all in progress
All see from whence their living comes.
Now we implore you that when the earth warms again that sus-
    taining food may grow.
This we ask by the power of the incense tobacco,
Oh inhale it and listen to us,
Oh you, our great ancestor,
You who dwell in the sky!

You thought that there should be veins and that there should be
    fountains of water;
Now this thought is made a fact and is occurring
So we ask that this shall continue.
Now again the smoke arises
To you the father of all men-beings,
To you who dwell in the sky!

Now you thought that there should be living creatures,
Inhabiting the waters, useful to the people.

Now your thoughts have happened and we implore you that it may
    not be withdrawn,
Oh you who were born of Earth,
Oh you who dwell in the sky!
But may continue as long as earth endures.

So now another.
You did think that there should be world
And that bushes should grow upon it for a help to the people,
That the bushes should yield various fruits for the benefit of men-
    beings,
Oh you who were born of Earth,
Oh you who dwell in the sky,
May this continue as long as earth endures!

Now again the smoke arises,
Oh inhale the incense and continue to listen
Oh you who were born of Earth
Oh you who dwell in the sky!

So now another.
Now you did think that there should be forests upon the earth
And that they might be a help to the people.
So now moreover you did think that there should be a certain tree
That should yield sweet water from its trunk.
Now that tree is the Maple and it is faithful to its design
May this continue to be,
Oh you who dwell in the sky!

Now again the smoke arises,
And the people pray that this may still continue when the earth
    becomes warm again!
So now this thing is done.
Our words are as straight as we could make them.
Only this can we do for we are all young
Oh you who were born of Earth,
Oh you who dwell in the sky!
So now this one thing ends.

So now another.
You have created wild animals that roam in the forests,
You did think that they would be a pleasure to men-beings

Who should remember and say, " We are his descendants."
Now may they continue so to be,
Oh you who were born of Earth,
Oh you who dwell in the sky!

So now another.
The people are speaking;
They are continuing from the commencement of creation
Discussing those things that you didst think would be a benefit to
    men-beings,
Oh you who were born of Earth,
Oh you who dwell in the sky!

Now the birds that inhabit the air,
Birds from the low world to the great birds,
Birds that float above the clouds.
All these you did think would be a benefit to mankind.
Oh you who were born of Earth,
Oh you who dwell in the sky!
Now we ask that this thought should be forever
Even as long as earth endures.

Now again the smoke arises,
Continue to listen as you inhale this incense,
For we are discussing the things of your creation
That you did think should be a benefit to mankind,
Oh you who were born of Earth,
Oh you who dwell in the sky!
Now you did think that there should be a world and that it should
    become cold,
At a recurring season become cold again.
Now we implore thee that it should not be too great a cold
And likewise when the earth becomes warm again,
That the heat should be moderate and comfortable.
Now again the smoke arises
To you who were born of Earth,
To you who dwell in the sky!

So now another.
Continue to listen!
You did think that there should be a wind
And that it should be a help to the world.

Now the wind is here.
And the people pray that it may continue to be so as long as earth
  endures.

Now again the smoke arises
To you who were born of Earth,
To you who dwell in the sky!
Now they came from the west.
Ti′sŏt we call them,
Our great grandfathers the Thunderers;
You did make them our relatives.
They were placed in a high position
That they might care for the earth
And feed the waters that flow over the world and purify them,
And freshen all things that grow.
A certain season was appointed for their activity
The season when the earth commences to become warm again.
Now again the smoke arises,
It lifts our words to you,
Oh inhale the incense and continue to listen,
Oh you who were born of Earth,
Oh you who dwell in the sky!
Now the whole world prays that you will listen,
May all these things continue as long as earth endures,
Oh you who were born of Earth,
Oh you who dwell in the sky!

So now again another.
You did think that there should be a sky
And that within it should be something to illuminate the world,
Ĕndē′ka gää′′kwa, our great brother, the mighty warrior, the Sun,
And that so it should be called so.
He has a high position that shall last as long as earth endures.
Now again the smoke arises and so smoke tobacco as you listen,
Oh you who were born of Earth,
Oh you who dwell in the sky!
Now the people of all earth with one voice implore you
That your plan may be carried out and continue as long as earth
  endures,
So do your descendants pray.

So now another.

It is of Soi'kā gää"kwa, our grandmother, the Moon in the sky.

You did make her a sign for reckoning the years of children.

Now she has fulfilled the design of her creation so far.

Now again the smoke arises.

Inhale the incense as you continue to listen,

Oh you who were born of Earth,

Oh you who dwell in the sky!

Through the smoke we pray that this may be so as long as earth
    endures,

So pray your descendants,

Oh you who were born of Earth,

Oh you who dwell in the sky!

So have they said,

Oh you who were born of Earth,

Oh you who dwell in the sky!

Now you did think that there should be a sky

And that spots should be in the sky

For signs unto the people.

So did you design this to be so as long as the earth endures.

And the people implore thee that this may continue to be as long
    as the earth endures.

Now again the smoke arises,

And through it the people speak.

Oh inhale as you continue to listen,

Oh you who were born of Earth,

Oh you who dwell in the sky!

Now you did design all that which should occur in the world,

And planned the four sacred ceremonies

That should be perpetuated forever

And celebrated by the people each year.

Be celebrated by these who call themselves your descendants;

That there should be head ones and their assistants

To perpetuate the four ceremonies.

Now as many men-beings as remain on earth are here,

Gathered about this pole.

Now then you have seen that we commenced at the new part of
    day.

Now you shall know that you are invited to listen to thanking
    songs this day!

[The head chief yells Yokadi!,Gowagannie!
The people answer wo' wo' wo'!]

Now tomorrow morning you must consider yourself invited to the
Great Feather Dance!

[Cries by the head chief Hioh, hiu, hiu, hiu!
The people answer Io' io' io' io' io'!]

Two parts will be celebrated, the Great Feather Dance and the
Harvest Thanksgiving.

[Cries by the head chief ¡Ganio⁻ganio ganio!
Answers by the the people Ho-ni ho-ni!]

These two ceremonies will be in progress tomorrow,
Oh you who were born of Earth,
Oh you who dwell in the sky
And the next day you are invited to the sacred game.

[Cries by the head chief, Ba-a'! ba-a'! ba-a'! ba-a'! ba-a'!
Answers by the people, Hoie! hoie! hoie! hoie!]

Now again the smoke arises
The incense of the sacred tobacco,
To you who were born of Earth,
Yet dwell in the sky
Only this can we do
To fulfil the law.
All the things of your creation that you have made visible to us
We thank you for and for all the things that you have created.
In the manner that you did think, we have thanked you,
From low earth upward to the great sky where you are living.
With all their strength the people thank you and you have seen it,
Oh you who were born of Earth,
Oh you who dwell in the sky!
So now it is done.
Now you did think that you would appoint four messengers whose
work should be to watch over earth
And the people that dwell in the world
To keep them all from harm,
For men-beings are your children.
Now do I say, the voices of the people combine as one
To thank you.
We have done as best we can in giving thanks to the four
messengers.
Now again the smoke arises,
And we speak through its incense.
Inhale the smoke as you do listen.
Oh the great Handsome Lake!

We believe that he is happy in the place that you have prepared
  for him.
Moreover we thank him.
Oh you who were born of Earth,
Oh you who dwell in the sky!
Now only this can we do.
You thought that it should be this way,
Oh you that were born of Earth,
Oh you who dwell in the sky!
Now we thank you, the Creator of the World.
Here are gathered so many people as remain,
Few head men remain.
Only this can we do,
And they say how the people should act.
Of the head men and their cousins only so many are left,
[But they with] the men and the women
The children that run and the children that creep
As one man-being offer you thanks.
They are your descendants,
Oh you who dwell in the sky!
Now you did think that we should offer you tobacco when we
  addressed you.
And we have fulfilled your request and used tobacco.
We leave our words with you until the next great thanksgiving,
Until then may the people continue in health.
Now the smoke arises!
Oh inhale as you do listen!
Only this can we do
For all the words are spoken
To you, our great ancestor,
Oh you who dwell in the sky.
Oh you who were born of Earth!

NE GANEOWO[1]

One of the four sacred ceremonies of the Seneca

The Gānē'onwon is a ceremonial thanksgiving in which two
"preachers," standing on either side of a long bench around which
a company of religious dancers have arranged themselves, alternately intone sections of the Gānē'onwon ritual. At the end of

---

[1] Ne"gānē'onwon, recorded and translated at Newtown, Cattaraugus reservation, January 1906.

each section the speaker starts a chant which is taken up by the singers who sit on the benches. A drummer keeps time by beating a water drum and the dancers gracefully circle around the benches. The direction of this dance, as all Iroquois dances, is counterclockwise. When the chant and dance have continued a period deemed sufficient by the opposite speaker, he halts the singing and dancing by the exclamation " Gwi''yă' ! " and then commences his intonation.

The writer had recorded the entire Gānē'o^nwo^n ritual, speeches and songs, on a set of phonograph records, especially for preservation by the New York State Education Department. Unfortunately these perished in the Capitol fire of March 29, 1911. About 100 other ceremonial records on wax cylinders were also destroyed at that time.

[PRELIMINARY] TRANSLATION OF THE GANEOWO RITUAL OF THE SENECA

I Gwi''ya' !
Now the whole assemblage is offering thanks!
This day [there] is occurring what the Creator has made pleasing for his own self.
We are thankful that what he has made for himself is accomplished.
[Singing and dancing].

II Gwi''ya' ! [Singing and dancing stop].
Now the whole assemblage is offering thanks!
The Creator thought that there should be men-beings,
And he thought that there should be chiefs to regulate the actions of these men-beings.
So now we thank him that what he thought has come to pass!
[Singing and dancing are resumed].

III Gwi''ya' ! [Singing and dancing stop].
Now the whole assemblage is offering thanks!
Now he thought that there should be two sexes,
That one should be the female
That children might grow from her.
We thank the women that they are doing their duty in fulfilling the design of their creation.
[Singing and dancing resumed].

IV   Gwi"ya'! [Singing and dancing stop].
     Now the whole assemblage is offering thanks!
     He thought that there should be a difference in the length
       of lives,
     And that children should run about and some creep.
     So this is what he has done.
     We are thankful that this is fulfilled.
     [Singing and dancing resumed].

 V   Gwi"ya'! [Singing and dancing stop].
     Now the whole assemblage is offering thanks!
     He thought that certain ones should be the leaders of the
       people,
     The same for both male and female, to preserve the four
       ceremonies.
     So we thank these head ones that they are dutiful to the
       calling of their Creator.
     [Singing and dancing resumed].

VI   Gwi"ya'! [Singing and dancing stop].
     Now the whole assemblage is offering thanks!
     He thought that there should be a world and that people
       should be upon the world,
     That they should draw their sustenance from the world.
     So we thank the Creator that what he thought has come
       to pass.
     [Singing and dancing resumed].

VII Gwi"ya'! [Singing and dancing stop].
     Now the whole assemblage is offering thanks!
     He thought that there should be things in the world for
       sustenance
     And that people should labor for their sustenance.
     Now we petition the Creator that we may again see the
       season of things growing from which our living is.
     [Singing and dancing resumed].

VIII Gwi"ya'! [Singing and dancing stop].
     Now the whole assemblage is offering thanks!
     He thought that there should be herbs of different kinds
     And that these should grow when the earth is warm
     And that these herbs should be a help to the people when
       medicine was needed.

So we thank the Creator that what he thought is now
    occurring.
[Singing and dancing resumed].

IX Gwi"ya'! [Singing and dancing stop].
Now the whole assemblage is offering thanks!
He thought that there should be two different varieties of
    trees and that one should yield fruit.
Now the first fruit of the year is the strawberry
And he thought that when the strawberries are ripe his
    creatures should thank him,
Thank him in a great feast and dance ceremony.
Now I ask that the time of strawberries may return again.
[Singing and dancing resumed].

X Gwi"ya'! [Singing and dancing stop].
Now the whole assemblage offers thanks!
He thought that there should be trees for a help to the
    people of earth.
So now we thank the Creator because what he thought is
    fulfilled and is a help to the people.
[Singing and dancing resumed].

XI Gwi"ya'! [Singing and dancing stop].
Now the whole assemblage offers thanks!
He thought that there should be a certain tree to bear
    fruit.
So we are thankful that all things are that he has or-
    dained
And shall be as long as the world endures.
[Singing and dancing resumed].

XII Gwi"ya'! [Singing and dancing stop].
Now the whole assemblage is offering thanks!
He thought that there should be forests upon the earth
That these should be a help to the people of earth.
So we thank the Creator that what he thought has come to
    pass.
[Singing and dancing resumed].

XIII Gwi"ya'! [Singing and dancing stop].
Now the whole assemblage is offering thanks!
He thought that there should be a certain tree

From which sweet waters should flow when the earth
warmed.

That this tree should be the maple and that men-beings
should tap it,

And that this should be a help to the people.

So we thank the Creator that what he thought is occurring.

[Singing and dancing resumed].

XIV Gwi''ya'! [Singing and dancing stop].

Now the entire assemblage is offering thanks!

He thought that there should be a certain tree to yield
nuts,

So we are thankful that what he thought is so.

[Singing and dancing resumed].

XV Gwi''ya'! [Singing and dancing stop].

Now the whole assemblage is offering thanks!

He thought that he would create wild beasts

And that men-beings should derive benefits from them.

So we thank the Creator that they are [yet] for our help.

[Singing and dancing resumed].

XVI Gwi''ya'! [Singing and dancing stop].

Now the whole assemblage is offering thanks!

He thought that there should be certain ones who should
be his servants,

And that they should come from the west and care for
the world,

That they should cause the earth to become wet

Thereby feeding the springs and waters that flow

Moreover that they should be called Hadiwĕnnoda'diĕ's,
the Thunderers.

So we thank the Creator that they have always fulfilled
the purpose of their creation.

Now we put everything together and say

We are thankful that all things are doing that for which
they were created.

[Singing and dancing resumed].

XVII Gwi''ya'! [Singing and dancing stop].

Now the whole assemblage is offering thanks!

He thought that there should be a sky over head;

He thought that there should be stars in that sky

That the men-beings that he put upon the earth might be
   guided thereby;
That certain stars should guide the people,
So we thank the Creator that what he thought is so.
[Singing and dancing resumed].

XVIII   Gwi"ya'! [Singing and dancing stop].
Now the whole assemblage is offering thanks!
Now he thought that there should be a certain one in the
   sky.
And that he should give light a certain period of time
And that they should call him "our brother, ĕndē'-
   ka gä'äkwa',"
Now, as we are all gathered together, we thank the sun
   that he is eternally dutiful.
[Singing and dancing resumed].

XIX   Gwi"ya'! [Singing and dancing stop].
Now the whole assemblage is offering thanks!
He thought that there should be another in the heavens
Who should reveal itself when the sun went under
And that people should call it ăksō'ōt, our grandmother,
   'Soi'kägä'äkwa.
Now, as we are all gathered together, we thank the moon
   that she is eternally dutiful.
[Singing and dancing resumed].

XX   Gwi"ya'! [Singing and dancing stop].
Now the whole assemblage is offering thanks!
He thought that there must be a certain one who should
   reveal what he thought.
He thought that he should lay the Gai'wiio' before the
   people,
So he revealed the Gai'wiio' to Ganio'dai'io'
And he did his duty as the Creator had ordained,
He preached and taught until he died.
So we all render our thanks for he has done his duty
For we now follow in the way he taught
And we will remember forever.
[Singing and dancing resumed].

XXI   Gwi"ya'! [Singing and dancing stop].
Now the whole assemblage is offering thanks!

He thought that he should have four beings for his messengers

Who should watch over the people of earth and that on
their strength their living should be.

Now we thank the four messengers that they are faithful
to the design of their creation.

[Singing and dancing resumed].

XXII Gwi"ya'! [Singing and dancing stop].

Now the whole assemblage is offering thanks!

He thought that the people should commence with the
lower earth to thank him

For all that he had created and should offer thanks for
things from below up to himself in the high world.

We therefore, gathered together in this assemblage, thank
our Creator,

Yea all of his creatures who are living in this world.

[Singing and dancing resumed].

XXIII Gwi"ya'! [Singing and dancing stop].

Now all the people offer thanks!

He thought that there should be certain persons to sing
for the dances he had made.

Now you who have sung and are singing, we thank you.

[Singing and dancing resumed].

[Speaker exhorts all the people to join in the dance].

OUTLINES OF THE CORNPLANTING AND THE MAPLE THANKSGIVINGS

AN OUTLINE PROGRAM OF WAANO''NAOGWA''CIOT, THE CORN-
PLANTING CEREMONY

1 Opening address by a chief
2 A Thanksgiving speech
3 Ne''äskä'nīe', the women's dance
4 Ne''ga'dā'ciot, the jubilee dance
5 Ne''gusshēdon'dada', the jug shaking dance
6 Ne''äskän'īe', the women's dance
7 Ne''yiĕndonĕsshontă', the old women's song
8 Ne''äskä'nīe', the women's dance
9 Ne''gaianon'gayonka
10 Ne''ostō'wägo'wa, the great feather dance
11 Closing address
12 Distribution of the feast

The object of the Cornplanting ceremony is to secure divine favor and help in the spring planting. Everyone is invoked to till the ground and earn the bread they eat. The ceremony lasts about four or five hours.

THE MAPLE FESTIVAL

A council is called to set the time for this festival which has no exact day but varies according to the weather. However, it takes place soon after the sap commences to run. Its object is to thank all trees for their services to man and invoke their protection and good will for the coming year.

Outline program

1 The address to the maple tree. A fire is built at the foot of a large maple tree. The people gather around and a special officer advances with a basket of tobacco which he sprinkles on the fire as he recites the address to the maple:

> Ne' nĕngä' gägwä'ani saiwisa'ane gäni'sĕ swĕn'iio'
> Seane ganigä'o ne''niganigai'isek
> One'' dīq' oyän'kwa(owe)soi'yĕ'
> Negihedahadondi gaiyehonoshäs henizaiwissahon'
> Onen'' dīq' kejedai' soñgwäni, etc.

The prayer at the maple festival
Wa"da Tadinion'nio'o'
Maple Thanksgiving

Ĕsⁿwaiyĭgwa'showine" odēha'donni. Ne"wainnondoi'shoñk

Oh partake of this tobacco the forests.   This we petition
nega'dogä nayŭt'däoⁿ näĕtgonĕ'igais näwä"dä
may you continue the production of sweet water Oh maple
Hawe'oⁿ Nawĕnniio' ĕⁿgäoⁿdadegaoⁿ ĕⁿgani'gaiksēk
The will of the Creator that a certain tree water flows from
Ne"nĕⁿgä' ĕⁿgä'oñk hadieo"shä deodoⁿoⁿ ne" hē"hadidŭk'kēnoⁿdiēs
This it   may not accidents   occur   the running about
hadĭksä'shoⁿ'o' gahadĕgonⁿshoⁿ
the children   in the woods.

Ne" neⁿgä" wănĭshäde' īs' ĕsswai'ya'dagwäni'yothet
Now this   day   you   it belongs to you to enjoy
ⁿĕⁿgä" wănĭshä de'.
this   day.

Djasayawa'godŭk Hawĕn'iio' cia"dadē gäoya'gē'tciojo".
We give thanks   oh God   to you   the dweller of the heavens.
Agwai'wayiis   ne"gaiyiwanda'kho.
We have done it   what devolved upon us.
Osŭt'gät'ho   djogwŭtgwēnio'.
You have seen   what we have done.
Da'nē'ho'.
So, it is.

The address to the maple, the chief of trees and the prayer to the
Creator

A Seneca ceremony

The priest stands at the roots of a maple. A fire is burning and
the priest casts tobacco in the fire and as its smoke arises he says:

To the tree:

" O partake of this incense,
You the forests!
We implore you
To continue as before,
The flowing waters of the maple.

Plate 22

Ceremonial march of the Toń'wïsas Company. The leader carries an armful of ears of corn in one arm and a tortoise shell rattle in her outstretched right hand. From a drawing by Jesse Cornplanter, Ganundaiyeoh, a Seneca boy)

Plate 23

Purification ceremony of the Society of Otters, a Seneca women's winter ceremony

Drawn by
J.Complanter—

To the Creator and the tree:

> It is the will of the Creator
> That a certain tree
> Should flow such water.
> Now may no accidents occur
> To children roaming in the forests.
> Now this day is yours
> May you enjoy it,— this day.

To the Creator:

> We give thanks, oh God, to you,
> You who dwell in heaven.
> We have done our duty
> You have seen us do it.
> So it is done."

SPECIAL ANNUAL CEREMONIES

I   Dä′nondinônnio″ Ĕdē‘kwa gää′kwa‘, the Sun Dance.
II   Dä′nondinônnio″ Soi′ka gää′kwa‘, the Moon Dance.
III Wasaze,[1] the Thunder Dance.

I

1 Dä′nondinônnio″ Ĕndē′ka gää′kwa‘, the Sun dance, is designed to honor the sun.

2 This ceremony has no certain time for its celebration but may be called by anyone, at any time, who dreams it necessary for the welfare of the settlement.

3 The ceremony begins at noon when arrows are shot up toward the sun while the populace shout their war cries.

4 A fire is built outside and tobacco is thrown by a priest who chants the sun-rite.

5 Three times during this ceremony a shower of arrows are shot up to the sun accompanied by a chorus of cries, intended to notify him that they are addressing him.

6 Immediately afterward the Osto′wägowa is engaged in as the only fitting dance to perform before the mighty Sun.

II

1 Dä′nondinônnio″ Soikagää′kwa‘, the Moon Dance ceremony, is convened by anyone who dreams it necessary or by the advice of a clairvoyant.

---

[1] Meaning, Dakota, or Sioux.

2 A thanksgiving speech is recited by a chief while he burns the tobacco offering to the moon.

3 As the peach stone gambling game is thought especially pleasing to the moon, the company gambles away the evening.

4 The distribution of the feast terminates the ceremony.

III

1 Wasaze, the Thunder Dance, is one designed to please the spirit of Thunder, Hi"no^n.

2 A council is called when the first thunder of the year is heard and a time as immediate as possible set for the Wasaze.

3 The dancers assemble without the council house, an opening address is made by a priest or chief and the dance immediately starts.

4 The line of dancers dance into the long house.

5 Hi"no^n is supposed to delight in war songs and these are sung to please him.

6 Tobacco is burned and a thanksgiving speech made to Hi"no^n, for his services in the past and he is prayed to continue his favors.

LEGEND OF THE COMING OF DEATH [1]

When the world was first made, men-beings did not know that they must die some time. In those days everyone was happy and neither men, women nor children were afraid of anything. They did not think of anything but doing what pleased them. At one time, in those days, a prominent man was found on the grass. He was limp and had no breath. He did not breathe. The men-beings that saw him did not know what had happened. The man was not asleep because he did not awaken. When they placed him on his feet he fell like a tanned skin. He was limp. They tried many days to make him stand but he would not. After a number of days he became offensive.

A female man-being said that the man must be wrapped up and put in the limbs of a tree. So the men did so and after a while the flesh dropped from the bones and some dried on. No one knew what had happened to cause such a thing.

Soon afterward a child was found in the same condition. It had no breath. It could not stand. It was not asleep, so they said. The men-beings thought it was strange that a girl man-being should act this wise. So she was laid in a tree. Now many others did these things and no one knew why. No one thought that he himself would do such a thing.

There was one wise man who thought much about these things and he had a dream. When he slept the Good Minded spirit came to him and spoke. He slept a long time but the other men-beings noticed that he breathed slowly. He breathed [nevertheless]. Now after a time this man rose up and his face was very solemn. He called the people together in a council and addressed the people. The head men all sat around with the people.

The wise man spoke and he said, " The Good Minded spirit made every good thing and prepared the earth for men-beings. Now it appears that strange events have happened. A good word has come to me from the Good Minded spirit. He says that every person must do as you have seen the other persons do. They have died. They do not breathe. It will be the same with all of you. Your minds are strong. The Good Minded spirit made them that way so that you could endure everything that happened. So then do not be downcast when I tell you that you all must die. Listen

---

[1] Related by Edward Cornplanter, March 1906.

further to what I say. The name of the one that steals away your breath is S'hondowĕk'owa. He has no face and does not see any one. You can not see him until he grasps you. He comes sometimes for a visit and sometimes he stays with us until many are dead. Sometimes he takes away the best men and women and passes by the lesser ones. I was not told why he does this thing. He wants to destroy every person. He will continue to work forever. Every one who hears me and every one not yet born will die. There is more about you than living. Any moment you may be snatched by S'hondowĕk'owa, he who works in the thick darkness.

You must now divide yourselves into nine bands, five to sit on one side of the fire and four on the other and these bands shall care for its members. You must seek out all good things and instruct one another, and those who do good things will see when they die the place where the Maker of all things lives."

THE FUNERAL ADDRESS [1]

Awēyondo' Gawen'notgä'o

Now all hearken to what must be said!

We are gathered here because of what our Creator has done. He made it so that people should live only a certain length of time-none to be more favored than another.

Now our uncles made provisions for this event, and our grandfathers and the chiefs when they first thought of this thing [death] in those days. They had never seen death [before]. Their first knowledge came when they saw a person in an assembly die. [Strangely] no one was surprised. Soon afterwards they saw another death in the manner of the first. Soon again another died. Then did the chiefs consider the matter, saying, " We were not born to live forever." Then did the people see that they were not to live forever but only for a certain period of time. Therefore, they made certain rules. Then did they divide the people into clans, kashadenioh. Then did they divide the clans into two divisions. Now when a death occurred the other division [phratry] was to officiate at the funeral. The side that lost one of its members must quietly mourn and say nothing. The cousins must do the speaking. They must speak telling the mourners what they must think. So now first they should say, " Keep your minds up."

The preacher then turns to the mourners and addresses them as follows:

There are many of your own relations yet remaining, there are old folk and there are children. So let these lift up your minds. Moreover here is the earth upon which we tread, everything upon it is for our comfort. There is water, springs of water and streams of water flowing over the earth. There are different plants and trees. All of these our Creator has given us. So let this lift up your minds.

So now then another.

There is the sky above our heads. There are many things there. In the forms of the stars are signs to guide us. The sun gives us light. The moon gives us light. She is our grandmother. The sun is our brother. All these are performing that for which they were created. So let this lift up your minds.

So now then another.

---

[1] Related by Skidmore Lay, Cattaraugus chief, March 1906.

It is the Gai'wiio', the good word of our Creator. Our Creator thought that the people should hear what was in his mind. So he sent word down to the earth. He thought that the people should know what his words were. Now this should lift up your minds.

So now then another.

It is the four geniewage [ceremonies]. Now this should lift up your minds.

[If the dead person is a chief the preacher here ceases to give the chief on the mourning side an opportunity to reply. The reply is as follows]:

Cousin! I have heard all that you have laid before us — how we should keep our minds. We have commenced from the beginning of the world when the Creator made us. We have thought of the water, the springs and the streams of water. We have thought of the sky and everything therein, the sun and the moon, the words of our Creator and the four ceremonies. These things you have pointed out, Oh Cousin! These things will lift up our minds. Now, Cousin, you should know that we accept all that you have said. We can not say that we do not accept what you have said. Now we put all of your words together; we accept them all. So is the reply.

[The preacher then arises and continues]:

So now again listen, all of you!

Now let every one listen.

[The preacher makes an extemporaneous speech in which he addresses the entire assembly. Afterward he selects passages from the Gai'wiio' among which the following is always repeated]:

So now another message.

Now it is said that your people must change certain customs. It has been the custom to mourn at each recurring anniversary of the death of a friend or relative. It is said that while you are on earth you do not realize the harm that this works upon the departed.

[Now moreover, it is said that when an infant is born upon the earth with which the parents are dissatisfied it knows and says, " I will return to my home above the earth."]

Now it is said that grief adds to the sorrows of the dead. It is said that it is not possible to grieve always. Ten days shall be the time for mourning and when our friends depart we must lay grief aside. When you, the beings of the earth, lose one of your number you must bury your grief in their grave. Some will die today and some tomorrow, for all our days are numbered. So hereafter do not grieve. Now it is said that when the ten days have elapsed to prepare a feast and the soul of the dead will return and partake of it with you. It is said moreover that you can journey with the dead only as far as the grave. It is said that when you follow a body to the grave you must have prepared for that journey as if to travel afar. Put on your finest clothing for every human creature is on its journey graveward. It is said that the bodies of the dead have intelligence and know what transpires about them. It is true.

So they said and he said. Eniaiehuk. (Section 67 of the Gai'wiio'.)

[The preacher then announces certain decisions of "the dead side" and then continues with the established funeral rite, as follows]:

When the body of the dead is buried we must become resigned to our loss. It can not be helped.

[The preacher speaks to the fathers]:

Now do you also do the same as the dead side and become resigned to your sorrow?

[The preacher addresses the relatives afar off]:

And now you afar off who are the relatives of the dead, do you become resigned also when you hear of the loss?

The things of the past shall continue. It [death] should not hamper or stop any ordination of the Creator. Let not a death stop an event in course of progress. Let us fulfil the law of mourning for a ten-day period and have the feast at the end. We believe that the dead will return at the end of ten days. Now the Creator said, "The customs ordained by the early chiefs [regarding mourning] are right. They had no knowledge of what would happen in the future when they made the customs but the Creator soke to Ganio'dai'io and said, 'True and good is the ceremony of your grandfathers for the time of mourning and also the death feast.'"

[When the face of the dead is unwrapped for its friends to look upon for the last time the preacher says]:

Now let all journey to the grave with the body of the dead for it is as far as we can go.

[At the grave the preacher turns to the crowd and says]:

So now we thank all those who have come to this funeral ceremony to help us. So it is done.

[The body is then covered with earth.]

THE DEATH FEAST [1]

Wainonjää''koⁿ'

Now let all listen, all ye who are here assembled!

Cousins! We all are familiar with the happening of a few days ago. We are [therefore] here because of what the Creator has done.

Now the relatives have made arrangements. They have promised to obey the commands of the four messengers who said, " It is right to have a feast for the dead. Therefore this thing should be done."

Ten days have passed. Now the relatives of the dead have made preparations and the feast is ready for the dead. Now let this be in your minds, all ye who are here present.

[The preacher here pauses. At his side sits the speaker for the mourners. In his charge is a bundle containing various gifts for those who have aided the bereaved family. The speaker has been told to whom the various presents are to go, and as the preacher pauses and bends down to receive the formal instructions he hands him the first gift. Sitting among the women mourners is a woman, the " mistress of the ceremonies," whose duty is to deliver the gifts to the intended recipients.

After listening to the directions of the speaker the preacher resumes] :

So now the bereaved offer thanks. They thank the one who cared for the body of the dead and dressed it for burial. To that one they give this as a testimony. [The preacher names the article and the matron rising from her seat receives it and delivers it to the person named].

[The preacher again bends to the speaker at his side and receives the " second word." Again facing the audience he proceeds] :

So now of another they have thought. It is of the night watcher [or night watchers]. To this one [or to these ones], they give this roll of cloth [or skins]. And this is your thanks.

[The speaker hands the preacher the roll and he hands it to the matron who delivers it. Stooping and listening to the whispered instructions for the delivery of the next gift, the preacher after making sure that he understands straightens and again speaks]:

---

[1] Related by Edward Cornplanter, March 1906.

Now to him who wrapped the body in its burial covering [or made the coffin], the relatives offer thanks.

[The gift is bestowed as previously described.]

Now the matron who has managed the funeral receives a gift of thanks.

[This named person being the one who has first received and given the gifts now remains seated while the wife or sister of the preacher rises and receiving the gift bestows it. According to Iroquois etiquette it would be an improper thing for the matron to receive her own gift and bear it before the eyes of the crowd to her seat. The recipients are supposed not to be eager to receive the gifts, the things that once belonged to the dead. Besides according to Iroquois philosophy one can not give one's self a thing.]

Now she who notified the people — the relatives desire to give thanks and offer this gift.

Now those who dug the grave — to you the relatives give thanks and offer gifts.

And now you the good friends and relatives, of what is remaining receive you this gift. [The preacher names each person for whom a gift is intended, repeating the formula given. If property of considerable value as live stock or lands is left, the speaker for the mourners in behalf of the council of heirs tells the preacher their decisions and they are announced before the audience. The modern "death feast law" provides that in the event of a man's death his property must go to his children. If he is without issue, then it reverts to his wife. If he was unmarried it was given to the nearest of kin. The law further provides that the property must be divided and apportioned at the "death feast." By the old law the nearest of kin on the clan (maternal) side received the property. Children did not ordinarily inherit their father's property, but their mother's. Their "mother's husband's" belongings went to the kin of the clan to which he belonged.]

[If the dead were an officer of any kind, the preacher announced who was to take his or her place. In order that this election be valid the person chosen must stand, if possible, in the very spot where the dead person expired.]

Now I have finished speaking for the relatives.

Now listen to another matter, all ye who are here present.

Now at this time let the [mourning] relatives cease their grieving. Now may they go and do whatsoever they wish. They are the same as ever and may speak as they please again. Now can they be notified of things to be done. They have now the right to engage in any current happening. No longer think their hands must be held back. If it is possible to do, now do, for the time of mourning has passed.

So now we have done our part for you, cousins. So I have done.

[The preacher resumes his seat.]

[The speaker for the mourning side arises and addresses the officiating side]:

Now listen cousins!

We have heard all that you have said and [know that] you have done your part. We believe that you have done your part. You must hold in your minds that we thank you for what you have done for us. Now I give you this [the object is named] for your trouble.

[Although the speaker is standing at the side of the preacher, the latter can not receive the gift direct, but the matron rising from her seat takes the offering and holds it out to him. Even then he does not take it but points to his wife or mother, indicating that it is to be placed in her keeping.]

[The speaker continues]:

Now we must ask your pardon for giving so small a gift; it is small and your services have been great.

Now we relieve you of your duties, the duties for which we bound you. Now you are relieved.

[The preacher rises and says]:

Now all listen to a few more words that I shall say!

Let all the people here gathered keep silent. Now is the time for the distribution of the feast. It will now be distributed, for it has been prepared and we must eat. Now let they who did the cooking distribute. Let all tarry until the feast is finished. Let hard feelings affect no one and let the matrons divide equally and overlook none. So it is finished.

SECRET MEDICINE SOCIETIES OF THE SENECA[1]

During the last six years the writer has made a detailed field study of the various phases of Iroquois culture, special attention being directed to the rites and ceremonies of the semisecret orders and societies that yet survive among the so-called pagan Iroquois. It was only after diligent inquiry that the actual existence of these societies was clearly established. The False Face Company and the Secret Medicine Society, better termed The Little Water Company, have been known to ethnologists for some time, but no one has adequately described them or has seemed fully aware of their significance. Likewise certain dances, such as the Bird, the Bear, the Buffalo, the Dark, and the Death dances, have been mentioned. Ceremonies also, such as the Otter ceremony and the Woman's song, have been listed, but that back of all these ceremonies there was a society never seems to have occurred to anyone. The Indians do not volunteer information, and when some rite is mentioned they usually call it a dance. Through this subterfuge the existence of these societies has long been concealed, not only from white investigators but from Christian Indians as well, the latter usually professing ignorance of the "pagan practices" of their unprogressive brothers.

Even so close an observer as Lewis H. Morgan says: "The Senecas have lost their Medicine Lodges, which fell out in modern times; but they formerly existed and formed an important part of their religious system. To hold a Medicine Lodge was to observe their highest religious mysteries. They had two such organizations, one for each phratry, which shows still further the natural connection of the phratry and the religious observances. Very little is now known concerning these lodges or their ceremonies. Each was a brotherhood into which new members were admitted by formal initiation."[2]

Morgan's experience is that of most observers, close as their observation may be. The writer, with the assistance of his wife, however, living with the "pagans" and entering fully into their rites, discovered that the "medicine lodges," so far from having become extinct, are still active organizations, exercising a great

---

[1] Adapted from the author's article in American Anthropologist, 2:2, April-June, 1909.

[2] Morgan, Ancient Society, p. 97, ed. 1907.

amount of influence not only over the pagans but also over the nominal Christians.

It was found that the organization and rites of the societies might best be studied among the Seneca, who have preserved their rituals with great fidelity. The Onondaga, although keeping up the form of some, have lost many of the ancient features and look to the Seneca for the correct forms.

The teachings of Ganio'dai'io', Handsome Lake, the Seneca prophet, revolutionized the religious life of the Iroquois to a large extent, its greatest immediate effect being on the Seneca and Onondaga. Later it greatly influenced the Canadian Iroquois, excepting perhaps the Mohawk about the St Lawrence. Handsome Lake sought to destroy the ancient folk-ways of the people and to substitute a new system, built of course upon the framework of the old. Finding that he made little headway in his teachings, he sought to destroy the societies and orders that conserved the older religious rites, by proclaiming a revelation from the Creator. The divine decree was a command that all the animal societies hold a final meeting at a certain time, throw tobacco in the ceremonial fires, and dissolve. The heavenly reason for this order, Handsome Lake explained, was that men were acquainted with the effects of their familiarity with the spirits of the animals, which, although they might bring fortune and healing to the members of the animal's order, might work terrible harm to men and to other animals.

The chiefs who were friendly to the prophet and others who were frightened by his threats met in counsel and proclaimed that all the animal and mystery societies should immediately dissolve, and, by their order, were dissolved and disbanded. This they did without holding a hayänt'wŭtgŭs, tobacco-throwing ceremony, as directed. The members of the societies, therefore, declared that the order of the council was illegal and not binding, that the sin of disobedience was upon the chiefs and not upon the body of members. The societies consequently continued their rites, although they found it expedient to do so secretly, for they were branded as witches and wizards,[1] and the members of one society at least were executed as sorcerers when they were found practising their arts.

The existence of the societies became doubly veiled. The zealous proselytes of the New Religion denied their legality and even their existence, and the adherents of the old system did not care to

---

[1] The modern Iroquois call all sorcerers and conjurers, regardless of sex, "witches." They never use the masculine form.

express themselves too strongly in the matter of proclaiming their sacred orders still very much alive. The rites of the societies were performed in secret places for a number of years after the advent of the prophet, but as the adherents of the New Religion became more conservative, the societies again gradually entered into public ceremonies held in the council houses on thanksgiving occasions. At such times some of them gave public exhibitions of their rites ; others had no public ceremonies whatsoever. With the gradual acceptance of the New Religion by the great majority of the people, the older religious belief was blended into the new. The Iroquois regard it, as their Old Testament. The tabooed societies became bolder in their operations, and the new religionists entered their folds with few if any qualms.

It was about this time that their policy seems to have changed, for after some inquiry the writer can find no restriction placed on membership by reason of phratry or clanship. Candidates might join any society regardless of clan except the society of Men-who-assist-the-women's-ceremonies, which is not a secret organization. This society consists of two divisions, the membership of a division being determined by phratry. It is purely a benevolent society, however, and has nothing to do with " medicine." The various societies of all kinds had, and still have, individual lodges, each of which is nominally independent of any jurisdiction save that of its own officers. The leaders, however, confer and keep their rites uniform. At present, especially in the Little Water Company, it is not even necessary for the song-holder, the chief officer, to be a pagan. This company is the only one which can boast of any great Christian membership or of a lodge composed entirely of nominal Christians. This lodge is the Pleasant Valley Lodge of the Little Water Company on the Cattaraugus reservation. Mrs Harriet Maxwell Converse joined this lodge in 1892, afterward joining the pagan lodge at Newtown.

A careful study of the Iroquois societies will lead to the conclusion that most of the societies are of ancient origin and that their rituals have been transmitted with little change for many years. Indeed, that under the circumstances any changes should have been made would be stranger than that none had occurred at all. Most of the rituals are chanted in unison by the entire company of members, and any change in note, syllable, or word would immediately be detected. Rites transmitted by song are more difficult to change than simple recitals where musical rhythm is not correlated with the word. Some of the rituals, moreover, contain archaic words and expressions, and even entire sentences are not understood by the singers.

Each society has a legend by which its origin and peculiar rites are explained. Most of these legends portray the founder of the society as a lost hunter, an outcast orphan, or a venturesome youth curious to know what was farther on. The founder got into strange complications, saw strange or familiar animals engaged in their rites, was discovered, forgiven, adopted, kept a captive, and finally, after long study and many warnings, was sent back to his people to teach them the secrets of the animals and how their favor could be obtained. The secrets were to be preserved by the society which the hero was to found.[1] There are some variations of this abstract, but it covers the general features of most of the legends.

The study of the societies was commenced by the writer in 1902, and during the years 1905–6 an almost uninterrupted study was made for the New York State Education Department, and the results deposited in the State Library. Since that time the research has been continued for the New York State Museum. Paraphernalia have been collected, phonograph records have been made of many of the songs and ceremonial speeches, texts have been recorded and translated, legends have been gathered, and some music has already been transcribed. There still remains an enormous amount of work to be done, and it is greatly to be regretted that a multiplicity of duties bars the way for as speedy progress in this work as might be desirable, especially since many of the informants are old people and in ill health.

A brief outline of the various societies is presented in this paper. It is impossible for the sake of brevity to present a fair compend or even a systematic outline. The main features of the less known organizations and some neglected facts of the few that are better known are mentioned, it being hoped that even such statements may be useful to students of ethnology. The list follows.[2]

NIGANĔGA″A‘ OĂ‘ NO’, OR NE″ HONO″TCINO″GĂ. THE LITTLE WATER
COMPANY

This society is perhaps the best organized of all the Seneca folk-societies. It holds four meetings each year, but only on three occasions is the night song, Ganoda, chanted. To describe ade-

---

[1] Myths and Legends of the Iroquois, N. Y. State Mus. Bul. 125, p. 176.

[2] A description of some of these societies was prepared for incorporation in the Fifth Annual Report of the Director of the State Museum, 1909.

quately the rites of this society would require a small volume. For the purposes of this paper, since the society has been described at greater length elsewhere, only a few notes can be given.

The company is organized to perform the rites thought necessary to preserve the potency of the " secret medicine," niganĕga"a', known as the " little-water powder." The meetings, moreover, are social gatherings of the members in which they can renew friendship and smoke away mutual wrongs, if any have been committed. It is contrary to the rules to admit members having a quarrel unless they are willing to forgive and forget. Both men and women are members. Its officers, in order of their importance, are: the song-holder, the chief matron, the watcher of the medicine, the feast-makers, invoker, flute-holder, and announcers and sentinels. There are two altars, the Altar of the Fire and the Altar of the Mystery. The ritual consists of three sets of songs describing the various adventures of the founder, known as the Good Hunter. At the close of each section the feast-makers pass bowls of berry juice, giving each singer a draft from a ladle. In some lodges a pipe is passed. An intermission then follows, during which the members, men and women alike, smoke the native home-grown tobacco. The singing is accompanied by the shaking of gourd rattles, and each member shakes one while he sings. Only purified members are supposed to enter. Unclean men or women, even though members, are debarred. The society has no public ceremony and no dances. Only members are supposed to know the precise time and place of meeting. The songs must never be sung outside of the lodge-room, but special meetings are sometimes called for the purpose of instructing novices. The office of song-holder by the Cattaraugus Seneca is hereditary to the name O'dän'kot, Sunshine. The present song-holder of the Ganun'dasē lodge, the pagan lodge at Newtown, Cataraugus reservation, is a youth who is learning the song, George Pierce, the former O'dän'kot, having recently died. Visitors may listen to the songs in an outer room, but are debarred from viewing the " mysteries." Each member, on entering, deposits his medicine packet on the Altar of the Mystery and places his contribution of tobacco in the corn-husk basket. The tobacco is thrown into the fire by the invoker as he chants his prayer to the Creator, the Thunder Spirit, and to the Great Darkness. The flute-song is played during the second and third sections. At the close of the ceremony a pig's head is passed and pieces of the boiled meat are torn from the head with the teeth, the members cawing in imitation of crows. In early times a bear's head was eaten. The food is then distributed, and the meeting or

Fig. 3   The medicine outfit, husk tray, medicine bundle, rattle and flute

" sitting " is concluded. The ceremony commences at about 11 o'clock p. m. and is adjourned at daybreak. The sun " must not see the rites." The business of the society is all conducted before the ceremony commences: reports of the officers are given and the treasurer's report read. The paraphernalia of this society consist of the medicine bundles, the flute, gourd rattles for each singer, the sacred tobacco basket and a bark dipper. The necessary furnishings are a table and a fireplace, these being the " altars," and a lamp. The " medicine " is not used in the ceremonies; it is simply " sung for." Its power is conserved for use by the medicine people in healing ceremonies. The singing of the ritual is conducted in total darkness, the lights being brought in only during the intermissions.

DEWANONDIISSO[n]DAIK'TA', PYGMY SOCIETY, THE DARK DANCE
CEREMONY

The ritual of this society consists of 102 songs, divided into four
sections, as follows: The first section, 15 songs; the second, 23
songs; the third, 30 songs, and the fourth, 34 songs. The order of
the ceremony is somewhat like that of the Medicine Company. All
the songs are sung in darkness. It is believed that the spirit members of the society come and join in the singing, and their voices
are thought to be audible at times.

The water drum and the horn rattle are used in this ceremony
for keeping time. There is a brief dance. The Dark ceremony is
designed to appease certain spirits and to procure the good offices of
others. Meetings are called at any time for the purpose of appeas-
ing the spirits of certain charms that have become impotent or which
may become so, or are called by members and even by nonmembers
who are troubled by certain signs and sounds, such as the drumming of the water fairies or stone throwers, pygmies, who by their
signs signify their desire for a ceremony. Nonmembers become
members by asking for the services of the society. The rites are
preeminently the religion of the " little folk " whose good will is
sought by all Indians living under the influence of the Ongwe''-
oñwe'ka', Indian belief. The Pygmies are thought to be " next to
the people " in importance, and to be very powerful beings. They
demand proper attention or they will inflict punishment upon those
who neglect them. This society, however, " sings for " all the
" medicine charms " and all the magic animals. These magic animals are members of the society, and in order of their importance
are: Jo[n]gä'o[n], Elves or Pygmies; Jodi''gwado[n], the Great Horned
Serpent; Shondowĕk'owa, the Blue Panther, the herald of
death; Dewŭtiowa'is, the Exploding Wren. Other members, equal
in rank, are: Diatdagwŭt', White Beaver; O'nowaot'gont, or
Gane''onttwŭt, the Corn-bug; Otnä'yont, Sharp-legs; O'wai'ta,
Little Dry Hand; Dagwŭn'noyaĕnt, Wind Spirit, and Nia''gwahē,
Great Naked Bear.

These charm-members are called Ho'tcine'gada. The charms or
parts of these members, which the human members keep and sing
for, are: none of the first two, because they are very sacred and
" use their minds " only for charms; panther's claw; feathers; white
beaver's castor; corn-bug dried; bone of sharp-legs; dry hand; hair
of the wind, and bones of Nia''gwahē. Some of these charms bring
evil to the owners, but must not be destroyed under any circum-

stance. Their evil influence can be warded off only by the ceremonies. The owner or his family appoints someone to " hold the charm " after the first owner's death. Other charms are only for benevolent purposes, but become angry if neglected. Of the evil charms, the sharp bone may be mentioned; and of the good charms the exploding bird's feathers. Most of them are regarded, however, as ot'gont. The members of this society save their fingernail parings and throw them over cliffs for the Pygmies.

The ceremonies of the societies are always opened with a speech by the invoker. The following speech is that of the Pygmy Society, and in a general way is the pattern of nearly all opening invocations.

Yotdondak'o', Opening Ceremony of the Pygmy Society

We now commence to thank our Creator.

Now we are thankful that we who have assembled here are well.

We are thankful to the Creator for the world and all that is upon it for our benefit.

We thank the Sun and the Moon.

We thank the Creator that so far tonight we are all well.

Now I announce that A B is to be treated.

Now this one, C D, will throw tobacco in the fire.

Now these will lead the singing, E and F.

So I have said.

[The " tobacco thrower " advances to the fire and, seating himself, takes a basket of Indian tobacco and speaks as follows:]

Now the smoke rises!

Receive you this incense!

You who run in the darkness.

You know that this one has thought of you

And throws this tobacco for you.

Now you are able to cause sickness.

Now, when first you knew that men-beings were on earth, you said,

" They are our grandchildren."

You promised to be one of the forces for men-beings' help,

For thereby you would receive offerings of tobacco.

So now you get tobacco — you, the Pygmies. [Sprinkles tobacco on the fire.]

Now is the time when you have come;

You and the member have assembled here tonight.

Now again you receive tobacco — you, the Pygmies.   [Throws tobacco.]

You are the wanderers of the mountains;

You have promised to hear us whenever the drum sounds,

Even as far away as a seven days' journey.

Now all of you receive tobacco.   [Throws tobacco.]

You well know the members of this society,

So let this[1] cease.

You are the cause of a person, a member, becoming ill.

Henceforth give good fortune for she (or he) has fulfilled her duty and given you tobacco.

You love tobacco and we remember it;

So also you should remember us.

Now the drum receives tobacco,

And the rattle also.

It is our belief that we have said all,

So now we hope that you will help us.

Now these are the words spoken before you all,

You who are gathered here tonight.

So now it is done.

DAWANDO', THE SOCIETY OF OTTERS

This is a band of women organized to propitiate the otters and other water animals who are supposed to exercise an influence over the health, fortunes, and destinies of men.   The otter, which is the chief of the small water animals, including the fish, is a powerful medicine-animal, and besides having his own special society is a member of the Yĕ'dos, or I''dos, and the Hono''tcino''gä'.

The Otters may appear at any public thanksgiving, as the Green Corn dance and the Midwinter ceremony.   After a tobacco-throwing ceremony, hayänt'wŭtgŭs, the three women officers of the Dawan'do' each dip a bucket of the medicine-water from the spring or stream, dipping down with the current, and carry it to the council house where they sprinkle everyone they meet by dipping long wisps of corn husk in the water and shaking them at the people.   If the women succeed in entering the council house and sprinkling everyone without hindrance, they go for more water and continue until stopped.   The only way in which they may be forced to discontinue their sprinkling is for someone, just before she sprinkles him, to snatch the pail and throw the entire contents over her head.

---

[1] The malific influence causing sickness.

The Otter woman will then say, " Hat'gaiï', niawē' ! "— meaning,
" Enough, I thank you! "   She will then retire.

The Otters are especially active during the Midwinter ceremony,
and when the water is thrown over their heads it very often freezes,
but this is something only to be enjoyed.   When possessed with the
spirit of the otter, the women are said to be unaware of their actions,
and sometimes, when they are particularly zealous, the whistle of
the otter is heard.   This greatly frightens the people, who regard it
as a manifestation of the presence of the " great medicine otter."
The women afterward deny having imitated the otter's call, saying
that they were possessed of the otter and had no knowledge of what
they did.

The Otter Society has no songs and no dances.   Its members
are organized simply to give thanks to the water animals and to
retain their favor.   When one is ungrateful to the water animals,
as a wasteful fisherman, or a hunter who kills muskrats or beaver
without asking permission or offering tobacco to their spirits, he
becomes strangely ill, so it is believed.   The Otters then go to a
spring and conduct a ceremony, after which they enter the sick
man's lodge and sprinkle him with spring water, hoping thereby to
cure him.

I″DOS OÄ′NO‛, SOCIETY OF MYSTIC ANIMALS

The I″dos Company is a band of " medicine " people whose object is to preserve and perform the rites thought necessary to keep
the continued good will of the " medicine " animals.   According
to the traditions of the company, these animals in ancient times
entered into a league with them.   The animals taught them the
ceremonies necessary to please them, and said that, should these be
faithfully performed, they would continue to be of service to mankind.   They would cure disease, banish pain, displace the causes of
disasters in nature, and overcome ill luck.

Every member of the company has an individual song to sing in
the ceremonies, and thus the length of the ceremony depends on
the number of the members.   When a person enters the I″dos, he
is given a gourd rattle and a song.   These he must keep with care,
not forgetting the song or losing the rattle.

The head singers of the I″dos are two men who chant the dance
song.   This chant relates the marvels that the medicine man is able
to perform, and as they sing he proceeds to do as the song directs.
He lifts a red-hot stone from the lodge fire and tosses it like a ball
in his naked hands; he demonstrates that he can see through a

carved wooden mask having no eyeholes, by finding various things about the lodge; he causes a doll to appear as a living being, and mystifies the company in other ways. It is related that new members sometimes doubt the power of the mystery-man and laugh outright at some of the claims of which he boasts. In such a case he approaches the doll, and though his face be covered by a wooden mask, cuts the string that fastens its skirt. The skirt drops, exposing the legs of the doll. Then the doubting woman laughs, for everyone else is laughing, at the doll she supposes, but shortly she notices that everyone is looking at her, and to her utmost chagrin discovers that her own skirt-string has been cut and that she is covered only by her undergarments. Immediately she stops laughing and never afterward doubts the powers of the medicine-man, who, when he cut the doll's skirt-string by his magic power, cuts hers also.

The I″dos is said to have been introduced among the Seneca by the Huron. The ritual, however, is in Seneca, though some of the words are not understood. The principal ceremonies are: (a) Gai'yowĕ^n'ogowa, The sharp point; (b) Gahadi'yago^n, At the wood's edge; (c) Gai″'do^n, The great Gai″'do^n. Other ceremonies are: O'to'do^{n}gwa″, It is blazing; and Tci'gwawa, The other way around. During ceremonies b and c only individual members sing. The chief of the society is said to be a man who is able to see through a wooden mask which has no eye-openings. By his magic power he is able to discover hidden things previously concealed by the members, probably by some particular member. He discovers the ceremonial, no matter where hidden, and juggles with a hot stone drawn from the fire. When the ceremonies are finished the members feast on a pig's head. In early times a deer's head was used. As do the members of the Medicine Lodge upon such an occasion, the members tear the meat from the head with their teeth. The ceremonies of the society are now considered an efficacious treatment for fevers and skin diseases. The rites are supposed to be strictly secret.

The writer has transcribed the entire text of the I″dos ritual in Seneca and has translated it. Three masks are used in the rites — the Conjuror's mask, the Witch mask, and the Dual-spirit's mask. These masks are never used in the rites of the False Face Company, and differ from them in that they have no metal eyes. A flashlight picture of a corner of the I″dos lodge was made by the writer in January 1909, but the session of the lodge was not one of the " regular " ones.

SHA''DOTGE'A, THE EAGLE SOCIETY

The ritual of the Eagle Society consists of ten songs and a dance. The song is called Ganĕ''gwaē oä''no'. Every member participating in the ceremony paints on each cheek a round red spot. No one but members may engage in its ceremonies, even though these be performed publicly. The Eagle Society's ceremony is regarded as most sacred, in this respect next to the Great Feather Dance, O'stowä'gowa. It is believed that the society holds in its songs the most potent charms known. It is said that the dying, especially those afflicted with wasting diseases, and old people, have been completely restored by its ceremonies. This is because the Dew Eagle, to which the society is dedicated, is the reviver of wilting things.[1] The membership is divided into two classes by phratryship. A person may become a member by dreaming such a thing necessary, or by receiving the rites of the society in case of illness. Special costumes are worn in the ceremonies. In the dance the members divide and stand opposite each other according to phratry, the animals opposite the birds. Two dancers from each phratry are chosen, and one singer from each. The dancers assume a squatting posture and imitate the motions of birds. The physical exertion is intense and requires constant interruption. The dancers and singers continue to dance and sing until completely exhausted, unless someone strikes the signal pole and makes a speech. The dancers then retire to their benches until the speech ends, when the singers take up their song and the dance is continued. After his speech, the speaker, who may be any member, presents the dancers for whom he speaks with a gift of money, tobacco, or bread; but the old custom was to give only such things as birds liked for food. The speeches are usually in praise of one's own clan and in derision of the opposite phratry. At the close, the speakers all apologize for their clannish zeal, and say, as if everyone did not known it, that their jibes were intended only as jests. The dancers each hold in their left hands a calumet fan, made by suspending six heron or four eagle feathers parallel and horizontally from a rod or reed. In their right hands they hold small gourd rattles with wooden handles, or small bark rattles made of a folded strip of hickory bark patterned after the larger False-face bark rattles. The signal pole and the striking stick are spirally striped with red paint. After the

---

[1] The Dew Eagle refreshed the scalp of the Good Hunter by plucking a feather from its breast and sprinkling the scalp with dew from the lake in the hollow of its back.

ceremony, when held in a private lodge, the members feast on a pig's head; but this is a modern substitute for a bear's or a deer's head, though crows' heads once were eaten also.

NIA'GWAI" OÄ"NO', THE BEAR SOCIETY

The ritual of the Bear Society consists of twenty songs and a dance. During the intermissions in the dance, that is, between songs, the participants eat berries from a pan on the dance-bench, or, in winter, eat honey, taking portions of the comb and eating it as they walk about the bench. The ceremony is opened by making a tobacco offering to the spirits of the bears, during which the chief Bear-man makes an invocation. The high officer of the society, however, is a woman. The symbol of membership is a black streak drawn diagonally across the right cheek. The object of the society is to cure the diseases of its members and candidates by chanting and dancing. The ceremony is believed to be a remedy for fevers and rheumatism, as well as to bring good fortune. In a healing ceremony the chief woman blows on the head of the patient. After a ceremony the members carry home with them pails of bear pudding, a sweetened corn pudding mixed with sunflower oil. The Bears use the water drum and horn rattles. All Seneca dances are counterclockwise.

Fig. 4   Horn Rattle used in the Seneca Bear Dance

DEGI'YA'GO^n OÄ"NO', THE BUFFALO SOCIETY

The ritual of this society consists of a number of songs which relate the story of the origin of the order. After a ceremony in which there is a dance, the members depart, carrying with them the buffalo pudding. The dancers imitate the action of buffalo when stamping off flies, and the pudding is supposed to be of the consistency of the mud in which the buffalo stamps. When it is eaten it acts as a charm that "stamps off" disease or ill fortune. The Buffalos use the water drum and horn rattles.

O‘GI‘WĒ OÄ‘NO‘, CHANTERS FOR THE DEAD

The O‘gi‘wē ceremony is called for by any member who dreams of the restless spirit of some former member, relative, or friend. At the ceremony the set of songs is sung, the large water drum beaten, and a feast indulged in. The food is supposed to satisfy the hungry ghosts that for some reason are " earth-bound," as spiritists might express it. The O‘gi‘wē ceremony must not be confused with the Death Feast ceremony, which is a clan affair. The diviner of the O‘gi‘wē people is able to identify the unknown spirit which may be troubling the dreams of a member. The sickness and ill fortune caused by evil ghosts may be dispelled by the ceremony. The chief officer is a woman.

DESWADENYATIONDOTTŬ‘, THE WOMAN'S SOCIETY

This society preserves the ritual by which good fortune and health are obtained for women. The singers, fourteen in number at Cattaraugus, are all men. During their singing the women dance. The office of chief singer is hereditary. The women join in a chorus as the men sing. Horn rattles and water drums are used.

TOWII‘SAS, SISTERS OF THE DIO‘HĒ‘KO

This society is composed of a body of women whose special duty is to offer thanks to the spirits of the corn, the beans, and the squashes, Dio‘hē‘ko (these sustain our lives). By their ceremonies of thanksgiving the Towii‘sas propitiate the spirits of growth, and people are assured of a good harvest. The Towii‘sas have a ceremonial song and a march, but no dances. The legend of the society relates that the entire band of Towii‘sas, in the latter part of the seventeenth century, was captured by the Cherokee and carried down the Ohio river. Thereafter two men were admitted as escorts in their march through the woods. At the closing of the ceremony the head-woman chants the Dio‘hē‘ko song as she leads her band about a kettle of corn pudding. She carries an armful of corn on the cob; in her right hand she holds some loose beans, and in her left some squash seeds, the emblems of fertility. The Towii‘sas hold one ceremony each year, unless some calamity threatens the harvest. The rattle of this society is made of a land tortoise (box-turtle) shell. These are often found in graves, but their exact use in the Iroquois territory has not generally been known to archeologists. The leg rattle is another variety having several perforations.

HADIGO[n]'SA SHO[n]O', THE FALSE FACE COMPANY

This organization is one of the better known societies of the Iroquois, and its rites have often been described, though not always correctly interpreted. There are three divisions of the False Faces, and four classes of masks — doorkeeper or doctor masks, dancing masks, beggar masks, and secret masks. The beggar and thief masks form no part of the paraphernalia of the true society, and the secret masks are never used in public ceremonies in the council house at the midwinter ceremony. The False Face ceremonies have been well described, though by no means exhaustively, by Morgan[1] and Boyle.[2] The main features are generally known.

Fig. 5 Typical medicine mask

The paraphernalia of this society consist of the masks previously mentioned, turtle-shell rattles (snapping turtles only), hickory bark rattles, head throws, a leader's pole upon which is fastened a small husk face, a small wooden false face, and a small turtle rattle, and a tobacco basket.

There are two Seneca legends setting forth the origin of the False Faces, and three with the Mohawk story. These stories, however, explain the origin of different classes of masks. Each mask has a name. One story relates that the False Faces originated with the Stone Gaints. However this may be, the writer obtained in 1905, from a woman claiming to be the keeper of the secret masks, a mask representing the Stone Gaint's face. With it was a mask made of wood, over which was stretched a rabbit skin stained with blood. This mask was supposed to represent the face of a traitor as he would look when drowned for his infamy. Chief Delos Kettle said it was used to cure veneral diseases.

There is some dispute as to the antiquity of the False Face Company. Doctor Beauchamp, in his History of the Iroquois,[3] says it is comparatively recent. From a study of the Seneca society, however, the writer is inclined to believe that it is quite old with them,

---

[1] Morgan, Fifth Annual Report New York State Cabinet (Museum), 1852, p. 98.
[2] Boyle, Archaeological Report, Provincial Museum, Toronto, 1898, p. 157.
[3] N. Y. State Mus. Bul. 78, p. 141.

although it may be more recent with the other Iroquois. Early explorers certainly could not have seen everything of Iroquois culture, especially some of the secret things, and their lack of description may be regarded as negative testimony rather than as positive evidence of the nonexistence of certain features which later students have found. It is quite possible that the author of " Van Curler's " Journal of 1634–35 mentions a false face when he writes: " This chief showed me his idol; it was a head with the teeth sticking out; it was dressed in red cloth. Others have a snake, a turtle, a swan, a crane, a pigeon for their idols. . . ." The Seneca at present · drape their false faces when they hang them up for safe keeping, and use them as well as turtle and snake charms as bringers of good fortune. Some pipes from seventeenth-century graves seem to represent blowing masks. Mr M. R. Harrington and the writer found one in 1903 while excavating a seventeenth-century site, since learned to be of Seneca occupancy, on Cattaraugus creek, near Irving. The counterpart of this pipe was found by R. M. Peck on the Warren site, near West Bloomfield, N. Y. The Indians say it is a False Face blowing ashes, and such it may represent. Mr Harrington, and the writer as well, have found what may be false face eye-disks, as well as turtle-shell rattles, in Seneca and Erie graves.

The principal False Face ceremonies are: Ganoi''iowi, Marching Song; Hodigosshos'ga, Doctors' Dance, and Yea^{n}sĕ^{n}dădi'yas, Doorkeepers' Dance.

THE OPENING OR TOBACCO THROWING CEREMONY OF THE FALSE FACE COMPANY

Now receive you this tobacco, you, Shagodiowĕ^{nʹ}gowa, the great false face.

Now it is that you have come to where your grandchildren are gathered.

Now you are taking the place of the great false faces who are wandering in the rocky valleys and mountains.

Now you are the ones who think much of this sacred tobacco.

Now we wish to make a request of you. So we always offer this sacred tobacco [literally, real tobacco], when we ask anything of you.

We pray that you help us with your power.

You can go over all the earth.

In the center of the earth is a great pine tree and that is the place of your resting. It is there that you rub your rattle when you come to rest.

Now then this tree receives this tobacco.

We ask that you watch over us and exercise your power to protect us from anything harmful.

We hold in mind that you have ever done your duty in past times and we ask that you continue [vigilant] henceforth.

We use this tobacco when we ask favors of you for you are very fond of this tobacco.

Now your cane gets tobacco. The great pine tree to its top is your cane.

Now you, the husk faces, you get tobacco also.

You have been associated with the false faces in times past. Now you receive tobacco for you have done your duty.

So it is finished.

GAJI''SASHOⁿO', THE HUSK-FACES

This society seems rather loosely organized among the Seneca, but its chief members act as water doctors. They endeavor to cure certain diseases by spraying and sprinkling water on the patients. Two Husk-faces are admitted with the False Faces in their midwinter long-house ceremony, and act as door-openers. As a company they also have a ceremony in which the Grandfather's Dance is featured. The grandfather is attired in rags, and, holding a cane stationary, dances in a circle about it, using the cane as a pivot. The company dance is one in which all the members participate. Nonmembers may partake of the medicine influence of the ceremony by joining in the dance at the end of the line when the ceremony is performed in the council house at the midwinter festival.

That the foregoing so-called societies are in fact organizations, and that their rites are not merely open ceremonies in which anyone may engage, is apparent from the following considerations:

1 The organizations have permanent officers for the various parts of their rites.

2 They have executive officers.

3 They have certain objects and stand for specific purposes.

4 They have stable and unchangeable rituals.

5 Those who have not undergone some form of an initiatory rite are not allowed to enter into their ceremonies.

6 They have legends by which the origin and objects of the rites are explained.

7 It is not permissible to recite the rituals or to chant any of the songs outside of the lodge to anyone who has not been inducted into the society.

Some of the societies have other features, such as stated meetings and officers' reports, but the foregoing characteristics apply to all the Seneca secret or semisecret ceremonies and entitle them to the name of *societies*.

When an Indian is afflicted with some disorder which can not be identified by the native herb doctors, the relatives of the patient consult a clairvoyant, who names the ceremony, one of those above described, believed to be efficacious in treating the ailment. Some times several ceremonies are necessary, and as a final resort a witch-doctor is called upon.

As to the influence of these organizations on the people, while it must be confessed that they foster some " superstitions " inconsistent with the modern folk-ways of civilized society, they serve more than any other means to conserve the national life of the people. The strongest body of Iroquois in New York today are the two bands or divisions of the Seneca, and the Seneca have the largest number of " pagans." They are perhaps likewise the most patriotic, and struggle with greater energy to retain their tribal organization and national identity.

The customs of these adherents of the old Iroquois religion react on and influence the entire body of the people, " pagans " and Christians alike.

IROQUOIS SUN MYTHS[1]

The Iroquois of New York and Canada still retain vestiges of their former adoration of the sun, and observe certain rites, very likely survivals of more elaborate sun ceremonies.

The writer has witnessed several so-called " sun dances " among the Iroquois; but in every case the dance was the Ostowä"gowa, or Great Feather Dance, the prime religious dance of the Gai'wiio' religion. This modern religion was originated about 1800 by Ganio'dai'io' (" Handsome Lake " the Seneca prophet) and almost entirely revolutionized the religious system of the Iroquois of New York and Ontario. Few of the early folk beliefs have survived the taboo of the prophet; and these beliefs are not easily traced, or even discovered, unless one has before him the Gai'wiio' of Handsome Lake and the Code of Dekanowi'da, the founder of the Confederacy.

The Seneca sun ceremony, Ëndéka Dä'kwa Dännon'dinon'nio' (" Day Orb-of-light Thanksgiving "), is called by any individual who dreams that the rite is necessary for the welfare of the community. The ceremony begins promptly at high noon, when three showers of arrows or volleys from muskets are shot heavenward to notify the sun of the intention to address him. After each of the volleys the populace shout their war cries, " for the sun loves war." A ceremonial fire is built — anciently by the use of a pump-drill, modernly by a match — and the sun-priest chants his thanksgiving song, casting from a husk basket handfuls of native tobacco upon the flames as he sings. This ceremony takes place outside the long house, where the rising smoke may lift the words of the speaker to the sun. Immediately after this, the entire assemblage enters the long house, where the costumed Feather dancers start the Ostowä"gowa.

Among the Onondaga of the Grand River reserve in Ontario, the leader of the sun ceremony carries an effigy of the sun. This is a disk of wood ten inches in diameter, fastened to a handle perhaps a foot long. The disk is painted red in the center, and has a border of yellow. Around the edge are stuck yellow-tipped down-feathers from some large bird. The New York Iroquois have no such effigies, and the writer seriously doubts that the preachers of Handsome Lake's Gai'wiio' would permit such a practice, it being a viola-

---

[1] A. C. Parker in the Journal of American Folk Lore, October–December 1910.

tion of the prophet's teaching. The Canadian Iroquois, however, received the revelations later than their New York brethren, and were longer under the influence of the older religion, which may account for the survival and use of the sun-disk.

The writer has discovered several sun myths among the Seneca, the one which follows being related by Edward Cornplanter, Soson'dowa (" Great Night "), the recognized head preacher of the Gai'wiio' of Handsome Lake. Cornplanter is a Seneca, and a descendant of Gaiänt'waka, the prophet's brother.

The fragments of the cosmological myths which conclude this article are from a mass of ethnological and folk-lore data which it is hoped will shortly be edited and published.

THREE BROTHERS WHO FOLLOWED. THE SUN UNDER THE SKY'S RIM

This happened in old times, when there were not many people. There were three brothers and they were not married. They were hunters and had spent their lives hunting. When the brothers were young they enjoyed the excitement of hunting; but as they grew older it did not give them so much pleasure. The youngest brother suggested that for new experiences they walk to the edge of the earth, where the sky comes down and touches the big sea of salt water. There is salt water west, and this world is an island. The other brothers thought the plan a good one; and when they had prepared everything they started on the journey. They traveled a good many years and a good many things happened to them. They always went straight westward.

At last the brothers came to a place where the sun goes under the sky's edge. The sky bends down there and sinks into the water. They camped there for a month and watched the things that happened there. They noticed how the sun got under the rim of the sky and went away quickly. Some men came there and tried to get under the edge of the sky, but it descended quickly and crushed them. There is a road there. Now they noticed that when the sky came up, the water sank lower; and that when the sky went in the water, the water rose higher.

The younger brothers desired to pass under the rim of the sky when the sun slipped under on his road; but the elder brother said that the happenings were too evilly mysterious, and that he was afraid. The younger brothers ran under the rim of the sky quickly, and the rim was very thick. They kept on the road, and water was on each side. They were afraid that the sky would come down and crush them. Now, the oldest brother, it is said, watched them; and when he saw that nothing happened to injure his brothers, he began to run after them. The younger brothers turned from their safe place to encourage him; but the sky came down on the sun's road and crushed him, but they saw his spirit (notwai'shäⁿ) shoot by quickly. The brothers felt sad.

On the other side of the sky everything is different, so it is said. Before the brothers was a large hill; and when they had ascended it, they saw a very large village in the distance. A man came running toward them. He was in the distance; but he came nearer, and he called out, "Come!" It was their elder brother. "How did you come so quickly, brother?" they asked. "We did not see you come."

The brother answered only, "I was late." He passed by on a road.

An old man came walking toward them. He was youthful and his body was strong, but his hair was long and white. He was an old man. His face was wise-looking, and he seemed a chief. "I am the father of the people in the Above-the-Sky-Place," he said. "Hawĕni'io' is my son. I wish to advise you because I have lived here a long time. I have always lived here, but Hawĕni'io' was born of the woman on the island. When you see Hawĕni'io', call quickly, 'Niawĕⁿ'skänoⁿ!' If you fail to speak first, he will say, 'You are mine,' and you will be spirits, as your brother is."

The brothers proceeded and saw a high house made of white bark. They walked up the path to the door. A tall man stepped out quickly, and the brothers said, "Niawĕⁿ'skänoⁿ!" and the great man said, "Dogĕⁿs', I have been watching you for a long time." The brothers entered the house. Now, when they were in the house, the man said, "In what condition are your bodies?" The brothers answered, "They are fine bodies." The great man answered, "You do not speak the truth. I am Hawĕni'io', and I know all about your bodies. One of you must lie down, and I will purify him, and then the other."

One brother lay down, and Hawĕni'io' placed a small shell to his lips, and put it on the brother's mouth. He also tapped him on the neck, and sealed the shell with clay. He began to skin the brother. He took apart the muscles, and then scraped the bones. He took out the organs and washed them. Then Hawĕni'io' built the man again. He loosened the clay and rubbed his neck. He did this with both brothers; and they sat up, and said, "It seems as if we had

slept." Hawĕni'io' said, " Every power of your bodies is renewed.
I will test you."

The brothers followed Hawĕni'io' to a fine grove of trees surrounded by a thick hedge. All kinds of flowers were blooming
outside. " My deer are here," said Hawĕni'io'.

A large buck with wide antlers ran toward them. " He is the
swiftest of my runners. Try and catch him," said Hawĕni'io'.

The men ran after the deer, and rapidly overtook him. " He has
given us good speed," the brothers said. They soon discovered that
they had many surpassing abilities, and the great man tested them
all on that day.

They returned to the white lodge, and the brothers saw a messenger running toward them. Upon his wide chest was a bright ball of
light. It was very brilliant. In some unknown language he shouted
to Hawĕni'io' and dashed on.

" Do you understand his words, or do you know that man? "
asked Hawĕni'io'. " He is the sun, my messenger. Each day he
brings me news. Nothing from east to west escapes his eye. He
has just told me of a great war raging between your people and
another nation. Let us look down on the earth and see what is
happening."

They all went to a high hill in the middle of the country, and
looked down through a hole where a tree had been uprooted. They
saw two struggling bands of people and all the houses burning.
They could hear people crying and yelling their war cries.

" Men will always do this," said Hawĕni'io', and then they went
down the hill.

The brothers stayed a long time in the upper world, and learned
so much that they never could tell it all. Sometimes they looked
down on the earth and saw villages in which no one lived. They
knew that they were waiting for people to be born and live there.
In the upper world they saw villages, likewise, awaiting the coming
of people. Hawĕni'io' told them a good many things, and after a
time told a messenger to lead them to the path that the sun took
when he came out on the earth in the morning. They followed the
messenger and came out on the earth. They waited until the
sun went over the earth and had gone to the west. Again then
they went under the edge of the sky in the east, and came out in
their country again. It was night, and they slept on the ground.
In the morning they saw their own village, and it was overgrown
with trees. They followed a path through the woods and came

upon another village. Their own people were there, and they went into a council house and talked. They told their story; and no one knew them except their own sister, who was an aged woman.

"The war of which you speak took place fifty years ago," the sister said.

The brothers did not care for the earth now, but wished themselves back in the upper world. They were not like other men, for they never grew tired. They were very strong and could chase animals and kill them with their hands. Nothing could kill them, neither arrows nor disease. After a while, both were struck by lightning, and then they were both killed.

It seems quite likely that there are modern features in this legend; but my informant assured me that the portion relating to the sky and the sun was very old. He said also that he had always heard the upper world described as related in the legend. He added that the sun loved the sound of war, and would linger in his morning journey to see a battle, but that after he reached midheaven he traveled at his usual speed.

Mrs Asher Wright, who spoke Seneca perfectly, and who labored as a missionary among them for fifty years, recorded two Seneca myths as they had been related to her by Esquire Johnson, an old Seneca chief. One describes the origin of good and evil, and says that the sun was made by the Good-minded spirit from the face of his mother. That legend makes the first woman the mother of the twins. The second manuscript, dated 1876, relates practically the same story, but mentions the Sky-woman as having borne first a daughter, who became, without any knowledge of man, the mother of the twins. The mother, having died at their birth, was buried by her mother. The Sky-woman, the grandmother, then turned and addressed the Good-minded spirit, according to Esquire Johnson, quoted by Mrs Wright, as follows:

"Now you must go and seek your father. When you see him, you must ask him to give you power." Pointing to the east, she said, "He lives in that direction. You must keep on until you reach the limits of the Island, and then upon the waters until you reach a high mountain which rises up out of the water, and which you must climb to the summit. There you will see a wonderful being sitting on the highest peak. You must say, 'I am your son.'"

The "wonderful being" appears from the succeeding text to be the sun, although not specifically so named.

We thus have three conflicting ideas presented — the sun as the messenger of the Creator and as the patron of war, as the face of the first mother, and as the father of mankind of earthly origin, although this latter conclusion may be disputed by some for lack of a definite reference.

This leads us to the fact that Iroquois mythology in its present state has been derived from several sources. This has been caused, without doubt, by the policy of adopting the remnants of conquered tribes. Thus we may expect that in Iroquois mythology are the survivals of early Huron, Neutral, Erie, and Andaste elements. It is now possible to trace only the Huron. Algonquian elements came in through the Delaware, the Chippewa, the Shawnee, the Munsee, the Mahikan, and possibly the Nanticoke. It is not difficult to trace Siouan influence.

The writer has been able to trace some of the influencing elements to their sources, but it is nevertheless admitted that the problem of critically sifting and comparing Iroquois myths is a delicate task.

ANECDOTES OF CORNPLANTER

Related by Emily Tallchief, his great great granddaughter

CORNPLANTER MAKES PEACE

" Now these stories are true and came to Solomon Obail from Cornplanter, and Solomon, my father, told me.

" The Cornplanter reservation Senecas often traveled by canoes down the Allegany river to Pittsburgh. On a certain occasion Cornplanter went with a party of canoeists down the Allegany to Pittsburgh. While on his journey one of the paddlers sang Woine'owi as he paddled. Now as he sang the party was startled by a voice that called from the cliff above, ' Halt ye! ' The paddler grounded the canoe and Cornplanter went ashore, where, ascending the cliff, he found a number of Indians gathered about a tree to which a white man was bound. ' So now Cornplanter,' said the chief of the band, ' I have called you to kill this man. You may now do as you please with him and we will be satisfied.' Cornplanter drew forth his long hunting knife and feeling of its sharp edge said ' So I may do as I wish. Truly then I shall do so.' So saying he rushed toward the man with upraised knife and brought it down with a flourish. The man was not injured but instead stepped out from the tree free, for Cornplanter's knife had severed the thongs. ' Now,' said Cornplanter, after some conversation with the man, ' I will hire a guide to take this man back to his home in Philadelphia.' A warrior accepted the commission and guided the prisoner safely back to his home where he found him to be a man of prominence, a chief among his people."

"So I say this," added Mrs Tallchief, "to show that my grandfather was a good man, just and kind. Because of these qualities he became influential."

CORNPLANTER AND WASHINGTON

"Now during the war of the thirteen fires against the king of Great Britain, we, the Iroquois, were loyal to our old allies, the British. We fought for them, but, alas for us they were beaten. Now Washington, the great leader of the thirteen fires, was determined to punish us for our part in the war, for he did not realize that we were but keeping our treaties with the British when we fought. So Washington said, 'Depart from among us and go to the west far from the white people.' But Cornplanter said, 'Not so. We are determined not to move. We have long lived here and intend to continue in our own territory as long as we are able to hold it.' 'Not so,' answered Washington, 'you fought against us and therefore you must move on to the west and if you refuse we shall compel you.' 'Then,' answered Cornplanter, 'we will resist you by force of arms. If you win we will have to go, otherwise we will remain where we now are.'

"Cornplanter returned from Washington to his people and spread the news. Quickly it traveled among all the Indians to the south, the east and the west. All were very angry and said, 'We will fight. When the white man tries to move us as they please it is time that we moved a few white men.' Then the western Indians began to massacre the settlers. The news came to Washington. 'It is a mistake to encourage another Indian war,' he said and then sent for Cornplanter. 'I want to settle our difficulties,' said he, 'and I wish peace. I do not wish war, therefore you, Cornplanter, must pacify your people.' 'I care not to meddle further with matters,' said Cornplanter. 'But you must go,' insisted Washington, 'you are the only man who can restore peace and good will.' Thus it was that Cornplanter accepted the commission. He returned home and collecting a party of chiefs sent abroad declarations of peace. The delegation went through Sandusky into the farther west. There Cornplanter called a council and said, 'We must be peaceful with the white men and cease tormenting them.' Now the tribe was a very fierce one and was very angry that Cornplanter advised peace. They mixed poison with the food which they served the delegation and a number died. Cornplanter also was made severely ill. Then Cornplanter became very angry and calling a council said, ' You have acted with treachery. Now I cease to plead. I now command that you let the white people live in peace. Do not kill another one. If you do I will bring the whole Five Nations against you and with a great army of white men will kill every one of you. The Senecas are the greatest nation of all nations and whatever they plan they do. We are always successful and always victorious in sport, debate or battle. So beware.' Now the western Indians councilled among themselves and said, ' We must hastily agree for if the Senecas come against us we surely will be defeated.' "

ORIGIN OF THE NAME CORNPLANTER

" Gaiänt'wakĕ', the great chief, once went to Philadelphia.

" ' How do your people procure food? ' asked a white man, a Quaker.

" ' We are hunters,' answered the chief.

" ' Have you not observed our great fields of corn and grain? ' asked the white man, ' and did you know that we never have famines as you do? Why do your people not cultivate gardens of size and till large fields of grain? '

" ' My people used to do so,' said the chief, ' and not many years ago when they dwelt in the valley of the Genesee. Now I think that I will encourage this practice again.'

" This conversation so impressed the chief that when he returned he spoke of the matter before the councils and exhorted people in private to plant more and hunt less. Because of this he received the name of *The Planter,* but the whites called him Cornplanter."

KEY TO PHONIC SYSTEM

a   as in *father, bar;* Germ. *haben*

ā   the same sound prolonged

ă   as in *what;* Germ. *man*

ä   as in *hat, man, ran*

ai   as in *aisle,* as i in *mine, bind;* Germ. *Hain*

au   as ou in *out,* as ow in *how;* Germ. *Haus*

c   as sh in *shall;* Germ. sch in *schellen;* cio-sho as in *show*

d   pronounced with the tip of the tongue touching the upper teeth

e   as e in *they,* as a in *may;* Fr. *ne*

ě   as in *met, get, then;* Germ. *denn;* Fr. *sienne*

g   as in *gig;* Germ. *geben;* Fr. *gout*

h   as in *has, he;* Germ. *haben*

i   as in *pique, machine;* ie as ye in English *yea*

ī   the same sound prolonged io as yo in *you*

ĭ   as in *pick, pit*

j   as in *judge*

k   as in *kick, kin*

n   as in *no, nun, not*

ñ   as ng in *ring, sing*

o   as in *note, boat*

q   as ch in Germ. *ich*

s   as in *see, sat*

t   pronounced with the tip of the tongue on the upper teeth

u   as in *rule;* Germ. *du;* Fr. ou in *doux*

ŭ   as in *rut, shut*

w   as in *wit, win*

y   as in *yes, yet*

dj   as j in *judge*

tc   as ch in *church;* tci-chee as in *cheese*

n   marks nasalized vowels as a^n, e^n, $ě^n$, o^n, $ă^n$, ai^n, etc.

'   indicates an aspiration or soft emission of the breadth which is initial or final, thus 'h, ěn', o', etc.

'   marks a sudden closure of the glottis preceding or following a sound, thus 'a, o', ä', ă', etc.

'   marks the accented syllable of a word

t and *h* in this system are always pronounced separately

GLOSSARY OF SENECA WORDS

(For key to pronunciation see page 139)

Adanidä'oshä — (cooperative labor), 39

Adekwe'oⁿge — (green corn thanksgiving), 43

Adĭstowä'e — (feather wearing; name applied to conservative Indians by the more radical), 14

Adoⁿdär'ho — (meaning snaky headed), 5

Adoⁿ'wĕⁿ — (thanking or cheer songs), 41; figure, 84

Askä'nīe' — (women's dance), 101

Awē'yondo' gawen'-notgä'o — (the funeral address), 107

Dagwŭn'noyaĕnt — (the wind spirit), 119

Daitdagwŭt' — (white beaver), 119

Dänondinõñ'yo — (Thanksgiving), 103

Dawan'do' — (other ceremony), 121

Degi'ya'goⁿ oä''no' — (Buffalo Society), 125

Dewŭtiowa'is — (exploding wren), 119

Dioge''djaie — (grassy place), 75

Diohe''koⁿ — (the corn, bean and squash triad; the word means, They sustain us), 39, 54, 86

Diondēgă' — (Seneca name of Pittsburgh)

Dion'dot — (tree), 75

Dionĭ'hogä'wĕ — (Open Door; or Door Keeper, name of Seneca war sachem, once held by Gen. Ely S. Parker), 12

Diono'sade'gĭ — (place of burnt houses; the Seneca name for Cornplanter village), 20, 52

Djĭs'gäⁿdă'taha' — (ghost talker), 68

Dogĕⁿs' — (truly a reply), 113

Ĕndē'ka gää''kwa — (daytime brilliant orb, the sun), 91

Enīa'iehŭk — (it was once that way; the closing word of each section of the Gai' wiio')

Gadă'ciot — (the trotting dance), 82, 101

Gadägĕs'käoⁿ — (fetid banks), Cattaraugus

Gagwē'goⁿ — (all, everyone, entirely), 33

Gahadi yago — (at the wood's edge, a ceremony), 123

Gaiänt'wakă — (The Planter, commonly called Cornplanter. A Seneca pine tree chief name. The half brother of Handsome Lake), 23, 24, 44, 50

Gai"doⁿ (an I"dos ceremony), 123
Gai'yowĕⁿ'ogowă (the sharp point; a ceremony), 123
Gai'wiio' (meaning the good message; pronounced as if spelled guy-we-you), 5, 6, 26, 43
Gai'wiios'tŭk (the Christian religion), 57
Gaji"sashoⁿo' (husk false face), 129
Gaknowe'haat (to copulate), 73
Găko'go' (she is a gluttonous beast, a name), 74
Ganäwĕⁿ'gowa (great bowl game), 41
Gänä'yasta' (midwinter ceremony), 81
Ganĕ"gwaē (the Eagle dance song), 124
Gane'oⁿwoⁿ (the harvest thanksgiving ceremony), 21, 26, 41, 94
Ganio'dai'io (Handsome or Beautiful Lake, the title of the sachem name held by the prophet), 5, 18, 22, 46, 80
Ganōda (night song), 116
Gănonjoni'yon (Kittle Hangs, a name), 74
Ganonktiyuk'gegäo (name of Onondaga), 76
Ganos'ge' (house of the tormentor), 56
Gănoⁿ'wagĕs (fetid water, Seneca name for their village near present site of Avon, Livingston co., N. Y.), 9, 78
Ganowoñ'goⁿ (in the rapids, name of Warren, Pa.), 20
Ganŭn'dasē' (Ga-nun-da-se, meaning a town new or Newtown. Name of non-Christian Seneca village on Cattaraugus reservation)
Ganŭndase"ge' (place of a new town; Seneca name of Geneva), 79
Ganuñg'sĭsnē'ha (long house people), 7
Gat'goⁿ' (witchcraft), 27
Gawĕnnodŭs'hä (compelling charm; charm used to compel persons to obey the charm holder), 29, 30
Gayänt'gogwus (tobacco thrown down, " Dipped " Tobacco, a woman's name), 24
Go'diodia'se (a lying tale, slander), 37
Gonoigä'nongi (drunken), 20
Gowonoⁿ"gowa (Large Talker, a name), 74
Gushēdon'dada (jug shaking dance), 101
Gwi"yă' (an exclamation in the ganē'wo song), 85, 100

Hanïssē'ono	(ha-nĭs-sē'-o-no, the devil), 18
Hadēiyäyo'	(new year announcers), 82
Hadidji'yontwŭs	(the new year ceremony), 75
Hadigoⁿ'săshoⁿo'	(False Face company), 127
Hadioⁿyă"geono	(they are messengers; the four angels), 19, 25
Hadiwĕnnoda'dies	(the thunderers), 98
Ha'dji'no	(male), 73
Haiyon'wĕntha	(Hai-yon'-wĕnt-ha, a sachemship title meaning, *he has lost it and searches, knowing where to find it.* The Seneca name for Hiawątha)
Hanä'sishĕ	(new year ceremonial officers), 82
Hasan'owānĕ'	(exalted name, the word applied to a chief), 44
Hătgwi'yot	(the son-in-law of Handsome Lake), 23
Hawĕni'o'	(good ruler, God; the name mostly used by the Christian Seneca), 48, 133
Hayänt'wŭtgŭs	(tobacco throwing ceremony), 121
Hĕnne'yoⁿ'	(a clairvoyant), 49
Hi"noⁿ	(the Thunderer), 104
Hodiänok'dooⁿ Hĕd'-iohe'	(the Creator), 19, 48
Honio"oⁿ	(white man), 20
Ho'noⁿ'gwae	(a nest), 47
Honon'diont	(overseer of the ceremonies), 411, 421
Hono"tcino"gä	(the guardian company), 116
Ho'tcine'gada	(company of charm holders; note that "tci" is pronounced as "chee" in *cheese*), 119
Hoyā'nĕ	(noble born, good in character, applied as a title to sachems. The Mohawk form Rhoya'nĕ' is sometimes translated "lord"), 9, 22
I"dos	(a charm society), 121, 122
Jodi"gwadoⁿ'	(a great horned serpent), 119
Joⁿgä'oⁿ	(elves of pygmies), 119
Joi'ise	(New Voice, a man's name), 76
Niagă'hos'säă'	(small bundle of magic substance), 29
Nia"gwahē	(great naked bear or mammoth bear, a mythical beast), 28; footnote, 40; 119

Nia'gwai"	(bear, bear ceremony), 125
Niawĕⁿ'	(thanks are given), 36
Niawĕ"skänoⁿ'	(thank you, you are strong), a greeting, 133
Nĭganĕga"a'	(little water) a medicine powder, 116
Niio'	(so be it, or it is well, " all right "), 22
Nĭs'a	(name of a month), 86
Nĭsko'wŭkni	(nĭs-ko'-wŭk-ni, the moon of midwinter), 6, 53
Notwai'shäⁿ	(spirit), 133
Oä'no'	(a dance, or society)
Odä'eo	(the veil over the world), 67
O'dän'kot	(Sunshine, a name), 117
Odjis'kwăthēⁿ	(Pudding Dry, a man's name), 24
O'g'i'wē	(the death chant, a ceremony), 21, 26, 50, 126
Ohĭ'īo'	(river beautiful, name applied to the Allegany river), 20
Ondē'yä	(ceremonial officers, " buffalo robed "), 81
One'gă	(whiskey or rum), 9, 27
Oñgwe"oñwe	(real men, Iroquois), 18, 45
Oñgwe"oñwekä'	(Oñgwe"-oñwe-kä', literally, *men beings — real* — emphatically so), 6
Ono'ityi'yĕnde	(witch poison), 29, 72
Onondaga	(meaning, upon the hills)
Osto'wä'gō'wa	(Great Feather dance, the chief religious dance), 25, 42
Ot'go'ä	(wampum), 57
Otnä'yont	(sharp bone charm), 119
O'to'doⁿgwa"	(it is blazing, a ceremony), 123
Owa'ĕtgäⁿ	(road bad; a rough road), 69
O'wai'ta	(dried hand charm), 119
Sagoyĕ'wa'thă'	(pronounced Sa-go-yĕ'-wā-t'hă'; means, he keeps them awake. Name of Red Jacket, a Seneca leader and orator), 68
Sedékonĭ"	(you come to eat), 36
Sedē'tciä	(early in the morning), 6
Sedwā'gowā'nĕ'	(Se-dwā'-go-wā'-nĕ') Teacher-great, name applied to Handsome Lake, 71; footnote, 53; 67
Segaⁿhedŭs	(*He resurrects;* Christ), 67
Segoewa't'ha	(the tormentor, devil), 48

INDEX

BOOK THREE

The Constitution of the Five Nations

Contents

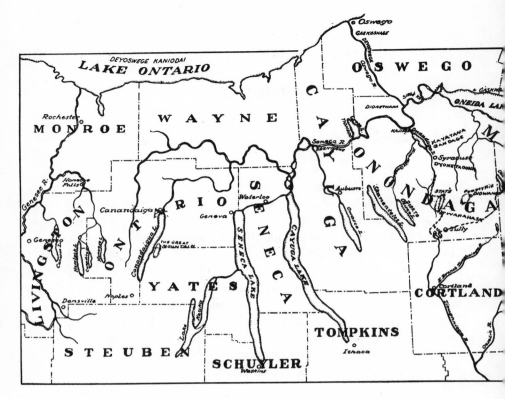

Map of the Central Portion of New York
The Long House Country

This area covers the principal region traversed by Dekanawida and Hiawatha in their efforts to effect the formation of the Five Nations' Confederacy. The dotted line from Onondaga Lake through the Mohawk Valley shows approximately the route taken by Hiawatha in his journey to meet Dekanawida.

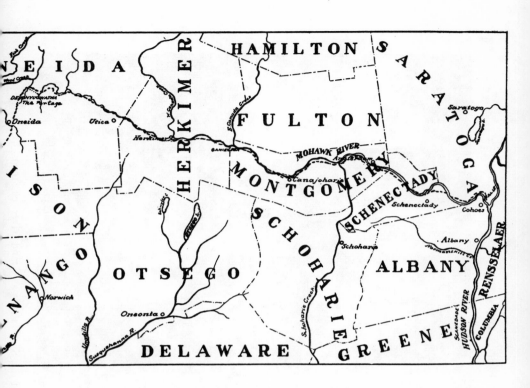

Plate 1

Council of the Six Nations at Grand River, ca. 1900.

The Constitution of the Five Nations

OR

The Iroquois Book of the Great Law

ARTHUR C. PARKER

THE IROQUOIS CONSTITUTION

The constitution of the Iroquois League is known to the Iroquois as the Great Binding Law, or the Great Immutable Law. Their term for it is Ne" Gayänĕshä"gowā. It was transmitted orally from one generation to another through certain of the lords or sachems of the confederacy who had made it their business to learn it. Not until recently have the Iroquois attempted to put their code in written form. For many generations its knowledge has been preserved by a collection of wampum belts and strings, each of which served to recall each law or regulation. Many of the belts and strings became lost or destroyed, and fearing a total destruction of their ancient archives, the Six Nations[1] of New York Indians in 1898 elected The University of the State of New York the official custodian of their wampums. The University accepted the charge and the Legislature passed suitable laws governing the custody of the wampums. In 1908 the Director of the State Museum was proclaimed the keeper of the wampums by Sa-ha-whi, president of the Six Nations.

---

[1] The Five Nations became the Six Nations, with the admission of the Tuscarora in 1724.

The Iroquois constitution is mentioned by both Morgan and Hale, but neither seems to have been able to make a transcript and translation of it. All the Iroquois nations were acquainted with it and extracts from the law are found in many of the speeches of their sachems, as recorded by historians, notably the French explorers and Colden.

The version of the constitution now held authentic by the Iroquois of New York and Ontario, embraces a narrative of the events in the lives of Hiawatha and Dekanawida that lead up to its foundation. Its special interest lies in the fact that it is an attempt of the Iroquois themselves to explain their own civic and social system. It is therefore an invaluable guide to many interesting branches of Iroquois ethnology. Many of the facts contained in this document are familiar to students, but that they formed a part of a definite system of law will perhaps be new. Several of the wampum belts in the New York State Museum are constitutional belts or memorials.

Originally the Five Nations of Iroquois were similar to other Indian tribes or bands — independent bodies with similar dialects and similar customs but with no political coherence. Each man and each tribe to itself, was the rule. Often the individual nations warred with one another, and with external enemies pressing them from all quarters they found themselves in a precarious situation. The very peril in which they lived developed their strategic ability and fostered diplomacy. It likewise produced leaders and finally the great lawgiver who should bring about peace and unity and make the Iroquois the " Indians of Indian," the " Romans of the New World." Hale referred to Hiawatha as the " lawgiver of the Stone age "[1] but Hiawatha does not deserve the title. He was only the spokesman of a greater mind. The Mohawk nation recognizes in Dekanawida its great culture hero and the founder of its civic system, giving Haiyentwatha (Hiawatha) a second place. Nearly all authorities among the other nations of the five agree in this and attribute to Dekanawida the establishment of the Great Peace. The prefatory articles of the Great Immutable Law recognize him as such and represent him as saying:

> I am Dekanawideh and with the Five Nations' confederate lords I plant the Tree of the Great Peace. I plant it in your territory Adodarhoh and the Onondaga Nation, in the territory of you who are fire keepers.
> I name the tree the Tree of the Great Long Leaves. Under the shade of this Tree of the Great Peace we spread the soft, white, feathery down of the globe thistle as seats for you, Adodarhoh and your cousin lords.

[1] Proc. Amer. Ass'n. Adv. Sci., 30:324. 1881.

.   .   .   There shall you sit and watch the council fire of the Confederacy of the Five Nations.

Roots have spread out from the Tree of the Great Peace   .   .   . and the name of these roots is the Great White Roots of Peace.   If any man of any nation outside of the Five Nations shall show a desire to obey the laws of the Great Peace   .   .   .   they may trace the roots to their source   .   .   .   and they shall be welcomed to take shelter beneath the Tree of the Long Leaves.

The smoke of the confederate council fire shall ever ascend and shall pierce the sky so that all nations may discover the central council fire of the Great Peace.

I, Dekanawideh, and the confederate lords now uproot the tallest pine tree and into the cavity thereby made we cast all weapons of war.   Into the depths of the earth, down into the deep underearth currents of water flowing into unknown regions, we cast all weapons of strife.   We bury them from sight forever and plant again the tree.   Thus shall all Great Peace be established and hostilities shall no longer be known between the Five Nations but only peace to a united people.

As one goes further into the unique document, the method by which universal peace is to be established is revealed.   All nations were to sit beneath the peace tree and acknowledge the imperial regency of the Five Nations' council.   To the Five Nations this seemed a very simple thing for they called themselves Ongweoweh, Original Men, a term that implied their racial superiority.   Thus to them it seemed quite natural that other nations should acknowledge their right to rule.   They never doubted the justness of their claim or saw that it possibly could be disputed.   With them it was the basis for universal action.   Other nations were inclined to dispute that the Iroquois were inherently superior and naturally rebelled at the idea of submission, even though it might be for their own ultimate benefit.

From tribe to tribe, tradition shows,[1] the emissaries of the Great Peace went carrying with them the messages in their wampum strands, and inviting delegates to sit beneath the Peace Tree and " clasp their arms about it " and to discuss the advantages of an alliance.

The political success of the Iroquois as a result of their system gave them phenomenal strength and likewise excited widespread jealousy.   Thus the Iroquois found themselves plunged in a war for existence and without friends to call upon.

How a government calling itself the Great Peace provided for war is shown in the part of the great immutable law called " Skanawatih's Laws of Peace and War."   Extracts from these laws follow:

When the proposition to establish the Great Peace is made to a foreign nation it shall be done in mutual council.   The nation is to be persuaded

---

[1] See, for example, The Passamaquoddy Wampum Records by J. D. Prince, page 483, Proc. Amer. Phil. Soc., v. 36.   Also Appendix, page 119 of this bulletin.

by reason and urged to come into the Great Peace. If the Five Nations
fail   .   .   .   after a third council   .   .   .   the war captain of the
Five Nations shall address the head chief of the rebellious nation and
request him three times to accept the Great Peace. If refusal steadfastly
follows the war captain shall let a bunch of white lake shells fall from
his outstretched hand and shall bound quickly forward and club the
offending chief to death. War shall thereby be declared and the war
captain shall have his men at his back to support him in any emergency.
War shall continue until won by the Five Nations.   .   .   .   Then shall
the Five Nations seek to establish the Great Peace by a conquest of the
rebellious nation.

When peace shall have been established by the termination of the
war   .   .   .   then the war captain shall cause all weapons of war to be
taken from the nation. Then shall the Great Peace be established and
the nation shall observe all the rules of the Great Peace for all time to
come.

Whenever a foreign nation is conquered or has by their own free will
accepted the Great Peace, their own system of internal government may
continue so far as is consistent but they must cease all strife with other
nations.

In this manner and under these provisions and others every
rebellious tribe or nation, almost without exception, was either
exterminated or absorbed. The Erie, the Neutral, the Huron, the
Andaste and other cognate tribes of the Iroquoian stock were broken
up and the scattered bands or survivors settled in the numerous
Iroquois towns to forget in time their birth nation and to be known
forever after only as Iroquois. The law read, " Henceforth let no
one so adopted mention the name of his birth nation. To do so
will hasten the end of the Great Peace." The Lenni Lenape or
Delaware, the Nanticoke, the broken bands of the Minsi and the
Shawne, the Brothertown and other Algonquian tribes yielded to
the armed persuasions to accept the Great Peace; likewise did the
Tutelo and Catawba of the eastern Siouan stock, and the Choctaw
of the Muskoghean yield, and to that action is due the fact that
they have descendants today.

The Iroquois policy of adopting captives led to the mixture of
widely scattered stocks. The Iroquois therefore became an ethnic
group of composite elements. Thus from the ideas of universal
peace and brotherhood grew universal intermarriage, modified of
course by clan laws.

According to the great immutable law the Iroquois confederate
council was to consist of fifty rodiyaner (civil chiefs) and was to
be divided into three bodies, namely, the older brothers, the Mohawk
and the Seneca; the younger brothers, the Cayuga and the Oneida;
and the fire keepers, the Onondaga. Each brotherhood debated a
question separately and reported to the fire keepers, who referred
the matter back and ordered a unanimous report. If the two
brotherhoods still disagreed the fire keepers had the casting vote.

If, however, the brotherhoods agreed and their decision was not in accord with the wishes of the fire keepers, the fire keepers could only confirm the decision, for absolute unanimity was the law and required for the passage of any question. Provisions to break speedily any deadlock were provided. All the work of the council was done without an executive head, save a temporary speaker appointed by acclamation. Adodarhoh, in spite of his high title, was only the moderator of the fire keepers.

These "lords" or civil chiefs were nominated by certain noble women in whose families the titles were hereditary; the nominations were confirmed by popular councils both of men and of women and finally by the confederate council. Women thus had great power for not only could they nominate their rulers but also depose them for incompetency in office. Here, then, we find the right of popular nomination, the right of recall and of woman suffrage, all flourishing in the old America of the Red Man and centuries before it became the clamor of the new America of the white invader. Who now shall call Indians and Iroquois savages!

Not only were there popular councils to check an overambitious government, but both the men and the women had in their "war chief" a sort of aboriginal public service commissioner who had authority to voice their will before the council. Men of worth who had won their way into the hearts of the people were elected pine tree chiefs with voice but no vote in the governing body. The rights of every man were provided for and all things done for the promotion of the Great Peace.

Among the interesting things in this Iroquois constitution are the provisions for the official symbols. Many of these symbols, such as the point within a circle, the bundle of arrows, the watchful eagle, are described in detail. The fifteenth string of the Tree of the Long Leaves section, for example, reads:

"Five arrows shall be bound together very strongly and each arrow shall represent one nation. As the five arrows are strongly bound, this shall symbolize the union of the nations. . . ."

This reference to the arrows bound together was quoted by King Hendrick in 1755 in his talk with Sir William Johnson.

Perhaps a more striking paragraph to students of Indian history will be the reference to a certain wampum belt:

"A broad, dark belt of wampum . . . having a white heart in the center on either side of which are two white squares all connected with the heart by white rows shall be the emblem of the unity of the Five Nations. The white heart in the middle . . .

means the Onondaga nation . . . and it also means that the heart of the Five Nations is single in its loyalty to the Great Peace. . . ."

This belt is sometimes called the Hiawatha belt and is one of the most valuable Iroquois belts now extant. It is now on exhibition in the Congressional Library.

The Great Peace as a governmental system was an almost ideal one for the stage of culture with which it was designed to cope. I think it will be found to be the greatest ever devised by barbaric man on any continent. By adhering to it the Five Nations became the dominant native power east of the Mississippi and during the colonial times exercised an immense influence in determining the fate of English civilization on the continent. They, as allies of the British, fought for it and destroyed all French hopes for colonization.

The authors of the great immutable law gave the Iroquois two great culture heroes, heroes almost without equal in American Indian annals. Through the law as a guiding force and through the heroes as ideals the Iroquois have persisted as a people, preserved their national identity and much of their native culture and lore. Today in their various bodies they number more than 16,000 souls. This is a remarkable fact when it is considered that they are entirely surrounded by a dominant culture whose encroachments are persistent and unrelenting in the very nature of things.

The Canadian Iroquois indeed govern themselves by the laws contained in these codes, proving their utility even in modern days.

The two principal manuscripts that form the basis of this work were found in the Six Nations Reservation, Ontario, Canada, in 1910.

The first manuscript was a lengthy account of the Dekanawida legend and an account of the Confederate Iroquois laws. This material has been brought together by Seth Newhouse, a Mohawk, who has expended a large amount of time and given the subject a lengthy study. His account written in Indian English was submitted to Albert Cusick, a New York Onondaga-Tuscarora, for review and criticism. Mr Cusick had long been an authority on Iroquois law and civic rites, and had been a chief informant for Horatio Hale, William M. Beauchamp and in several instances for the present writer. Mr Cusick was employed for more than a month in correcting the Newhouse manuscript until he believed the form in which it is now presented fairly correct and at least as accurate as a free translation could be made.

The second manuscript was compiled by the chiefs of the Six Nations council and in the form here published has been reviewed and corrected by several of their own number, including Chiefs John Gibson, Jacob Johnson and John William Elliott. The official copy was made by Hilton Hill, a Seneca, then employed by the Dominion superintendent for the Six Nations. It has been reviewed and changes were suggested by Albert Cusick.

The Newhouse code was divided into three sections. These were, " The Tree of the Long Leaves," " The Emblematical Union Compact," and " Skanawatih's Law of Peace and War." Each law was associated with a wampum belt or string of wampum beads. The string number and the section of the code from which it is extracted is indicated after each law, as given in the text.

In examining this code of Iroquois law it will be noted that no reference is made in the Canadian codes to the " Long House of the Five Nations." Various reasons are assigned for this. Mr Newhouse cut out all reference to it from his original manuscript because some of the older chiefs said that Handsome Lake, the destroyer of the old religious system, had successfully associated his religious teachings with the Long House. The force of this fact is apparent when we learn that a follower of the Handsome Lake religion is called among other names, Gānūñ'sisnē'ha, " Long House Lover." Another reason is that the historic Long House territory is in New York State, and that the Ontario Iroquois who left New York after the Revolution to cling to the British, dislike any reference to their former habitation that seems to bind them to it. The Dekanawida code provides a refuge for the confederacy in distress, and in Canada they believe they have found " the great elm " under which they may gather in safety to continue their national existence.

In presenting these documents the original orthography has been retained. The only attempt to record Iroquois names and words phonetically is in the notes. This will account for some variations in spelling. The Mohawk and Onondaga writers in their manuscripts used Ayonhwatha and Hayonhwatha interchangeably and there are other variations.

THE DEKANAWIDA LEGEND[1]
DEKANAWIDA'S BIRTH AND JOURNEY

North of the beautiful lake (Ontario) in the land of the Crooked Tongues, was a long winding bay and at a certain spot was the Huron town, Ka-ha-nah-yenh. Near by was the great hill, Ti-ro-nat-ha-ra-da-donh. In the village lived a good woman who had a virgin daughter. Now strangely this virgin conceived and her mother knew that she was about to bear a child. The daughter about this time went into a long sleep and dreamed that her child should be a son whom she should name Dekanawida. The messenger in the dream told her that he should become a great man and that he should go among the Flint people to live and that he should also go to the Many Hill Nation and there raise up the Great Tree of Peace. It was true as had been said the virgin gave birth to a boy and the grandmother greatly disliked him and she rebuked her daughter.

"You refuse to tell me the father of the child," she said, "and now how do you know that great calamity will not befall us, and our nation? You must drown the child."

So then the mother took the child to the bay and chopped a hole in the ice where she customarily drew water and thrust him in, but when night came the child was found at his mother's bosom. So then the mother took the child again and threw him in the bay but at night the child returned. Then the third time the grandmother herself took the child and drowned him but in the morning the child nestled as before on its mother's own bosom.

So the grandmother marveled that the child, her grandson, could not be drowned. Then she said to her daughter:

"Mother, now nurse your child for he may become an important man. He can not be drowned, we know, and you have borne him without having marriage with any man. Now I have never heard of such an occurrence nor has the world known of it before."

Beginning with that time the mother took great care of her child and nursed him. She named him Dekanawida in accord with the instruction of her dream.

The child rapidly grew and was remarkably strong and healthy. His appearance was noticed for its good aspect and his face was most handsome.

When Dekanawida had grown to manhood he was greatly abused

---

[1] From the Newhouse version.

by the Huron people because of his handsome face and his good mind. He was always honest and always told what he believed was right. Nevertheless he was a peculiar man and his people did not understand him.

Many things conspired to drive him away for the Crooked Tongues had no love for such a man. Their hearts were bitter against a man who loved not war better than all things.

After a journey by canoe across the lake he came into the hunting territory of the Flint Nation. He journeyed on to the lower fall of the river of the Flint Nation and made a camp a short way from the fall on the flat land above it. He sat beneath a tall tree and smoked his pipe in quiet meditation.

A man of the Flints passed by and seeing the fire and the stranger approached him cautiously to discover what weapon he bore, if any. Carefully the man of the Flint reconnoitered but saw no weapon, but only the stranger quietly smoking. Returning to the town a short distance away the presence of the odd stranger was reported. Then the chiefs and their men went out and assembled about the man who smoked. One of the head men was delegated to question the stranger and so he asked " From whence came you?"

" I am from Ka-ka-na-yenh," the stranger replied.

" I am of the Wyandots, whom you call the Crooked Tongues because our speech is slightly different," answered the stranger, " My mother is a virgin woman."

" Then," said the speaker, " By what name are you known?"

" I am Dekanawidah, so named because my virgin mother dreamed that it should be so and no one else shall ever be named by this name."

" What brought you here to us," asked the speaker.

So then Dekanawidah answered, " The Great Creator from whom we all are descended sent me to establish the Great Peace among you. No longer shall you kill one another and nations shall cease warring upon each other. Such things are entirely evil and he, your Maker, forbids it. Peace and comfort are better than war and misery for a nation's welfare."

Then answered the speaker of the Flints, "All that you say is surely true and we are not able to contradict it. We must have proof, however, before we submit ourselves to you whereby we may know that you indeed possess rightful power to establish the Great Peace."

So answered Dekanawida, " I am able to demonstrate my power for I am the messenger of the Creator and he truly has given me my choice of the manner of my death."

" Choose then," said the speaker, "a manner of destruction for we are ready to destroy you." Dekanawida replied, " By the side of the falls at the edge of a precipice stands a tall tree. I will climb the tree and seat myself in the topmost branches. Then shall you cut down the tree and I shall fall into the depths below. Will not that destroy me? "

Then said the speaker, " Let us proceed at once."

Dekanawida ascended the tree and it was chopped down. A multitude of people saw him fall into the chasm and plunge into the water. So they were satisfied that he was surely drowned. Night came but Dekanawida did not appear and thus were the people sure of his death, and then were they satisfied.

The next morning the warriors saw strange smoke arising from the smoke hole of an empty cabin. They approached cautiously and peering in the side of the wall where the bark was loosened they saw Dekanawidah. He was alive and was not a ghost and he was cooking his morning meal.

So the watchers reported their discovery and then were the chiefs and people truly convinced that indeed Dekanawidah might establish the Great Peace.

THE TROUBLED NATIONS

The Ongwe-oweh had fought long and bravely. So long had they fought that they became lustful for war and many times Endeka-Gakwa, the Sun, came out of the east to find them fighting. It was thus because the Ongwe-oweh were so successful that they said the Sun loved war and gave them power.

All the Ongwe-oweh fought other nations sometimes together and sometimes singly and, ah-gi! ofttimes they fought among themselves. The nation of the Flint had little sympathy for the Nation of the Great Hill, and sometimes they raided one another's settlements. Thus did brothers and Ongwe-oweh fight. The nation of the Sunken Pole fought the Nation of the Flint and hated them, and the Nation of the Sunken Pole was Ongwe.

Because of bitter jealousy and love of bloodshed sometimes towns would send their young men against the young men of another town to practise them in fighting.

Even in his own town a warrior's own neighbor might be his enemy and it was not safe to roam about at night when Soi-ka-Gakwa, our Grandmother, the Moon, was hidden.

Everywhere there was peril and everywhere mourning. Men were ragged with sacrifice and the women scarred with the flints, so everywhere there was misery. Feuds with outer nations, feuds with brother nations, feuds of sister towns and feuds of families and of clans made every warrior a stealthy man who liked to kill.

Then in those days there was no great law. Our founder had not yet come to create peace and give united strength to the Real Men, the Ongwe-oweh.

In those same days the Onondagas had no peace. A man's life was valued as nothing. For any slight offence a man or woman was killed by his enemy and in this manner feuds started between families and clans. At night none dared leave their doorways lest they be struck down by an enemy's war club. Such was the condition when there was no Great Law.

South of the Onondaga town lived an evil-minded man. His lodge was in a swale and his nest was made of bulrushes. His body was distorted by seven crooks and his long tangled locks were adorned by writhing living serpents. Moreover, this monster was a devourer of raw meat, even of human flesh. He was also a master of wizardry and by his magic he destroyed men but he could not be destroyed. Adodarhoh was the name of the evil man.

Notwithstanding the evil character of Adadarhoh the people of Onondaga, the Nation of Many Hills, obeyed his commands and though it cost many lives they satisfied his insane whims, so much did they fear him for his sorcery.

The time came, however, when the Onondaga people could endure him no longer. A council was called to devise a way to pacify him and to entreat him to cease his evil ways. Hayonwatha called the council for he had many times sought to clear the mind of Adodarhoh and straighten his crooked body. So then the council was held in the house of Hayontawatha. It was decided that half the people should go by boat across the creek where it widens and that others should skirt the shore. Adodarhoh was not in his nest in the swale but in a new spot across the wide place in the creek.

The boats started and the people walked. From the bushes that overhung the shore a loud voice sounded. " Stand quickly and look behind you for a storm will overwhelm you."

In dismay the people arose in their canoes and turned about. As they did so the canoes overturned and the men were plunged into the water and many were drowned. A few escaped and then all survivors returned to the village. So had Adodarhoh frustrated the attempt to meet with him.

Again the people prepared to conciliate Adodarho. Three times they agreed to attempt the undertaking. So on the second occasion they go by canoe and by land, those who go by canoe follow the shore and those who go by land walk on the pebbles close to the water's edge.

Again the cunning Adodarho sees them and calling down Hagoks he shook him, and the people in a wild rush scramble for the feathers, for the plumes of Hagoks are most beautiful and men are proud when their heads are adorned with them. There is a tumult and blows are struck. Evil feelings arise and in anger the people return to the village still contending. The mission of conciliation is forgotten.

The next day Ayonhwatha called the people to their promise and for the third time to attempt a council with Adodarho. Moreover, they promised to obey every instruction and listen neither to a voice outside nor an omen nor any commotion.

Another council was held in the lodge of a certain great dreamer. He said, " I have dreamed that another shall prevail. He shall come from the north and pass to the east. Hayonwhatha shall meet him there in the Mohawk country and the two together shall prevail. Hayonwhatha must not remain with us but must go from us to the Flint land people."

So when the journey across the lake was attempted there was a division and the dreamer's council prevailed.

Then the dreamer held two councils and those who believed in him conspired to employ Ohsinoh, a famous shaman.

Hayonwhatha had seven daughters whom he loved and in whom he took great pride. While they lived the conspirators knew he would not depart. With the daughters dead they knew the crushing sorrow would sever every tie that bound him to Onondaga. Then would he be free to leave and in thinking of the welfare of the people forget his own sorrow.

Hayonwhatha could not call the people together for they refused further to listen to his voice. The dreamer's council had prevailed.

At night Osinoh climbed a tree overlooking his lodge and sat on a large limb. Filling his mouth with clay he imitated the sound of a screech owl. Calling the name of the youngest daughter he sang:

> " Unless you marry Osinoh
> You will surely die, -whoo-hoo! "

Then he came down and went to his own home.

In three days the maiden strangely died. Hayonwhatha was disconsolate and sat sitting with his head bowed in his hands. He mourned, but none came to comfort him.

In like manner five other daughters passed away and the grief of Hayonwhatha was extreme.

Clansmen of the daughters then went to the lodge of Hayonwhatha to watch, for they knew nothing of Osinoh's sorcery. They gathered close against the large trees and in the shadows of bushes. The clansmen suspected some evil treachery and were there to discover it.

There was no moon in the sky when Osinoh came. Cautiously he came from habit but he was not afraid. He drove his staff in the ground, he breathed loud like a magic totem animal snorting and then he climbed the tree. He spat the clay about the tree to imitate the screech owl and as he did he said: " Si-twit, si-twit, si-twit." Then he sang:

> " Unless you marry Osinoh
> You shall surely die, whoo-hoo! "

The morning came and Osinoh descended. As he touched the ground a clansman shot an arrow and transfixed him. Prostrate fell Osinoh and the clansman rushed at him with a club.

Osinoh looked up. " You are unable to club me," he said. " Your arm has no power at all. It weakens. Today I shall recover from this wound. It is of no purpose to injure me."

It was true indeed; the clansman could not lift the club to kill Osinoh. Then Osinoh arose and went home and in three days the daughter died. So perished all by the evil magic arts of Osinoh.

The grief of Hayonwhatha was terrible. He threw himself about as if tortured and yielding to the pain. No one came near him so awful was his sorrow. Nothing would console him and his mind was shadowed with the thoughts of his heavy sorrow.

" I shall cast myself away, I shall bury myself in the forest, I shall become a woodland wanderer," he said. Thus he expressed his desire to depart. Then it was known that he would go to another nation.

Hayonwhatha " split the heavens," Watanwhakacia, when he departed and his skies were rent asunder.

Toward the south he went and at night he camped on the mountain. This was the first day of his journey. On the second day he descended and camped at the base of the hill. On the third day

he journeyed onward and when evening came he camped in a hickory grove.   This he named O-nea-no-ka-res-geh, and it was on
the morning he came to a place where round jointed rushes grew.
He paused as he saw them and made three strings of them and
when he had built a fire he said: "This would I do if I found
anyone burdened with grief even as I am.   I would console them
for they would be covered with night and wrapped in darkness.
This would I lift with words of condolence and these strands of
beads would become words with which I would address them."

So at this place he stayed that night and he called the spot O-hon-
do-gon-wa, meaning Rush-land.

When daylight came he wandered on again and altering the
course of his journey turned to the east.   At night he came to a
group of small lakes and upon one he saw a flock of ducks.   So
many were there and so closely together did they swim that they
seemed like a raft.

"If I am to be truly royaneh (noble)," he said aloud to himself,
"I shall here discover my power."   So then he spoke aloud and
said: "Oh you who are 'floats' lift up the water and permit me
to pass over the bottom of the lake dryshod."

In a compact body the ducks flew upward suddenly and swiftly,
lifting the water with them.   Thus did he walk down the shore and
upon the bottom of the lake.   There he noticed lying in layers the
empty shells of the water snail, some shells white, and others purple.   Stooping down he filled a pouch of deer skin with them, and
then passed on to the other shore.   Then did the ducks descend
and replace the water.

It was here that Hayonwhatha desired for the first time to eat.
He then killed three ducks and roasted them.   This was the evening
of the fifth day.

In the morning he ate the cold meat of the roasted ducks and
resumed his journey.   This was the sixth day and on that day he
hunted for small game and slept.

On the morning of the seventh day he ate again and turned his
way to the south.   Late in the evening he came to a clearing and
found a bark field hut.   There he found a shelter and there he
erected two poles, placed another across the tops and suspended
three shell strings.   Looking at them he said: "Men boast what
they would do in extremity but they do not do what they say.   If
I should see anyone in deep grief I would remove these shell strings
from the pole and console them.   The strings would become words
and lift away the darkness with which they are covered.   Moreover what I say I would surely do."   This he repeated.

A little girl discovered smoke arising from the field lodge and she crept up and listened. She advanced and peered in a chink in the bark. Then she ran homeward and told her father of the strange man.

"The stranger must be Hayonwhatha," said the father, " I have heard that he has departed from Onondaga. Return, my daughter, and invite him to our house."

The girl-child obeyed and Hayonwhatha went to her house. "We are about to hold a council," the father said. " Sit in that place on one side of the fire and I will acquaint you with our decisions."

The council was convened and there was a great discussion. Before darkness every evening the council dissolved and at no time was Hayonwhatha called upon for advice nor was anything officially reported to him.

On the tenth day of his journey during the debate in the council Hayonwhatha quietly left and resumed his wandering. Nothing had been asked of him and he felt himself not needed by the people. Late in the evening he came to the edge of another settlement and as was his custom he kindled a fire and erected a horizontal pole on two upright poles. On this he placed three strings of the wampum shells. Then he sat down and repeated his saying: " Men boast what they would do in extremity but they do not do what they promise. If I should see any one in deep grief I would remove these shells from this pole and console him. The shells would become words and lift away the darkness with which they are covered. Moreover, I truly would do as I say." This he repeated.

The chief man of the village saw the smoke at the edge of the forest and sent a messenger to discover who the stranger might be. Now when the messenger reached the spot he saw a man seated before a fire and a horizontal pole from which three strings of small shells were suspended. He also heard the words spoken as the stranger looked at the strings. So then when he had seen all he returned and reported what he had seen and heard.

Then said the chief man, " The person whom you describe must truly be Hayonwhatha whom we have heard left his home at Onondaga. He it is who shall meet the great man foretold by the dreamer. We have heard that this man should work with the man who talks of the establishment of peace."

So then the chiefs sent a messenger who should say, " Our principal chief sent me to greet you. Now then I wish you would come into our village with me."

Hayonwhatha heard the messenger and gathered up his goods and went into the village and when he had entered the chief's house the chief said, " Seat yourself on the opposite side of the fire so that you may have an understanding of all that we do here in this place."

Then Hayonhwatha sat there for seven days and the chiefs and people talked without arriving at any decision. No word was asked Hayonhwatha and he was not consulted. No report was made officially to him. So he did not hear what they talked about.

On the eighteenth night a runner came from the south. He was from the nation residing on the seashore. He told the chiefs of the eminent man who had now come to the town on the Mohawk river at the lower falls. Then the messenger said: "We have heard of the dream of Onodaga which told of the great man who came from the north. Now another great man who shall now go forward in haste to meet him shall change his course and go eastward to meet in the Flinty land village (Kanyakahake), the great man. There shall the two council together and establish the Great Peace." So said the messenger from the salt water seashore, who came to tell Hayonwhatha to journey east.

So the chiefs of the town where Hayonhwatha was staying chose five men as an escort for Hayonhwatha. They must go with him until he reached the house where Dekanawida was present. So then on the next day the chief himself went with the party and watched carefully the health of Hayonhwatha. The journey lasted five days and on the fifth day the party stopped on the outskirts of the town where Dekanawida was staying and then they built a fire. This was the custom, to make a smoke so that the town might know that visitors were approaching and send word that they might enter without danger to their lives. The smoke was the signal of friends approaching.[1] The Mohawks (People of the Flinty Country) knew the meaning of the signal so they sent messengers and invited the party into the village.

When Hayonhwatha had entered the house where the people had gathered the chief asked him whom he would like to see most. Then Ayonhwatha answered, " I came to see a very great man who lately came from the north." The chief said, " I have with you two men who shall escort you to the house where Dekanawida is

---

[1] In those days it was necessary to build a fire on the outskirts of a village about to be entered. If necessary to kill an animal for food, its pelt must be hung on a tree in plain sight because it is the property of the nation in whose territory it is killed. This information was given to me by Albert Cusick and Seth Newhouse.

Plate 2

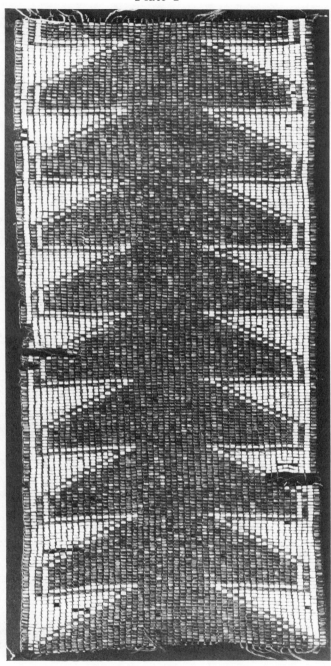

Great Belt of the Confederacy symbolizing the Gayänĕsshä"gowä as an
ever growing tree

Plate 3

Belt of the covenant. Displayed by the speaker of the confederate council.

present." Then the people went out and the two men escorted Hayonhwatha to Dekanawida. This was on the twenty-third day. Then Dekanawida arose when Hayonhwatha had entered and he said: " My younger brother I perceive that you have suffered from some deep grief. You are a chief among your people and yet you are wandering about."

Hayonhwatha answered, " That person skilled in sorcery, Osinoh, has destroyed my family of seven daughters. It was truly a great calamity and I am now very miserable. My sorrow and my rage have been bitter. I can only rove about since now I have cast myself away from my people. I am only a wanderer. I split the heavens when I went away from my house and my nation."

Dekanawida replied, " Dwell here with me. I will represent your sorrow to the people here dwelling."

So Hayonhwatha had found some one who considered his distress and he did stay. Then Dekanawida told of his suffering and the people listened.

The five escorts were then dismissed and Hayonhwatha gave thanks to them and told them to return to their own region again. Then the escorts said, " Now today it has happened as was foretold in a dream. The two are now together. Let them now arrange the Great Peace." Then they returned home.

When Dekanawida laid the trouble before the council he promised to let Hayonhwatha know their decision. The chiefs deliberated over the sad events and then decided to do as Dekanawida should say. He then should remedy the trouble. Then Dekanawida went in perplexity to his lodge and as he came to it he heard Hayonhwatha say, " It is useless, for the people only boast what they will do, saying ' I would do this way,' but they do nothing at all. If what has befallen me should happen to them I would take down the three shell strings from the upright pole and I would address them and I would console them because they would be covered by heavy darkness." Dekanawida stood outside the door and heard all these words. So then Dekanawida went forward into the house and he went up to the pole, then he said: " My younger brother, it has now become very plain to my eyes that your sorrow must be removed. Your griefs and your rage have been great. I shall now undertake to remove your sorrow so that your mind may be rested. Have you no more shell strings on your pole? "

Hayonhwatha replied, " I have no more strings but I have many shells in a tanned deer's skin." So he opened his bundle and a great quantity of shells fell out. So then Dekanawida said, " My younger brother, I shall string eight more strands because there must be eight parts to my address to you." So then Hayonhwatha permitted the stringing of the shells and Dekanawida made the strings so that in all there were thirteen strings and bound them in four bunches. These must be used to console the one who has lost by death a near relative. " My younger brother, the thirteen strings are now ready on this horizontal pole. I shall use them. I shall address you. This is all that is necessary in your case."

So then he took one bunch off the pole and held it in his hand while he talked. While he talked one after another he took them down and gave one to Hayonhwatha after each part of his address.

The words that he spoke when he addressed Hayonhwatha were eight of the thirteen condolences.

When the eight ceremonial addresses had been made by Dekanawida the mind of Hayonhwatha was made clear. He was then satisfied and once more saw things rightly.

Dekanawida then said, " My younger brother, these thirteen strings of shell are now completed. In the future they shall be used in this way: They shall be held in the hand to remind the speaker of each part of his address, and as each part is finished a string shall be given to the bereaved chief (Royaneh) on the other side of the fire. Then shall the Royaneh hand them back one by one as he addresses a reply; it then can be said, ' I have now become even with you.' "

Dekanawida then said, " My junior brother, your mind being cleared and you being competent to judge, we now shall make our laws and when all are made we shall call the organization we have formed the Great Peace. It shall be the power to abolish war and robbery between brothers and bring peace and quietness.

"As emblems of our Royoneh titles we shall wear deer antlers and place them on the heads of Royaneh men."

Hayonhwatha then said, " What you have said is good, I do agree."

Dekanawida said, " My younger brother, since you have agreed I now propose that we compose our Peace song. We shall use it on our journey to pacify Adodarhoh. When he hears it his mind shall be made straight. His mind shall then be like that of other men. This will be true if the singer remembers and makes no error in his singing from the beginning to the end, as he walks before Adodarhoh."

Hayonhwatha said, "I do agree, I truly believe the truth of what you say."

Then Dekanawida said, "My younger brother, we shall now propose to the Mohawk council the plan we have made. We shall tell our plan for a confederation and the building of a house of peace. It will be necessary for us to know its opinion and have its consent to proceed."

The plan was talked about in the council and Dekanawida spoke of establishing a union of all the nations. He told them that all the chiefs must be virtuous men and be very patient. These should wear deer horns as emblems of their position, because as he told them their strength came from the meat of the deer. Then Hayonhwatha confirmed all that Dekanawida had said.

Then the speaker of the Mohawk council said, " You two, Dekanawida and Hayonhwatha, shall send messengers to the Oneida (People of the Stone) and they shall ask Odatshedeh if he will consider the plan."

When Odatshedeh had been asked he replied, " I will consider this plan and answer you tomorrow."

When the tomorrow of the next year had come, there came the answer of the Oneida council, " We will join the confederation."

So then the Mohawks (Kanyenga) sent two messengers to Onondaga asking that the nation consider the proposals of Dekanawida. It was a midsummer day when the message went forth and the Onondaga council answered, "Return tomorrow at high sun." So the two great men returned home and waited until the next midsummer. Then the midday came and the Onondaga council sent messengers who said, " We have decided that it would be a good plan to build the fire and set about it with you." Dekanawida and Hayonhwatha heard this answer.

So then at the same time Dekanawida and Hayonhwatha sent messengers to the Cayuga nation and the answer was sent back. The Cayugas said they would send word of their decision tomorrow, upon the midsummer day. The next year at midsummer the Cayugas sent their answer and they said, " We do agree with Dekanawida and Hayonhwatha."

Now the People of the Great Hill were divided and were not agreed because there had been trouble between their war chiefs, but messengers were sent to them but the Senecas could not agree to listen and requested the messengers to return the next year. So when the messengers returned the councils did listen and considered the proposals. After a year had passed they sent messengers to say that they had agreed to enter into the confederacy.

Then Dekanawida said, " I now will report to the Mohawk council the result of my work of five years." Hayonhwatha then said, " I do agree to the report."

THE ESTABLISHMENT OF THE GREAT PEACE

Dekanawida requested some of the Mohawk chiefs to call a council, so messengers were sent out among the people and the council was convened.

Dekanawida said, " I, with my co-worker, have a desire to now report what we have done on five successive midsummer days, of five successive years. We have obtained the consent of five nations. These are the Mohawks, the Oneidas, the Onondagas, the Cayugas and the Senecas. Our desire is to form a compact for a union of our nations. Our next step is to seek out Adodarhoh. It is he who has always set at naught all plans for the establishment of the Great Peace. We must seek his fire and look for his smoke."

The chief speaker of the council then said, " We do agree and confirm all you have said and we wish to appoint two spies who shall volunteer to seek out the smoke of Adodarhoh."

Two men then eagerly volunteered and Dekanawida asked them if they were able to transform themselves into birds or animals, for such must be the ability of the messengers who approached Adodarhoh. The two men replied, " We are able to transform ourselves into herons and cranes."

" Then you will not do for you will pause at the first creek or swamp and look for frogs and fish."

Two men then said, " We have magic that will transform us into humming birds. They fly very swiftly."

" Then you will not do because you are always hungry and are looking for flowers."

Two other men then said, " We can become the Dare, the white crane."

" Then you will not do because you are very wild and easily frightened. You would be afraid when the clouds move. You would become hungry and fly to the ground looking about for ground nuts."

Then two men who were crows by magic volunteered but they were told that crows talked too loudly, boasted and were full of mischief.

So then in the end two men who were powerful by the magic of the deer and the bear stepped before the council and were chosen. The speaker for the council then reported to Dekanawida that the spies were ready to go. Then they went.

Now Dekanawida addressed the council and he said, " I am Dekanawida and with me is my younger brother. We two now lay before you the laws by which to frame the Ka-ya-neh-renh-ko-wa. The emblems of the chief rulers shall be the antlers of deer. The titles shall be vested in certain women and the names shall be held in their maternal families forever." All the laws were then recited and Hayonhwatha confirmed them.

Dekanawida then sang the song to be used when conferring titles. So in this way all the work and the plans were reported to the Mohawk council and Hayonhwatha confirmed it all. Therefore the council adopted the plan.

When the spies returned the speaker of the council said, " Ska-non-donh, our ears are erected." Then the spies spoke and they said, "At great danger to ourselves we have seen Adodarhoh. We have returned and tell you that the body of Adodarhoh has seven crooked parts, his hair is infested with snakes and he is a cannibal."

The council heard the message and decided to go to Onondaga at midsummer.

Then Dekanawida taught the people the Hymn of Peace and the other songs. He stood before the door of the longhouse and walked before it singing the new songs. Many came and learned them so that many were strong by the magic of them when it was time to carry the Great Peace to Onondaga.

When the time had come, Dekanawida summoned the chiefs and people together and chose one man to sing the songs before Adodar-hoh. Soon then this singer led the company through the forest and he preceded all, singing the Peace songs as he walked. Many old villages and camping places were passed as they went and the names were lifted to give the clan name holders. Now the party passed through these places:

Old Clearing
Overgrown with bushes
A temporary place
Protruding rocks
Between two places
Parties opposite at the council fire
In the Valley

Drooping Wing
On the Hillside
Man Standing
I have daubed it
Lake Bridge
Between two side hills
Lake Outlet
At the forks
Long Hill
Broken Branches Lying
The Spring
White
Corn Stalks on both sides
Two Hillsides
The Old Beast

All these places were in the Mohawk country.

Now they entered the Oneida country and the great chief Odat-shedeh with his chiefs met them. Then all of them marched onward to Onondaga, the singer of the Peace Hymn going on ahead.

The frontier of the Onondaga country was reached and the expedition halted to kindle a fire, as was customary. Then the chiefs of the Onondagas with their head men welcomed them and a great throng marched to the fireside of Adodarhoh, the singer of the Peace Hymn leading the multitude.

The lodge of Adodarhoh was reached and a new singer was appointed to sing the Peace Hymn. So he walked before the door of the house singing to cure the mind of Adodarhoh. He knew that if he made a single error or hesitated his power would be weakened and the crooked body of Adodarhoh remain misshapen. Then he hesitated and made an error. So another singer was appointed and he too made an error by hesitating.

Then Dekanawida himself sang and walked before the door of Adodarhoh's house. When he finished his song he walked toward Adodarhoh and held out his hand to rub it on his body and to know its inherent strength and life. Then Adodarhoh was made straight and his mind became healthy.

When Adodarhoh was made strong in rightful powers and his body had been healed, Dekanawida addressed the three nations. He said, " We have now overcome a great obstacle. It has long stood in the way of peace. The mind of Adodarhoh is now made right and his crooked parts are made straight. Now indeed may we establish the Great Peace.

"Before we do firmly establish our union each nation must appoint a certain number of its wisest and purest men who shall be rulers, Rodiyaner. They shall be the advisers of the people and make the new rules that may be needful. These men shall be selected and confirmed by their female relations in whose lines the titles. shall be hereditary. When these are named they shall be crowned, emblematically, with deer antlers."

So then the women of the Mohawks brought forward nine chiefs who should become Rodiyaner and one man, Ayenwaehs, as war chief.

So then the women of the Oneidas brought forward nine chiefs who should become Rodiyaner, and one man, Kahonwadironh, who should be war chief.

So then the Onondaga women brought forward fourteen chiefs who should become Rodiyaner, and one man, Ayendes, who should be war chief.

Each chief then delivered to Dekanawida a string of lake shell wampum a span in length as a pledge of truth.

Dekanawida then said: "Now, today in the presence of this great multitude I disrobe you and you are not now covered by your old names. I now give you names much greater." Then calling each chief to him he said: "I now place antlers on your head as an emblem of your power. Your old garments are torn off and better robes are given you. Now you are Royaner, each of you. You will receive many scratches and the thickness of your skins shall be seven spans. You must be patient and henceforth work in unity. Never consider your own interests but work to benefit the people and for the generations not yet born. You have pledged yourselves to govern yourselves by the laws of the Great Peace. All your authority shall come from it.

"I do now order that Skanawateh shall in one-half of his being be a Royaneh of the Great Peace, and in his other half a war chief, for the Rodiyaner must have an ear to hear and a hand to feel the coming of wars."

Then did Dekanawida repeat all the rules which he with Ayonhwatha had devised for the establishment of the Great Peace.

Then in the councils of all the Five Nations he repeated them and the Confederacy was established.

THE COUNCIL OF THE GREAT PEACE

THE GREAT BINDING LAW, GAYANASHAGOWA

1 I am Dekanawidah and with the Five Nations' Confederate Lords[1] I plant the Tree of the Great Peace. I plant it in your territory, Adodarhoh, and the Onondaga Nation, in the territory of you who are Firekeepers.

I name the tree the Tree of the Great Long Leaves. Under the shade of this Tree of the Great Peace we spread the soft white feathery down of the globe thistle as seats for you, Adodarhoh, and your cousin Lords.

We place you upon those seats, spread soft with the feathery down of the globe thistle, there beneath the shade of the spreading branches of the Tree of Peace. There shall you sit and watch the Council Fire of the Confederacy of the Five Nations, and all the affairs of the Five Nations shall be transacted at this place before you, Adodarhoh, and your cousin Lords, by the Confederate Lords of the Five Nations. (1–I, TLL).[2]

2 Roots have spread out from the Tree of the Great Peace, one to the north, one to the east, one to the south and one to the west. The name of these roots is The Great White Roots and their nature is Peace and Strength.

If any man or any nation outside the Five Nations shall obey the laws of the Great Peace and make known their disposition to the Lords of the Confederacy, they may trace the Roots to the Tree and if their minds are clean and they are obedient and promise to obey the wishes of the Confederate Council, they shall be welcomed to take shelter beneath the Tree of the Long Leaves.

We place at the top of the Tree of the Long Leaves an Eagle who is able to see afar. If he sees in the distance any evil approaching or any danger threatening he will at once warn the people of the Confederacy. (2–II, TLL).

3 To you Adodarhoh, the Onondaga cousin Lords, I and the other Confederate Lords have entrusted the caretaking and the watching of the Five Nations Council Fire.

When there is any business to be transacted and the Confederate Council is not in session, a messenger shall be dispatched either to

---

[1] Royaneh is always translated "lord."

[2] The abbreviations after each law refer to the sections in the original code and their numbers. TLL, means Tree of the Long Leaves; EUC Emblematical Union Compact, and LPW, Skanawita's Laws of Peace and War. The first number in Roman numerals refers to the original number of the law, the second number, in Arabic numerals, to the section number in the division of the law named by the abbreviation following.

Adodarhoh, Hononwirehtonh or Skanawatih, Fire Keepers, or to their War Chiefs with a full statement of the case desired to be considered. Then shall Adodarho call his cousin (associate) Lords together and consider whether or not the case is of sufficient importance to demand the attention of the Confederate Council. If so, Adodarhoh shall dispatch messengers to summon all the Confederate Lords to assemble beneath the Tree of the Long Leaves.

When the Lords are assembled the Council Fire shall be kindled, but not with chestnut wood,[1] and Adodarhoh shall formally open the Council.

Then shall Adodarhoh and his cousin Lords, the Fire Keepers, announce the subject for discussion.

The Smoke of the Confederate Council Fire shall ever ascend and pierce the sky so that other nations who may be allies may see the Council Fire of the Great Peace.

Adodarho and his cousin Lords are entrusted with the Keeping of the Council Fire. (4–IV, TLL).

4 You, Adodarho, and your thirteen cousin Lords, shall faithfully keep the space about the Council Fire clean and you shall allow neither dust nor dirt to accumulate. I lay a Long Wing before you as a broom. As a weapon against a crawling creature I lay a staff with you so that you may thrust it away from the Council Fire. If you fail to cast it out then call the rest of the United Lords to your aid. (3–III, TLL).

5 The Council of the Mohawk shall be divided into three parties as follows: Tekarihoken, Ayonhwhathah and Shadekariwade are the first party; Sharenhowaneh, Deyoenhegwenh and Oghrenghrehgowah are the second party, and Dehennakrineh, Aghstawenserenthah and Shoskoharowaneh are the third party. The third party is to listen only to the discussion of the first and second parties and if an error is made or the proceeding is irregular they are to call attention to it, and when the case is right and properly decided by the two parties they shall confirm the decision of the two parties and refer the case to the Seneca Lords for their decision. When the Seneca Lords have decided in accord with the Mohawk Lords, the case or question shall be referred to the Cayuga and Oneida Lords on the opposite side of the house. (5–V, TLL).

6 I, Dekanawidah, appoint the Mohawk Lords the heads and the leaders of the Five Nations Confederacy. The Mohawk Lords are

---

[1] Because chestnut wood in burning throws out sparks, thereby creating a disturbance in the council.

the foundation of the Great Peace and it shall, therefore, be against the Great Binding Law to pass measures in the Confederate Council after the Mohawk Lords have protested against them. (6–VI, TLL).

No council of the Confederate Lords shall be legal unless all the Mohawk Lords are present. (13–XIII, TLL).

7 Whenever the Confederate Lords shall assemble for the purpose of holding a council, the Onondaga Lords shall open it by expressing their gratitude to their cousin Lords and greeting them, and they shall make an address and offer thanks to the earth where men dwell, to the streams of water, the pools, the springs and the lakes, to the maize and the fruits, to the medicinal herbs and trees, to the forest trees for their usefulness, to the animals that serve as food and give their pelts for clothing, to the great winds and the lesser winds, to the Thunderers, to the Sun, the mighty warrior, to the moon, to the messengers of the Creator who reveal his wishes and to the Great Creator[1] who dwells in the heavens above, who gives all the things useful to men, and who is the source and the ruler of health and life.

Then shall the Onondaga Lords declare the council open.

The council shall not sit after darkness has set in. (7–VII, TLL).

8 The Firekeepers shall formally open and close all councils of the Confederate Lords, they shall pass upon all matters deliberated upon by the two sides and render their decision.

Every Onondaga Lord (or his deputy) must be present at every Confederate Council and must agree with the majority without unwarrantable dissent, so that a unanimous decision may be rendered. (8–VIII, TLL).

If Adodarho or any of his cousin Lords are absent from a Confederate Council, any other Firekeeper may open and close the Council, but the Firekeepers present may not give any decisions, unless the matter is of small importance. (9–IX, TLL).

9 All the business of the Five Nations Confederate Council shall be conducted by the two combined bodies of Confederate Lords. First the question shall be passed upon by the Mohawk and Seneca Lords, then it shall be discussed and passed by the Oneida and Cayuga Lords. Their decisions shall then be referred to the Onondaga Lords, (Fire Keepers) for final judgment. (10–X, TLL).

The same process shall obtain when a question is brought before the council by an individual or a War Chief. (11–XI, TLL).

---

[1] Hodiänok'doon Hĕdiohe' (Seneca).

10 In all cases the procedure must be as follows: when the Mohawk and Seneca Lords have unanimously agreed upon a question, they shall report their decision to the Cayuga and Oneida Lords who shall deliberate upon the question and report a unanimous decision to the Mohawk Lords. The Mohawk Lords will then report the standing of the case to the Firekeepers, who shall render a decision (17–XVII, TLL) as they see fit in case of a disagreement by the two bodies, or confirm the decisions of the two bodies if they are identical. The Fire Keepers shall then report their decision to the Mohawk Lords who shall announce it to the open council. (12–XII, TLL).

11 If through any misunderstanding or obstinacy on the part of the Fire Keepers, they render a decision at variance with that of the Two Sides, the Two Sides shall reconsider the matter and if their decisions are jointly the same as before they shall report to the Fire Keepers who are then compelled to confirm their joint decision. (18–XVIII, TLL).

12 When a case comes before the Onondaga Lords (Fire Keepers) for discussion and decision, Adodarho shall introduce the matter to his comrade Lords who shall then discuss it in their two bodies. Every Onondaga Lord except Hononwiretonh shall deliberate and he shall listen only. When a unanimous decision shall have been reached by the two bodies of Fire Keepers, Adodarho shall notify Hononwiretonh of the fact when he shall confirm it. He shall refuse to confirm a decision if it is not unanimously agreed upon by both sides of the Fire Keepers. (19–XIX, TLL).

13 No Lord shall ask a question of the body of Confederate Lords when they are discussing a case, question or proposition. He may only deliberate in a low tone with the separate body of which he is a member. (21–XXI, TLL).

14 When the Council of the Five Nation Lords shall convene they shall appoint a speaker for the day. He shall be a Lord of either the Mohawk, Onondaga or Seneca Nation.

The next day the Council shall appoint another speaker, but the first speaker may be reappointed if there is no objection, but a speaker's term shall not be regarded more than for the day. (35–XXXV, TLL).

15 No individual or foreign nation interested in a case, question or proposition shall have any voice in the Confederate Council except to answer a question put to him or them by the speaker for the Lords. (41–XLI, TLL).

16 If the conditions which shall arise at any future time call for an addition to or change of this law, the case shall be carefully considered and if a new beam seems necessary or beneficial, the proposed change shall be voted upon and if adopted it shall be called, "Added to the Rafters." (48–XLVII, TLL).

Rights, duties and qualifications of Lords

17 A bunch of a certain number of shell (wampum) strings each two spans in length shall be given to each of the female families in which the Lordship titles are vested. The right of bestowing the title shall be hereditary in the family of females legally possessing the bunch of shell strings and the strings shall be the token that the females of the family have the proprietary right to the Lordship title for all time to come, subject to certain restrictions hereinafter mentioned. (59–LIX, TLL).

18 If any Confederate Lord neglects or refuses to attend the Confederate Council, the other Lords of the Nation of which he is a member shall require their War Chief to request the female sponsors of the Lord so guilty of defection to demand his attendance of the Council. If he refuses, the women holding the title shall immediately select another candidate for the title.

No Lord shall be asked more than once to attend the Confederate Council. (30–XXX, TLL).

19 If at any time it shall be manifest that a Confederate Lord has not in mind the welfare of the people or disobeys the rules of this Great Law, the men or the women of the Confederacy, or both jointly,[1] shall come to the Council and upbraid the erring Lord through his War Chief. If the complaint of the people through the War Chief is not heeded the first time it shall be uttered again and then if no attention is given a third complaint and warning shall be given. If the Lord is still contumacious the matter shall go to the council of War Chiefs. (66–LXVI, TLL). The War Chiefs shall then divest the erring Lord of his title by order of the women in whom the titleship is vested. When the Lord is deposed the women shall notify the Confederate Lords through their War Chief, and the Confederate Lords shall sanction the act. The women will then select another of their sons as a candidate and the Lords shall elect him. Then shall the chosen one be installed by the Installation Ceremony. (123–XLI, EUC), (Cf. 42–XLII).

---

[1] See sections 94 and 95 for right of popular councils.

When a Lord is to be deposed, his War Chief shall address him as follows:

"So you, —————————, disregard and set at naught the warnings of your women relatives. So you fling the warnings over your shoulder to cast them behind you.

"Behold the brightness of the Sun and in the brightness of the Sun's light I depose you of your title and remove the sacred emblem of your Lordship title. I remove from your brow the deer's antlers, which was the emblem of your position and token of your nobility. I now depose you and return the antlers to the women whose heritage they are."

The War Chief shall now address the women of the deposed Lord and say:

"Mothers, as I have now deposed your Lord, I now return to you the emblem and the title of Lordship, therefore repossess them."

Again addressing himself to the deposed Lord he shall say:

"As I have now deposed and discharged you so you are now no longer Lord. You shall now go your way alone, the rest of the people of the Confederacy will not go with you, for we know not the kind of mind that possesses you. As the Creator has nothing to do with wrong so he will not come to rescue you from the precipice of destruction in which you have cast yourself. You shall never be restored to the position which you once occupied."

Then shall the War Chief address himself to the Lords of the Nation to which the deposed Lord belongs and say:

"Know you, my Lords, that I have taken the deer's antlers from the brow of —————————, the emblem of his position and token of his greatness."

The Lords of the Confederacy shall then have no other alternative than to sanction the discharge of the offending Lord. (42–XLII, TLL).

20 If a Lord of the Confederacy of the Five Nations should commit murder the other Lords of the Nation shall assemble at the place where the corpse lies and prepare to depose the criminal Lord. If it is impossible to meet at the scene of the crime the Lords shall discuss the matter at the next Council of their nation and request their War Chief to depose the Lord guilty of crime, to "bury" his women relatives and to transfer the Lordship title to a sister family.

The War Chief shall address the Lord guilty of murder and say:
" So you, ——————— (giving his name) did kill ———————
(naming the slain man), with your own hands! You have committed
a grave sin in the eyes of the Creator. Behold the bright light of
the Sun, and in the brightness of the Sun's light I depose you of
your title and remove the horns, the sacred emblems of your Lordship title. I remove from your brow the deer's antlers, which was
the emblem of your position and token of your nobility. I now
depose you and expel you and you shall depart at once from the
territory of the Five Nations Confederacy and nevermore return
again. We, the Five Nations Confederacy, moreover, bury your
women relatives because the ancient Lordship title was never intended to have any union with bloodshed. Henceforth it shall not
be their heritage. By the evil deed that you have done they have
forfeited it forever."

The War Chief shall then hand the title to a sister family and he
shall address it and say:
" Our mothers, ———————, listen attentively while I address
you on a solemn and important subject. I hereby transfer to you
an ancient Lordship title for a great calamity has befallen it in
the hands of the family of a former Lord. We trust that you, our
mothers, will always guard it, and that you will warn your Lord
always to be dutiful and to advise his people to ever live in love,
peace and harmony that a great calamity may never happen again."
(47–XLVII, TLL).

21 Certain physical defects in a Confederate Lord make him ineligible to sit in the Confederate Council. Such defects are infancy, idiocy, blindness, deafness, dumbness and impotency. When
a Confederate Lord is restricted by any of these conditions, a
deputy shall be appointed by his sponsors to act for him, but in
case of extreme necessity the restricted Lord may exercise his
rights. (29–XXIX, TLL).

22 If a Confederate Lord desires to resign his title he shall
notify the Lords of the Nation of which he is a member of his intention. If his coactive Lords refuse to accept his resignation he
may not resign his title.

A Lord in proposing to resign may recommend any proper candidate which recommendation shall be received by the Lords, but
unless confirmed and nominated by the women who hold the title
the candidate so named shall not be considered. (31–XXXI,
TLL).

23 Any Lord of the Five Nations Confederacy may construct shell strings (or wampum belts) of any size or length as pledges or records of matters of national or international importance.

When it is necessary to dispatch a shell string by a War Chief or other messenger as the token of a summons, the messenger shall recite the contents of the string to the party to whom it is sent. That party shall repeat the message and return the shell string and if there has been a summons he shall make ready for the journey.

Any of the people of the Five Nations may use shells (or wampum) as the record of a pledge, contract or an agreement entered into and the same shall be binding as soon as shell strings shall have been exchanged by both parties. (32–XXXII, TLL).

24 The Lords of the Confederacy of the Five Nations shall be mentors of the people for all time. The thickness of their skin shall be seven spans — which is to say that they shall be proof against anger, offensive actions and criticism. Their hearts shall be full of peace and good will and their minds filled with a yearning for the welfare of the people of the Confederacy. With endless patience they shall carry out their duty and their firmness shall be tempered with a tenderness for their people. Neither anger nor fury shall find lodgement in their minds and all their words and actions shall be marked by calm deliberation. (33–XXXIII, TLL).

25 If a Lord of the Confederacy should seek to establish any authority independent of the jurisdiction of the Confederacy of the Great Peace, which is the Five Nations, he shall be warned three times in open council, first by the women relatives, second by the men relatives and finally by the Lords of the Confederacy of the Nation to which he belongs. If the offending Lord is still obdurate he shall be dismissed by the War Chief of his nation for refusing to conform to the laws of the Great Peace. His nation shall then install the candidate nominated by the female name holders of his family. (34–XXXIV, TLL).

26 It shall be the duty of all of the Five Nations Confederate Lords, from time to time as occasion demands, to act as mentors and spiritual guides of their people and remind them of their Creator's will and words. They shall say:

" Hearken, that peace may continue unto future days!

"Always listen to the words of the Great Creator, for he has spoken.

" United People, let not evil find lodging in your minds

" For the Great Creator has spoken and the cause of Peace shall not become old.

" The cause of peace shall not die if you remember the Great Creator."

Every Confederate Lord shall speak words such as these to promote peace. (37–XXXVII, TLL).

27 All Lords of the Five Nations Confederacy must be honest in all things. They must not idle or gossip, but be men possessing those honorable qualities that make true royaneh. It shall be a serious wrong for anyone to lead a Lord into trivial affairs, for the people must ever hold their Lords high in estimation out of respect to their honorable positions. (45–XLV, TLL).

28 When a candidate Lord is to be installed he shall furnish four strings of shells (or wampum) one span in length bound together at one end. Such will constitute the evidence of his pledge to the Confederate Lords that he will live according to the constitution of the Great Peace and exercise justice in all affairs.

When the pledge is furnished the Speaker of the Council must hold the shell strings in his hand and address the opposite side of the Council Fire and he shall commence his address saying: " Now behold him. He has now become a Confederate Lord. See how splendid he looks." An address may then follow. At the end of it he shall send the bunch of shell strings to the opposite side and they shall be received as evidence of the pledge. Then shall the opposite side say:

" We now do crown you with the sacred emblem of the deer's antlers, the emblem of your Lordship. You shall now become a mentor of the people of the Five Nations. The thickness of your skin shall be seven spans — which is to say that you shall be proof against anger, offensive actions and criticism. Your heart shall be filled with peace and good will and your mind filled with a yearning for the welfare of the people of the Confederacy. With endless patience you shall carry out your duty and your firmness shall be tempered with tenderness for your people. Neither anger nor fury shall find lodgement in your mind and all your words and actions shall be marked with calm deliberation. In all of your deliberations in the Confederate Council, in your efforts at law making, in all your official acts, self interest shall be cast into oblivion. Cast not over your shoulder behind you the warnings of the nephews and nieces should they chide you for any error or wrong you may do, but return to the way of the Great Law which is just and right. Look and listen for the welfare of the whole people and have always in view not only the present but also the coming generations, even those whose faces are yet beneath the surface of the ground — the unborn of the future Nation." (51–LI, TLL).

29 When a Lordship title is to be conferred, the candidate Lord shall furnish the cooked venison, the corn bread and the corn soup, together with other necessary things and the labor for the Conferring of Titles Festival. (50–L, TLL).

30 The Lords of the Confederacy may confer the Lordship title upon a candidate whenever the Great Law is recited, if there be a candidate, for the Great Law speaks all the rules. (XLIV–44, TLL).

31 If a lord of the Confederacy should become seriously ill and be thought near death, the women who are heirs of his title shall go to his house and lift his crown of deer antlers, the emblem of his Lordship, and place them at one side. If the Creator spares him and he rises from his bed of sickness he may rise with the antlers on his brow.

The following words shall be used to temporarily remove the antlers:

" Now our comrade Lord (or our relative Lord) the time has come when we must approach you in your illness. We remove for a time the deer's antlers from your brow, we remove the emblem of your Lordship title. The Great Law has decreed that no Lord should end his life with the antlers on his brow. We therefore lay them aside in the room. If the Creator spares you and you recover from your illness you shall rise from your bed with the antlers on your brow as before and you shall resume your duties as Lord of the Confederacy and you may labor again for the Confederate people." (XXVII–27, TLL).

32 If a Lord of the Confederacy should die while the Council of the Five Nations is in session the Council shall adjourn for ten days. No Confederate Council shall sit within ten days of the death of a Lord of the Confederacy.

If the Three Brothers (the Mohawk, the Onondaga and the Seneca) should lose one of their Lords by death, the Younger Brothers (the Oneida and the Cayuga) shall come to the surviving Lords of the Three Brothers on the tenth day and console them. If the Younger Brothers lose one of their Lords then the Three Brothers shall come to them and console them. And the consolation shall be the reading of the contents of the thirteen shell (wampum) strings of Ayonhwhathah. At the termination of this rite a successor shall be appointed, to be appointed by the women heirs of the Lordship title. If the women are not yet ready to place their nominee before the Lords the Speaker shall say, " Come let us go out." All shall then leave the Council or the place of gathering. The installation shall then wait until such a time as the women are ready. The Speaker shall lead the way from the house by saying, " Let us depart to the edge of the woods and lie in waiting on our bellies."

When the women title holders shall have chosen one of their sons the Confederate Lords will assemble in two places, the Younger Brothers in one place and the Three Older Brothers in another. The Lords who are to console the mourning Lords shall choose one of their number to sing the Pacification Hymn as they journey to the sorrowing Lords. The singer shall lead the way and the Lords and the people shall follow. When they reach the sorrowing Lords they shall hail the candidate Lord and perform the rite of Conferring the Lordship Title. (22–XXII, TLL).

33 When a Confederate Lord dies, the surviving relatives shall immediately dispatch a messenger, a member of another clan, to the Lords in another locality. When the runner comes within hailing distance of the locality he shall utter a sad wail, thus: " Kwa-ah, Kwa-ah, Kwa-ah!" The sound shall be repeated three times and then again and again at intervals as many times as the distance may require. When the runner arrives at the settlement the people shall assemble and one must ask him the nature of his sad message. He shall then say, " Let us consider." Then he shall tell them of the death of the Lord. He shall deliver to them a string of shells (wampum) and say " Here is the testimony, you have heard the message." He may then return home.

It now becomes the duty of the Lords of the locality to send runners to other localities and each locality shall send other messengers until all Lords are notified. Runners shall travel day and night. (23–XXIII, TLL).

34 If a Lord dies and there is no candidate qualified for the office in the family of the women title holders, the Lords of the Nation shall give the title into the hands of a sister family in the clan until such a time as the original family produces a candidate, when the title shall be restored to the rightful owners.

No Lordship title may be carried into the grave. The Lords of the Confederacy may dispossess a dead Lord of his title even at the grave. (24–XXIV, TLL).

Election of Pine Tree chiefs

35 Should any man of the Nation assist with special ability or show great interest in the affairs of the Nation, if he proves himself wise, honest and worthy of confidence, the Confederate Lords may elect him to a seat with them and he may sit in the Confederate Council. He shall be proclaimed a *Pine Tree sprung up for the Nation* and be installed as such at the next assembly for the installation of Lords. Should he ever do anything contrary to the rules of the Great Peace, he may not be deposed from office — no one shall cut him down[1]— but thereafter everyone shall be deaf to his voice and his advice. Should he resign his seat and title no one shall prevent him. A Pine Tree chief has no authority to name a successor nor is his title hereditary. (LXVIII–68, TLL).

Names, duties and rights of war chiefs

36 The title names of the Chief Confederate Lords' War Chiefs shall be:
Ayonwaehs, War Chief under Lord Takarihoken (Mohawk)
Kahonwahdironh, War Chief under Lord Odatshedeh (Oneida)
Ayendes, War Chief under Lord Adodarhoh (Onondaga)
Wenenhs, War Chief under Lord Dekaenyonh (Cayuga)
Shoneradowaneh, War Chief under Lord Skanyadariyo (Seneca)
The women heirs of each head Lord's title shall be the heirs of the War Chief's title of their respective Lord. (52–LII, TLL).
· The War Chiefs shall be selected from the eligible sons of the female families holding the head Lordship titles. (53–LIII, TLL).

37 There shall be one War Chief for each Nation and their duties shall be to carry messages for their Lords and to take up the arms of war in case of emergency. They shall not participate in the proceedings of the Confederate Council but shall watch its progress and in case of an erroneous action by a Lord they shall receive the complaints of the people and convey the warnings of the women to him. The people who wish to convey messages to the Lords in the Confederate Council shall do so through the War Chief of their Nation. It shall ever be his duty to lay the cases, questions and propositions of the people before the Confederate Council. (54–LIV, TLL).

38 When a War Chief dies another shall be installed by the same rite as that by which a Lord is installed. (56–LVI, TLL).

---

[1] Because, " his top branches pierce the sky and if his roots are cut he will not fall but hang upright before the people."

39 If a War Chief acts contrary to instructions or against the provisions of the Laws of the Great Peace, doing so in the capacity of his office, he shall be deposed by his women relatives and by his men relatives. Either the women or the men alone or jointly may act in such case. The women title holders shall then choose another candidate. (55–LV, TLL).

40 When the Lords of the Confederacy take occasion to dispatch a messenger in behalf of the Confederate Council, they shall wrap up any matter they may send and instruct the messenger to remember his errand, to turn not aside but to proceed faithfully to his destination and deliver his message according to every instruction. (57–XLVII, TLL).

41 If a message borne by a runner is the warning of an invasion he shall whoop, " Kwa-ah, Kwa-ah," twice and repeat at short intervals; then again at a longer interval.

If a human being is found dead, the finder shall not touch the body but return home immediately shouting at short intervals, " Koo-weh! " (23–XXIII, TLL).

Clans and consanguinity

42 Among the Five Nations and their posterity there shall be the following original clans: Great Name Bearer, Ancient Name Bearer, Great Bear, Ancient Bear, Turtle, Painted Turtle, Standing Rock, Large Plover, Little Plover, Deer, Pigeon Hawk, Eel, Ball, Opposite-Side-of-the-Hand, and Wild Potatoes. These clans distributed through their respective Nations, shall be the sole owners and holders of the soil of the country and in them is it vested as a birthright. (94–XI, EUC).

43 People of the Five Nations members of a certain clan shall recognize every other member of that clan, irrespective of the Nation, as relatives. Men and women, therefore, members of the same clan are forbidden to marry. (98–XV, EUC).

44 The lineal descent of the people of the Five Nations shall run in the female line. Women shall be considered the progenitors of the Nation. They shall own the land and the soil. Men and women shall follow the status of the mother. (60–LX, TLL).

45 The women heirs of the Confederate Lordship titles shall be called Royaneh (Noble) for all time to come. (61–LXI, TLL).

46 The women of the Forty Eight (now fifty) Royaneh families shall be the heirs of the Authorized Names for all time to come.

Plate 4

1   2

1 Nomination belt used to confirm the nomination of the civil chiefs
2 Welcome belt used in welcoming delegates

Plate 5

Reciting the Laws of the Confederacy

From an engraving in Lafitau's, Moeurs des Sauvages Ameriquains, published in 1724

When an infant of the Five Nations is given an Authorized Name at the Midwinter Festival or at the Ripe Corn Festival, one in the cousinhood of which the infant is a member shall be appointed a speaker. He shall then announce to the opposite cousinhood the names of the father and the mother of the child together with the clan of the mother. Then the speaker shall announce the child's name twice. The uncle of the child shall then take the child in his arms and walking up and down the room shall sing: "My head is firm, I am of the Confederacy." As he sings the opposite cousinhood shall respond by chanting, "Hyenh, Hyenh, Hyenh, Hyenh," until the song is ended. (95–XII, EUC).

47 If the female heirs of a Confederate Lord's title become extinct, the title right shall be given by the Lords of the Confederacy to the sister family whom they shall elect and that family shall hold the name and transmit it to their (female) heirs, but they shall not appoint any of their sons as a candidate for a title until all the eligible men of the former family shall have died or otherwise have become ineligible. (25–XXV, TLL).

48 If all the heirs of a Lordship title become extinct, and all the families in the clan, then the title shall be given by the Lords of the Confederacy to the family in a sister clan whom they shall elect. (26–XXVI, TLL).

49 If any of the Royaneh women, heirs of a titleship, shall wilfully withhold a Lordship or other title and refuse to bestow it, or if such heirs abandon, forsake or despise their heritage, then shall such women be deemed buried and their family extinct. The titleship shall then revert to a sister family or clan upon application and complaint. The Lords of the Confederacy shall elect the family or clan which shall in future hold the title. (28–XXVIII, TLL).

50 The Royaneh women of the Confederacy heirs of the Lordship titles shall elect two women of their family as cooks for the Lord when the people shall assemble at his house for business or other purposes.

It is not good nor honorable for a Confederate Lord to allow his people whom he has called to go hungry. (62–LXII, TLL).

51 When a Lord holds a conference in his home, his wife, if she wishes, may prepare the food for the Union Lords who assemble with him. This is an honorable right which she may exercise and an expression of her esteem. (38–XXXVIII, TLL).

52 The Royaneh women, heirs of the Lordship titles, shall, should it be necessary, correct and admonish the holders of their titles. Those only who attend the Council may do this and those

who do not shall not object to what has been said nor strive to undo the action. (63–LXIII, TLL).

53 When the Royaneh women, holders of a Lordship title, select one of their sons as a candidate, they shall select one who is trustworthy, of good character, of honest disposition, one who manages his own affairs, supports his own family, if any, and who has proven a faithful man to his Nation. (64–LXIV, TLL).

54 When a Lordship title becomes vacant through death or other cause, the Royaneh women of the clan in which the title is hereditary shall hold a council and shall choose one from among their sons to fill the office made vacant. Such a candidate shall not be the father of any Confederate Lord. If the choice is unanimous the name is referred to the men relatives of the clan. If they should disapprove it shall be their duty to select a candidate from among their own number. If then the men and women are unable to decide which of the two candidates shall be named, then the matter shall be referred to the Confederate Lords in the Clan. They shall decide which candidate shall be named. If the men and the women agree to a candidate his name shall be referred to the sister clans for confirmation. If the sister clans confirm the choice, they shall refer their action to their Confederate Lords who shall ratify the choice and present it to their cousin Lords, and if the cousin Lords confirm the name then the candidate shall be installed by the proper ceremony for the conferring of Lordship titles. (65–LXV, TLL).

Official symbolism

55 A large bunch of shell strings, in the making of which the Five Nations Confederate Lords have equally contributed, shall symbolize the completeness of the union and certify the pledge of the nations represented by the Confederate Lords of the Mohawk, the Oneida, the Onondaga, the Cayuga and the Seneca, that all are united and formed into one body or union called the Union of the Great Law, which they have established.

A bunch of shell strings is to be the symbol of the council fire of the Five Nations Confederacy. And the Lord whom the Council of Fire Keepers shall appoint to speak for them in opening the council shall hold the strands of shells in his hands when speaking. When he finishes speaking he shall deposit the strings on an elevated place (or pole) so that all the assembled Lords and the people may see it and know that the council is open and in progress.

When the council adjourns the Lord who has been appointed by his comrade Lords to close it shall take the strands of shells in his hands and address the assembled Lords. Thus will the council adjourn until such a time and place as appointed by the council. Then shall the shell strings be placed in a place for safekeeping.

Every five years the Five Nations Confederate Lords and the people shall assemble together and shall ask one another if their minds are still in the same spirit of unity for the Great Binding Law and if any of the Five Nations shall not pledge continuance and steadfastness to the pledge of unity then the Great Binding Law shall dissolve. (14–XIV, TLL).

56 Five strings of shell tied together as one shall represent the Five Nations. Each string shall represent one territory and the whole a completely united territory known as the Five Nations Confederate territory. (108–XXV, EUC).

57 Five arrows shall be bound together very strong and each arrow shall represent one nation. As the five arrows are strongly bound this shall symbolize the complete union of the nations. Thus are the Five Nations united completely and enfolded together, united into one head, one body and one mind. Therefore they shall labor, legislate and council together for the interest of future generations.

The Lords of the Confederacy shall eat together from one bowl the feast of cooked beaver's tail. While they are eating they are to use no sharp utensils for if they should they might accidentally cut one another and bloodshed would follow. All measures must be taken to prevent the spilling of blood in any way. (15–XV, TLL).

58 There are now the Five Nations Confederate Lords standing with joined hands in a circle. This signifies and provides that should any one of the Confederate Lords leave the council and this Confederacy his crown of deer's horns, the emblem of his Lordship title, together with his birthright, shall lodge on the arms of the Union Lords whose hands are so joined. He forfeits his title and the crown falls from his brow but it shall remain in the Confederacy.

A further meaning of this is that if any time any one of the Confederate Lords choose to submit to the law of a foreign people he is no longer in but out of the Confederacy, and persons of this class shall be called " They have alienated themselves." Likewise such persons who submit to laws of foreign nations shall forfeit all birthrights and claims on the Five Nations Confederacy and territory.

You, the Five Nations Confederate Lords, be firm so that if a tree falls upon your joined arms it shall not separate you or weaken your hold. So shall the strength of the union be preserved. (16–XIV, TLL).

59 A bunch of wampum shells on strings, three spans of the hand in length, the upper half of the bunch being white and the lower half black, and formed from equal contributions of the men of the Five Nations, shall be a token that the men have combined themselves into one head, one body and one thought, and it shall also symbolize their ratification of the peace pact of the Confederacy, whereby the Lords of the Five Nations have established the Great Peace.

The white portion of the shell strings represent the women and the black portion the men. The black portion, furthermore, is a token of power and authority vested in the men of the Five Nations.

This string of wampum vests the people with the right to correct their erring Lords. In case a part or all the Lords pursue a course not vouched for by the people and heed not the third warning of their women relatives, then the matter shall be taken to the General Council of the women of the Five Nations. If the Lords notified and warned three times fail to heed, then the case falls into the hands of the men of the Five Nations. The War Chiefs shall then, by right of such power and authority, enter the open council to warn the Lord or Lords to return from their wrong course. If the Lords heed the warning they shall say, " we will reply to-morrow." If then an answer is returned in favor of justice and in accord with this Great Law, then the Lords shall individually pledge themselves again by again furnishing the necessary shells for the pledge. Then shall the War Chief or Chiefs exhort the Lords urging them to be just and true.

Should it happen that the Lords refuse to heed the third warning, then two courses are open: either the men may decide in their council to depose the Lord or Lords or to club them to death with war clubs. Should they in their council decide to take the first course the War Chief shall address the Lord or Lords, saying: " Since you the Lords of the Five Nations have refused to return to the procedure of the Constitution, we now declare your seats vacant, we take off your horns, the token of your Lordship, and others shall be chosen and installed in your seats, therefore vacate your seats."

Should the men in their council adopt the second course, the War Chief shall order his men to enter the council, to take positions beside the Lords, sitting between them wherever possible. When this is accomplished the War Chief holding in his outstretched hand a bunch of black wampum strings shall say to the erring Lords: " So now, Lords of the Five United Nations, harken to these last words from your men. You have not heeded the warnings of the women relatives, you have not heeded the warnings of the General Council of women and you have not heeded the warnings of the men of the nations, all urging you to return to the right course of action. Since you are determined to resist and to withhold justice from your people there is only one course for us to adopt." At this point the War Chief shall let drop the bunch of black wampum and the men shall spring to their feet and club the erring Lords to death. Any erring Lord may submit before the War Chief lets fall the black wampum. Then his execution is withheld.

The black wampum here used symbolizes that the power to execute is buried but that it may be raised up again by the men. It is buried but when occasion arises they may pull it up and derive their power and authority to act as here described. (SPW 81 XII).

60 A broad dark belt of wampum of thirty-eight rows, having a white heart in the center, on either side of which are two white squares all connected with the heart by white rows of beads shall be the emblem of the unity of the Five Nations.[1]

The first of the squares on the left represents the Mohawk nation and its territory; the second square on the left and the one near the heart, represents the Oneida nation and its territory; the white heart in the middle represents the Onondaga nation and its territory, and it also means that the heart of the Five Nations is single in its loyalty to the Great Peace, that the Great Peace is lodged in the heart (meaning with Onondaga Confederate Lords), and that the Council Fire is to burn there for the Five Nations, and further, it means that the authority is given to advance the cause of peace whereby hostile nations out of the Confederacy shall cease warfare; the white square to the right of the heart represents the Cayuga nation and its territory and the fourth and last white square represents the Seneca nation and its territory.

White shall here symbolize that no evil or jealous thoughts shall creep into the minds of the Lords while in council under the Great

[1] This is the " Hiawatha Belt " purchased by John Boyd Thatcher of Albany and now in the Congressional Library.

Peace. White, the emblem of peace, love, charity and equity surrounds and guards the Five Nations. (84–EUC, 1).

61 Should a great calamity threaten the generations rising and living of the Five United Nations, then he who is able to climb to the top of the Tree of the Great Long Leaves may do so. When, then, he reaches the top of the Tree he shall look about in all directions, and, should he see that evil things indeed are approaching, then he shall call to the people of the Five United Nations assembled beneath the Tree of the Great Long Leaves and say: "A calamity threatens your happiness."

Then shall the Lords convene in council and discuss the impending evil.

When all the truths relating to the trouble shall be fully known and found to be truths, then shall the people seek out a Tree of Ka-hon-ka-ah-go-nah,[1] and when they shall find it they shall assemble their heads together and lodge for a time between its roots. Then, their labors being finished, they may hope for happiness for many days after. (II-85, EUC).

62 When the Confederate Council of the Five Nations declares for a reading of the belts of shell calling to mind these laws, they shall provide for the reader a specially made mat woven of the fibers of wild hemp. The mat shall not be used again, for such formality is called the honoring of the importance of the law. (XXXVI–36, TLL).

63 Should two sons of opposite sides of the council fire agree in a desire to hear the reciting of the laws of the Great Peace and so refresh their memories in the way ordained by the founder of the Confederacy, they shall notify Adodarho. He then shall consult with five of his coactive Lords and they in turn shall consult their eight brethren. Then should they decide to accede to the request of the two sons from opposite sides of the Council Fire, Adodarhoh shall send messengers to notify the Chief Lords of each of the Five Nations. Then they shall despatch their War Chiefs to notify their brother and cousin Lords of the meeting and its time and place.

When all have come and have assembled, Adodarhoh, in conjunction with his cousin Lords, shall appoint one Lord who shall repeat the laws of the Great Peace. Then shall they announce who they have chosen to repeat the laws of the Great Peace to the two sons. Then shall the chosen one repeat the laws of the Great Peace. (XLIII–43, TLL).

---

[1] A great swamp Elm.

64 At the ceremony of the installation of Lords if there is only one expert speaker and singer of the law and the Pacification Hymn to stand at the council fire, then when this speaker and singer has finished addressing one side of the fire he shall go to the opposite side and reply to his own speech and song. He shall thus act for both sides of the fire until the entire ceremony has been completed. Such a speaker and singer shall be termed the " Two Faced " because he speaks and sings for both sides of the fire. (XLIX–49, TLL).

65 I, Dekanawida, and the Union Lords, now uproot the tallest pine tree and into the cavity thereby made we cast all weapons of war. Into the depths of the earth, down into the deep underearth currents of water flowing to unknown regions we cast all the weapons of strife. We bury them from sight and we plant again the tree. Thus shall the Great Peace be established and hostilities shall no longer be known between the Five Nations but peace to the United People.

Laws of adoption

66 The father of a child of great comliness, learning, ability or specially loved because of some circumstance may, at the will of the child's clan, select a name from his own (the father's) clan and bestow it by ceremony, such as is provided. This naming shall be only temporary and shall be called, "A name hung about the neck." (XII–96, EUC).

67 Should any person, a member of the Five Nations' Confederacy, specially esteem a man or a woman of another clan or of a foreign nation, he may choose a name and bestow it upon that person so esteemed. The naming shall be in accord with the ceremony of bestowing names. Such a name is only a temporary one and shall be called "A name hung about the neck." A short string of shells shall be delivered with the name as a record and a pledge. (XIV–97, EUC).

68 Should any member of the Five Nations, a family or person belonging to a foreign nation submit a proposal for adoption into a clan of one of the Five Nations, he or they shall furnish a string of shells, a span in length, as a pledge to the clan into which he or they wish to be adopted. The Lords of the nation shall then consider the proposal and submit a decision. (XXI–104, EUC).

69 Any member of the Five Nations who through esteem or other feeling wishes to adopt an individual, a family or number of families may offer adoption to him or them and if accepted the

matter shall be brought to the attention of the Lords for confirmation and the Lords must confirm the adoption. (XXII–105, EUC).

70 When the adoption of anyone shall have been confirmed by the Lords of the Nation, the Lords shall address the people of their nation and say: " Now you of our nation, be informed that such a person, such a family or such families have ceased forever to bear their birth nation's name and have buried it in the depths of the earth, Henceforth let no one of our nation ever mention the original name or nation of their birth. To do so will be to hasten the end of our peace. (XXIII–106, EUC).

Laws of emigration

71 When any person or family belonging to the Five Nations desires to abandon their birth nation and the territory of the Five Nations, they shall inform the Lords of their nation and the Confederate Council of the Five Nations shall take cognizance of it. (XXXIX–39, TLL).

72 When any person or any of the people of the Five Nations emigrate and reside in a region distant from the territory of the Five Nations Confederacy, the Lords of the Five Nations at will may send a messenger carrying a broad belt of black shells and when the messenger arrives he shall call the people together or address them personally displaying the belt of shells and they shall know that this is an order for them to return to their original homes and to their council fires. (XL–40, TLL).

Rights of foreign nations

73 The soil of the earth from one end of the land to the other is the property of the people who inhabit it. By birthright the Oñgwehonweh (Original beings) are the owners of the soil which they own and occupy and none other may hold it. The same law has been held from the oldest times.

The Great Creator has made us of the one blood and of the same soil he made us and as only different tongues constitute different nations he established different hunting grounds and territories and made boundary lines between them. (LXIX–69, TLL).

74 When any alien nation or individual is admitted into the Five Nations the admission shall be understood only to be a temporary one. Should the person or nation create loss, do wrong or cause suffering of any kind to endanger the peace of the Confederacy,

Plate 6

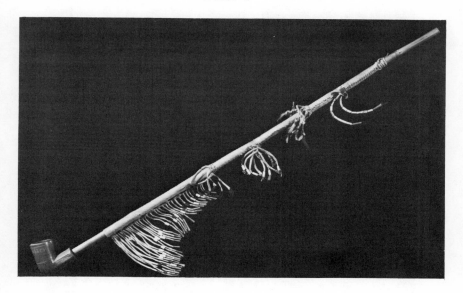

Council pipe used in the ceremonies of raising a civil chief. This pipe was last owned by Albert Cusick, who presented it to the State Museum in 1911.

Plate 7

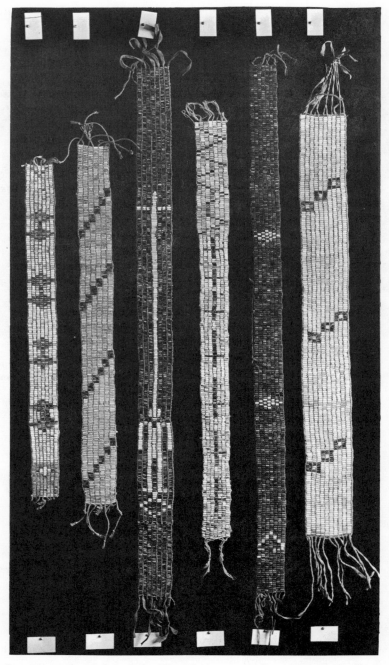

Commemoration belts of the Five Nations recording events and alliances

the Confederate Lords shall order one of their war chiefs to repri-
mand him or them and if a similar offence is again committed the
offending party or parties shall be expelled from the territory of
the Five United Nations. (XXVI–119, EUC).

75 When a member of an alien nation comes to the territory
of the Five Nations and seeks refuge and permanent residence, the
Lords of the Nation to which he comes shall extend hospitality and
make him a member of the nation. Then shall he be accorded equal
rights and privileges in all matters except as after mentioned.
(XXXVII–120, EUC).

76 No body of alien people who have been adopted temporarily
shall have a vote in the council of the Lords of the Confederacy,
for only they who have been invested with Lordship titles may
vote in the Council. Aliens have nothing by blood to make claim
to a vote and should they have it, not knowing all the traditions
of the Confederacy, might go against its Great Peace. In this
manner the Great Peace would be endangered and perhaps be
destroyed. (XXXVIII–121, EUC).

77 When the Lords of the Confederacy decide to admit a foreign
nation and an adoption is made, the Lords shall inform the adopted
nation that its admission is only temporary. They shall also say
to the nation that it must never try to control, to interfere with
or to injure the Five Nations nor disregard the Great Peace or
any of its rules or customs. That in no way should they cause
disturbance or injury. Then should the adopted nation disregard
these injunctions, their adoption shall be annulled and they shall
be expelled.

The expulsion shall be in the following manner: The council
shall appoint one of their War Chiefs to convey the message of
annulment and he shall say, "You (naming the nation) listen to
me while I speak. I am here to inform you again of the will of the
Five Nations' Council. It was clearly made known to you at a
former time. Now the Lords of the Five Nations have decided
to expel you and cast you out. We disown you now and annul
your adoption. Therefore you must look for a path in which to
go and lead away all your people. It was you, not we, who committed wrong and caused this sentence of annulment. So then
go your way and depart from the territory of the Five Nations
and from the Confederacy." (XXXIX–122, EUC).

78 Whenever a foreign nation enters the Confederacy or accepts
the Great Peace, the Five Nations and the foreign nation shall

enter into an agreement and compact by which the foreign nation shall endeavor to pursuade other nations to accept the Great Peace. (XLVI–46, TLL).

Rights and powers of war

79 Skanawatih shall be vested with a double office, duty and with double authority. One-half of his being shall hold the Lordship title and the other half shall hold the title of War Chief. In the event of war he shall notify the five War Chiefs of the Confederacy and command them to prepare for war and have their men ready at the appointed time and place for engagement with the enemy of the Great Peace. (I–70, SPW).

80 When the Confederate Council of the Five Nations has for its object the establishment of the Great Peace among the people of an outside nation and that nation refuses to accept the Great Peace, then by such refusal they bring a declaration of war upon themselves from the Five Nations. Then shall the Five Nations seek to establish the Great Peace by a conquest of the rebellious nation. (II–71, SPW).

81 When the men of the Five Nations, now called forth to become warriors, are ready for battle with an obstinate opposing nation that has refused to accept the Great Peace, then one of the five War Chiefs shall be chosen by the warriors of the Five Nations to lead the army into battle. It shall be the duty of the War Chief so chosen to come before his warriors and address them. His aim shall be to impress upon them the necessity of good behavior and strict obedience to all the commands of the War Chiefs. He shall deliver an oration exhorting them with great zeal to be brave and courageous and never to be guilty of cowardice. At the conclusion of his oration he shall march forward and commence the War Song and he shall sing:

> Now I am greatly surprised
> And, therefore, I shall use it,—
> The power of my War Song.
> I am of the Five Nations
> And·I shall make supplication
> To the Almighty Creator.
> He has furnished this army.
> My warriors shall be mighty

> In the strength of the Creator.[1]
> Between him and my song they are
> For it was he who gave the song
> This war song that I sing!
> (III–72, SPW).

82 When the warriors of the Five Nations are on an expedition against an enemy, the War Chief shall sing the War Song as he approaches the country of the enemy and not cease until his scouts have reported that the army is near the enemies' lines when the War Chief shall approach with great caution and prepare for the attack. (IV–73, SPW).

83 When peace shall have been established by the termination of the war against a foreign nation, then the War Chief shall cause all the weapons of war to be taken from the nation. Then shall the Great Peace be established and that nation shall observe all the rules of the Great Peace for all time to come. (V–74, SPW).

84 Whenever a foreign nation is conquered or has by their own will accepted the Great Peace their own system of internal government may continue, but they must cease all warfare against other nations. (VI–75, SPW).

85 Whenever a war against a foreign nation is pushed until that nation is about exterminated because of its refusal to accept the Great Peace and if that nation shall by its obstinacy become exterminated, all their rights, property and territory shall become the property of the Five Nations. (VII–76, SPW).

86 Whenever a foreign nation is conquered and the survivors are brought into the territory of the Five Nations' Confederacy and placed under the Great Peace the two shall be known as the Conqueror and the Conquered. A symbolic relationship shall be devised and be placed in some symbolic position. The conquered nation shall have no voice in the councils of the Confederacy in the body of the Lords. (VIII–77, SPW).

87 When the War of the Five Nations on a foreign rebellious nation is ended, peace shall be restored to that nation by a withdrawal of all their weapons of war by the War Chief of the Five Nations. When all the terms of peace shall have been agreed upon a state of friendship shall be established. (IX–78, SPW).

---

[1] It will be recalled that when the Eries demanded by what power the Five Nations demanded their surrender, the Iroquois replied "The Master of Life fights for us!"

88 When the proposition to establish the Great Peace is made to a foreign nation it shall be done in mutual council. The foreign nation is to be persuaded by reason and urged to come into the Great Peace. If the Five Nations fail to obtain the consent of the nation at the first council a second council shall be held and upon a second failure a third council shall be held and this third council shall end the peaceful methods of persuasion. At the third council the War Chief of the Five Nations shall address the Chief of the foreign nation and request him three times to accept the Great Peace. If refusal steadfastly follows the War Chief shall let the bunch of white lake shells drop from his outstretched hand to the ground and shall bound quickly forward and club the offending chief to death. War shall thereby be declared and the War Chief shall have his warriors at his back to meet any emergency. War must continue until the contest is won by the Five Nations (X–79, SPW).

89 When the Lords of the Five Nations propose to meet in conference with a foreign nation with proposals for an acceptance of the Great Peace, a large band of warriors shall conceal themselves in a secure place safe from the espionage of the foreign nation but as near at hand as possible. Two warriors shall accompany the Union Lord who carries the proposals and these warriors shall be especially cunning. Should the Lord be attacked, these warriors shall hasten back to the army of warriors with the news of the calamity which fell through the treachery of the foreign nation. (XI–80, SPW).

90 When the Five Nations' Council declares war any Lord of the Confederacy may enlist with the warriors by temporarily renouncing his sacred Lordship title which he holds through the election of his women relatives. The title then reverts to them and they may bestow it upon another temporarily until the war is over when the Lord, if living, may resume his title and seat in the Council. (XII–82, SPW).

91 A certain wampum belt of black beads shall be the emblem of the authority of the Five War Chiefs to take up the weapons of war and with their men to resist invasion. This shall be called a war in defense of the territory. (XIV–83, SPW).

Treason or secession of a nation

92 If a nation, part of a nation, or more than one nation within the Five Nations should in any way endeavor to destroy the Great Peace by neglect or violating its laws and resolve to dissolve the

Confederacy, such a nation or such nations shall be deemed guilty of treason and called enemies of the Confederacy and the Great Peace.

It shall then be the duty of the Lords of the Confederacy who remain faithful to resolve to warn the offending people. They shall be warned once and if a second warning is necessary they shall be driven from the territory of the Confederacy by the War Chiefs and his men. (III–86, EUC).

Rights of the people of the Five Nations

93 Whenever a specially important matter or a great emergency is presented before the Confederate Council and the nature of the matter affects the entire body of Five Nations, threatening their utter ruin, then the Lords of the Confederacy must submit the matter to the decision of their people and the decision of the people shall affect the decision of the Confederate Council. This decision shall be a confirmation of the voice of the people. (XV–84, SPW).

94 The men of every clan of the Five Nations shall have a Council Fire ever burning in readiness for a council of the clan. When it seems necessary for a council to be held to discuss the welfare of the clans, then the men may gather about the fire. This council shall have the same rights as the council of the women. (V–88, EUC).

95 The women of every clan of the Five Nations shall have a Council Fire ever burning in readiness for a council of the clan. When in their opinion it seems necessary for the interest of the people they shall hold a council and their decision and recommendation shall be introduced before the Council of Lords by the War Chief for its consideration. (IV–87, EUC).

96 All the Clan council fires of a nation or of the Five Nations may unite into one general council fire, or delegates from all the council fires may be appointed to unite in a general council for discussing the interests of the people. The people shall have the right to make appointments and to delegate their power to others of their number. When their council shall have come to a conclusion on any matter, their decision shall be reported to the Council of the Nation or to the Confederate Council (as the case may require) by the War Chief or the War Chiefs. (VI–89, EUC).

97 Before the real people united their nations, each nation had its council fires. Before the Great Peace their councils were held. The five Council Fires shall continue to burn as before and they

are not quenched. The Lords of each nation in future shall settle their nation's affairs at this council fire governed always by the laws and rules of the council of the Confederacy and by the Great Peace. (VII–90, EUC).

98 If either a nephew or a niece see an irregularity in the performance of the functions of the Great Peace and its laws, in the Confederate Council or in the conferring of Lordship titles in an improper way, through their War Chief they may demand that such actions become subject to correction and that the matter conform to the ways prescribed by the laws of the Great Peace. (LXVII–67, TLL).

Religious ceremonies protected

99 The rites and festivals of each nation shall remain undisturbed and shall continue as before because they were given by the people of old times as useful and necessary for the good of men. (XVI–99, EUC).

100 It shall be the duty of the Lords of each brotherhood to confer at the approach of the time of the Midwinter Thanksgiving and to notify their people of the approaching festival. They shall hold a council over the matter and arrange its details and begin the Thanksgiving five days after the moon of Dis-ko-nah is new. The people shall assemble at the appointed place and the nephews shall notify the people of the time and the place. From the beginning to the end the Lords shall preside over the Thanksgiving and address the people from time to time. (XVII–100, EUC).

101 It shall be the duty of the appointed managers of the Thanksgiving festivals to do all that is needful for carrying out the duties of the occasions.

The recognized festivals of Thanksgiving shall be the Midwinter Thanksgiving, the Maple or Sugar-making Thanksgiving, the Raspberry Thanksgiving, the Strawberry Thanksgiving, the Corn-planting Thanksgiving, the Corn Hoeing Thanksgiving, the Little Festival of Green Corn, the Great Festival of Ripe Corn and the complete Thanksgiving for the Harvest.

Each nation's festivals shall be held in their Long Houses. (XVIII–101, EUC).

102 When the Thanksgiving for the Green Corn comes the special managers, both the men and women, shall give it careful attention and do their duties properly. (XIX–102, EUC).

103 When the Ripe Corn Thanksgiving is celebrated the Lords of the Nation must give it the same attention as they give to the Midwinter Thanksgiving. (XX–103, EUC).

104 Whenever any man proves himself by his good life and his knowledge of good things, naturally fitted as a teacher of good things, he shall be recognized by the Lords as a teacher of peace and religion and the people shall hear him. (X–93, EUC).

The installation song

105 The song used in installing the new Lord of the Confederacy shall be sung by Adodarhoh and it shall be:

" Haii, haii Agwah wi-yoh
   "   "   A-kon-he-watha,
   "   "   Ska-we-ye-se-go-wah
   "   "   Yon-gwa-wih
   "   "   Ya-kon-he-wa-tha

Haii, haii, It is good indeed
   "   "   (That) a broom,—
   "   "   A great wing,
   "   "   It is given me
   "   "   For a sweeping
             instrument.

(LVIII–58, TLL).

106 Whenever a person properly entitled desires to learn the Pacification Song he is privileged to do so but he must prepare a feast at which his teachers may sit with him and sing. The feast is provided that no misfortune may befall them for singing the song on an occasion when no chief is installed. (XXIV–107, EUC).

Protection of the house

107 A certain sign shall be known to all the people of the Five Nations which shall denote that the owner or occupant of a house is absent. A stick or pole in a slanting or leaning position shall indicate this and be the sign. Every person not entitled to enter .the house by right of living within it upon seeing such a sign shall not approach the house either by day or by night but shall keep as far away as his business will permit. (IX–92, EUC).

Funeral addresses

108 At the funeral of a Lord of the Confederacy, say: " Now we become reconciled as you start away. You were once a Lord of the Five Nations' Confederacy and the United People trusted you. Now we release you for it is true that it is no longer possible for us to walk about together on the earth. Now, therefore, we lay it (the body) here. Here we lay it away. Now then we say to you, ' Persevere onward to the place where the Creator dwells in peace. Let not the things of the earth hinder you. Let nothing that transpired while yet you lived hinder you. In hunting you once took delight; in the game of Lacrosse you once took delight and in the feasts and pleasant occasions your mind was amused, but now do not allow thoughts of these things to give you trouble. Let not your relatives hinder you and also let not your friends and associates trouble your mind. Regard none of these things.'

" Now then, in turn, you here present who were related to this man and you who were his friends and associates, behold the path that is yours also! Soon we ourselves will be left in that place. For this reason hold yourselves in restraint as you go from place to place. In your actions and in your conversation do no idle thing. Speak not idle talk neither gossip. Be careful of this and speak not and do not give way to evil behavior. One year is the time that you must abstain from unseemly levity but if you can not do this for ceremony, ten days is the time to regard these things for respect."

109 At the funeral of a War Chief, say:
" Now we become reconciled as you start away. You were once a war chief of the Five Nations' Confederacy and the United People trusted you as their guard from the enemy. (The remainder is the same as the address at the funeral of a Lord). (XXVII–110, EUC).

110 At the funeral of a Warrior say:
" Now we become reconciled as you start away. Once you were a devoted provider and protector of your family and you were ever ready to take part in battles for the Five Nations' Confederacy. The United People trusted you. (The remainder is the same as the address at the funeral of a Lord). (XXVIII–111, EUC).

111 At the funeral of a young man, say:
" Now we become reconciled as you start away. In the beginning of your career you are taken away and the flower of your life is withered away. (The remainder is the same as the address at the funeral of a Lord). (XXIX–112, EUC).

112 At the funeral of a chief woman say:

" Now we become reconciled as you start away. You were once a chief woman in the Five Nations' Confederacy. You once were a mother of the nations. Now we release you for it is true that it is no longer possible for us to walk about together on the earth. Now, therefore, we lay it (the body) here. Here we lay it away. Now then we say to you, ' Persevere onward to the place where the Creator dwells in peace. Let not the things of the earth hinder you. Let nothing that transpired while you lived hinder you. Looking after your family was a sacred duty and you were faithful. You were one of the many joint heirs of the Lordship titles. Feastings were yours and you had pleasant occasions. . . .' (The remainder is the same as the address at the funeral of a Lord). (XXX–113, EUC).

113 At the funeral of a woman of the people, say:

" Now we become reconciled as you start away. You were once a woman in the flower of life and the bloom is now withered away. You once held a sacred position as a mother of the nation. (Etc.) Looking after your family was a sacred duty and you were faithful. Feastings . . . (Etc.) (The remainder is the same as the address at the funeral of a Lord.) (XXXI–114, EUC).

114 At the funeral of an infant or young woman say:

" Now we become reconciled as you start away. You were a tender bud and gladdened our hearts for only a few days. Now the bloom has withered away . . . (Etc.) Let none of the things that transpired on earth hinder you. Let nothing that happened while you lived hinder you. (The remainder is the same as the address at the funeral of a Lord). (XXXII–115, EUC).

115 When an infant dies within three days, mourning shall continue only five days. Then shall you gather the little boys and girls at the house of mourning and at the funeral feast a speaker shall address the children and bid them be happy once more, though by a death, gloom has been cast over them. Then shall the black clouds roll away and the sky shall show blue once more. Then shall the children be again in sunshine. (XXXIII–116, EUC).

116 When a dead person is brought to the burial place, the speaker on the opposite side of the Council Fire shall bid the bereaved family cheer their minds once again and rekindle their hearth fires in peace, to put their house in order and once again be in brightness for darkness has covered them. He shall say that the black clouds shall roll away and that the bright blue sky is

visible once more. Therefore shall they be in peace in the sunshine again. (XXXIV–117, EUC).

117 Three strings of shell one span in length shall be employed in addressing the assemblage at the burial of the dead. The speaker shall say:

"Hearken you who are here, this body is to be covered. Assemble in this place again ten days hence for it is the decree of the Creator that mourning shall cease when ten days have expired. Then shall a feast be made."

Then at the expiration of ten days the Speaker shall say: "Continue to listen you who are here. The ten days of mourning have expired and your minds must now be freed of sorrow as before the loss of the relative. The relatives have decided to make a little compensation to those who have assisted at the funeral. It is a mere expression of thanks. This is to the one who did the cooking while the body was lying in the house. Let her come forward and receive this gift and be dismissed from the task. In substance this shall be repeated for every one who assisted in any way until all have been remembered. (XXXV–118, EUC).

THE CODE OF DEKANAHWIDEH

TOGETHER WITH

THE TRADITION OF THE ORIGIN OF THE FIVE NATIONS' LEAGUE

Prepared by the committee of chiefs appointed by the Six Nations' Council of Grand River, Canada, and adopted by Council of Chiefs, July 3, 1900.

The committee was as follows:

Chief Peter Powless	Mohawk
Chief J. W. M. Elliott	Mohawk
Chief Nicodemus Porter	Oneida
Chief Thomas William Echo	Onondaga
Chief William Wage	Cayuga
Chief Abram Charles	Cayuga
Chief John A. Gibson	Seneca
Chief Josiah Hill	Tuscarora
Chief John Danford	Oneida of the Thames
Chief Isiah Sickles	Oneida of the Thames

INTRODUCTORY

For several hundred years the Five Nations (since 1715 the Six Nations) have existed without a written history chronicled by themselves, of their ancient customs, rites and ceremonies, and of the formation of the Iroquois League. Books have been written by white men in the past, but these have been found to be too voluminous and inaccurate in some instances.

Of the existence of the Five Nations therefore, before the formation of the League of Great Peace by Dekanahwideh, living as they did apart from one another as separate nations and having nothing in common, much might be written, but at this juncture our object will only admit of the relation of the formation of the League of the Five Nations, which as far as can be ascertained took place about the year 1390.

The purpose for which this league or confederation of the Five Nations was organized was to enable them to protect themselves against the invasion of their vast domains by other nations who were hostile to them, and also the formation of a form of government among themselves. Ever since the birth of the league this government has existed with but very slight modifications.

The student of ethnology may find something which may be of interest to him in this record, compiled as it is by the elder ceremonial chiefs who are now among those who are ruling the people of the Six Nations as chiefs or lords, under the old régime of dynastical lords in perpetuation of that system of government by hereditary succession as it was constituted by Dekanahwideh and his associates at the time of the formation of the League of the Iroquois.

This account is not intended to be a concise history of this interesting people, but simply a record of those interesting traditions which have been for centuries handed down from father to son in connection with the formation of the league.

There is no doubt in the minds of the writers of this preface that many of the ancient traditions of the Six Nations have become much modified, and some have been long relegated to oblivion owing to the fact that in the earlier history of these peoples there were for a long time no members of the various nations capable of rendering these traditions in writing and thus preserving them intact to their posterity.

It is a noteworthy fact that the League of the Five Nations (now known as the Six Nations) as constituted centuries ago by Dekanahwideh and his associates, has been followed in accordance with the rules of the confederacy as laid down by this founder of the league, and that the installation of the lords (chiefs) as rulers of the people as laid down in these unwritten rules hundreds of years ago is still strictly observed and adhered to by the chiefs of the Six Nations and their people.

With reference to the origin or birth, character and doings of Dekanahwideh as herein chronicled, it will be observed that they present an analogy or similarity to Hebrew biblical history and teachings. This is portrayed strongly in the narration of the birth of Dekanahwideh and also in certain extraordinary powers which he is attributed to have possessed.

There is little doubt that some of this influence was brought about as a result of the labors and teachings of the Jesuit fathers among them. In the early discovery of the Five Nations the Jesuit fathers made an effort to christianize them.

These precepts as taught and inculcated in the minds of the people by these missionaries have been assimilated to some extent and wrought into their own religious belief, as well perhaps as into the story of the traditional nativity of this founder of the Iroquois Confederacy.

It was in recognition of the fact that all nations have a traditional history similar to this one (and some of them have long since become enlightened and educated to better things) which originated with these people while they were yet in a crude state (notably, for example, may be cited the English, Irish and Scotch legends and traditions) that this small fragment of Iroquois traditional history was written by the chiefs, so that they might preserve it as other nations have done.

It is only natural for a people undergoing a transition from a state of barbarism to that of civilization and christianity to evince a desire to have their past mythological legends and crude history preserved.

It was therefore at the request of, and by the authority of the Six Nations' Council, that that portion of the traditional history of this people relating to the formation of the League of the Five Nations, together with the condolence ceremonies, now used in the creation and induction into office of new chiefs as successors to deceased members of the council, was written from dictation by the ceremonial chiefs as follows: Chiefs Peter Powless, Mohawk; Nicodemus Porter, Oneida; William Wage and Abram Charles, Cayuga; John A. Gibson, Seneca; Thomas William Echo, Onondaga; and Josiah Hill, Tuscarora. Chiefs Josiah Hill and J. W. M. Elliott were appointed to act as secretaries, with the express purpose of having it published by the Department of Indian Affairs, so that the future generations of the people of the Six Nations may have preserved to them these traditions of their forefathers which otherwise in time would become lost.

Signed. at Ohsweken Council House, Six Nations Reserve, Ontario, Canada, August 17, 1900.

JOSIAH HILL, *Secretary Six Nations' Council.*

J. W. M. ELLIOTT, *Mohawk Chief, Secretary of the ceremonial committee of Indian rites and customs.*

Indian words

The meanings of some of the more difficult Indian words to be found in this work are as follows:

1 A-ka-rah-ji-ko-wah—A great swamp elm
2 Ska-reh-heh-se-go-wah—The great tall tree

3 Jo-neh-rah-de-se-go-wah—The great long leaves

4 Djok-de-he-sko-na—The great white roots

5 Ka-ya-neh-renh-ko-wah—The great peace

6 Karihwiyoh—Good tidings of peace and power

7 Rodiyanesho'o—Lords or chiefs

8 Hoyane (Royaneh) — Lord or chief

9 Ehkanehdodeh—A pine tree, applied to earned or self-made chiefs

10 Kwa-ah — The mourning cry used by a chief warrior to convey the news of the death of a lord or head chief

11 Kanekonketshwaserah — The condolence ceremony used upon the death of a lord or chief

THE TRADITIONAL NARRATIVE

OF THE

ORIGIN OF THE CONFEDERATION OF THE FIVE NATIONS

COMMONLY KNOWN AS THE IROQUOIS

Together with an account of the ancient customs, usages and ceremonies in use by these nations in the choice and installation into office of their Ro-de-ya-ner-shoh (lords or chiefs), including traditions relating to the lives and characters of Dekanahwideh, the framer of the league, Hay-yonh-wa-tha (Hiawatha), the lawgiver, Tha-do-da-ho and other leaders.

The peculiar beginning of the Great Peace,[1] or the Great League of the Five Nations at a time most ancient, is here told.

The name of the place mentioned as the birthplace of Dekanahwideh[2] was called Kah-ha-nah-yenh,[3] somewhere in the neighborhood of the Bay of Quinte.

According to tradition, a woman[4] was living in that neighborhood who had one daughter of stainless character who did not travel away from home, but remained with her mother constantly, and when she had attained the age of womanhood she had held no manner of intercourse with any man. In the course of time, notwithstanding, she showed signs of conception and her mother was very much aggrieved. The mother, therefore, spoke to her daughter and said: "I am going to ask you a question and I want you to tell me the truth. What has happened to you and how is it that you are going to bear a child?" Then the daughter replied and said, "Mother I will tell you the truth, I do not know how I became with child."[5]

Then the mother said: "The reply you give me is not sufficient to remove my grief. I am sure that you did not tell me the full truth concerning what I asked you." Then the daughter replied: "I have indeed told you the whole truth concerning what you asked me." Then the sorrowing mother said: "Of a truth, my daughter, you have no love for me."

---

[1] Gaya"nässhägo, in Onondaga; Gayanĕs'shä"gowa, in Seneca. Derived from Gayanĕs'shä, *A compelling rule of virtue,* and gowa, *great, exalted.*

[2] Dekanăwï'da, *Two water currents flowing together.*

[3] Kanyĕⁿ'gĕ (Onon.), *Among the flints, Flinty peace,* cf. Hadineyĕ"ge'gä, *They are flint people.*

[4] No father or husband; that is, no male is mentioned in this family until Dekanahwideh appears.

[5] A virgin (female) is called deyĕn'nowädon'; (masc.) dehaⁿnowä'doⁿ' meaning, *He is hidden;* from nowä'doⁿ', *hidden.* Ye'wayei' is the word for *pure.*

Then she began to ill-treat her daughter, and then the daughter also began to feel aggrieved because of this ill-treatment from her mother.

It so happened that as the time approached when the daughter would deliver the child, that the mother dreamed [1] that she saw a man whom she did not know, and that he said that he appeared as a messenger to her on account of her troubled mind, caused by the condition of her daughter who had in so mysterious a manner conceived a child.

" I am here to deliver to you a message and now I will ask you to cease your grieving and trouble of mind, and the ill-treatment of your daughter from day to day because it is indeed a fact that your daughter does not know how she became with child. I will tell you what has happened. It is the wish of the Creator that she should bear a child, and when you will see the male child you shall call him Dekanahwideh. The reason you shall give him that name is because this child will reveal to men-beings (Oñg'wĕoⁿwĕ'), the Good Tidings of Peace and Power [2] from Heaven, and the Great Peace shall rule and govern on earth, and I will charge you that you and your daughter should be kind to him becauses he has an important mission to perform in the world, and when he grows up to be a man do not prevent him from leaving home."

Then the old woman, (Iăgĕⁿ'tci) asked the messenger, what office the child should hold.

The messenger answered and said: " His mission is for peace and life to the people both on earth and in heaven."

When the old woman woke up the next morning she spoke to her daughter and said: " My daughter, I ask you to pardon me for all the ill-treatment I have given you because I have now been satisfied that you told me the truth when you told me that you did not know how you got the child which you are about to deliver."

Then the daughter also was made glad, and when she was delivered of the child, it was as had been predicted; the child was a male child, and the grandmother called him Dekanahwideh.

The child grew up rapidly, and when he had become a young man he said: " The time has come when I should begin to perform my duty in this world. I will therefore begin to build my canoe and by tomorrow I must have it completed because there is work for me to do tomorrow when I go away to the eastward."

---

[1] *She dreamed,* waagoi'shĕⁿdŭksĕⁿá. To guess the meaning of a dream, third person, plural, present, Hodinowaiya'ha.

[2] Ne"gä'ihwiio'ne"skäñ'noⁿ'khu (Seneca), literally, *The good message* (or edict), *the power.*

Then he began to build his canoe out of a white rock, and when he had completed it, Dekanahwideh said: " I am ready now to go away from home and I will tell you that there is a tree[1] on top of the hill and you shall have that for a sign whenever you wish to find out whether I shall be living or dead. You will take an axe and chop the tree and if the tree flows blood[2] from the cut, you will thereby know that I am beheaded and killed, but if you find no blood running from this tree after you have chopped a chip from it, then you may know that my mission was successful. The reason that this will happen is because I came to stop forever the wanton shedding of blood among human beings."

Then Dekanahwideh also said: " Come to the shore of the lake and see me start away."

So his mother and his grandmother went together with him and helped to pull the boat to the lake and as they stood at the lake, Dekanahwideh said: " Good bye, my mothers, for I am about to leave you for I am to go for a long time. When I return I will not come this way."

Then the grandmother said " How are you going to travel since your canoe is made out of stone. It will not float."

Then Dekanahwideh said, " This will be the first sign of wonder that man will behold; a canoe made out of stone will float."

Then he bade them farewell, put his canoe in the lake and got in. Then he paddled away to the eastward and the grandmother and his mother with wonder beheld him and saw that his canoe was going swiftly. In a few moments he disappeared out of their sight.

It happened at that time a party of hunters had a camp on the south side of the lake now known as Ontario and one of the party went toward the lake and stood on the bank of the lake, and beheld the object coming toward him at a distance, and the man could not understand what it was that was approaching him; shortly afterwards he understood that it was a canoe, and saw a man in it, and the moving object was coming directly toward where he stood, and when the man (it was Dekanahwideh) reached the shore he came out of his boat and climbed up the bank.

Then Dekanahwideh asked the man what had caused them to be where they were, and the man answered and said: " We are here

---

[1] Djirhonathäradadon'.
[2] That men enter into or become trees is an old Iroquois conception. The sap of the tree becomes blood that flows when the tree is injured.

for a double object. We are here hunting game for our living and also because there is a great strife in our settlement."

Then Dekanahwideh said, "You will now return to the place from whence you came. The reason that this occurs is because the Good Tidings of Peace and Friendship have come to the people, and you will find all strife removed from your settlement when you go back to your home. And I want you to tell your chief that the Ka-rih-wi-yoh[1] (Good Tidings of Peace and Power) have come and if he asks you from whence came the Good Tidings of Peace and Power, you will say that the Messenger of the Good Tidings of Peace and Power will come in a few days.

Then the man said: "Who are you now speaking to me?"

Dekanahwideh answered: "It is I who came from the west and am going eastward and am called Dekanahwideh in the world."

Then the man wondered and beheld his canoe and saw that his canoe was made out of white stone.

Then Dekanahwideh said, "I will go and visit Tyo-den-he deh[2] first." Dekanahwideh then went down the bank and got into his boat, and passed on. Then the man also turned away and went home, and when he came back to the camp he said: "I saw a strange man coming from the lake with a canoe made out of white stone and when he landed he came up the bank and I had a conversation with him. First, he asked me where I came from and when I told him he understood everything.[3] Then he said: "You will all go home for there is now peace, and all strife has been removed from the settlement."

Then the party went home and as soon as they reached home, they went and told the Royaner[4] (lord) and said that the Good Tidings of Peace and Power had come. Then the lord asked the speaker who told him the message and then he said that he saw a man who was called Dekanahwideh in the world. Then the lord asked him from whence the Good Tidings of Peace and Strength were coming.

---

[1] Karhihwiio, or in Seneca, Ne"Gā'ihwiio, meaning a proclamation of good ... ... .terally the word is interpreted, *A good message.* The mis-sionaries use the word gā-i-hwi-io for *Gospel.* The power of the new civil government is called skĕñ'noⁿ', meaning *inherent potence.*

[2] Tiodenhe'dĕ, meaning He (having died) lives again, cf. Siga'hedŭs, *He resurrects,* used as a name for Christ.

[3] Dekanawida is reputed to have been a clairvoyant.

[4] Royaner is hoya'ne in Seneca. The Mohawk root-equivalent is Ya"nerhe. Royaner means *excellent, noble, good, exalted, pure.* Thus as a title the name is translated *Lord.* Missionaries so use the name, cf. Hale Book of Rites, p. 65.

Then the man said: " It is coming and will come soon."

Then the lord said: " Where did you see the man?" He replied, " I saw him in the lake with his canoe; he came from the west and he is going eastward."

Then the lord began to wonder and said that he thought the settlement should remain in silence, for all would be glad and satisfied.

Dekanahwideh continued his journey and came to where the great wizard Toh-do-dah-ho[1] lived. This man was possessed with great power as a wizard and no man could come to him without endangering his life and it is related that even the fowls of the air whenever they flew directly over his place of abode would die and fall down on his premises, and that if he saw a man approaching him he was sure to destroy him or kill him. This man was a cannibal, and had left the settlement to which he belonged for a long time and lived by himself in an isolated place.

Dekanahwideh came[2] and approached the abode of the cannibal and saw him carrying a human body into his house and shortly he saw him come out again and go down to the river and draw some water. Dekanahwideh went closer and when he had come to the house he went up onto the roof and from the chimney opening[3] he looked in and saw the owner come back with a pail of water, put up a kettle on the fireplace to cook his meal and after it was cooked he saw him take the kettle from the fire and place it at the end of the fireplace and say to himself, " I suppose it is now time for me to have my meal and after I am finished I will go where I am required on business."

Dekanahwideh moved still closer over the smoke hole and looked straight down into the kettle. The man Tah-do-dah-ho was then moving around the house and when he came back to take some of the meat from the kettle he looked into it and saw that a man was looking at him from out of the kettle. This was the reflection of Dekanahwideh. Then the man Tah-do-dah-ho moved back and sat down near the corner of the house and began to think seriously and he thought that it was a most wonderful thing which had happened. He said to himself that such a thing had never occurred before as long as he had been living in the house. " I did not

---

[1] Thadoda'ho.

[2] He came on a tour of inspection. The Onondaga version says it was Hiawatha.

[3] Albert Cusick, the Onondaga informant, says this incident is an interpolation.

know that I was so strange a man," he said. "My mode of living must be wrong." Then he said: "Let me look again and be sure that what I have seen is true." Then he arose, went to the kettle and looked into it again, and he saw the same object — the face of a great man and it was looking at him. Then he took the kettle and went out and went toward the hillside and he emptied it there.

Then Dekanahwideh came down from the roof and made great haste toward the hillside, and when Tha-do-dah-ho came up the hill he met Dekanahwideh.

Dekanahwideh asked Tah-do-dah-ho where he came from and he said, "I had cooked my meal and I took the kettle from the fire and placed it on the floor. I thought that I would take some of the meat out of the kettle and then I saw a man's face looking at me from the kettle. I do not know what had happened; I only know such a thing never occurred to me before as long as I have been living in this house. Now I have come to the conclusion that I must be wrong in the way I am and the way I have been living. That is why I carried the kettle out of my house and emptied it over there by the stump. I was returning when I met you." Then he said, "From whence did you come?"

Dekanahwideh answered, "I came from the west and am going eastward."

Then the man said, "Who are you that is thus speaking to me?"

Then Dekanahwideh said, "It is he who is called Dekanahwideh in this world." Dekanahwideh then asked: "From whence have you come?"

The man then said: "There is a settlement to which I belong but I left that settlement a long time ago."

Then Dekanahwideh said, "You will now return, for peace and friendship have come to you and your settlement and you have now repented the course of wrong doing which you pursued in times past. It shall now also occur that when you return to your settlement you, yourself, shall promote peace and friendship for it is a fact that peace is now ruling in your settlement and I want you to arrange and settle all matters." Then Dekanahwideh also said: "I shall arrive there early tomorrow morning. I shall visit the west first. I shall visit there the house of the woman, Ji-kon-sah-seh. The reason why I shall do this (go and visit this woman first) is because the path passes there which runs from the east to the west."

Then after saying these words Dekanahwideh went on his way and arrived at the house of Ji-kon-sah-seh and said to her that he had come on this path which passed her home and which led from the east to the west, and on which traveled the men of blood-thirsty and destructive nature.

Then he said unto her, " It is your custom to feed these men when they are traveling on this path on their war expeditions." He then told her that she must desist from practising this custom. He then told her that the reason she was to stop this custom was that the Karihwiyoh[1] or Good Tidings of Peace and Power had come. He then said: " I shall, therefore, now change your disposition and practice." Then also, "I now charge you that you shall be the custodian of the Good Tidings of Peace and Power, so that the human race may live in peace in the future." Then Dekanahwideh also said, " You shall therefore now go east where I shall meet you at the place of danger (to Onondaga), where all matters shall be finally settled and you must not fail to be there on the third day. I shall now pass on in my journey."

Then he journeyed on a great way and went to another settlement. Here he inquired who their Royaner was and after he had ascertained his abode he went to his home and found him, and when they met, Dekanahwideh said, " Have you heard that the Good Tidings of Peace and Power are coming?" The lord then said: " I truly have heard of it."

Then Dekanahwideh asked him what he thought about it.

Then the lord said, " Since I have heard of the good news I have been thinking about it and since then I have not slept." Then Dekanhwideh said, " It is now at hand — that which has been the cause of your sleeplessness."

Then Dekanahwideh said, " You shall hereafter be called Hayyonh-wa-tha [2] (Hiawatha)."

Then the lord said, " To whom am I speaking? " Dekanahwideh answered and said: " I am the man who is called on earth by the name of Dekanahwideh, and I have just come from the west and am now going east for the purpose of propagating peace, so that the shedding of human blood might cease among you."

Then the Lord Hahyonhwatha asked, " Will you wait until I go and announce the news to my colleagues? " Dekanahwideh then

---

[1] Djikonsă′sĕ′, *The wild cat* (fat faced), known as the "mother of nations." This was the most honored female title among the Huron Iroquois. She is sometimes call the Peace Queen. She was of the Neuter Nation and her lodge was on the east side of the Niagara, at Kai-a-nieu-ka. Often she was termed Ye-go-wa-neh, the great woman.

[2] Haiyonhwat′hă, meaning *He has misplaced something but knows where to find it*.

said that he could wait as he was on this good mission.   Then the Lord Hahyonhwatha announced to his colleagues and people that they assemble to hear Dekanahwideh, and when they were assembled Hahyonhwatha asked Dekanahwideh what news he had for the people.   Dekanahwideh answered that the proclamation of the Good Tidings of Peace and Power had arrived and that he had come on a mission to proclaim the Good News of Peace and Power that bloodshed might cease in the land, as the Creator, he had learned, never intended that such should ever be practised by human beings.

Lord Hahyonhwatha answered the people: " We have now heard the Good News of Peace and Power from this man Dekanahwideh." He then turned and asked his colleagues and all the people what answer they should give.   Then one of the chief warriors asked: " What shall we do with the powerful tribes on the east and on the west[1] of our villages who are always hostile to us?"

Then Dekanahwideh answered and said that the hostile nations referred to had already accepted the Good News of Peace and Power.

Then the chief warrior answered and said: " I am still in doubt and I would propose (as a test of power) that this man (Dekanahwideh) climb up a big tree by the edge of a high cliff and that we then cut the tree down and let it fall with him over the cliff,[2] and then if he does not die I shall truly believe the message which he has brought us."

Then the deputy chief warrior said: " I also am of the same opinion and I approve of the suggestion of the chief warrior."

Then Dekanahwideh said: " I am ready and most willingly accede to your request, because the Good News of Peace and Power has come unto us, I now confidently place myself in your hands."

Then the lord said: " It has now been decided.   We will therefore all go to where the tree stands."   They then started to go there and when they arrived where the tree stood, the lord said: " We have now arrived where the tree that we have decided upon stands."

Then the chief warrior said to Dekanahwideh: " I made this proposal and therefore you will now climb this tree so that it will

---

[1] To the west of the Onondagas were the Seneca and Cayuga nations; to the east the Oneida and Mohawk.   It is possible, however, that the New England Indians on the east and the Neuters on the west were meant by this paragraph.   Consult J. D. Prince, Wampum Records of the Passamaquoddy Documents, Annals N. Y. Acad. Sci. No. 15, p. 369–77.   1898.

[2] The Newhouse version (q.v.) gives more details of this incident.

be a sign of proof, and the people may see your power.   If you live to see tomorrow's sunrise then I will accept your message."

Then Dekanahwideh said, " This shall truly be done and carried out."   He then climbed the tree and when he had reached the top of the tree[1] he sat down on a branch, after which the tree was cut down, and it fell over the cliff with him.

Then the people kept vigilant watch so that they might see him, but they failed to see any signs of him.   Then the chief warrior said, " Now my proposition has been carried out and Dekenahwideh has disappeared and so now we will vigilantly watch at sunrise tomorrow morning.   Then the Lord Hahyonhwatha said, " We shall now return home."

Now when the new day dawned one of the warriors arose before sunrise and at once went to the place where the tree had been cut and when he had arrived there he saw at a short distance a field of corn, and near by the smoke from a fire[2] toward which the warrior went.   When he arrived there he saw a man sitting by the fire and after seeing the man he at once returned to the Lord Hahyonhwatha and when he arrived there he said that he had seen the man sitting by the fire, and that it was he who was on the tree which was cut the evening before.

Then Hahyonhwatha charged him to convey these tidings to his colleagues and all the people and in a short time all the people had assembled.   Then the Lord Hahyonhwatha said, " We will now call Dekanahwideh," and he then commissioned the chief warrior and the deputy chief warrior to go after him and they went to where Dekanahwideh had his fire and when they arrived they told him that the Lord Hahyonhwatha had sent them to bring him and that they would escort him to the home of Hahyonhwatha.

Then Dekanahwideh said: " It is right.   I shall go with you."

They then returned and when they arrived back at the abode of Hahyonhwatha, the chief warrior spoke and said, " We have returned with Dekanahwideh, and he is now in your charge."   Lord Hahyonhwatha then said: " I am now surely ready to fully accept the Good News of Peace and Power, and it now rests with you as your opinion in this matter."

---

[1] This event took place on the cliff overlooking the lower falls of the Mohawk.   The tree was a bitter hickory, (gŭs′thik), which stood at the doorway of a woman named De′siio′.   When Dekanawida climbed the tree he sang the air of " the six songs of the pacification hymn."

[2] The column of smoke from Dekanawida's fire is said always to have " pierced the sky."   The term is, Wagayĕⁿgwa′i′dĕⁿwagaiyaestä′, *It forms smoke, smoke pierces the sky.*

The chief warrior then said: "I was in great doubt, but have now truly concluded to accept the Good News of Peace and Power." Then Royaner (Lord) Hahyonhwatha said: "Now faithfully see these matters are settled and finished."

Then he further said: "Dekanahwideh, you may now listen to the answer we have concluded to give you. We have received the message which you brought us, and we have jointly concluded to accept the message of Good News of Peace and Power and we have now concluded all we have to say, and the matter shall now rest with you entirely."

Dekanahwideh then said: "This day is early and yet young, so is the new mind also tender and young, so also is the Good Tidings of Peace and Power, and as the new sun of Good Tidings of Peace and Power arose, so it will proceed on its course and prosper; so also will the young mind, and the Good Tidings of Peace and Power shall prevail and prosper. Therefore in the future your grandchildren forever shall live in peace."

Then Dekanahwideh answered again: "You, chief warrior, you have had power in warfare, but now this is all changed. I now proclaim that since you had doubts, you shall be hereafter known in the land by the name of Tha-ha-rih-ho-ken (De-ka-ri-ho-ken),[1] which means doubting or hesitating over two things as to which course to adopt."

And Dekanahwideh said: "You, the deputy chief warrior, I charge you that you shall be called and known hereafter in the land by the name of Sa-de-ga-rih-wa-den[2] (one-who-respects-all-matters-as-important-equally) because you truly have concurred in and justly confirmed all that you have heard."

Then Dekanahwideh also said: "I shall now pass on and go east, and we shall meet again tomorrow[3] to add to what we have already accomplished."

Then Dekanahwideh passed on in his journey.

Then in Lord Hahyonhwatha's family composed of three[4] daughters, the eldest was taken ill and in a little time she died.[5]

---

[1] In Onondaga, Degaihō'kĕⁿ'. His name appears first on the roll of "Rodiyaner."

[2] Tcă'dekaiiwāt'dĕ, sometimes translated, *Two stories diverging in conclusions.*

[3] "Tomorrow," or "on another day" frequently means the next year. Dekanawida in going east possibly went to the Abenaki or other New England Indians. See Prince, *op. cit.*

[4] Newhouse says seven.

[5] A Mohawk account. Cf. Newhouse, who says the daughters all perished through the witchcraft of Osi'no'. One account says that he took the form

The mind of Hahyonhwatha was troubled. His colleagues and the people assembled at his home and condoled with him and admonished him to forget his sorrow, and he acceded to their desire.

Shortly afterwards the second daughter took sick and in a short time died. Then the sorrow and trouble of the Lord Hahyonhwatha was greatly increased, and again his colleagues and people assembled at his abode and again they tried to induce him to forget his sorrow and trouble, but he could not answer them. So Deharihoken said: " I will not tell you my mind (my purpose). I think that we should look for something which would console the mind of our lord in his trouble and bereavement." Then he also said: " I would lay before you warriors, for your consideration, that you cheer him by playing a game of lacrosse." [1]

Then Sadekarihwadeh said: " I will now tell you my mind, first let the people all assemble to console him. This shall be done as alas our lord has now only one daughter left alive."

Then Dekarihoken confirmed all that Sadekarihwadeh had said.

Then the people assembled at the home of the Lord Hahyonhwatha and they spoke unto him words of condolence that he might forget his grief and bereavement.

But the lord did not answer them. So then the warriors decided that they would play a game of lacrosse in order to cheer him and during the time that they were playing, the last daughter of Hahyonhwatha came out of the family abode to go after some water and when she had gone half way to the spring she saw flying high up in the air above a beautiful bird. [2] She paused in her journey and the bird flew downwards toward her. She cried out aloud, being frightened, and said, " O, see this bird! " after which she ran away.

Then the warriors saw it and as it was then flying low, the warriors followed it, and as they were looking at the bird they did not notice the daughter of Hahyonhwatha before them and in their haste they ran over and trampled her to death, and it transpired that the daughter of Hahyonhwatha was with child.

Then Sadekarihwadeh went and told Hahyonhwatha that a strange bird called Teh-yoh-ronh-yoh-ron (a high flying bird which

---

of a screech owl and conjured from a tree overlooking the daughters' lodge; another that he became a poison shadow at the bottom of a spring.

[1] Each game had a reputed medicinal effect.

[2] This was the magic Hä'goks, sometimes called " the wampum eagle." Another descriptive name is given later in the text.

pierces the skies) had come amongest them and that it was due to the visit of the bird that his daughter was killed.

Then Hahyonhwatha answered sadly and said: " I have now lost all my daughters and in the death of this, my last daughter, you have accidently and unwittingly killed two beings." [1]

And Hahyonhwatha further said: " I must now go away to the west," and he started immediately on his way. He met Dekanahwideh on the trail and Dekanahwideh warned him of the danger on his way, especially with reference to a certain man who was watching, saying as follows:

" There is danger in front of you, there is a man watching your way in front of you. It is necessary for you to approach him without his becoming aware of your coming until you get to him. If you can get up to him while he is unaware of your approach then we shall surely prosper in our mission. You will then speak to him and ask him what thing he is watching for. He will answer you and say that he is watching to protect the fields of corn as the people of other nations and also animals destroy the crops and he is watching therefore that the crops might be preserved, so that the children might live from the harvest."

Then Hahyonhwatha proceeded on his journey and when he arrived where the man was sitting beside a fire near a big tree and watching; he quickly spoke, asking, " What are you doing? " And the man answered and said: " I am watching the fields of corn to protect them from other nations and also from animals that our children might live from the harvest."

Hahyonhwatha then said to the man: " Return home now and tell your lord that the Good News of Peace and Power has come." So he returned and told his Lord the message given to him by Hahyonhwatha. Then the lord said: " Who is it who told you this strange news? " Then the man who had been watching said: "A man suddenly appeared to me when I was watching the fields of corn and he told me the news."

Hahyonhwatha went to the other end of the corn field and there met Dekanahwideh. Dekanahwideh said: " We have now announced the (Ka-ya-ne-reh) Good Tidings of Peace and Power, therefore you shall abide in this hut near these corn fields, which you will only leave when you receive an invitation from the people.

---

[1] Other versions say that this event took place before Hiawatha met Dekanawida, his grief over his losses, driving him into a self-imposed exile, during which he lamented all evil conditions. Later he met Dekanawida. A. Cusick, and Baptist Thomas, New York Onondagas, both concurred in this.

You must not go unless the invitation is official. A woman shall first come to you early tomorrow morning who will be the first to see you, then you shall cut and prepare some elderberry twigs.[1] You shall cut them into pieces and remove the heart pulp and then you shall string them up." "Then the lord (Royaner) shall send a messenger to you to invite you, but you must not accept the invitation until he shall send to you a string of twigs similar to your own."

Then Hahyonhwatha went on his journey and found the hut beside the cornfield and built a fire, and in the morning a woman came to the cornfield and saw the smoke from the fire at the end of the cornfield and when she arrived there she saw a man sitting with his head hanging down. Then the woman hurried home and went straightway to where the lord (Royaner) lived and when she arrived she told him that she had seen a strange man sitting beside a fire in the cornfield.

Then the lord asked her: "What thing was this man doing there?" And the woman answered and said that the man was sitting there quietly looking on the ground.[2]

Then the lord said: "This must be the man who sent the message of the Good Tidings of Peace and Power. I shall therefore now send a messenger to bring him hither."

He then summoned the chief warrior and the deputy chief warrior to come to him and when the two had come, the lord said to them: "You shall go after the man who is at the fire in the cornfield and bring him to me. The lord then said to the deputy chief warrior: "I send you to go after him," and the deputy chief warrior went to bring this man, and when he arrived at the place where the man had built the fire, he saw a man sitting there and he was looking at a string of elderberry twigs which was hanging on a pole horizontally placed in front of him.

Then the deputy chief warrior said: "I am sent after you by the lord (Royaner)."

The man did not answer and so the deputy chief warrior repeated the message of the lord three times, but the man did not give any

---

[1] Wampum at first seems to have been any kind of cylindrical bead, large or small. The Mohawk name is o'tgo'rha; Seneca, o'tko'ä'. The quills of feathers and porcupines were used as wampum (o'tgo'rha). Indeed Baptist Thomas, an Onondaga informant, says porcupine quills were used and not elderberry twigs as stated in this version.

[2] Hiawatha kept repeating the phrase, äsanatcik, meaning, *they should give me a wampum token.*

reply. Then the deputy chief warrior turned and returned to the lord, and when he arrived, he said to the lord: "He did not reply."

The lord then asked: "What did you see?" Then the deputy chief warrior answered and said, "I saw a string of elderberry twigs hanging on a pole in front of him and he was looking at it." Then the lord answered and said: "I now understand; I shall therefore make a similar string out of quills which will cause him to come." The lord then made two strings of quills and put them on a thong.

The lord then said: "I have now completed the strings and you shall both go after him and bring him here. You shall therefore take these strings of quills with you to him and they shall become words and that will induce him to come. They then went on their errand and when they had arrived at the fire the chief warrior said: "The lord has again sent us after you, and this string of quills are his words which are to bring you to him."

Then Hahyonhwatha answered and said: "This is what should have been done." He then took the string of quills and said: "After I get through smoking[1] I shall go to the lord."

They then returned to the lord and when they had arrived they said that the man had now answered and that when he had finished smoking his pipe he would come.

The lord then told them to tell the people so that they would all assemble when the man should arrive.

The chief warrior and the deputy chief warrior then went to tell the people to assemble as soon as possible to the abode of the lord.

The people had therefore all assembled when Hahyonhwatha arrived. The lord said to him: "You have come amongst us and doubtless you have some important matter to convey to us. The people have already assembled and are prepared to listen to the matter which you may have to communicate to us."

Then Hahyonhwatha answered: "I have come here to deliver to you the message of Good Tidings of Peace and Power so that our children in the future may live in peace."

Then the lord said: "We shall defer answering you until the return of a certain man for whom we are waiting, but in the meantime we desire that you shall remain in our village with us."

Then Hahyonhwatha answered and said: "This can be safely

---

[1] To have gone in haste without a semblance of deliberation would have been considered insulting.

done as I came to you with the message of Good Tidings of Peace and Power."

Then the lord said: " I shall therefore entertain you myself. This will be done because the message which you have brought to us may be the same as the other man's for which we are waiting, and he has sent word that he is coming." Then Hahyonhwatha said: " I approve of all this."

The assembled people then dispersed and when night came the lord told Hahyonhwatha that he could sleep in the inner room. Then he (Hahyonhwatha) went in and retired. Shortly after he heard a voice outside which said: "Are you stopping here?" and Hahyonhwatha replied, " Yes." Now the voice from outside said that it was very urgent for him to come out.

So Hahyonwatha went out and he saw Dakanahwideh standing outside. Dekanahwideh then said: " It is now urgent that we proceed directly on our journey.[1] You have now accomplished all that is necessary to be done here at present; we can go to another settlement now and afterwards return. The man you are now waiting for will likely have returned by that time."

" There is one settlement left to be visited, although I have been there before and had conversation with the man. I have promised him that I will visit him again and for that reason when you left home you heard a loud toned voice in front of you saying, 'A-son-kek-ne-eh.'[2] We will now proceed on our journey."

They then went and while they were on their way Dekanahwideh said, " Let us stop here and wait a while, and you will look toward the southeast. So they stood still and Hahyonhwatha looked toward the southeast and saw the smoke arising and reaching to the sky.

Then Dekanahwideh asked: " What do you see?"

Hahyonhwatha said: " I see smoke piercing the sky."

Then Dekanahwideh answered: " That smoke which you saw is where the abode of Dyon-yon-ko is. The reason you see the smoke piercing the sky is because the Good Tidings of Peace and Power have come to the people of that settlement but unfortunately, owing to the selfishness and lack of energy of these people, the Good Tidings of Peace and Power have not prospered and have not extended to other settlements.[3] It is thus good that these people

---

[1] Baptist Thomas says Hiawatha left this council because of a dispute on the part of the people, who forgot him in their effort to honor another man.
[2] " It has not yet occurred," asoñ'de'nëi'.
[3] It is said that the New England Indians (Adirhon'daks), the Cherokee (Oya'de), the Wyandott (Thăstăhetci), the Tionante (Tyonontate'ka'), the

have received the Good Tidings of Peace and Power. We shall
therefore take power from them which will enable us to complete
the work we have undertaken to accomplish."

They then heard the loud toned voice saying: "A-soh-kek-ne
———eh" (it is not yet; which means, impatiently waiting). Then
Dekanahwideh said: "It is now very urgent for us to proceed on
our journey to the place from whence this voice proceeds." They
then went and they had not gone far when they came to a lake.
Then Dekanahwideh said: "It is now left with you to decide
what we shall do; you have seen the lake and it is beside this lake
that the man lives whose loud voice you have heard saying:
'Asohkene———eh.'"

Dekanahwideh then also said: "There are two ways which we
can pursue to get across the lake, and you can have your choice.
We can take the boat which you see lying flat on the ground and
paddle over or we can magically pass above the lake, and so get
over it." Dekanahwideh also said: "That man whom you heard
calling in a loud voice is able to cause the boat to upset if he sees
it and the people within it to become drowned; he has ended the
lives of many people in this way in the lake."[1]

Then Hahyonhwatha said: "My choice is that we pass over
above the lake." Then Dekanahwideh said: "It is best to approach this man from behind; the reason we should do this is that
he has been so long impatiently waiting that it would not be wise
to approach him from the front and it might cause trouble." Then
Dekanahwideh also said: "We shall now therefore proceed on
our journey."

Then they went on their journey and arrived at the other side
of the lake. They had not gone far when Hahyonhwatha saw the
man sitting on a high knoll where it was his custom to sit. When
silently they arrived where he was sitting, Dekanahwideh stood on
the right side and Hahyonhwatha on the left. The man had not yet
seen them when he called again: "A-soh-kek-ne———eh!"

Then Hahyonhwatha saw what this man was doing and as soon
as the man called out in the loud voice the lake became very rough
and troubled and great billows formed on its surface.

Then Dekanahwideh spoke and said: "I have now returned

Neuter Nation (Atirhagenrat), the Erie (Djikon'saseoano') and others,
including the Delaware and some southern tribes, were invited into the
confederacy.

[1] Onondaga lake at a point near the present village of Liverpool.

and according to my promise. I promised to bring some one with me and I have now fulfilled this promise."

Then the man who was sitting down turned around and saw Dekanahwideh and said: "Who is the man that has come with you?"

Dekanahwideh then said: "Look to your left and you will see." Then he looked to his left and saw the man standing there; then he said to the man (Hahyonhwatha): "What are you doing here?"

Hahyonhwatha answered and said: "I am standing here beside you because our minds are with you and are turned toward you, for the Good Tidings of Peace and Power have now arrived. You will therefore now see as you turn around in every direction the columns of smoke arising." [1]

Then the man raised his head and carefully looked around and he asked: "Who will accomplish this, that the Good Tidings of Peace and Power be propagated?"

Dekanahwideh said: "Tomorrow in the day time the delegates will come and approach you; then all things will be completed."

Then the man said: "I shall wait until all the delegates shall have arrived."

Then Dekanahwideh said: "We must now return but we must all meet again tomorrow."

So Dekanahwideh and Hahyonhwatha went away and returned again to the abode of the lord where Hahyonhwatha had been lodging when Dekanahwideh called him out and when they had arrived there the lord found out that Hahyonhwatha had returned. Then the lord called him in and told him that the man for whom they had been waiting had returned and said: "We are now ready to answer your message."

Then Hahyonhwatha said: "I am also now ready and I am accompanied by my coworker."

Then the lord answered and said: "You will now bring him in." Then Hahyonhwatha called Dekanahwideh and he came in.

Then the lord said: "The man for whom we have been waiting has now returned and he has delivered his message fully and according to our understanding it is the same as your message. We now understand and we therefore have now decided to accept your message."

---

[1] Smoke arises from settlements of people at peace with each other. The tall column of smoke symbolized the establishment of the Gayanĕsshä"gowa.

Then Dekanahwideh said: "We shall now conclude the object of this message." He then asked the question: "To whom among us did the message of the Good Tidings of Peace and Power first come?"

The lord answered and said: "It is to the man who was guarding the cornfield."

Then Dekanahwideh said: "Where is the man? You shall now bring him here." So the lord called him in and when he had come the lord said: "This is the man who guarded the fields of corn so that our children might live on the harvest."

Dekanahwideh said: "I now ask you if you are indeed the man who guards the cornfields and what your magical power is when you are so guarding the cornfields."

Then the man answered and said: "I rely entirely on my bow and arrows and when I go to the cornfields I take all my arrows with me."

Then Dekanahwideh asked the question: "How or in what manner·do you carry your power?" (meaning his bows and arrows).

The man then answered and said: "I place them in a quiver and place the quiver on my back."

Then Dekanahwideh said: "You shall now therefore be called "Oh-dah-tshe-deh"[1] (meaning, the quiver bearer), as your duty as a guardian of the cornfields is now changed because the Good News of Peace and Power has now come. Your duty hereafter shall now be to see that your children (instead of fields) shall live in peace."

Then Dekanahwideh again asked the lord: "In the past (during the long time he had been guarding the cornfields), what did you do with reference to that part of the crops which were damaged?"

Then the lord answered and said: "I used to send the warriors to gather the damaged crops and they brought them to me and I would divide the corn in equal shares among the people."

Then Dekanahwideh said: "You shall now therefore hereafter be called Ka-non-kwe-yo-da.[2] It shall therefore now be your duty to propagate the Good Tidings of Peace and Power so that your children may live in peace."

Then Dekanahwideh said: "Where is the man for whom you have been waiting?" The lord then called this man and when

---

[1] Odatcē"te', quiver bearer, principal Oneida chief.
[2] Kanonkwenyō'don', *A row of ears of corn standing upright.*

he had arrived, Dekanahwideh said: "Are you the man for whom this people have been waiting so long to return?" Then the man answered, " I am that man." Then Dekanahwideh said: " What was the cause of your long delay in coming?" The man answered and said, " I was waiting for that other man who passed here, and who promised to return but who did not return, and while I was vigilantly watching and waiting for him I could not see him and he failed to return as promised, and when I was on the point of returning I tore down my hut which I had built, then I looked back to my home for the path by which I had come. It had been plainly open before me but now on each side of the path was the forest. I then left and came home here and then I found that already the people had all heard of the Good News which I wished to bring them, so I simply corroborate what they have already heard (from Hahyonhwatha)."

Then Dekanahwideh said: "Everything is now completed, and as you have now torn down your hut, your duty is now changed. You looked back and saw plainly the path through the forest. You shall therefore be known in the land by the name of De-yo-ha'-kwe-de.[1] Your duty shall therefore be to propagate the Good Tidings of Peace and Power so that your children in the future may live in peace." Then Dekanahwideh also said: " I will now tell you that the people through whose settlements I have passed have all accepted the Good Tidings of Peace and Power. Hahyonhwatha shall therefore now go after his colleagues and I shall now visit the settlement at the big mountain [2] and see what is happening there. I have been there before but I have not yet received an answer and what I think now is that we ought to join together in this great work for it is now urgent that it would be done for our time is getting shortened and we have only until tomorrow [3] to complete the whole compact." Then he, Dekanahwideh, also said: " It would be best to appoint two delegates to go and find the smoke."

Then Hahyonhwatha said: " Where shall we meet again?"

Dekanahwideh answered and said: " We shall meet again by the lake shore where my boat lies." [4]

Then Ohdahtshedeh spoke and said: " I shall lie across the pathway like a log and when you come to me you will come in

---

[1] Teyoha'gwĕñtĕ', *Hollow voice in the throat.*

[2] Ganundawao, Bare Hill, the Seneca capitol.

[3] The term " tomorrow " means *a year hence.*

[4] At the mouth of the Oswego river; Oswē'geⁿ', meaning, *the place of the outpouring.*

contact with a log and I shall then join with you" (meaning that he, Ohdahtshedeh, would be lying in wait for them and when they should come to the log, which means his settlement, he could accompany them). Then Ohdahtshedeh further said that he would agree to appoint two delegates to go and look for smoke (smoke means settlements).

Then Ohdahtshedeh said: "It is now left with you, the warriors, as to which of you will volunteer to go."

Then the chief warrior said: "I shall be one of those who volunteer to go." Then Ohdahtshedeh also said: "There is one more required to go; who will therefore volunteer?"

For a long time no one gave answer. Then Ohdahtshedeh asked the question anew and still again no one answered. Then Ohdahtshedeh said: "I shall ask the question once again, for the last time, and if any one desires to volunteer let him speak at once", and from the outside of the gathering a man spoke out and said that he would be one of the volunteers.

Then Dekanahwideh said, "Go and call that man who is speaking from the outside." The man was called in and he was asked to stand by the chief warrior in the meeting. Then Dekanahwideh said to the chief warrior: "You are the first to accede to the request of the lord to volunteer, therefore, your duty shall be to obey orders whenever the (lord) has any duties to give you." Then Dekanahwideh said to the warrior who was the second to volunteer: "As you came from the outside of the meeting, you shall therefore in the future be an assistant to the chief warrior in his duties, and whenever the chief warrior assigns his duties to you, you shall perform his duties and carry out his instructions." Then Dekanahwideh said: "It is now completed; you have all been assigned your duties. You will now go and search for the smoke and wherever you see smoke you shall go there and when you arrive there you shall see the lord of the settlement, then you shall tell him your message. You will say we were sent here by the lords (Ro-de-ya-ners-onh) who take you by the hand and invite you to the place of meeting. You will say to the lord you will send delegates and on their way to the conference to pass where the lord lives at the big mountain and you shall invite him to accompany you. Then if the lord asks you the place of meeting you shall say, ' by the lake where lives the Great Wizard who calls out in the loud-toned voice.'"

They then separated, the chief warrior and his assistant going on their mission, and Dekanahwideh and Hahyonhwatha going to their own home settlements, and when Hahyonhwatha had arrived home he said, "Everything is now completed and we shall (all colleagues) now all go to the conference. You shall therefore all make ready."

The people watched the two volunteer delegates· start on their mission and saw them become transformed into high-flyers (a species of hawk)[1] and they arose high in the air and soared southward and when they descended and alighted near the settlement they were retransformed and proceeded to the village.[2] Here they inquired the abode of the lord, and they were conducted to him and when they had arrived they saw a man. Then the chief warrior asked: "Are you the lord?"

And he answered and said: "I am. Are you seeking for me?"

The chief warrior then said: "Yes, truly we are looking for you."

Then the lord said: "I will now ask you upon what mission have you come here."

Then the chief warrior said: "We are sent by the lords (Rodeyanersonh) who invite you to go to the meeting place of the conference, and you are to take your power with you" (meaning peaceful intent). "You shall therefore invite the lord who lives on the great mountain to accompany you."

Then the lord spoke and said, "Where shall we meet in conference," and the chief warrior answered and said, "By the lake."

Then the lord said: "I have known about this for a long time. I shall therefore now accept your message." Then he took his pipe and said: "When I finish smoking I shall attend the conference" and the chief warrior and his assistant saw the pipe which was an exceedingly large one and larger than any pipe which they had ever seen before. They then returned to their own settlement and when they had returned Ohdahtshedeh asked, "Did you discover the smoke?" Then the chief warrior answered and said: "Everything is right, all is well, and we have discovered the object which you desired; when we saw the smoke we went there and when we arrived we found the lord and we repeated to him fully all our message, and when he had heard all, he answered and said, 'I had known about this for a long time, and knew that I was required to attend the great conference and I now therefore accept and

---

[1] The two birds into which the messengers were transformed were Hă'goks' and Skadjiĕ'na.

[2] To the Cayuga capitol town. The Cayuga have the council name of Sononawendo'na, Great Pipe People.

approve the message.' He promised to pass on his way to the
conference, the settlement at the great mountain,[1] and the people
there are to accompany him to the conference."

Then Ohdahtshedeh said: " It is now time that Hahyonhwatha
should return, and as soon as he returns we shall at once go to the
conference."

Dekanahwideh himself had also gone to the settlement of the
great mountain and when he had arrived at the abode of the lord
of the settlement he said: " It is now very urgent that you should
reply to the message which I have left here before."

The lord answered and said: " The chief warrior and his
deputy have failed to unanimously agree with me to accept the
message of Good Tidings of Peace and Power, and I am now
bewildered and I am at loss to discover any course which might
lead me to overcome this difficulty. The reason why we are thus
placed is that the chief warrior and his deputy, who have the power
and the control of the people, have disagreed with us to accept the
message."

Then Dekanahwideh said: " That which has occurred with you
will not make a difference. The reason why it will not make any
difference is that you, being the lord, have accepted the message.
You are not alone, for they are many who have now accepted the
message and they will assist you to successfully consider the difficulty in which you are placed."

Then moreover Dekanahwideh said: " You will now notify the
brother lord whose abode is on the *other side of the river* [2] that it
is now urgent for him to come over the river, so that we might
meet together here." Then the lord sent a messenger to notify the
lord, whose abode was on the other side of the river, and shortly
after the lord arrived at the appointed place.

Then Dekanahwideh said: " We have now all met together. I
will therefore ask your mind."

Then the lord who had come from over the river spoke and
said: " We lords on either side of the river have decided to accept
your message which you left. The only difficulty which we have
now to contend with is that our chief warrior and his deputy have
failed to agree with us to accept the message, and they have the
power to control the people, and we lords on either side of the

---

[1] The Seneca capitol. The Senecas were divided into two bands, one of
which seems to have been allied with the Erie.
[2] Probably the Genesee river. " The other lord " means the chief of the
trans-Genesee Seneca.

river are totally bewildered and fail to see a way out of the difficulty." [1]

Then Dekanahwideh said: " I now fully understand everything and I will encourage you with reference to this matter which has occurred to you. You are not alone for many have accepted the message of Good Tidings of Peace and Power. Therefore, owing to that which has occurred to you, you (the lord) whose abode is on this east side of the river and to whom the message first came shall be known in the land by the name of Ska-nya-dah-ri-yoh,[2] and you, the lord who came from over the river who has agreed in mind with your colleague on this side of the river, shall be called in the land by the name of Sa-denka-ronh-yes." [3]

Then Dekanahwideh also said: " This is now completed Now it is for you to make ready, for in a little while a man will come whom you will accompany to the conference." They then in the distance heard the man call, "A-soh-kek-ne————eh," meaning " It is not yet."

Then Hahyonhwatha distinctly heard where he was. Then Hahyonhwatha said to his colleague: " The time is now come when we should go to the conference." They then started to go to the place appointed for the conference and they arrived at the place where the log (the Lord Ohdahtshedeh) was lying across the path.

Ohdahtshedeh said: " We have been impatiently waiting for we have heard the man calling with a loud voice now for a long time. It is at the place appointed for the meeting of the conference."

Then Hahyonhwatha said: " Let us now proceed to the conference." They then went to the conference. Then Dekanahwideh said, " I shall now return to my abode and we shall all meet at the place appointed for the conference." Then the Lords Deh-ka-eh-yonh, Ji-non-dah-weh-hon [4] and Dyon-yonh-koh came from their settlement and when they arrived at the abode of Skanyadahriyoh, they said that the lords had decided and arranged that all should call here on their way to the conference and that they were to invite all to accompany them.

---

[1] The difficulties of the Senecas are related in all versions of this tradition. Two separate bodies of the Senecas are described in nearly all stories of the origin of the league.

[2] Ganiodai'io' (Seneca), Handsome Lake.

[3] Sadegai'yēs (Onondaga), or Dyădegaihyēs.

[4] Djinondawē'hon'.

Then Skanyadariyoh said: "We are ready now and we have been waiting for a long time."

They then journeyed on their way to the conference. Dekanahwideh had arrived at the place of meeting first, and after him arrived Hahyonhwatha, Ohdahtshedeh and their colleagues and shortly afterwards Skanyadariyoh, Dehkaehyonh and their colleagues arrived.

After they had all assembled in conference, Dekanahwideh stood up and said:

" This conference met here composed of four nations being now assembled, you will therefore now first consider what we shall do with reference to a certain woman, our mother, who has not yet arrived." They then considered the matter and they decided that they would proceed with the business on hand and the matter would be in progress when she arrived.

Then Dekanahwideh said: " The first thing we shall do will be to cross over the lake and it shall be Hahyonhwatha and Ohdahtshedeh and Dehkaehyonh and Skanyadariyoh and Sadehkaronhyes, who are the rulers with power who shall cross first. If these lords can safely get across the lake and make peace, then you, the whole delegation, can cross. Therefore you shall now watch and you shall see a display of power when they leave the shore in their boat. I shall therefore appoint Hahyonhwatha to guide the boat."

They then entered the boat and he (Dekanahwideh) stood in front of the boat and Hahyonhwatha sat in the stern and the rest of the lords then noticed that the boat was made of white marble. Then they embarked in this boat from the shore and they had not proceeded far on their journey when they heard a voice calling out, "A-soh-kek-ne————eh," and as soon as this voice had called out a strong wind arose and caused the lake to become very rough and troubled and great billows[1] formed upon its surface and more especially around the boat. Then those in the boat became frightened and said: " We are now going to die," but Dekanahwideh spoke and said: " There is no danger because Peace has prevailed."

Then Dekanahwideh further said to the wind and lake, " Be thou quiet, Gä-hä",[2] and rest." Then the wind and the roughness of the lake ceased. They had not gone much farther when the man across the lake called out "Asohkekne————eh," and then the wind and roughness of the lake became still more violent. Then again

---

[1] The lake was troubled because certain ceremonial words were spoken, making it become alive.
[2] The Wind God.

Dekanahwideh said: "You, the wind and the lake, be still, for we have not crossed the water yet." Then again the lake became calm. Then Hahyonhwatha began to paddle hard and the boat went so swiftly that when they reached the shore, the boat plowed deeply into the dry land on the shore bank.

Then Dekanahwideh said: "We will now get out of the boat for we have now arrived at the place where we desire to go." Then he got out and the other lords followed him and they continued on their journey and they had only gone a short distance when they beheld a man sitting on a high, round knoll and when they arrived where he was sitting they stood all around him and Dekanahwideh stood directly in front of him, then he spoke and said: "We have now arrived, we representing the four nations. You will therefore now answer the message which we have left here with you. These lords who now stand all around you have now accepted the Good Tidings of Peace and Power, which signifies that hereafter the shedding of human blood shall cease, for our Creator the Great Ruler never intended that man should engage in any such work as the destruction of human life. There are many who have perished in the direction you are now facing, and these lords have come to induce you to join them so that the shedding of human blood might cease and the Good Tidings of Peace and Power might prevail."

Then the man looked around and saw these men (the lords) standing all around him, but he did not answer but kept silent. Then these lords looked at his head while he was sitting on the ground and they saw his hair moving as if it were all alive and they saw that the movements of the hair greatly resembled that of serpents, and they looked at his hands and saw that his fingers were twisting and contorting continually in all directions and in all manner of shapes, and they became impatient because he would not answer the message.

Then Dekanahwideh said to Hahyonhwatha: "You shall now recross the lake and the chief warrior and De-ha-rih-ho-ken and Dyon-yonh-koh and our mother Ji-kon-sah-seh, shall accompany you back in the boat (when you return here)."

Then the man who was sitting on the ground smiled a little. Then Hahyonhwatha hurriedly went back and reembarked in the boat and recrossed the lake and when he had come to shore on the other side of the lake, they asked what had occurred.

Hahyonhwatha answered and said: "It is not yet complete, I have therefore come after the chief warrior, De-ha-rih-ho-ken and

Dyon-yonh-koh and our mother Ji-kon-sah-seh," [1] and they answered him and said: " She has now arrived."

Then all those whom he had named got into the boat. Then Hahyonhwatha said: " You will take as a sign that if we can get across the lake in safety and the lake remains calm all the way across then our message of peace will be accepted." They then embarked on the lake [2] and the boat was rapidly propelled and as they looked at the lake they saw that it was calm all the way across and they arrived on to the shore in safety, and when they had returned to where the man was sitting, Hahyonhwatha said, " Everything is completed, we are now all assembled here."

Then Dekanahwideh said: " We shall now first give thanks to the Great Ruler. We will do this because our power is now completed." He also said: " It shall be that each nation shall now have a voice in the thanksgiving and I shall therefore be the first to lead. He then exclaimed " Yo———hen! "

Then Ohdahtshedeh also repeated " Yo———hen " and after him followed Dehkaehyonh who also repeated " Yo———hen." The next in order was Skanyadahriyoh who also repeated " Yo——— hen " and after him Hahyonhwatha repeated " Yo———hen."

When Dekanahwideh started to address this man, the man became troubled and after all of the lords finished addressing the man his sympathy was affected and he shed tears. Then Dekanahwideh said: " We, the delegates of all the nations who have accepted the Good Tidings of Peace and Power, are now assembled here.

" The course, therefore, that we shall now pursue is that of the representatives of each nation giving utterance to their opinion upon this matter."

Ohdahtshedeh was the first to address the assembly and he said: " I shall be the first to give utterance to my opinion upon this matter. In my opinion this man may approve of our mission if we all lay our heads before him." (This means that the nations here represented would be submissive to this man Tha-do-dah-ho).

Then Dekanahwideh and Skanyadahriyoh spoke and said: " We acquiesce to all that Ohdahtshedeh has said."

Then Dekanahwideh said to Thadodahho: " Now you will answer and state if you are satisfied with the submission of these

---

[1] Djikon'sase is a character who should be better known in Iroquois mythology. There are several traditions about her, in the various events of Iroquois tradition. The name passed as a title from one generation to another.

[2] Mud Lake, or Diok'to, Otisco Lake.

lords who have laid their heads before you," but even then Thadodah-ho did not answer.

Then Dekanahwideh said: "You Dyon-yonh-koh will now give utterance and express your opinion on this matter, as you now have the authority."

Then Dyon-yonh-koh spoke and said to Thadodah-ho: "The Creator, the Great Ruler, created this day which is now shedding its light upon us; he also created man and he also created the earth and all things upon it. Now look up and see the delegates of the Four Nations sitting around you, also see the chief warrior and this great woman our mother (Jiknosahseh), standing before you, all of whom have approved of this message. The lords and all the chief warriors and this great woman, our mother, have all agreed to submit the Good Tidings of Peace and Power to you, and thus if you approve and confirm the message, you will have the power and be the Fire-Keeper of our Confederate Council, and the smoke from it will arise and pierce the sky, and all the nations shall be subject to you."

Then the twisting movements of the fingers and the snakelike movements of the hair of Thadodahho ceased.

Then he spoke and said: "It is well. I will now answer the mission which brought you here. I now truly confirm and accept your message, the object of which brought you here."

THE DEER'S HORNS THE EMBLEM OF POWER

Then Dakanahwideh said: "We have now accomplished our work and completed everything that was required with the exception of shaping and transforming him (by rubbing him down), removing the snake-like hair from him and circumcising him."

The lords therefore all took part in doing this and Ohdahtshedeh was the first to rub down Thadodahho and the others followed his example so that the appearance of Thaddodahho might be like that of other men.

When this had been done then Dekanahwideh again said: "You, the chief warrior, and you, our mother, you have the control of the power (the authority), and we will now put upon him a sign, by placing upon his head the horns of a buck deer. The reason why we do this is because all people live upon the flesh of the deer, and the reason that we take the emblem of the deer horns is that this institution, the Great Peace, shall be the means of protecting our children hereafter."

Then Dekanahwideh also said: "We shall now use these symbolic deer's horns by placing them upon the heads of each other. It shall be thus then that these horns shall be placed upon the head of a man who shall be called a lord by his people — he shall have the power to rule his people." Then Dekanahwideh further said: "And now you, the chief warrior and our mother, shall place these horns upon the head of him, Thadodahho."

Then they looked and saw antlers lying on the ground in the midst of them, and Dekanahwideh said: " Pick these horns up and put them upon him." Then the mother went forward and picked them up. Then the chief warrior and the woman each grasped the horns and placed them on his head.

Then Dekanahwideh said to the man who was still sitting on the ground: " Now arise," and the man stood up.

Then Dekanahwideh said: " You, the nations who are assembled here, behold this man who stands up before us. We have now placed the deer's horns upon his head as an emblem of authority. The people shall now call him Lord Tha-do-dah-ho, in the land." Then Dekanahwideh said: " It shall now, in the future among us, the United Nations, thus be a custom that whenever a lord is to be created we shall all unite in a ceremony (such as this)."

POSITIONS OF THE CONFEDERATE LORDS

Then Dekanahwideh said: " Skanyadahriyoh and Sadehkarohyhes shall be the uncles of Dehkaehyonh. We have now formed the confederacy, and we shall now have two sets of lords, one on each side of the council fire.

" Then also Hahyonhwatha and Ohdahtshedeh, father and son, shall sit and face each other, one on each side of the council fire.

" Then Skanyadahriyoh and Sadehkaronhyes shall sit on one side of the council fire and their nephew Dehkaehyonh shall sit on the opposite side.

" On one side of the council fire shall then be seated Hayonhwatha, Skanyadahriyoh and Sadehkaronhyes and on the opposite side shall sit Ohdahtshedeh and Dehkaehyonh and it shall be that we shall place Thadodahho in the center between the two sets of lords in the council.

We shall establish this relationship as follows: You, Thadodahho, shall be the father of Ohdahtshedeh and Dehkaehyonh and Hahyonhwatha, Skanyadahriyoh and Sadehkaronhyes shall be your brothers and you shall be the principals of the confederation which we have just made and completed.

"The first matter which I shall lay before you for your consideration is that as clans[1] are already established among the people, that the several clans form relations as brothers and cousins. .

So the lords answered and said: "We have decided to adopt your· suggestion."

Then he, Dekanahwideh said: "You, Hahyonhwatha, shall be the first to come and appoint your colleagues; you are of the Turtle Clan and shall therefore appoint your colleagues of the same clan."

Then when this was done Hahyonhwatha said: "This is now all ready, they have accepted and they are as follows: De-ha-rih-ho-ken, Sa-de-ka-rih-wa-deh."

Then Dekanahwideh said: "These shall therefore be your brother colleagues, you of the Turtle Clan. The brethern of the Wolf Clan shall be Sa-renh-ho-wa-neh,[2] De-yon-heh-kon[3] and On-renh-reh-ko-wah[4] and our cousins of the Bear Clan[5] shall be De-hen-nah-ke-re-neh,[6] Ah-stah-weh-seh-ron-ron-tha[7] and Soh-sko-ha-roh-wa-neh."[8]

Then Dekanahwideh said: "You, Hahyonhwatha, have now completed appointing your colleagues of your nation, as the Good Tidings of Peace and Power first originated at Kan-yen-geh, you shall be called Ka-nyen-geh-ha-kah[9] (Mohawk)."

Then Dekanahwideh said to Hahyonhwatha: "Now it shall fall upon your son Ohdahtshedeh who sits upon the opposite side of the council fire to appoint his brother colleagues." Then Ohdaht-shedeh appointed his brother colleagues of the Turtle Clan as follows: So-non-sehs[10] (Long House), Tho-nahonh-ken-ah[11] and A-tye-donj-eneh-tha.[12] And then he, Ta-na-o-ge-a, appointed his cousins of the Bear Clan as follows: Deh-ha-da-weh-de-yons,[13] Deh-ha-nyen-da-sah-deh[14] and Roh-wa-tsha-don-hon.[15]. These being the

---

[1] In some traditions the origin of the clans is stated as coeval with the beginning of the Confederacy; the more accurate view is that clans had long existed.
[2] Saihowa'ne.
[3] Dionhekwi.
[4] Orhehe"gowa.
[5] Hodigwaho".
[6] Dehenagai'ne', Dragging horns.
[7] Hastamĕ'sĕntä', Dropped rattle.
[8] Soskohai'ine'.
[9] Kanyĕⁿgĕhä'kä, Flint people; cf. kanyeñgĕ', flinty place.
[10] Sono"s'es.
[11] Tonaogeⁿ"ä.
[12] Hadyä'donent'ha, Swallows his own body.
[13] Dehadahoⁿdĕⁿyonk.
[14] Dehanye'däsäyeñ', Two legs together.
[15] Howashadoⁿonkho'.

second nation who accepted the message of Peace and Power and as
their settlement (from whence they came) was where the great
historic stone was situated, O-neh-yont, they were called O-neh-yo-
deh-ha-ka.[1] (Oneidas).

Then Dekanahwideh said: " It shall now rest with you, the
uncles, Skanyadahriyoh and Sadehkaronhyes, to appoint your
colleagues." Then Skanyadahriyoh said: " I (myself) shall appoint two of my brothers and my cousin, Sa-deh-ka-ronh-yes, shall
appoint two of his brethern." Then Skanyadahriyoh of the Turtle
Clan also said: " I therefore now appoint Ka-no-kye [2] of the Turtle
Clan and Sa-tye-na-wat [3] of the Bear Clan as my colleagues."

Then Sa-deh-ka-ronh-yes of the Snipe clan said: " I now appoint
Sa-ken-jo-wah-neh [4] of the Pigeon Hawk Clan and Nis-ha-yeh-
nehs [5] of the Snipe Clan as my colleagues."

Then Dekanahwideh said: " You have all appointed your colleagues and Kanokye [6] and Sakenhiwahneh [7] shall be cousins, and
Nishayehnehs and Satyenawat [8] shall be cousins." He then said,
" You, Skanyadahriyoh and Sadehkaronhyes of the Seneca Nation,
have now completed appointing your colleagues. Your settlement
is at the big mountain and you shall therefore be called O-neh-do-
wah-ka [9] (people of the big mountain) Senecas."

Then Dekanahwideh also said: "And now your son Deh-ka-eh-
yonh,[10] who sits on the opposite side of the council fire, shall name
and appoint his colleagues."

Then Dehkaehyonh of the Big Bear Clan appointed his colleagues,
saying as follows: " I shall now appoint my son Ji-non-dah-weh-
honh [11] of the Ball Clan and my mother Ka-da-gwa-seh [12] of the
Bear Clan and my brother Sho-yonh-wehs [13] of the Young Bear
Clan and Hathatrohneh [14] of the Turtle Clan, Dyon-yonh-koh [15] of
the Hand Clan, and ·Deh-yoh-doh-weh-kon [16] of the Wolf Clan, and

---

[1] Onäyont, or Hadiniyutgä".
[2] Ga'noⁿgäï'.
[3] Sadyĕ'nawat.
[4] Sagendjo'nä.
[5] Nishayene'/thä'.
[6] Ga'noⁿgä-ï'.
[7] Gakĕⁿiwanĕ'.
[8] Sadyĕ'nawat.
[9] Onundawäga, Nundawä'g'g, The hill people.
[10] De'hagä'eⁿyok.
[11] Djinon'däwe'hoⁿ.
[12] Kadăgwä'dji.
[13] Sho'yoñwĕs, Long wind.
[14] Ha-tha"troh-ne'.
[15] Dion'yoñko'.
[16] Diotowĕ"kon, Two colds.

Dyon-weh-thoh [1] of the Snipe Clan. These are the brother colleagues.

Then Deh-ka-eh-yonh appointed the cousin of the chief so named as follows: Nah-don-dah-heh-ha [2] of the Plover Clan and Des-da-heh [3] of the Young Bear Clan.

Then Dekanahwideh said: " You, Deh-ka-eh-yonh [4] of the Cayuga Nation, have now finished appointing your colleagues and you shall therefore be called Queh-you-gwe-hah-ka [5] (Cayuga) from your custom of portaging your canoe at a certain point in your settlement."

Then Dekanahwideh also said: " I shall now leave it to you, Tha-do-dah-ho, to appoint your colleagues."

Then Thadodahho of the Bear Clan said: " The first I shall appoint will be Onh-neh-sah-heh,[6] my cousin of the Beaver Clan, and Ska-nya-da-ge-wak [7] of the Snipe Clan and Ah-weh-ken-yath [8] of the Ball Clan and Deh-ha-yat-kwa-eh [9] of the Turtle Clan, and these are all brothers."

Then Thadodahho appointed their son, Ho-noh-we-yeh-deh [10] of the Wolf Clan, and then Thadodahho appointed his (Ho-noh-we-yeh-dehs) uncles as follows: Kon-weh-neh-senh-don of the Deer Clan and Ha-he-honk also of the Deer Clan and then their brothers as follows: Ho-yonh-nye-neh [11] of the Eel Clan and So-deh-kwa-seh [12] also of the Eel Clan and Sa-ko-ken-o-heh [13] of the Pigeon Hawk Clan, and then he (Thadodahha) appointed the sons of the latter as follows: Ho-sah-ha-wa [14] of the Deer Clan and Ska-nah-o-wa-da [15] of the Small Turtle Clan.

Then Dekanahwideh spoke and said: " We have now come to appointing the lords of the Five Nations hereby represented. These lords have now all been crowned with deer's horns in conformity and in a similar manner to Thadodahho who was first crowned. Therefore we have now accomplished and completed the work of laying the foundation of the confederation."

---

[1] Dionwäthoⁿ".
[2] Nadondahě'hä'.
[3] Desgä'hě'.
[4] De'hagä'eⁿyok.
[5] Gwⁱioⁿ'gwehä'ka, drawn up from the water people.
[6] Oni'säähä'.
[7] Skanyä'dadji'wak, Bitter throat.
[8] Awekeⁿ"yat, Near the shore.
[9] Dehayatgwa'iěⁿ. Red spots on wings.
[10] Honowiyě"ghï.
[11] Hoyoⁿnyěⁿ"ni'.
[12] Sodě'gwasěⁿ', Bruised all over.
[13] Sägogěⁿ"hě', I shall see them again.
[14] Hosähähwi.
[15] Skanawä'di.

PACIFICATION OF THE SENECA CHIEFS

Then Dekanahwideh spoke again and said: "I will now lay before your confederate council for your consideration one matter, and that is with reference to the conduct of the chief warriors of O-non-do-wa-ka (Senecas) who have refused to act in conjunction (or accord) with the lords in accepting the message of Good Tidings of Peace and Power."

Then the lords sent messengers for these two chief warriors of the Onondowaka (Senecas) to appear. And when they had come to the council, Lord Hahyonhwatha addressed these two chief warriors and said: "This Confederate Council now in session, together with their warriors, have unanimously accepted the message of Peace and Power and only you two chief warriors have not yet accepted and neither have expressed yourselves on this matter." Then Hayonhwatha further said: "This Confederate Council and their chief warriors have unanimously decided to leave all the war power and military control of the people in your hands providing you accept the message so that in case of war with other nations you shall be the leaders of the people of the Confederate Nations in defense of their confederacy." Then one of these two warriors spoke and said: "We are agreed to accept the message."

Then Dekanahwideh continued his address and said: "Now our power is full and complete and the two chief warriors of the Onondowaka (Senecas) have agreed to accept the message of Good Tidings; therefore we shall now add to the number of the lords of the confederacy (Eh-ji-twa-nah-stah-soh-de-renh),[1] we shall call it Ka-na-stah-ge-ko-wah[2] and these two chief warriors shall represent the door of the long house. Ka-noh-hah-ge-ko-wah,[3] meaning *the great black door through which all good and evil messages must come to reach the confederate house of lords or council,* shall be the name of the door, and if any person or nation has any news, message or business matter to lay before the Confederate Council, he or they must come through this door."

Then Dekanahwideh again further said, "We shall now crown these two chief warriors with deer's horns[4] and make them lords also. We shall now first crown with deer's horns Deyohneohkaweh[5] of the Wolf Clan and then we shall also crown Kanonkedahwe[6]

---

[1] Nedjitwanastashoñdä'.
[2] Kana'stadjigo'wa,˝Black timbers.
[3] Kanohwa'gēgo'na.
[4] Skänondonoñä"gä, Deer horns.
[5] Deyoñeñhogä"wĕ', Open door.
[6] Kanon'gida'hwĭ', Hair burned off.

of the Snipe Clan and these two shall be cousins and they shall guard the door of the long house.[1] And we shall now floor the doorway with slippery elm bark, and it shall be that whenever we have visitors from other nations who will have any message or any business to lay before the Confederate Council, these two door-keepers shall escort and convey them before the council, but whenever the visitor or visitors have come for evil purposes, then Kanonkedahwe shall take them by the hand and lead them in and they shall slip on the slippery elm bark and fall down and they shall be reduced to a heap of bones (He-yoh-so-jo-de-hah [2] in Onondaga language; Ehyohdonyohdaneh in Mohawk), and the bones of the enemy shall fall into a heap before the lords of the confederacy." (A heap of bones here signifies a conquered nation to be dealt with by the lords of the confederacy who shall decide as to what manner they will be allowed to exist in the future.)

LAWS OF THE CONFEDERACY

Then Dekanahwideh again said: " We have completed the Confederation of the Five Nations, now therefore it shall be that hereafter the lords who shall be appointed in the future to fill vacancies caused by death or removals shall be appointed from the same families and clans from which the first lords were created, and from which families the hereditary title of lordships shall descend."

Then Dekanahwideh further said: " I now transfer and set over to the women who have the lordships' title vested in them, that they shall in the future have the power to appoint the successors from time to time to fill vacancies caused by death or removals from whatever cause."

Then Dekanahwideh continued and said: " We shall now build a confederate council fire [3] from which the smoke shall arise and pierce the skies and all nations and people shall see this smoke. And now to you, Thadodahho, your brother and cousin colleagues shall be left the care and protection of the confederate council fire, by the Confederate Nations."

---

[2] The term " long house " as applied to the confederacy is not generally used by the Canadian Iroquois in their manuscript copies of the confederate laws and legends. A mistaken notion that the long house idea originated with Handsome Lake accounts for it. Newhouse used the term " long house " in his earlier manuscripts but later erased it supplying the word " confederacy." He explained this by saying that he had heard an old man say that long house meant Handsome Lake's new religion, the thing that destroyed the knowledge of the old ways. Thus the term was tabooed in connection with the confederacy.

[2] En'yosodjodä"ha.

[3] Gadjista'iĕn'.

Then Dekanahwideh further said: " The lords have unanimously decided to spread before you on the ground this great white wampum belt Ska-no-dah-ken-rah-ko-wah [1] and Ka-yah-ne-renh-ko-wah,[2] which respectfully signify purity and great peace, and the lords have also laid before you this great wing, Ska-weh-yeh-seh-ko-wah,[3] and whenever any dust or stain of any description falls upon the great belt of white wampum, then you shall take this great wing and sweep it clean." (Dust or stain means evil of any description which might have a tendency to cause trouble in the Confederate Council.)

Then Dekanahwideh said: " The lords of this confederacy have unanimously decided to lay by you this rod (Ska-nah-ka-res)[4] and whenever you see any creeping thing which might have a tendency to harm our grandchildren or see a thing creeping toward the great white wampum belt (meaning the Great Peace), then you shall take this rod and pry it away with it, and if you and your colleagues fail to pry the creeping, evil thing out, you shall then call out loudly that all the Confederate Nations may hear and they will come immediately to your assistance."

Then Dekanahwideh said: " Now you, the lords of the several Confederate Nations, shall divide yourselves and sit on opposite sides of the council fire as follows: " You and your brother colleagues shall sit on one side of the council fire (this was said to the Mohawks and the Senecas), and your sons, the Oneidas and Cayugas, shall sit on the opposite side of the council fire. Thus you will begin to work and carry out the principles of the Great Peace (Ka-yah-ne-renh-ko-wah) and you will be guided in this by the great white wampum belt (Ska-no-dah-ke-rah-ko-wah) which signifies Great Peace."

Then Dekanahwideh said: " You, Thadodahho, shall be the fire keeper, and your duty shall be to open the Confederate Council with praise and thanksgiving to the Great Ruler and close the same."

Then Dekanahwideh also said: " When the council is opened, Hayonhwatha and his colleagues shall be the first to consider and give their opinion upon any subject which may come before the council for consideration, and when they have arrived at a decision, then shall they transfer the matter to their brethren, the Senecas, for their consideration, and when they, the Senecas, shall have

---

[1] Skanon'dä'kerhagona.
[2] Gayanässhägona (Onon.).
[3] Another belt known as the great wing, Dega'yadonwa'ne (Onon.).
[4] Ganagä'is.

arrived at a decision on the matter then they shall refer it back to Hahyonhwatha and his colleagues. Then Hahyonhwatha will announce the decision to the opposite side of the council fire.   ·

"Then Ohdahtshedeh and his colleagues will consider the matter in question and when they have arrived at a decision they will refer the matter to their brethren, the Cayugas, for their consideration and after they have arrived at a decision, they will refer the matter back to Ohdahtshedeh and his colleagues. Then Ohdahtshedeh will announce their decision to the opposite side of the council fire. Then Hahyonhwatha will refer the matter to Thadodahho and his colleagues for their careful consideration and opinion of the matter in question and if Thadodahho and his colleagues find that the matter has not been well considered or decided, then they shall refer the matter back again to the two sides of the council fire, and they shall point out where, in their estimation, the decision was faulty and the question not fully considered, and then the two sides of the council will take up the question again and reconsider the matter, and after the two sides of the council have fully reconsidered the question, then Hahyonhwatha will again refer it to Thadohahho and his colleagues, then they will again consider the matter and if they see that the decision of the two sides of the council is correct, then Thadodahho and his colleagues will confirm the decision."

Then Dekanahwideh further said: "If the brethren of the Mohawks and the Senecas are divided in their opinion and can not agree on any matter which they may have for their consideration, then Hahyonhwatha shall announce the two decisions to the opposite of the council fire. Then Ohdahtshedeh and his brother colleagues, after they have considered the matter, and if they also are divided in their decision, shall so report, but if the divided factions each agree with the decision announced from the opposite side of the council, then Ohdahtshedeh shall also announce their two decisions to the other side of the council fire; then Hahyonhwatha shall refer the matter to Thadodahho and his colleagues who are the fire keepers. They will fully consider the matter and whichever decision they consider correct they will confirm."

Then Dekanahwideh said: "If it should so happen that the lords of the Mohawks and the lords of the Senecas disagree on any matter and also on the opposite side of the council fire, the lords of the Oneidas and the lords of the Cayugas disagree among themselves and do not agree with either of the two decisions of the

opposite side of the council fire but of themselves give two decisions which are diverse from each other, then Hahyonhwatha shall
refer the four decisions to Thadodahho and his colleagues who
shall consider the matter and give their decision and their decision
shall be final."

Then Dekanahwideh said: "We have now completed the system
for our Confederate Council."

Then Dekanahwideh further said: "We now, each nation, shall
adopt all the rules and regulations governing the Confederate
Council which we have here made and we shall apply them to all
our respective settlements and thereby we shall carry out the principles set forth in the message of Good Tidings of Peace and
Power, and in dealing with the affairs of our people of the various
dominions, thus we shall secure to them contentment and happiness."

Then he, Dekanahwideh, said: "You, Ka-nyen-ke-ha-ka (Mohawk), you, Dekarihoken, Hahyonhwatha and Sadekarihwadeh,
you shall sit in the middle between your brother lords of the Mohawks, and your cousin lords of the Mohawks, and all matters
under discussion shall be referred to you by your brother lords and
your cousin lords for your approval or disapproval.

"You, O-nen-do-wa-ka (Senecas), you, Skanyhadahriyoh and
Sadeh-ka-ronh-yes, you shall sit in the middle or between your
brother lords and your cousin lords of the Senecas and all matters
under discussion shall be referred to you by them for your approval
or disapproval.

"You, Ohnenyohdehaka (Oneidas), you, Ohdahtshedeh, Kanon-
kweyoudoh and Deyouhahkwedeh, you shall sit in the middle between your brother lords and your cousin lords of the Oneidas and
all matters under discussion shall be referred to you by them for
your approval or disapproval.

"You, the Que-yenh-kwe-ha-ka (Cayugas), you, Dekaehyonh
and Jinondahwehonh, you shall sit in the middle between your
lords and your cousin lords of the Cayugas and all matters under
discussion shall be referred to you by them for your approval or
disapproval."

Then Dekanahwideh said: "We have now completed arranging
the system of our local councils and we shall hold our annual Confederate Council at the settlement of Thadodahho, the capitol
or seat of government of the Five Nations' Confederacy."

Dekanahwideh said: "Now I and you lords of the Confederate
Nations shall plant a tree Ska-renj-heh-se-go-wah[1] (meaning a tall

---

[1] Skarhehe"gowa.

and mighty tree) and we shall call it Jo-ne-rak-deh-ke-wah [1] (the tree of the great long leaves).

"Now this tree which we have planted shall shoot forth four great, long, white roots (Jo-doh-ra-ken-rah-ko-wah).[2] These great, long, white roots shall shoot forth one to the north and one to the south and one to the east and one to the west, and we shall place on the top of it Oh-don-yonh [3] (an eagle) which has great power of long vision, and we shall transact all our business beneath the shade of this great tree. The meaning of planting this great tree, Skarehhehsegowah, is to symbolize Ka-yah-ne-renh-ko-wa, which means Great Peace, and Jo-deh-ra-ken-rah-ke-wah, meaning Good Tidings of Peace and Power. The nations of the earth shall see it and shall accept and follow the roots and shall follow them to the tree and when they arrive here you shall receive them and shall seat them in the midst of your confederacy. The object of placing an eagle, Skadji'enä', on the top of the great, tall tree is that it may watch the roots which extend to the north and to the south and to the east and to the west, and whose duty shall be to discover if any evil is approaching your confederacy, and he shall scream loudly and give the alarm and all the nations of the confederacy at once shall heed the alarm and come to the rescue."

Then Dekanahwideh again said: "We shall now combine our individual power into one great power which is this confederacy and we shall therefore symbolize the union of these powers by each nation contributing one arrow, which we shall tie up together in a bundle which, when it is made and completely tied together, no one can bend or break."

Then Dekanahwideh further said: "We have now completed this union by securing one arrow from each nation. It is not good that one should be lacking or taken from the bundle, for it would weaken our power and it would be still worse if two arrows were taken from the bundle. And if three arrows were taken any one could break the remaining arrows in the bundle."

Then Dekanahwideh continued his address and said: "We shall tie this bundle of arrows together with deer sinew which is strong, durable and lasting and then also this institution shall be strong and unchangeable. This bundle of arrows signifies that all the lords and all the warriors and all the women of the Confederacy have become united as one person."

[1] Onä"dedjisko'na skaskohäi'nä', Big long leaves, big limber tree.
[2] Djok'dehësgo'na.
[3] The "upper world eagle" is called skadji'ënä'.

Then Dekanahwideh again said: "We have now completed binding this bundle of arrows and we shall leave it beside the great tree (Skarehhehsegowah) and beside the Confederate Council fire of Thadodahho."

Then Dekanahwideh said: "We have now completed our power so that we the Five Nations' Confederacy shall in the future have one body, one head and one heart."

Then he (Dekanahwideh) further said: "If any evil should befall us in the future, we shall stand or fall united as one man."

Then Dekanahwideh said: "You lords shall be symbolized as trees of the Five Confederate Nations. We therefore bind ourselves together by taking hold of each other's hands firmly and forming a circle so strong that if a tree shall fall prostrate upon it, it could neither shake nor break it, and thus our people and our grandchildren shall remain in the circle in security, peace and happiness. And if any lord who is crowned with the emblem of deer's horns shall break through this circle of unity, his horns shall become fastened in the circle, and if he persists after warning from the chief matron, he shall go through it without his horns and the horns shall remain in the circle, and when he has passed through the circle, he shall no longer be lord, but shall be as an ordinary warrior and shall not be further qualified to fill any office."

Then Dekanahwideh further said: "We have now completed everything in connection with the matter of Peace and Power, and it remains only for us to consider and adopt some measure as to what we shall do with reference to the disposal of the weapons of war which we have taken from our people."

Then the lords considered the latter and decided that the best way which they could adopt with reference to the disposal of the weapons would be to uproot the great tall tree which they had planted and in uprooting the tree a chasm would form so deep that it would come or reach the swift current of the waters under it, into which the weapons of war would be thrown, and they would be borne and swept away forever by the current so that their grandchildren would never see them again. And they then uprooted the great tree and they cast into the chasm all manner of weapons of war which their people had been in the custom of using, and they then replaced the tree in its original position.

Then Dekanahwideh further continued and said: "We have completed clearing away all manner of weapons from the paths of our people."

Then Dekanahwideh continued and said: "We have still one matter left to be considered and that is with reference to the hunting grounds of our people from which they derive their living."

They, the lords, said with reference to this matter: "We shall now do this: We shall only have one dish (or bowl) in which will be placed one beaver's tail and we shall all have coequal right to it, and there shall be no knife in it, for if there be a knife in it, there would be danger that it might cut some one and blood would thereby be shed." (This one dish or bowl signifies that they will make their hunting grounds one common tract and all have a coequal right to hunt within it.[1] The knife being prohibited from being placed into the dish or bowl signifies that all danger would be removed from shedding blood by the people of these different nations of the confederacy caused by differences of the right of the hunting grounds.)

Then Dekanahwideh continued and said: "We have now accomplished and completed forming the great Confederacy of the Five Nations together with adopting rules and regulations in connection therewith."

Then he, Dekanahwideh, continued and said: "I will now leave all matters in the hands of your lords and you are to work and carry out the principles of all that I have just laid before you for the welfare of your people and others, and I now place the power in your hands and to add to the rules and regulations whenever necessary and I now charge each of you lords that you must never seriously disagree among yourselves. You are all of equal standing and of equal power, and if you seriously disagree the consequences will be most serious and this disagreement will cause you to disregard each other, and while you are quarreling with each other, the white panther [2] (the fire dragon of discord) [3] will come and take your rights and privileges away. Then your grandchildren will suffer and be reduced to poverty and disgrace."

Then he, Dekanahwideh, continued and said: "If this should ever occur, whoever can climb a great tree (Skarehhehsegowah) and ascend to the top, may look around over the landscape and will see if there is any way or place to escape to from the calamity of the threatening poverty and disgrace, so that our children may have a home where they may have peace and happiness in their day.

---

[1] Dioⁿdowĕs'tă', hunting ground.
[2] Usually translated *lion*.
[3] Oshondowĕk'gona.

And if it so occurs that he can not see any way or place to escape the calamity, he will then descend the tree. You will then look for a great swamp elm tree (Aka-rah-ji-ko-wah) [1] and when you have found one with great large roots extending outwards and bracing outwards from the trunk, there you will gather your heads together."

Then Dekanahwideh continued and said: " It will be hard and your grandchildren will suffer hardship. And if it may so occur that the heads of the people of the confederacy shall roll and wander away westward, if such thing should come to pass, other nations shall see your heads rolling and wandering away and they shall say to you, ' You belong to the confederacy, you were a proud and haughty people once,' and they shall kick the heads with scorn, and they shall go on their way, but before they shall have gone far they shall vomit up blood." (Meaning that the confederacy shall still have power enough to avenge their people.)

Then Dekanahwideh further said: " There may be another serious trouble. Other nations may cut or hack these four great roots which grow from the great tree which we have planted and one of the roots shoots to the north and one to the south and one to the east and one to the west. Whenever such thing happens, then shall great trouble come into the seat of your lords of the confederacy."

Then Dekanahwideh said: " I shall now therefore charge each of your lords, that your skin be of the thickness of seven spreads of the hands [2] (from end of thumb to the end of the great finger) so that no matter how sharp a cutting instrument may be used it will not penetrate the thickness of your skin. (The meaning of the great thickness of your skins is patience and forbearance, so that no matter what nature of question or business may come before you, no matter how sharp or aggravating it may be, it will not penetrate to your skins, but you will forbear with great patience and good will in all your deliberations and never disgrace yourselves by becoming angry.) You lords shall always be guided in all your councils and deliberations by the Good Tidings of Peace and Power."

Then Dekanahwideh said: " Now, you lords of the different nations of the confederacy, I charge you to cultivate the good feeling of friendship, love and honor amongst yourselves. I have now

---

[1] Gain'dadjikgo'na.
[2] Djaduk'nioyionk'gage', seven fingers.

fulfilled my duty in assisting you in the establishment and organization of this great confederacy, and if this confederation is carefully guarded it shall continue and endure from generation to generation and as long as the sun shines. I shall now, therefore, go home, conceal and cover myself with bark and there shall none other be called by my name."

Then Dekanahwideh further continued and said: " If at any time through the negligence and carelessness of the lords, they fail to carry out the principles of the Good Tidings of Peace and Power and the rules and regulations of the confederacy and the people are reduced to poverty and great suffering, I will return."

Then Dekanahwideh said: "And it shall so happen that when you hear my name mentioned disrespectfully without reason or just cause, but spoken in levity, you shall then know that you are on the verge of trouble and sorrow. And it shall be that the only time when it shall be proper for my name to be mentioned is when the condolence ceremonies are being performed or when the Good Tidings of Peace and Power which I have established and organized are being discussed or rehearsed."

Then the lords (Ro-de-ya-ner-shoh) said: " We shall begin to work and carry out the instructions which you, Dekanahwideh, have laid before us."

Then they said: " We shall therefore begin first with the Confederate Council of the Five Nations and other nations who shall accept and come under the Great Law of the confederacy will become as props, supports of the long house.

" The pure white wampum strings shall be the token or emblem of the council fire, and it shall be that when the fire keepers shall open the council, he shall pick up this string of wampum and hold it on his hand while he is offering thanksgiving to the Great Ruler and opening the council." And then they also said: " That while the council is in session the strings of the white wampum should be placed conspicuously in their midst and when they should adjourn then, the fire keepers should pick up these strings of wampum again, offer thanksgiving, close the council and all business in connection with the council should then be adjourned."

Then they said: " We shall now establish as a custom that when our annual Confederate Council shall meet we shall smoke the pipe of peace." [1]

---

[1] Swĕⁿno"ăndwahē'ⁿ'.

And they, the lords, then said: " We shall now proceed to define the obligations and position of the lords of the Confederacy as follows:

" If a lord is found guilty of wilful murder, he shall be deposed without the warning (as shall be provided for later on) by the lords of the confederacy, and his horns (emblem of power) shall be handed back to the chief matron of his family and clan.

" If a lord is guilty of rape he shall be deposed without the usual warning by the lords of the confederacy, and his horns (the emblem of power) shall be handed back to the chief matron of his family and clan.

" If a lord is found guilty of theft, he shall be deposed without the usual warning by the lords of the confederacy and his horns (the emblem of power) shall be handed back to the chief matron of his family and clan.

" If a lord is guilty of unwarrantably opposing the object of decisions of the council and in that his own erroneous will in these matters be carried out, he shall be approached and admonished by the chief matron of his family and clan to desist from such evil practices and she shall urge him to come back and act in harmony with his brother lords.

" If the lord refuses to comply with the request of the chief matron of his family and clan and still persists in his evil practices of unwarrantably opposing his brother lords, then a warrior of his family and clan will also approach him and admonish him to desist from pursuing his evil course.

" If the lord still refuses to listen and obey, then the chief matron and warrior shall go together to the warrior and they shall inform him that they have admonished their lord and he refused to obey. Then the chief warrior will arise and go there to the lord and will say to him: ' Your nephew and niece have admonished you to desist from your evil course, and you have refused to obey.' Then the chief warrior will say: ' I will now admonish you for the last time and if you continue to resist, refuse to accede and disobey this request, then your duties as lord of our family and clan will cease, and I shall take the deer's horns from off your head, and with a broad edged stone axe I shall cut down the tree' (meaning that he shall be deposed from his position as lord or chief of the confederacy). Then, if the lord merits dismissal, the chief warrior shall hand back the deer's horns (the emblem of power) of the deposed lord to the chief matron of the family or clan."

Whenever it occurs that a lord is thus deposed, then the chief matron shall select and appoint another warrior of her family or clan and crown him with the deer's horns and thus a new lord shall be created in the place of the one deposed.

The lords of each of the confederate nations shall have one assistant and their duty, each of them, shall be to carry messages through the forests between our settlements and also in the absence of the lord through illness or any other impediment he shall be deputed by him (his lord) to act in his place in council.

The lords then said: "We have now completed defining the obligations and positions of a lord (Royaner) and therefore in accordance with the custom which we now have established, it shall be that when a lord is deposed and the deer's horns (emblem of power) are taken from him, he shall no longer be allowed to sit in council or even hold an office again."

Then the lords continued and said: "What shall we do in case some of us lords are removed by sudden death and in whom so much dependence is placed?"

"In such case (this shall be done), the chief matron and the warriors of the family and clan of the deceased lord, shall nominate another lord from the warriors of the family and clan of the dead lord to succeed him, then the matter will be submitted to the brother lords and if they (the brother lords) confirm the nomination, then the matter will be further submitted to their cousin lords and if they also confirm the nomination, then the candidate shall be qualified to be raised by the condolence ceremony (Honda nas)."

Then the lords continued and said: "In case the family and clan in which a lordship title[1] is vested shall become extinct, this shall be done: It shall then be transferred and vested in the hands of the confederate lords and they will consider the matter and nominate and appoint[2] a successor from any family of the brother lords of the deceased lord, and the lords may in their discretion vest the said lordship title in some family, and such title will remain in that family so long as the lords are satisfied.

"If ever it should occur that the chief matron in a family or clan in which a lordship title is vested should be removed by death and leave female infants who, owing to their infancy can not nominate a candidate to bear their lordship title, then the lords (of the same nation) at their pleasure may appoint an adult female of a sister family who shall make a temporary appointment, shall

---

[1] Nihosĕnnodĕ', *the title.*
[2] The term is Nahoⁿyawădägä yä'dĕⁿ.

come before the lords and request that the lordship title be restored to them, then the lords must obtain the title and restore it accordingly."

Then the lords continued and said: "We now have completed laying the foundation of our rules and methods (Kayanehrenokowa) and we will now proceed to follow and carry out the working of these rules and methods of the confederacy, and the local affairs of our respective settlements, and whenever we discover a warrior who is wise and trustworthy and who will render his services for the benefit of the people and thus aid the lords of the confederacy, we will claim him into our midst and confer upon him the title of 'He has sprung up as a Pine Tree [1]' (Eh-ka-neh-do-deh) and his title shall only last during his lifetime[2] and shall not be hereditary and at his death it shall die with him."

Then the lords (Rodiyaner) again considered and said: "We have now completed the appointment of our lords. It may so occur that before we may be quietly reseated in our respective places, we may sustain another loss by death (of a lord) and in that case we shall do this: While yet the dying lord is suffering in the agonies of death, his brother lords will come and remove his deer's horns from his head and place them beside the wall and if by the will of the Great Ruler he recovers from his illness, he shall then reclaim his crown of deer's horns and resume the duties of a lord. They further considered this matter and said: "While the lord is ill we will place a string of black wampum at the head of his bed and if he dies anyone belonging to his clan may take this string of black wampum and announce his death to the whole circle of the confederacy as follows:

"If a Lord among the three brothers,[3] Mohawk, Seneca and Onondaga, dies, the chief warrior or a warrior will convey the string of black wampum to their son, Ohdahtshedeh or Dehkaehyonh, or their colleagues, and he will leave it there, and while on his way ·from the home of the dead lord he will repeat at regular intervals the mourning cry, three times thus —'Kwa – – – ah; Kwa – – – ah; Kwa – – – ah.'

"Then Ohdahtshedeh or Dehkaehyonh or their colleagues will convey the string of black wampum to their four brothers, and so

---

[1] Waganeda'nyŭk.

[2] Enkanedoden, *the pine tree shall grow.*

[3] A'sě'nihoñdadĕn"gĕn, three brothers.

on until the whole circle of the confederacy shall become aware of the death of the lord. And if a lord among the two (now four) brothers (the Oneida and Cayuga) dies, then the chief warrior or any warrior deputed will carry and convey the string of black wampum to Dekarihoken or Skanyadahriyoh or Thadodahho, or their brother colleagues, and the chief warrior or any warrior so deputed will, while on his way, repeat the mourning cry three times at regular intervals as follows: 'Kwa –––ah; Kwa –––ah; Kwa –––ah;'[1] and if a chief warrior on either side of the council dies (or now if a chief of Tuscarora, Delaware, Nanticoke or Tuteli member[2] of the council dies), then the mourning messenger will, while on his way to announce the death of either of these, repeat the mourning cry twice only as follows: 'Kwa –––ah; Kwa –––ah.' In case of the sudden death of a lord, then his colleagues will remove his crown of deer's horns and will put it to one side where the chief matron of the family or clan to which he belonged will find and take it up again.

"If from whatever cause the crown of deer's horns are not removed from the head of the lord at the time of his death, then his colleagues will remove the same at the time of his burial and will place it beside the grave where the chief matron will find and pick it up again."

Then the lords said: "If a lord dies we will do this: we will put up a pole horizontally, and we will hang a pouch upon it, and we will put into the pouch a short string of wampum, and the side of the council fire which has sustained the loss by death shall do it and the side which has not sustained the loss will depute one of their lords to take the pouch off the pole, then he shall follow the path and go to the opposite side of the council fire where the loss has been sustained, and when he arrives at the house where the lord died he will stand at one end of the hearth and he will speak consoling words to the bereaved, and he will cheer them up, and this will be our mode of condolence, and these shall consist of eleven passages to be expressed in this condolence (Ka-ne-kon-kets-kwa-se-rah)[3] and eleven wampum strings shall be used in this ceremony.

---

[1] Kwa ă".

[2] Captive or adopted tribes having a seat and a voice in their own national affairs but no voice in the confederate council.

[3] Ganigohagetc'gwĕn', Their spirits are lifted up.

THE CONDOLENCE CEREMONY

The beginning of the condolence ceremony used immediately after the death of a chief (or lord) and which is subsequently followed by the preliminary ceremony called, "At the wood's edge."

1 Now hear us our uncles, we have come to condole with you in your great bereavement.

We have now met in dark sorrow to lament together over the death of our brother lord. For such has been your loss. We will sit together in our grief and mingle our tears together, and we four brothers will wipe off the tear from your eyes, so that for a day period you might have peace of mind. This we say and do, we four brothers.

2 Now hear us again, for when a person is in great grief caused by death, his ears are closed up and he can not hear and such is your condition now.

We will therefore remove the obstruction (grief) from your ears, so that for a day period you may have perfect hearing again. This we say and do, we four brothers.

3 Continue to hear the expression of us four brothers, for when a person is in great sorrow his throat is stopped with grief and such is your case; now, we will therefore remove the obstruction (grief) so that for a day period you may enjoy perfect breathing and speech; this we say and do, we four brothers.

The foregoing part of the condolence ceremony is to be performed outside of the place of meeting.

Then the bereaved will appoint two of their chief warriors to conduct the four brothers into the place of meeting.

4 Continue to hear the expression of us four brothers, for when a person is in great grief caused by death, he appears to be deformed, so that our forefathers have made a form which their children may use in condoling with each other (Ja-wek-ka-ho-denh) which is that they will treat him a dose of soft drink (medicine) and which when it is taken and settled down in the stomach it will pervade the whole body and strengthen him and restore him to a perfect form of man. This we say and do, we four brothers.

5 Continue to hear the expression of us four brothers. Now

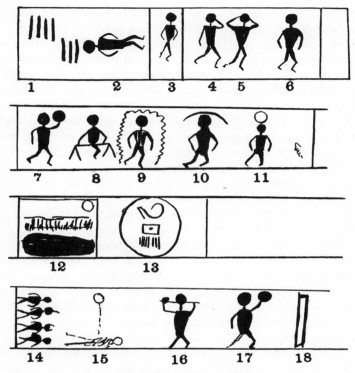

PICTOGRAPHS ON RECORD STAFF

(1) The seven parallel lines represent the four elder brothers and the three younger brothers of the eight clans who are mourning. (2) The prostrate figure is that of the dead chief of the eighth clan. (3) A chanter of condolence appears to comfort the sorrowing friends and relatives, (4) he lifts one hand to say, "we are mourning," (5) then both arms are raised to the heavens and he asks the people to look to the sun and be gladdened, and (6) then he points to the earth where sorrow shall be buried. (7) "Behold the sun in its brightness shining (8) for there sits the new chief (royaneh) on a bench with four legs, like the roots of the great tree." (9) Now the chief is in a bower of pine boughs where his enemies cannot discover him, there he sits and thinks of his duties. (10) Night covers him and he still meditates, (11) but the morning sun comes again like a circle of horns over his head and he approaches like the new sun. It shines over the new chief and (12) it shines over the grave of the chief who died. (13) Then shall the clans come in council and the new chief appears before them on a new mat, but the path is not yet clear or straight, until the (14) mourning clans arise and take their minds from (15) the dead chief whose spirit has gone after ten days from his body. Then (16) the new chief takes his staff and (17) goes forward with his sun before him, as a light to his mind and that people may see he is royaneh. Then (18) is his door open and his path made clear.

when a person is brought to grief by death, such person's seat or bed seems stained with human blood; such is now your case.

We therefore wipe off those stains with soft linen so that your seat and bed may be clean and so that you may enjoy peace for a day, for we may scarcely have taken our seats before we shall be surprised to hear of another death. This we say and do, we four brothers.

6 Continue to hear the expression of us four brothers. When a person is brought to grief through death, he is confined in the darkness of deep sorrow, and such is now the case of your three brothers. This we say, we four brothers.

7 When a person is brought to grief by death, he seems to lose sight of the sky (blinded with grief) and he is crushed with sorrow. We therefore remove the mist from your eyes, so that the sky may be clear to you. This we say and do, we four brothers.

8 When a person is brought to grief by death he seems to lose the sight of the sun; this is now your case. We therefore remove the mist so that you may see the sun rising over the trees or forest in the east, and watch its course and when it arrives in midsky, it will shed forth its rays around you, and you shall begin to see your duties and perform the same as usual. This we say and do, we four brothers.

9 Now when the remains are laid and cause the mound of clay (grave), we till the ground and place some nice grass over it and place a nice slab over it, so that his body (that of the dead lord) may quietly lay in his resting place, and be protected from the heavy wind and great rain storms. This we say and do, we four brothers.

10 Now continue to listen, for when a person is brought to grief, and such is your condition, the sticks of wood from your fire are scattered caused by death, so we the four brothers, will gather up the sticks of wood and rekindle the fire, and the smoke shall rise and pierce the sky, so that all the nations of the confederacy may see the smoke, and when a person is in great grief caused by the death of some of our rulers, the head is bowed down in deep sorrow. We therefore cause you to stand up again, our uncles and surround the council fire again and resume your duties. This we say and do, we four brothers.

11 Continue to listen for when the Great Spirit created us, he created a woman as the helpmate of man, and when she is called

Record staff containing the history of a condolence and raising ceremony of a royaneh or councellor.

away by death, it is grievously hard for had she been allowed to live she may have raised a family to inhabit the earth, and so we four brothers raise the woman again (to encourage and cheer up their downcast spirits) so that you may cheerfully enjoy peace and happiness for a day. This we say and do, we four brothers.

12 Now my uncle lords, you have two relations, a nephew and a niece. They are watching your course. Your niece may see that you are making a misstep and taking a course whereby your children may suffer ruin or a calamity, or it may be your nephew who will see your evil course and never bear to listen when the woman or warrior approach you and remind you of your duties, and ask you to come back and carry out your obligations as a Royaner or lord of the band. This we say and do, we four brothers.

13 They say it is hard for any one to allow his mind to be troubled too greatly with sorrow. Never allow yourself to be led to think of destroying yourself by committing suicide for all things in this world is only vanity. Now we place in your midst a torch. We all have an equal share in the said light, and would now call all the Rodhanersonh (lords) to their places and each perform the duties conferred upon each of them. This we say and do, we four brothers.

Now we return to you the wampum which we received from you when you suffered the loss by death. We will therefore now conclude our discourse. Now point out to me the man whom I am to proclaim as chief in place of the deceased.

THE HIAWATHA TRADITION

Related by Baptist Thomas (Sa ha whi) an Onondaga (Turtle Clan) as
he had it from Thomas Commissary (Ostowägō'nă* Big Feather).

When a man's heart is heavy with sorrow because of death he
wanders aimlessly (wa-hē-des-yas-sha-dā''-na').[1] That is why
Ha-yĕnt-watha went away from the Mohawks. His only sister — he
had only one sister — died. She was Da-si-yu' and she died. She
was not a comely woman but her brother loved her and so Ha-yent-
watha mourned and no one came to comfort him. Not one person
came to him in his grief to comfort him, therefore his mind was
clouded in darkness. His throat was dry and heavy and bitter.
So he went away for he did not wish to stay among a people who
had no hearts of sympathy for sorrow. The Mohawks had grown
callous and so accustomed to troubled times that they did not
care for the sorrows of others and even despised the tears of
mourners. They were always fighting. Even they sent out war
parties among their own relatives in other towns. Hayentwatha
often said this was wrong but no one listened to him. So when
his great sorrow came he went away. He took a canoe and went
upstream. He paddled up the Mohawk river and when he landed
to camp he talked to himself about his sorrow. " I would comfort others in sorrow," he said, " but no one comforts me."

After a long time he reached the portage and carried his canoe
to Wood creek.[2] Here he camped three days. He took up his
journey again and camped at one of two islands and went through
Oneida lake. Then he went up the river and came to Three River
point. Here he heard a broken branch creaking against a tree. It
cried giis, giis, giis, so he named this spot Dyo-neda-tonk. So then
he went up the river into Onondaga lake. He landed on the north
side, (near the present site of Liverpool),[4] and built a hut. Here
he made a camp fire and stayed for three days. Then he saw the
monster. He was a long way off and he was looking at Hayĕntwatha. So Hayĕntwatha moved his camp but the next morning
the monster came nearer. This being was Thă-do-dā'-ho'. So
the next evening Hayĕntwatha moved his camp again and in the

---

[1] Onondaga vocabulary.
[2] This portage is called De-hon-yugwha-tha.
[3] Odĭ-nĕs'-shi-yū, People of the sand and they shall be of the Snipe Clan.
[4] This spot he named Gă'skwasoëtge'.

morning again he saw the monster before his camp fire. It seems that he had snakes in his hair and covering his shoulders and one great one came up from his thighs and went over his shoulders. Hayĕntwatha looked at Thădodaho and said " Shon-nis'?" (who are you?) The monstrous being did not reply but his face looked very angry.

Again Hayĕntwatha changed his camp and built a shelter on one of the two islands in the lake. This spot he named Si-ye-ge. As before, the monster camped silently near him. He was nearer than ever before and seemed watching him from the corner of his eyes.

So then again Hayĕntwatha moved his camping place. He crossed the lake and camped at the point on the south shore. As he built his lodge he looked inland and saw seated on a knoll, the monster Thădodā'ho'. He then observed that what ever move he made the snake-bearing monster was ever before him. He seemed to anticipate his movements. This fact frightened Hayĕntwatha and he prepared to take up his journey again.

His sorrow was not diminished but hung like a black cloud over him. His heart was very heavy and there was no clear sky for him. He carried no war weapons and the monster frightened him. So Hayĕntwatha journeyed in his canoe up Onondaga creek. So in this manner he came to the Onondaga village. How long he stayed at the Onondaga town, my grandfather, Tom Commissary, did not say. Some say he stayed there and married. Some say he enjoined the Onondaga towns to be at peace and stop their quarreling. After a time when another great sorrow came, some say it was because his daughters died, he again continued his journey but Thădodā'ho' went before him and Hayĕntwatha saw him.

So Hayĕntwatha went south up Onondaga creek and he came to a certain spot where a brook enters the creek[1] and he saw there a pond and a grassy place. There it is said he saw a very large turtle and some women playing ball. Some say boys were playing ball but I say that women were playing ball because my grandfather said so. So Hayĕntwatha called this place Dwĕn-the'-gäs, and said from this spot comes the Ball Clan (Dwĕn-the-gäs Hadinya'-tĕnʼ) of the Great Turtle.

Hayĕntwatha continued his journey and went over Bear mountain.[2] First he camped at night at the foot of the high hill. Here

---

[1] A brook running through Cardiff, N. Y.
[2] Southwest of Cardiff, Lafayette township, Onondaga county.

he built a shelter. That night he heard a song and its words were what he believed and had spoken many times to the Onondaga chiefs and to the Mohawks.

In the morning he ascended the mountain and there he found five stalks of corn springing from four roots and there was only one large stalk at the root from which the five stalks grew. On each stalk were three large ears of ripe corn. Near the corn he saw a large turtle with a red and yellow belly and it was the turtle that danced. He danced the Ostowago'na, the great feather dance. So then Hayĕntwatha said "Did you sing last night? I heard singing." Then the turtle replied, " I sang. Now this is the great corn and you will make the nations like it. Three ears represent the three nations[1] and the five stalks from a single stalk represent the five nations and the four roots go to the north and west the south and the east."

Hayĕntwatha proceeded on his journey and after a time he came to a group of lakes. He called it Tgă-ni-yä-da-hä-nioñ (the lake group on hill) (the present Tully group of lakes). On one of these lakes were many ducks swimming very closely together. The ducks covered the lake. So Hayĕntwatha stopped to look at so strange a sight. " What are you doing there, so many of you?" he said all to himself. The ducks heard him and at the same moment, whoo! every one of them flew into the air and lifted up the water, so quickly did they fly up. The bottom of the lake was left dry and Hayĕntwatha walked across it. As he walked he saw many small shells and he gathered a deer skin full of shells so many were there. When he reached the opposite shore he saw a man limping toward him. He was dragging a large snapping turtle. " What troubles your walk?" asked Hayĕntwatha. " I have a blister on my crotch " answered the man.

Then said Hayĕntwatha to himself, " In the future this man and his brothers with all his female relations shall be known as Hodī-ho'ō'ĕn'h. They have blisters on their crotches and they shall be of the Small Turtle Clan."

Then again he proceeded on his journey and after a time he saw an old corn field and a field shelter house with a roof of stalks. So he went there for a camp.

The great sorrow had not left him so he sat by his campfire and talked to himself. Then he strung up the shells and placed three strings on a pole laid across two upright poles. He continued to talk.

---

[1] The original confederates were the Mohawk, Oneida and Onondaga.

A little girl saw the smoke of the campfire and went out into the field. She went close to the shelter house and listened to what Hayĕntwatha said. Then she returned and told her father what she had seen. He then sent two men to invite Hayĕntwatha to the village.

Hayĕntwatha did not reply to them but with his head bowed before his fire he said aloud to himself, " These people should know that every invitation should be confirmed by a string of shells such as hang before me; they should give me a strand (ä-sa-na-tcik')."

The men returned to their chief and told what they had heard. Then he ordered them to string up some beads of large porcupine quills and carry them to the stranger to become words of invitation. This they did and Hayĕntwatha said, " It is now right."

The warriors who came with the two messengers returned to the village and after smoking his pipe Hayĕntwatha went to the village with the two guides. At the settlement the council was in session and Hayĕntwatha was invited to sit on one side of the fire. The discussion was a spirited one and none of the head men could agree on any question. During the debate a great man came in. The room was crowded and the head man who had invited Hayĕntwatha arose and gave his place to the great man. The debate continued and Hayĕntwatha silently departed, angry at the slight he had received. In the council room the debate was as devoid of result as before when the head man arose and said, " I have staying with me a friend. He is a stranger and I do not know from whence he came. Perhaps he can settle our dispute."

Then everyone looked for the stranger but Hayĕntwatha was not there. The head man could not find him. So then the head man said, " I think I have made a great mistake. He must have been a great man and I have offended him. He has magically disappeared."

So the man who was able to settle the quarrel of the people was not there.

When Hayĕntwatha left the council he journeyed on to the outskirts of another settlement and made a camp. Here he commanded his two guardian birds to come to him. Their names were Hä'-goks' and Skadjiē'na.[1] He said, " Go and see if smoke arises from any settlement."

Then the birds arose and when they returned they said, " Smoke arises from the Oneida villages."

---

[1] Said by some informants to have been two human messengers bearing these names and not actually birds.

So then Hayĕntwatha went eastward and in all the Oneida towns he heard the people talking about the Great Law and about the Great Peace. Dekanawida had told of it but the people failed to understand it. So then Hayĕntwatha said, " I must meet that man for my mind is not yet unburdened." So he continued on his journey down the river, toward the Mohawk country, for he greatly wished to see Dekanawida.

APPENDIX A

THE PASSAMAQUODDY WAMPUM RECORDS

RECORDED BY J. D. PRINCE [1]

Many bloody fights had been fought, many men, women and children had been tortured by constant and cruel wars until some of the wise men among the Indians began to think that something must be done, and that whatever was to be done should be done quickly. They accordingly sent messengers to all parts of the country, some going to the south, others to the east, and others to the west and northwest. Some even went as far as the Wabanaki.[2] It was many months before the messengers reached the farthest tribes. When they arrived at each nation, they notified the people that the great Indian nations of the Iroquois, Mohawks and others had sent them to announce the tidings of a great Lagootwagon or general council for a treaty of peace. Every Indian who heard the news rejoiced, because they were all tired of the never-ending wars. Every tribe, therefore, sent two or more of their cleverest men as representatives to the great council.

When all the delegates were assembled they began to deliberate concerning what was best to do, as they all seemed tired of their evil lives. The leading chief then spoke as follows: "As we look back upon our blood-stained trail we see that many wrongs have been done by all of our people. Our gory tomahawks, clubs, bows and arrows must undoubtedly be buried for ever." It was decided, therefore, by all concerned to make a general Lagootwagon or treaty of peace, and a day was appointed when they should begin the rites.

For seven days, from morning till night, a strict silence was observed, during which each representative deliberated on the speech

---

[1] See "Klooskape, The Master." Funk & Wagnalls Co., 1899.
[2] According to Indian tradition, six Iroquoian tribes united in confederation in the interests of peace. This was the famous League of the Six Nations: Onondagas, Mohawks, Oneidas, Senecas, Cayugas and Tuscaroras. The first five of these completed their league as early as the middle of the fifteenth century under the Onondaga chief Hiawatha. The object of the federation was to abolish war altogether (see Brinton, The American Race, p.82,83). It is evident that the Passamaquoddy tradition embodied in this part of the Wampum Records refers to these proposals made by their Iroquois neighbors.

he should make and tried to discover the best means for checking the war. This was called the " Wigwam of silence."

After this, they held another wigwam called m'sittakw-wen tlewestoo, or " Wigwam of oratory." The ceremonies then began. Each representative recited the history of his nation, telling all the cruelties, tortures and hardships they had suffered during their wars and stating that the time had now come to think of and take pity on their women and children, their lame and old,. all of whom had suffered equally with the strongest and bravest warriors. When all the speeches had been delivered, it was decided to erect an extensive fence and within it to build a large wigwam. In this wigwam they were to make a big fire and, having made a switch or whip, to place " their father " as a guard over the wigwam with the whip in his hand. If any of his children did wrong he was to punish them' with the whip. Every child of his within the inclosure must therefore obey his orders implicitly. His duty also was to keep replenishing the fire in the wigwam so that it should not go out. This is the origin of the Wampum laws.

The fence typified a treaty of peace for all the Indian nations who took part in the council, fourteen in number, of which there are many tribes. All these were to go within the fence and dwell there, and if any should do wrong they would be liable to punishment with the whip at the hands of " their father." The wigwam within the fence represented a universal house for all the tribes, in which they might live in peace, without disputes and quarrels, like members of one family. The big fire (ktchi squt) in the wigwam denoted the warmth of the brotherly love engendered in the Indians by their treaty. The father ruling the wigwam was the great chief who lived at Caughnawaga. The whip in his hand was the type of the Wampum laws, disobedience to which was punishable by consent of all the tribes mentioned in the treaty.

After this, they proceeded to make lesser laws, all of which were to be recorded by means of wampum, in order that they could be read to the Indians from time to time. Every feast, every ceremony, therefore, has its own ritual in the wampum; such as the burial and mourning rites after the death of a chief, the installation of a chief, marriage etc. There were also salutation and visiting wampum.

CEREMONIES CUSTOMARY AT THE DEATH OF A CHIEF

When the chief of the tribe died, his flag pole was cut down and burnt, and his warlike appurtenances, bows and arrows, tomahawk and flag were buried with him. The Indians mourned for him one year, after which the Pwutwusimwuk or leading men were summoned by the tribe to elect a new chief. The members of one tribe alone could not elect their own chief; according to the common laws of the allied nations, he had to be chosen by a general wigwam. Accordingly, after the council of the leading men had assembled, four or six canoes were dispatched to the Micmac, Penobscot and Maliseet tribes if a Passamaquoddy chief had died.[1] These canoes bore each a little flag in the bow as a sign that the mission on which the messengers came was important. On the arrival of the messengers at their destination, the chief of the tribe to which they came called all his people, children, women and men, to meet the approaching boats. The herald springing to land first sang his salutation song (n'skawewintuagunul), walking back and forth before the ranks of the other tribe. When he had finished his chant the other Indians sang their welcoming song in reply.

As soon as the singing was over they marched to some imwewigwam or meeting house to pray together. The visiting Indians were then taken to a special wigwam allotted to their use over which a flag was set. Here they were greeted informally by the members of the tribe with hand-shaking etc. The evening of the first day was spent in entertaining the visitors.

On the next day the messengers sent to the chief desiring to see all the tribe assembled in a gwandowanek or dance hall. When the tribe had congregated there, the strangers were sent for, who, producing their strings of wampum to be read according to the law of the big wampum, announced the death of the chief of their tribe, " their eldest boy " (ktchi w'skinosismowal), and asked that the tribe should aid them to elect a new chief. The chief of the stranger tribe then arose and formally announced to his people the desire of the envoys, stating his willingness to go to aid them, his fatherless brothers, in choosing a new father. The messengers, arising once more, thanked the chief for his kindness and appointed a day to return to their own people.

The ceremony known as kelhoochun then took place. The chief notified his men that his brothers were ready to go, but that they

---

[1] From here on the recorder mentions only the neighboring Algonkin tribes as belonging to the federation which he has in mind. The northern Algonkin tribes were very probably in a loose federation with the Iroquois merely for purposes of intertribal arbitration. These Algonkin clans themselves, however, seem to have been politically interdependent, as one clan could not elect a chief without the consent of all the others.

should not be allowed to go so soon. The small wampum string called kellhoweyi or prolongation of the stay was produced at this point, which read that the whole tribe, men, women and children, were glad to see their brothers with them and begged them to remain a day or two longer; that "our mothers" (kigwusin), that is, all the tribal women, would keep their paddles yet a little while. This meant that the messengers were not to be allowed to depart so soon.

Here followed the ceremony called N'skahudin. A great hunt was ordered by the chief and the game brought to the meeting hall and cooked there. The noochila-kalwet or herald went about the village crying wikw-poosaltin, which was intelligible to all. Men, women and children immediately came to the hall with their birchbark dishes and sat about the game in a circle, while four or five men with long-handled dishes distributed the food, of which every person had a share. The feast was called kelhootwi-wikw-poosaltiu. When it was all over the Indians dispersed, but returned later to the hall when the messengers sang again their salutation songs in honor of their forefathers, in reply to which the chief of the tribe sang his song of greeting.

When the singing was over the chief seated himself in the midst of the hall with a small drum in one hand and a stick in the other. To the accompaniment of his drum he sang his k'tumasooi-n'tawagunul or dance songs, which was the signal for a general dance, followed by another feast.

The envoys again appointed a day to return, but were deterred in the same manner. As these feasts often lasted three weeks or a month, a dance being held every night, it was frequently a long time before they could go back to their own tribe, because the chief would detain them whenever they wished to return. Such was the custom.

THE CEREMONY OF INSTALLATION

When they reached home, however, and the embassies from the other Wabanaki tribes had also returned, the people of the bereaved tribe were summoned to assemble before the messengers, who informed them of the success of their mission. When the delegates from the other tribes, who had been appointed to elect the chief, had arrived and the salutation and welcome ceremonies had been performed, an assembly was called to elect the chief.

This took place about the second day after the arrival of the other Wabanaki representatives. A suitable person, a member of the bereaved tribe, was chosen by acclamation for the office of chief.

Plate 8

1   2

1 Wolf clan belt said to represent a pact of the Mohawk with the French
2 Tuscarora entrance belt

If there was no objection to him a new flag pole was made and prepared for raising, and a chief from one of the kindred tribes put a medal of wampum on the chief-elect who was always clothed in new garments. The installing chief then addressed the people, telling them that another "eldest boy" had been chosen, to whom they owed implicit obedience. Turning to the new chief, he informed him that he must act in accordance with the wishes of his people. The main duties of a chief were to act as arbiter in all matters of dispute, and to act as commander in chief in case of war, being ready to sacrifice himself for the people's good if necessary.

After this ceremony they marched to the hall, where another dance took place, the new chief singing and beating the drum. A wife of one of the other chiefs then placed a new deer skin or bear skin on the shoulders of the new chief as a symbol of his authority, after which the dance continued the whole night.

The officers of the new chief (geptins) were still to be chosen. These were seven in number and were appointed in the same manner and with the same ceremonies as the chief. Their duties, which were much more severe, were told them by the installing chief. The flag pole, which was the symbol of the chief, was first raised. The geptins stood around it, each with a brush in his hand, with which they were instructed to brush off any particle of dust that might come upon it. This signified that it was their duty to defend and guard their chief and that they should be obliged to spill their blood for him, in case of need and in defense of the tribe. All the women and children and disabled persons in the tribe were under the care of the geptins. The chief himself was not allowed to go into battle, but was expected to stay with his people and to give orders in time of danger.

After the tribal officers had been appointed, the greatest festivities were carried on; during the day they had canoe races, foot races and ball playing, and during the night, feasting and dancing. The Indians would bet on the various sports, hanging the prizes for each game on a pole. It was understood that the winner of the game was entitled to all the valuables hung on this pole. The festivities often lasted an entire month.

THE MARRIAGE CEREMONY: THE ANCIENT RITE

It was the duty of the young Indian man who wished to marry to inform his parents of his desire, stating the name of the maiden. The young man's father then notified all the relatives and friends of the family that his son wished to marry such and such a girl. If the friends and relations were willing, the son was permitted to offer his suit. The father of the youth prepared a clean skin of the bear, beaver or deer, which he presented to his son. Provided with this, the suitor went to the wigwam of his prospective bride's father and placed the hide at the back of the wigwam or nowteh. The girl's father then notified his relations and friends, and if there was no objection, he ordered his daughter to seat herself on the skin, as a sign that the young man's suit was acceptable. The usual wedding ceremonies were then held, namely, a public feast, followed by dancing and singing, which always lasted at least a week.

THE MARRIAGE CEREMONY IN LATER DAYS

After the adoption of the Wampum laws the marriage ceremony was much more complicated.[1]

When the young man had informed his parents of his desire to marry and the father had secured the consent of the relations and friends, an Indian was appointed to be the Keloolwett or marriage herald, who, taking the string of wampum called the Kelolwawei, went to the wigwam of the girl's father, generally accompanied by as many witnesses as cared to attend. The herald read the marriage wampum in the presence of the girl and her father, formally stating that such and such a suitor sought his daughter's hand in marriage. The herald, accompanied by his party, then returned to the young man's wigwam to await the reply. After the girl's father had notified his relatives and friends and they had given their consent, the wedding was permitted to go on.

The usual ceremonies then followed. The young man first presented the bride-elect with a new dress. She, after putting it on, went to her suitor's wigwam with her female friends, where she and her company formally saluted him by shaking hands. This was called wulisakowdowagon or salutation. She then returned to her father's house, where she seated herself with her following of old women and girls. The groom then assembled a company of his friends, old and young men, and went with them to the bride's wigwam to salute her in the same manner. When these salutations were over a great feast was prepared by the bride, enough for all the people, men, women and children. The bridegroom also prepared a similar feast. Both of these dinners were cooked in the

---

[1] Mitchell interpolated this remark.

open air and when the food was ready they cried out k'waltewall
" your dishes." Every one understood this, which was the signal
for the merry-makers to approach and fall to.

The marriage ceremonies, however, were not over yet. The
wedding party arrayed themselves in their best attire and formed
two processions, that of the bride entering the assembly wigwam
first. In later times it was customary to fire a gun at this point
as a signal that the bride was in the hall, whereupon the groom's
procession entered the hall in the same manner, when a second
gun was fired. The geptins of the tribe and one of the friends of
the bride then conducted the girl to the bridegroom to dance with
him. At midnight after the dancing a supper was served, to which
the bride and groom went together and where she ate with him
for the first time. The couple were then addressed by an aged
man (noiimikokemit) on the duties of marriage.

Finally, a number of old women accompanied the newly made
wife to her husband's wigwam, carrying with them her bed clothes.
This final ceremony was called natboonan, taking or carrying
the bed.

APPENDIX B

SKETCHES OF AN INDIAN COUNCIL, 1846

(From Schoolcraft's Census of 1845)

A grand council of the confederate Iroquois was held last week, at the Indian council house on the Tonawanda Reservation, in the county of Genesee. Its proceedings occupied three days, closing on the third instant. It embraced representatives from all the Six Nations — the Mohawk, the Onondaga, the Seneca; and the Oneida, the Cayuga and the Tuscarora. It is the only one of the kind which has been held for a number of years, and is the last which will ever be assembled with a full representation of all the confederate nations.

With the expectation that the council would commence on Tuesday, two or three of us had left Rochester so as to arrive at the council house Monday evening; but owing to some unsettled preliminaries, it had been postponed till Wednesday. The Indians from abroad, however, arrived at the council grounds, or in their immediate vicinity, on Monday; and one of the most interesting spectacles of the occasion, was the entry of the different nations upon the domain and hospitality of the Senecas, on whose ground the council was to be held. The representation of Mohawks, coming as they did from Canada, was necessarily small. The Onondagas, with the acting Tod-o-dah-hoh of the confederacy, and his two counsellors, made an exceedingly creditable appearance. Nor was the array of Tuscaroras, in point of numbers at least, deficient in attractive and imposing features.

Monday evening we called upon, and were presented to, Blacksmith, the most influential and authoritative of the Seneca sachems. He is about 60 years old, is somewhat portly, is easy enough in his manners, and is well disposed and even kindly towards all who convince him that they have no sinister designs in coming among his people.

Jemmy Johnson is the great high priest of the confederacy. Though now 69 years old, he is yet an erect, fine looking, and energetic Indian, and is both hospitable and intelligent. He is in possession of the medal presented by Washington to Red Jacket in 1792 which among other things of interest, he showed us.

It would be incompatible with the present purpose to describe all the interesting men who there assembled, among whom were Captain Frost, Messrs Le Fort, Hill, John Jacket, Doctor Wilson and others. We spent most of Tuesday, and indeed much of the time during the other days of the week in conversation with the chiefs and most intelligent Indians of the different nations, and gleaned from them much information of the highest interest in relation to the organization, government and laws, religion, customs of the people, and characteristics of the great men, of the old and once powerful confederacy. It is a singular fact, that the peculiar government and national characteristics of the Iroquois is a most interesting field for research and inquiry, which has never been very thoroughly, if at all, investigated, although the historic events which marked the proud career of the confederacy, have been perseveringly sought and treasured up in the writings of Stone, Schoolcraft, Hosmer, Yates and others.

Many of the Indians speak English readily; but with the aid and interpretations of Mr Ely S. Parker, a young Seneca of no ordinary degree of attainment, in both scholarship and general intelligence, and who with Le Fort, the Onondaga, is well versed in old Iroquois matters, we had no difficulty in conversing with any and all we chose to.

About midday on Wednesday, the council commenced. The ceremonies with which it was opened and conducted were certainly unique, almost indescribable; and as its proceedings were in the Seneca tongue, they were in a great measure unintelligible, and in fact profoundly mysterious to the pale faces. One of the chief objects for which the council had been convoked, as has been heretofore editorially stated in the *American,* was to fill two vacant sachemships of the Senecas, which had been made by the death of the former incumbents; and preceding the installation of the candidates for the succession, there was a general and dolorous lament for the deceased sachems, the utterance of which, together with the repetition of the laws of the confederacy — the installation of the new sachems — the impeachment and deposition of three unfaithful sachems — the elevation of others in their stead, and the performance of the various ceremonies attended upon these proceedings, consumed the principal part of the afternoon.

At the setting of the sun, a beautiful repast, consisting of an innumerable number of rather formidable looking chunks of boiled fresh beef, and an abundance of bread and succotash, was brought into the council house. The manner of saying grace on this occasion was indeed peculiar. A kettle being brought, hot and smoking from the fire, and placed in the center of the council house, there proceeded from a single person, in a high shrill key, a prolonged and monotonous sound, resembling that of the syllable *wah* or *yah*. This was immediately followed by a response from the whole multitude, uttering in a low and profoundly guttural but protracted tone, the syllable *whe* or *swe*, and this concluded grace. It was impossible not to be somewhat mirthfully effected at the first hearing of grace said in this novel manner. It is, however, pleasurable to reflect that the Indians recognize the duty of rendering thanks to the Divine Being in some formal way, for the bounties and enjoyments which he bestows; and were an Indian to attend a public feast among his pale faced brethern he would be effected, perhaps to a greater degree of marvel, at witnessing a total neglect of this ceremony, than we were at his singular way of performing it.

After supper commenced the dances. All day Tuesday, and on Wednesday, up to the time that the places of the deceased sachems had been filled, everything like undue joyfulness had been restrained. This was required by the respect customarily due to the distinguished dead. But now, the bereaved sachemships being again filled, all were to give utterance to gladness and joy. A short speech from Captain Frost, introductory to the employments of the evening, was received with acclamatory approbation; and soon eighty or ninety of these sons and daughters of the forest — the old men and the young, the maidens and matrons — were engaged in the dance. It was indeed a rare sight.

Only two varieties of dancing were introduced the first evening — the trotting dance and the fish dance. The figures of either are exceedingly simple, and but slightly different from each other. In the first named, the dancers all move round a circle, in a single file, and keeping time in a sort of trotting step to an Indian song of Yo-ho-ha, or yo-ho-ha-ha-ho, as sung by the leaders, or occasionally by all conjoined. In the other, there is the same movement file round a circle, but every two persons, a man and a woman, or two men, face each other, the one moving forward and the other backward, and all keeping step to the music of the singers, who are now, however, aided by a couple of tortoise or turtle shell rattles or an aboriginal drum. At regular intervals there is a sort of cadence in the music, during which a change of position by all the couples take place, the one who had been moving backward taking the place of the one **moving forward**, when all again move onward, one-half of the whole, of course, being obliged to follow on by advancing backward.

One peculiarity in Indian dancing would probably strongly commend itself to that class among pale-faced beaux and belles denominated the bashful; though perhaps it would not suit others as well. The men, or a number of them, usually begin the dance and the women, or each of them, selecting the one with whom she would like to dance, presents herself at his side as he approaches, and is immediately received into the circle. Consequently, the young Indian beau knows nothing of the tact required to handsomely invite and gallantly lead a lady to the dance; and the young Indian maiden presents her personage to the one she designs to favor, and thus quietly engage herself in the dance. And, moreover, while an Indian beau is not necessarily obliged to exhibit any gallantry as toward a belle, till she has herself manifested her own pleasure in the matter, so therefore the belle can not indulge herself in vacillant flirtations with any considerable number of beaux, without being at once detected.

On Tuesday the religious ceremonies commenced, and the council from the time it assembled, which was about 11 o'clock a. m., till 3 or 4 o'clock p. m., gave the most serious attention to the preaching of Jemmy Johnson, the great high priest, and the second in the succession under the new revelation. Though there are some evangelical believers among the Indians, the greater portion of them cherish the religion of their fathers. This, as they say, has been somewhat changed by the new revelation, which the Great Spirit made to one of their prophets about 47 years ago, and which, as they also believe, was approved by Washington. The profound regard and veneration which the Indian has ever retained toward the name and memory of Washington is most interesting evidence of his universally appreciated worth; and the fact that the red men regard him not merely as one of the best, but as the very best man that ever has existed, or that will ever exist, is beautifully illustrated in a single credence which they maintain even to this day, namely, that Washington is the only white man that has ever entered heaven, and is the only one who will enter there, till the end of the world.

Among the Senecas, public religious exercises take place but once a year. At these times Jemmy Johnson preaches hour after hour, for three days; and then rests from any public discharge of ecclesiastical offices the remaining 362 days of the year. On this, an unusual occasion, he restricted himself to a few hours in each of the last two days of the council. We were told by young Parker, who took notes of his preaching, that his subject matter on Tuesday abounded with good teachings, enforced by appropriate and happy illustrations and striking imagery. After he had finished, the council took a short respite. Soon, however, a company of warriors ready and eager to engage in the celebrated "corn dance," made their appearance. They were differently attired; while some were completely enveloped in a closely fitting and gaudy colored garb, others, though perhaps without intending it, had made wonderfully close approaches to an imitation of the costume said to have been so fashionable in many parts of the state of Georgia during the last hot summer, and which is also said to have consisted simply of a shirt collar and a pair of spurs. But in truth, these warriors, with shoulders and limbs in a state of ñudity, with faces bestreaked with paints, with jingling trinkets dangling at their knees, and with feather war-caps waving above them, presented a truly picturesque and romantic appearance. When the center of the council house had been cleared, and the musicians with the shell rattles had taken their places, the dance commenced; and for an hour and a half, perhaps two hours, it proceeded with surprising spirit and energy. Almost every posture of which the human frame is susceptible, without absolutely making the feet to be uppermost, and the head for once to assume the place of the understanding, was exhibited. Some of the attitudes of the dancers were really imposing, and the dance as a whole could be got up and conducted only by Indians. The women in the performance of the corn dance, are quite by themselves, keeping time to the beat of the shells, and gliding along sideways, scarcely lifting their feet from the floor.

It would probably be well if the Indians everywhere could be inclined to refrain at least from the more grotesque and boisterous peculiarities of this dance. The influence of these can not be productive of any good; and it is questionable whether it would be possible, so long as they are retained, to assimilate them to any greater degree of civilization or to more refined methods of living and enjoyment, than they now possess. The same may be said of certain characteristics of the still more vandalic war dance. This, however, was not introduced at the council.

A part of the proceedings of Friday, the last day of the council, bore resemblance to those of the preceding day. Jemmy Johnson resumed his preaching, at the close of which the corn dance was again performed, though with far more spirit and enthusiasm than at the first. Double the number that then appeared — all hardy and sinewy men, attired in original and fantastic style, among whom was one of the chiefs of the confederacy, together with forty or fifty women of the different nations — now engaged and for two hours persevered in the performance of the various complicated and fatiguing movements of this dance. The appearance of the dusky throng, with its increased numbers and, of course, apportionably increased resources for the production of shrill whoops and noisy stamping, and for the exhibition of striking attitudes and rampant motions, was altogether strange, wonderful and seemingly super-human.

After the dance had ceased another kind of " sport," a well-contested foot race, claimed attention. In the evening after another supper in the council house, the more social dances — the trotting, the fish, and one in which the women alone participated — were resumed. The fish dance seemed to be the favorite; and being invited to join it by one of the chiefs, we at once accepted the invitation, and followed in mirthful chase of pleasure, with a hundred forest children. Occasionally the dances are characterized by ebullitions of merriment and flashes of real fun; but generally a singular sobriety and decorum are observed. Frequently, when gazing at a throng of sixty or perhaps a hundred dancers, we have been scarcely able to decide which was the most remarkable, the staid and imperturbable gravity of the old men and women, or the complete absence of levity and frolicsomeness in the young.

The social dances of the evening, with occasional speeches from the sachems and chiefs, were the final and concluding ceremonies of this singular but interesting affair. Saturday morning witnesses the separation of the various nations, and the departure of each to their respective homes.

The writer would like to have said a word or two in relation to the present condition and prospects of the Indians, but the original design in regard to both the topics and brevity of this writing having been already greatly transcended, it must be deferred. The once powerful confederacy of the Six Nations, occupying in its palmy days the greater portion of New York State, now number only a little over 3000. Even this remnant will soon be gone. In view of this, as well as of the known fact that the Indian race is everywhere gradually diminishing in number, the writer can not close without invoking for this unfortunate people, renewed kindliness and sympathy and benevolent attention. It is true that, with some few exceptions, they possess habits and characteristics which render them difficult to approach; but still they are only what the Creator of us all has made them. And let it be remembered, it must be a large measure of kindliness and benevolence, that will repay the injustice and wrong that have been inflicted upon them.

R. S. G.

Rochester, October 7, 1845

APPENDIX C

MINUTES OF THE SIX NATIONS COUNCIL OF 1839[1]

LIST OF CHIEFS

Selected and inaugurated at the Six Nations' Council at
the Six Nations Onondaga Council House, July 17, 1839
Sen (.eca)

Of the Chicken Hawk Tribe
1 Shagĕhjowa, Joseph Silverheels of
Cattaraugus Reservation a Sachem of the
Long House of the Six nations
(Capt. Jones of Allegany, Gan'nage).
2 Sgăndiuhgwadi, Owen Blacksnake
James Robinson (Shaweegĕt) of Allegany
abdicated in favor of Blacksnake
A War Chief.

Of the Snipe tribe
1 Hah-jih-nya-wăs, Jacob Johnson
Walter Thomson (Honondahes) of Cattaraugus
Sachem of the Senecas
2 Degas swĕn'gaent, Davis Isaac
(English name not known) (Othowă) of Cattaraugus
War Chief.

Of the Swan tribe —
1 Deyúgăhăshă, John Mitten
(Old Greenblanket, Don dae hañ) of Buffalo reservation.
Sachem or as we might say sub-sachem for the Senecas, but
not entitled to a seat in the Six Nations' Council
2 Ga'năyuehse. James Pierce
English name not known (Toɔ'wihdoh)
War Chief.

Of the Deer Tribe
1 Swaowaeh, Jonah
White Chief Deganohsogă of Buffalo reservation
War Chief
2 Dóhsihdásgowa, John Baldwin
(George White Sa'gonondano of Buffalo.)
War Chief

[1] From the original manuscript.

3 Hăondyeyah, Lewis Kennedy
  (Capt. M'Gee Thoiwae) of Tonawanda
  Sachem of the Senecas.

These four clans are brethren
Of the Wolf tribe
1 Deonihhogă′hwă, Blacksmith
  Little Johnson of Buffalo (Jă-oyah-geăh) deposed
  of Tonawanda —
       Sachem of the Six Nations
2 Ganiyăs, John Dickie
  (No English name) (Dijihhnak) of Cattaraugus
       War chief and runner under the preceding.
3 Degaăont, John Kennedy jr
  (No English name) (Gagóh) of Buffalo
       War Chief
4 Gásgaodoh, John Joshua Bluesky
  (Two Guns) Gihdoondoh of Buffalo
  Killed in battle of Chippeway
       Sachem of the Senecas
5 Hayahsajih, Peter Johnson
  (Old Two Guns, brother
  of the preceding.)   (Degeyáhgoh)
       War Chief
6 Gayáhsodoh   George Green Blanket
  (No English name)   (Gonyus,)
                              Buffalo
       War Chief
7 Dagéhsahĕh   Isaac Shanks
  (Reuben James)   (Jiyakhoh)
                            Tonawandi
       Sachem of the Senecas
Of *the Turtle tribe.*
1 Hadogut   Jacob Shongo
  (No English name) Waonohsihdeh
                          of Allegany
       Sachem of Seneca
2 Gahnase   Abram John
  (No English name) (Ganăyáhseh)
                         Of Cattaraugus
       Sachem of Senecas

3 Ganïhdadėháoh
   (No English name) Danl Spring
                of Tonawandi
                   War Chief. James, Spring
4 Gahnăodoh   Ganänwĕhdŏoh
   (Thomson S. Harris)
   (deposed)   Buffalo
      War Chief
   Speaker for the women.
   Of the Beaver tribe
1 Aanishădekhah
   Abram Johny John
   Tall Chief   Howanyaondyo
   of Genesee   Buffalo
      Sachem for the Senecas
2 Ohgahdont   Isaac Johny John
   Guardian of the preceding during his minority
3 Doăhsah   Hemlock
   (Jack Berry)   (Jinohsowă)
                         Buffalo
      Sachem for the Senecas
4 Dayagodăhseh   George Turkey
   (Jack Snow)   (Dyneah)
                         Cattaraugus
      War Chief
5 Hayă'ndagă'nyahháh
   Joe Hemlock   Peter White
                Thayah'dah'ah
      War Chief   Cattaraugus
   Of the Bear Clan
1 Găhgwasah   Saul Logan
                      Shoiwagayăt
                      Buffalo

      War Chief
2 Aodogwĕh   Jack Doxtator
                      Hajă'anoh
                      Buffalo
      War Chief
   These five Clans are brothers like the preceding four.
      Of the Cayuga Nation
      Of the Swan Tribe

1 Wăọwawănaok,   Peter Wilson
  No English name   (Dyawegaathet)
                        Buffalo
      Sachem of the Cayugas
2 Ganyáh'geodoh   Jacob Seneca
                        Hahsegwih
                        Buffalo
    War Chief and runner for the preceding.
      Of the Snipe Clan.
1 Gendăohoh'   Joseph Peter
  James Young   Darhsas
        War Chief
The preceding minutes were taken at the time of the transaction recorded and are the original thereof.

ASHER WRIGHT

RECORD OF A CONDOLENCE COUNCIL
The Mourning Council for the raising of chiefs
See writing on letter & consult other interpreters for the full
meaning of the rest of the song.

Very mournful and solemn 'There lays a number of with their
horns on!! (Emblems of power like Hebrews)
Rehearsing the ancient custom that when they come we will
give them a part of the five, (as he did in the beginning of the
ceremony) Here ends the first song.

This was sung by Hyah'dajiwak after Col. Silversmith had presented the five as above. Then Elijah Williams answered by
alluding to the loss they had & gave a string of wampum, recounted the meanings of the several strings. Thanks them for
wiping away their tears & this day thank the Great Spirit that they
can thus cleanse away their grief and smoke the pipe of peace together, & then replies in a simular manner. We have come and
found you also mourning and we also wipe away your tears, etc.
Then Hayahdijiwak informed them that Gov. Blacksnake would
take the lead of the Oneida party.
  Then the Seneca side started —
  (Dan'a says that if any portion of the Six Nations should go
off he will be .... the confederacy)

Soon after the other side led by Blacksnake and young Jones repaired to the Council House and were received there by others who were seated there. Then came waiting & for many minutes one of the Oneidas second in the march walked the floor carrying the bag of old things & sang a wailing song, being frequently answered by the other side with a long wail & once by Elijah Williams. (What must be the feeling of these men.) Again Williams wails in a high tone & then others in a suppressed note an octave below. Wms. wails again & the low note is repeated & the bag bearer goes on singing. Now the wail and low tone are responded from the other side of the house. (I believe in his song he is repeating the names of the hadiyanne & then offices) of all the Six Nations. Now he is upon the Onondagas, and now they wail again as before. Now again. Now again. Is it repeated when he is coming to the names of the dead? Or is it at the finishing of those who belong to the same tribe? The latter I think or both.

Hai! Hai gayahaagweniohgwe!

Now he is upon the Cayugas. The exclamation hai! hai! seems a mourning interjection at the beginning of every sentence, between all the simple sentences & at the close of every paragraph. (Once Wms. made a little mistake & began to wail a word or two too soon & I noticed a little smiling) Now he is upon the Senecas. And now done & he has sat down by the side of Elijah Williams & now he has risen & began to speak instead of singing & desired them all to hear & said I have spoken the old way, continue it for one benefit, let it be followed forever.

Then silence and something which seemed like a consultation for several minutes followed. At length blankets were brought and a cord stretched across the Council House so as to separate the two parties from each other and cut off communication. Then another long interval of waiting. Then a bench was brought in to the Cayuga side and the wampum laid out before the masters of ceremonies, preparatory to the songs etc. These songs are the several articles of the ancient confederacy. Art 1 *Hai hai! Hai hi hi haih ne* etc. closing with a semitone downward slide of the voice etc.

It was so made everything was right when altogether they did it. There a relationship was made between them. (Song and response regular always interspersed with hai etc.) A chief warrior i. e. This wampum is so called, I suppose a chief or great woman. It was by their transaction that this operation goes forward.

After singing thus far he rose and made a wonderful speech to the dead man who invented the ceremonies, stating that, we have heard from our forefathers that these Nations will become extinct but we have now come to raise up chiefs and let the people hear the laws of our forefathers. Then he sung over the same speech.

Then Elijah Williams rose & recounted what was done in ancient times something like a declaration of independence repeating the names of the nations, or the others, united in one house & of the Sachems addressing the speech to "Ak sut" i. e. the other side, I suppose regarding them as the mother as it were of the Confederacy. (Here needs more inquiry)

Speaking of Ganinduiyes who used to live at Tonawanta, called him a Long Hickory Tree. After he had finished he received four papers of tobacco from the other side of the house & (shouted as it were.)

Then the other Oneida, Peter Williams, rose and took a string of wampum & explained the duties of a chief warrior as agreed by our forefathers that he must look to all the people and take care of them all old, young, women, children, creepers & the breast etc. So it was unanimously agreed (This was the black wampum)

---

2 A short wampum signifying that when a chief is buried his grave must be leveled as soon as possible (i. e. a new chief must be chosen)

3 As soon as done always gives over to the other side & Wm. had another   Comforting all who have been called to mourning by the death of Chiefs so as not to feel their loss always.

4 Now another sun breaks through the clouds and enlightened the faces which were sad before.

5 When the council five bands have been all scattered they must be gathered together again, i. e. when death has scattered the chiefs they must be collected again around the council fire and fill their places.

6 This is to comfort and pacify & satisfy the minds of the Chiefs, so that they can come together cheerfully to transact business.

7 If any of the chiefs go contrary to the law, the chiefs & chief warriors must consult the mother and follow her advice, thus, say we three of the children who are charging you.

8 We have poured water into the thirsty throats that they may be able to feel comfortable and speak freely.

9 He must carry his bag always whenever he goes anywhere he must go and stand by the corner of the fire and draw out his speech from the bag and if need be draw out his arrows also and declare war.

---

10 Requesting them to appoint men to fill the places of the dead and tell us that we may know who they are — (And then he joked a little and said we three brothers have got through, it is time to adjourn & we can get to the tavern.)

Then Hayahdajiwak rose and requested the three brothers to have patience.

The curtain was put up in the other side of the house and preparations made to send back another set of wampums to be kept by this party.

(Meanwhile the four papers of tobacco had been divided among the three brothers.)

Now the other side commence with a kind of a shout to call attention & a repetition of the Songs nearly as before with a wampum before them on the little bench.

(It is said the words are the same as used by the Oneidas, although sung by an Onondaga. Probably a form either compounded to suit the occasion or perhaps one of the ancient languages as it was hundreds of years ago.)

In the song on the other side they mentioned the death of the fathers. Now these sing that the children are alive yet (of course we are not in mourning as before). Oyehgwohdoh was the name of the founder of the confederacy.

Sing again we must always hear what our ancestors have said and hear the Chief Woman who can call a council of the women and tell their voice in council among the chiefs & they are obliged to listen, as to a chief (or perhaps more seriously).

Now the wampums are sent back beginning with the black one.

It is true as you have said we have experienced a great loss etc. & we will do as well as we can etc.

(Note certain of the wampums not brought or delayed.)

Note the peculiar manner of recitation accent on the first syllable spoken & then again on the last. I think these replies accompanying the several strings of wampum were (or mean) " Now

the word shall go forth in relation to what you have spoken."
" Our children (or younger brothers) all which you have said is
wise. It is a good matter. You are wise. Now hear, all which
you have spoken relative to this string of wampum is wise &
we will do accordingly "—
  But there is some variation in the words used according to the
particular charge given by the party.
  There are two sets of wampum & every time new chiefs are
elected these are exchanged and kept till the next election by the
two parties. (Did the two parties originate in the conjunction of
the two confederacies in ancient times?)
  Then he proceeded to bring forward the newly elected chiefs.
  1 Shagehjowa- Joseph Silverheels a sachem. Degahnoge

  You have requested us to tell us who we appoint to a co-worker
with the chiefs in accordance with the example of our forefathers
and now we have brought him forward, now know him, & know
that he is called such an one.

  2 In the place of Robinson i. e. next to the chief warrior,
Dyáñdiṇhgwadih, Owen Black Snake, Shaweegah'.
  3 Twenty Summers, John Mitten.
  (It is said that they have a string of wampum for every *name*
and that these are kept so that the names may not be lost.)
  4 A man not here, living at Alleghany in place of Ganáynihse,
dead James Pierce.

  5 In the place of Gaswăhgaah, lives at Cattaraugus, Chief
Warrior.

  6 Daandieyah, a young man at Tonawandi.

  7 Sgaowai, Jonah — White Chief, Gahnyagoh.

  8 Daáshihdasgowa, John Baldwin.

  9 Hahjihnyawăy Dea. Jacob Johnson
     Walter Thompson.
  10 In place of Little Johnson, (deposed) Dasnihogăhweh, Blacksmith of Tonawandi, Găoyah'gea.
  11 Janiyăhs, not present. John Dicker.
  12 Degaăout, John Kennedy.

13 Gasgaa-doh' John Joshua Sachem Gih'oh, in place of Two
Guns, father of Henry Two Guns and Daniel, killed in battle of
Chippeway—

14 Hayasajih, War Chief Gih'-oh.
  Peter Johnson
  (Degiyah'goh) in place of old Two Guns, brother of pre-
ceding.

---

15 Gayáhsodoh', George Green Blanket in place of his grandfather some time since dead.

---

16 Waádogut, Jacob Shongo, Dep. Sachem.

17 Dagehsadĕh young man from Tonawandi.

18 Gah'nase, Abram John sub Sachem.

---

19 Gah'neodoh' James Spring in place of T. S. Harris deposed.

---

20 Ganĕhdadĭhdãoh. A young man from Tonawandi.

Then Hayahdajiwak said that is all and Peter Williams begun
to speak when Col. Silversmith beckoned him down and Hayahdajiwak proceeded.

21 To put in Saul Logan Gaãhgwas-Chief or head of the
warriors.

---

22 Othaoh'dogwĕh. Jack Doxtader, a chief of the warriors.

23 In place of Jack Berry Doãsah (Sub Sachem) lives at the
falls.

---

24 Ohãneshadekhah'. Johnny Johnny John's son Sub-Sachem.

---

25 Isaac Johnny John. Guardian of preceding till he grew up.

26 Peter White of Cattaraugus Hayãndagãnyathah.

27 George Turkey, Do Da-yagodãhseh War chiefs.

Now he says we have finished for the Senecas, Doorkeepers.

Then Peter Williams ansd. and charged the chiefs to take care of
the people and not do anything contrary to the will of the people
and not to trust in their own wisdom because they are elevated not
to try to get above them but to promote their benefit and conform
to the laws of the Six Nations.

If it had not been for the wampums which have been preserved
it would have been difficult to have filled all these offices, of those
which are dead, etc. etc.

Congratulates them highly and says there is only one thing
lacking i. e. we begin to feel hungry — Then sat down but soon
after rose.   Held a wampum in his hand and made a speech &
proceeded to put Peter Wilson 1 Waowawăvaok, a Cayuga chief
in place of some old man and also Wm King resigned to him his
office.

2 Jacob G. Seneca was put in his second Ganyahgeodoh.

3 Joseph Satourette in place of James Young, Gĕhdăodoh.
— and made a speech afterward and presented a wampum but I
had no interpreter at hand & could not understand whether
another chief was put in or not.

About this time the provisions were brought in.

Peter Williams sat down & soon a shout was raised or wail.   I
do not know what to call it.   (Elevated note drawn out & then the
low octave followed) & was soon after repeated.   After some
moments repeated again and drawn out longer than before —

Then a long interval, while there were more provisions brought
in, in which the assembled seemed to get in promiscuous conversation in a low tone and many were going out and coming in as if
to relieve themselves after so long a confinement.

When Hayahdajiwak began to speak and as I supposed returned
thanks and compliments & gave some notices etc. and then invited
them according to the rule of our forefathers to take the food
before they go out that they may be strengthened & then took a
wampum and presented it to this side with an exhortation never
to flinch from duty nor fail to come when called to a council of
this kind.   We exhort you and exhort ourselves.

Then Peter Williams took the same wampum and gave an answer
that we were bound together again in fellowship according to the
rules of our forefathers.   We three brothers on this side of as you
on that side and all together and keep the council houses in order.
Thus we will all do according to the wishes of our forefathers.

Then Col. Silversmith sometime and exhorted them to keep the
rules and create the new tunes and alluded to the dancing of the

night and told them of strangers coming from abroad wish to have anything to do with our young women we shall not withhold them but shall act according to the rule and those who do not wish to have anything to do with these things can have an opportunity to stay away etc.

(According to the old custom of the Northern & perhaps of all other Indians)

(And let them take warning, Dea. White says in a whisper to them not to act so bad.)

Ayokhiyatgah agwus weetgat agwus weetgäh agwus.

APPENDIX D

MINUTES OF THE
COUNCIL OF THE SIX NATIONS,
UPON THE CATTARAUGUS RESERVATION[1]

Dec. 1st, 1862

Andrew Snow made a few remarks that all the chiefs take places.

Dewathaaseh made a few congratulatory remarks of thanks. According to Indian customs thanked the Great Spirit for having preserved of those as were, now represented in council. He further stated that it devolved upon the Canada Indians to proceed with the exposition of the law.

Nowineehdoh' & Ganohgaihdawih' then opened the bag of wampum.

Nowineehdoh' arose & spake saying that we are now got together. When our forefathers finished the law they in the first place would return thanks — that was passed.

As far as was proceeded they would go on with the exposition of the law — In the first place think this, we are poor it will therefore depend our brother on the other side of the fire. That was the arrangement.

Seneca Johnson then arose & spoke exhorting the people to listen.

There is a goodly number — We therefore give thanks to the whole — It was the conclusion of my brother on the other side of the fire to devolve upon me.

In the first place you were told the other day of how the law came into existance, lastly the Tuscaroras came into the confederacy. Our forefathers foretold of the destiny of the Indians at the commencement of All. council. We have now come to that.

Long House used to sing when we were in power they went on in harmony. Hense they foretold what would happen.

They have now gone to their grave.

Their footsteps are a great way off that made the law.

What I say I am responsible for

---

[1] From the original manuscript by N. H. Parker.

I will commence here. my told the truth in saying that the fire was here — Jonodagăantyewa. He was to have a stick when he could not do it he was to whoop and in less than no time the chiefs that is all true we could not go further than what was said by Hohsănehdeh'. The Long House says Six Nations — Tuscarora came in last —

5 nations made the law so & so — they were to be united by this law. If any one go through, his horns would fall off from his head. Or if any should fall another should be raised.

But if any should refuse to come back by three time — they should take them off — Thus they arranged it, as it was to last forever (the law)

It is true in what he said by saying that they should pull the tree &c.

A Brand was taken from the real fire & laid into Canada after the expedition against the Indians. The chief went across the river. They had a great council at Găndayĕh by name. They said we should put up a tha — so no one could not get one (or over (?))

They went to work — the law — here it is. We do not know all Deaigă — & sa — know it all they have it written.

Concerning the tree —

Dasdaegih to watch the west root — south root Cherochees to charge of done by Six Nations East root 7 nations St Regis took charge of the ocean — North root. Ojigweh nation took charge of.

Long House did this large wampum there at Canada.

When peace was declared Long House put fire there into Canada to watch the north region — This is why they said the great white root should grow, & we should put our heads there should anyone strike the root &c.

This is the sum and substance of what the Canadians have.

Presented a belt with 12 black crosses. the words of Otawatgaenoot the name where a great council was held all summer.

Gosiweh was the name of the chief dwah'gahah'

They was to kill the chief of the Six Nations Sawanoonoh took the law

I said just now — Canada nations presented the wampum with a dark spot in the middle represent a bowl or dish with beaver tail in it — they also made a road — also presented a wampum — I say nothing about this wampum presenting it being the british —

This belt represents the encircling of the Six Nations similar to the one at Onondaga —

Israel Jimeson wished the speaker to turn it to the females. You see they the chiefs cannot get through.

Now this belt show the 12 nations said &c.

All the nations of the Six Nations were represented.

Dish represented with beaver meat in it They should eat together — use no knife for fear they should cut and draw blood.

This belt is with hearts to represent one heart. This the to other nations.

This belt Brant & Niăondahgowa throwed into the fire representing their repentence. So all must do

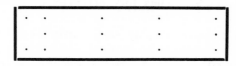

Again

I am merely what the proceedings were here and Canada 8 year council was held or called of all the nations & 4 years ago another was held of all the nations.

They were all united in the force of the law in Canada.

Now at this council many were present who were educated at that council.

As we now see here many are educated writing down the proceedings for future generations as it was the plan of our forefathers —

At this council a vote was taken whether they should adher to the law all rose.

This is all I can do as I fear I might injure feelings as there those present who made the law

But the main fire is not here Still it was your minds here to have the exposition of law again that was right. You now can see whether you have erred from the path of this law —

The white man has found his gun — now fighting. Let it not be so with us.

— Speech ended —

Additional remarks — It was the intention of the Long House wherever a council was held to bring the fires together. We heard that you was to take from us the fire that is the reason &c.

I will explain concerning this belt encircling the reason
6 arrows in a bundle
— We are weak —

The fathers & son's repentence this belt.

The Tuscarora said I am now at ease & therefore I shall not come to the fire.

I had a conversation with the British he asked me where I was going. I told him he said it was not right I protect you here — I said wonderful — your law & interest are connected by iron &c.

I said that those who erred were to be seen to &c.

S. S. D. Spoke It turned upon the Tuscaroras no chiefs here & it may true that he mind in peace as he is now able to take of chel,—

Sigwaih'seh is here installed at Onondaga he wishes to be in the confederacy —

Now and then you know they are divided still he will always be present & hopes that the other party will come to repentance —

Thomas Jimeson

Spoke & said he was happy to my friends — I wish to explain — before the sale of lands I used to talk with my friends old Canada. I thought I would try to live a different life — I bought lands — pay taxes — White man collected taxes first it was small 2d year I went & paid taxes again pd a little more than $20 — Path Master came next increased a little every year — came up to $40 — & 50 days roads Taxes. finally they petitioned for a corporation about 2 year it went through —City tax came in collector posted bills to pay on 1st of Oct. quite high about $110. Taxes must be pd or land sold — on the next Aug I pd again a little & on 1st of Dec since 5 year for 2 years I paid $50.— then officers changed time came. Tax fell off also on county Tax.

George Buck spoke in brief

The principal business of the day has gone by — it was concluded that the exposition of the law be made —

The council was called some time since Now you this day. You all Six Na have heard what was said by the keepers of the fire.

Both parties were here from Canada & here. you have heard all — ădwadegonih onăh

Detwathaahseh' spoke and said I will tell what happened where we came from — It was done in council. Sanctioned by Sardohahoh' Now I will tell about the chief. All claim him & for a reason — how we are to live encircling belt. I would say this is the same Six Nations joined in hands in the middle the house.

It is therefore important should he go through or over or go in ground to come out & some to do for the distruction of chil —

Again when he was chief he attended to interest of the land not to sell — also the interest of women chil — not to make chil.— or people cry — therefore his horns must fall on other nations west did not look to us — heads will roll

Chiefs skin must be thick & have patience,

Warriors beyond the circle & women (?) next therefore 3 times &c. chiefs must consider their (?) warriors then women

Then all shall come together to consider.

Again how a chief shall speak chiefs shall have control of Deaths of chiefs to sympathize with such family.

Chief shall hold office for life or good behavior.

Again we see our Canada friend. We see here the fire — the minds seems the same concerning the law. So you ought to do. I shall adher to it — Speech closed.

Wish to Amend

How the council should never speak of dividing land by disbanding the Na —

Again

When white man became brothers they traded land. Chiefs said All lands sold should be in common.

Nowineedoh' to speak for or in behalf of the chiefs from abroad.

listen brothers

You see us here Onondagas —All is exposed the law in full this day & all we can do —

You see us chiefs here this all they can do —

Their minds is, we have all construed the law should a council be called at some other place Then you may have the whole.

Again this thing is come to pass according to your mind —

It now devolve upon you to consider We all see our troubles — some day — it is therefore you should consider carefully.

How shall we do that our chil shall & have many days — Therefore you consider carefully in regard to this matter.

This much we say in brief — I would say again you are wise & you can see what to do.

Speech ended

Little Joe spoke

We have heard all the law exposed regard to what has been said. We have no time now tomorrow we will tell you.

Dec. 2d 1862

Council of the Six Nations resumed its deliberation by opening remarks of John Cook according to the custom of such councils —

Thanking the Great Spirit in preserving the lives of all now present & those who have come from abroad —

The council therefore was ready to proceed to *business.*

John Cook again spoke

saying his friends had now come from Canada as they were to do by and by.

It is this, that each tribe in N. Y. speak for themselves — to commune in order. When after all have spoken a certain one will be appointed to speak for the whole —

Tonawandas to council first, then Alle. then Catt — They were then ordered to take their accustomed seats

Tonawandas

Jubez Ground spoke as follows:

That it was the duty in all such gatherings to exchange words of thanks before proceeding to business.

It was announced that we were the first to explain our troubles in council — We have divided. Some of us thought we were not going right — Blksmith and Jemmy Johnson were strait till their death Had they been living it would not have been so —

The other side tells us that we have erred because we would not comply with the law. So we said to them

Hence the party thought it best to have a council called to hear the exposition of the law — Our party is strong in the faith of the law.

You understand how we stand We are divided. We stand on the Six Na law & will stand by it — This is the feeling of our party. So you understand.

They have firm reliance on the law —

Now we tell how large our party is who *will* adher to the law 282.

We were told that belt was left for repentance — We have none to leave as they not believe they have erred.

The above is the actual number who voluntarily wished to on our side joined us without threats. Thus much we explain to you and our position *in brief*

Seneca Johnson said

The No of your party as I understand is 282. Now I ask the whole No at Ton

Isaac Doctor said that we do not know exactly but the other side has the majority — our party was once over 300 but fell off to the other side by threats, such as you will have no more goods & money if you keep the other side & you go to Kansas.

Alle —

Isaac Halftown —

I am appointed to speak for Alle & I will be brief as respects the condition of our people — we have what the Ton have said

They say that the other side has the majority how they (?) will do in that case I do not know.

The Alle would be glad to get back.

They expect to take their band and explain to those left at home Daniel Two Guns said that he speaks for the old folks — they have not let go the law

They will in the first place have to talk with the Pres. The Pres. have erred from the contract

In respect to our party we have a party but cannot say how many So much in brief. Daniel 2 guns added

I said we do not know but we will go to work and see & let you know how many wish to adher to the Six Nations Law.

Isaac Halftown spoke again saying (the Alle) we will take hold of it.

I now ask concerning the wampum belt of repentance. You said &c

We Catt & Alle have erred we got white man law.

Shall we put the belt there too?

This is what I wish to know.

Little Joe said the thing today was going on what was to happen. The Cayugas also would have the privilege to speak he has erred it therefore may be of some help to those who have erred to hear them speak.

Joseph Isaac explained that they were ready to speak as soon Seneca Johnson:

In reference to the question, let my brothers have patience until we answer to all that may be said.

Dr. Wilson:

We will inform you how we feel we are much enlightened greatly in the exposition of the law — we therefore thank you — Now in reference to another matter, the white man long ago turned the Indians mind —

Concerning the arrows. This is to be of one mind — we come from the west through the white man's advice we now have small pieces of land. It now depends on you old folks to determine what to do —

Concerning the fires &c the white man has mixed his laws in criminal cases &c Then went on to relate the condition of Catt & Alle Reservations from the commencement up to this time, but still the idea is (our idea) that the old fellows are still chiefs in Six Nations Council —

Our idea is that there is lack in the exposition of the law. Still we hope that at some future time the whole will come together & still their faith remained the same relying on the law of the Six Nations

> *Adjourned to eat* —
> John Cook spoke for women
> Jisgoh'goh gave notice who was to make

answer —

Silverman spoke

Ganyodioyoh

Dewathaah'sech' said that our destruction is being brought about by the white man

In regard to murder and theft the laws of the white man has jurisdiction also in case of liquor Laws by U. S. made

Our condition is this Our old chiefs beg laws for the protection of timber.

APPENDIX E

CERTAIN IROQUOIS TREE MYTHS AND SYMBOLS[1]

A student of Iroquoian folklore, ceremony, or history will note the many striking instances in which sacred or symbolic trees are mentioned. One finds allusions to such trees not only in the myths and traditions that have long been known to literature, and in the speeches of Iroquois chiefs in council with the French and English colonists, but also in the more recently discovered wampum codes and in the rituals of the folk-cults.

There are many references to the "tree of peace" in the colonial documents on Indian relations. Cadwallader Colden, for example, quotes the reply of the Mohawk chief to Lord Effingham in Jul, 1684. The Mohawk agreed to the proposals for peace and their spokesman said: "We now plant a Tree who's tops will reach the sun, and its Branches spread far abroad, so that it shall be seen afar off; and we shall shelter ourselves under it, and live in Peace, without molestation." (Gives two beavers.)[2]

In a footnote Colden says that the Five Nations always express peace under the metaphor of a tree. Indeed, in the speech, a part of which is quoted above, the peace tree is mentioned several times.

In Garangula's reply to De la Barre, as recorded by Lahontan, are other references to the "tree." In his "harangue" Garangula said:

"We fell upon the Illinese and the Oumamis, because they cut down the Trees of Peace. . ." "The Tsonontouans, Gayogouans, Onnotagues, Onnoyoutes and Agnies declare that they interred the Axe at Cataracuoy in the Presence of your Predecessor the very Center of the Fort; and planted the Tree of Peace in the same place; 'twas then stipulated that the Fort should be used as a Place of Retreat for Merchants, and not as a Refuge for Soldiers. You ought to take care that so great a number of Militial Men as we now see . . . do not stifle and choke the Tree of Peace . . . it must needs be of pernicious Consequences to stop its Growth and hinder it to shade both your Country and ours with its Leaves." [3]

The examples cited above are only a few of many that might be quoted to show how commonly the Iroquois mentioned the peace

---

[1] A. C. Parker; an extract from Amer. Anthropologist, v. 14, No. 4, 1912.
[2] Colden, History of the Five Nations, reprint, p. 58, New York, 1866.
[3] Lahontan, Voyages, v. 1, p. 42. London, 1735.

tree. There are also references to the tree that was uprooted " to afford a cavity in which to bury all weapons of war," the tree being replanted as a memorial.

In the Iroquoian myth, whether Cherokee, Huron, Wyandot, Seneca or Mohawk, the "tree of the upper world" is mentioned, though the character of the tree differs according to the tribe and sometimes according to the myth-teller.

Before the formation of the lower or earth world the Wyandot tell of the upper or sky world and of the "big chief" whose daughter became strangely ill.[1] The chief instructs his daughter to "dig up the wild apple tree; what will cure her she can pluck from among its roots." David Boyle[2] wondered why the apple tree was called " wild " but that the narrator meant wild-apple and not wild apple is shown by the fact that in some versions the Seneca call the tree the crab-apple. The native apple tree with its small fruit was intended by the Indian myth-teller, who knew also of the cultivated apple and took the simplest way to differentiate the two.

With the Seneca this tree is described more fully. In manuscript left by Mrs Asher Wright, the aged missionary to the Seneca, I find the cosmologic myth as related to her by Esquire Johnson, a Seneca, in 1870. Mrs Wright and her husband understood the Seneca language perfectly and published a mission magazine in that tongue as early as 1838. Her translation of Johnson's myth should therefore be considered authentic. She wrote:

"There was a vast expanse of water. . . . Above it was the great blue arch of air but no signs of anything solid. . . . In the clear sky was an unseen floating island sufficiently firm to allow trees to grow upon it, and there were men-beings there. There was one great chief who gave the law to all the Ongweh or beings on the island. In the center of the island there grew a tree so tall that no one of the beings who lived there could see the top. On its branches flowers and fruit hung all the year round. The beings who lived on the island used to come to the tree and eat the fruit and smell the sweet perfume of the flowers. On one occasion the chief desired that the tree be pulled up. The great chief was called to look at the great pit which was to be seen where the tree had stood."

The story continues with the usual description of how the sky-mother was pushed into the hole in the sky and fell upon the wings of the waterfowl who placed her on the turtle's back. After this mention of the celestial tree in the same manuscript is the story of

[2] Connelley, W. E., Wyandot Folk Lore. Topeka, 1889.
[2] Boyle, The Iroquois, in Archeological Report of Ontario for 1905, p. 147.

the central world-tree. After the birth of the twins, Light One and Toadlike (or dark) One, the Light One, also known as Goodminded, noticing that there was no light, created the "tree of light." This was a great tree having at its topmost branch a great ball of light. At this time the sun had not been created. It is significant, as will appear later, that the Good-minded made his tree of light one that brought forth flowers from every branch. After he had continued experimenting and improving the earth, " he made a new light and hung it on the neck of a being, and he called the new light Gaagwaa (ga gwa) and instructed its bearer to run his course daily in the heavens." Shortly after he is said to have " dug up the tree of light, and looking into the pool of water in which the stump (trunk) had grown, he saw the reflection of his own face and thereupon conceived the idea of creating Ongwe and made them both a man and a woman."

The central world-tree is found also in Delaware mythology, though so far as I can discover it is not called the tree of light. The Journal of Dankers and Slyter[1] records the story of creation as heard from the Lenape of New Jersey in 1679. All things came from a tortoise, the Indians told them. " It had brought forth the world, and in the middle of its back had sprung a tree upon whose branches men had grown."[2] This relation between men and the tree is interesting in comparison with the Iroquois myth, as it is also conceived to be the central world-tree. Both the Lenape and the Iroquois ideas are symbolic and those who delight in flights of imagination might draw much from both.

The Seneca world-tree is described elsewhere in my notes as a tree whose branches pierce the sky and whose roots extend to the waters of the underworld. This tree is mentioned in various ceremonial rites of the Iroquois. With the False Face Company, Hadigo sa sho o, for example, the Great Face, chief of all the False Faces, is said to be the invisible giant that guards the world tree (gaindowa ne). He rubs his turtle-shell rattle upon it to obtain its power, and this he imparts to all the visible false faces worn by the company. In visible token of this belief the members of the company rub their turtle rattles on pine-tree trunks, believing that thereby they become imbued with both the earth power and the sky power. In this use of the turtle-shell rattle there is perhaps a recognition of

[1] Journal of Voyage to New York in 1679–80, by Jasper Dankers and Peter Slyter translated in Trans. L. I. Hist. Soc., v. I. 1867.
[2] With the New England Indians the idea was held that men were found by Glooskap in a hole by an arrow which he had shot into an ash tree.

the connection between the turtle and the world-tree that grows upon the primal turtle's back.

In the prologue of the Wampum Code of the Five Nations Confederacy we again find references to a symbolic "great tree." In the code of Dekanawide, the Iroquois culture hero exclaims:

"I am Dekanawide, and with the Five Nations' confederate lords (rodiyaner) I plant the Tree of the Great Peace. I plant it in your territory, Adodarho and the Onondaga nation, in the territory of you who are Fire Keepers.

"I name the tree the Tree of the Great Long Leaves. Under the shade of this Tree of Peace we spread the soft, feathery down of the globe thistle, there beneath the spreading branches of the Tree of Peace."

In the second "law" of the code, the four roots of the "tree" are described, and the law-giver says:

"If any individual or any nation outside of the Five Nations shall obey the laws of the Great Peace and make known their disposition to the lords of the confederacy, they may trace the roots of the tree, and if their minds are clean and obedient . . . they shall be welcome to take shelter beneath the Tree of the Long Leaves.

"We place in the top of the Tree of the Long Leaves an Eagle who is able to see afar; . . . he will warn the people."

In another place is the following:

"I, Dekanawide, and the union lords now uproot the tallest pine tree and into the cavity thereby made we cast all weapons of war. Into the depths of the earth, down into the deep underearth currents of water flowing to unknown regions we cast all the weapons of strife. We bury them from sight and we plant again the tree. Thus shall the Great Peace, Kaye narhe ko wa, be established."

These laws and figures of speech are evidently those which the Iroquois speakers had in mind when addressing "peace councils" with the whites.

Symbolic trees appear not only in Iroquois history, mythology, and folk beliefs, but also in their decorative art. The numerous decorative forms of trees embroidered in moose hair and porcupine quills by the eastern Algonquians, by the Hurons, and by the Iroquois appear to be attempts to represent the world-tree and the celestial tree, in some cases, with "all manner of fruits and flowers." Many, if not most, of the modern descendants of the old-time Indians, who copy these old designs, have forgotten their meanings, and some have even invented new explanations. A few of the more conservative, however, still remember the true meanings of their designs and from these much of interest has been learned.

INDEX